WORD RECOGNITION ACTIVITIES

PATTERNS AND STRATEGIES FOR DEVELOPING FLUENCY

Barbara J. Fox

North Carolina State University

Merrill
Prentice Hall

Upper Saddle River, New Jersey
Columbus, Ohio

Library of Congress Cataloging-in-Publication Data

Fox, Barbara J.
    Word recognition activities : patterns and strategies for developing fluency / Barbara J. Fox.—1st ed.
        p. cm.
    Includes bibliographical references.
    IBSN 0-13-030451-4
        1. Word recognition. I. Title
  LB1050.44 .F69 2002
  372.46'2—dc21

2002190245

Vice President and Publisher: Jeffery W. Johnston
Editor: Linda Ashe Montgomery
Production Editor: Mary M. Irvin
Design Coordinator: Diane C. Lorenzo
Project Coordination and Text Design: Carlisle Publishers Services
Cover Designer: Ali Mohrman
Cover Art: Drawn by Brandon Dini, age 5; colored by Jordan Baum, age 6
Production Manager: Pamela D. Bennett
Director of Marketing: Ann Castel Davis
Marketing Manager: Krista Groshong
Marketing Coordinator: Tyra Cooper

This book was set Novarese by Carlisle Communications, Ltd., and was printed and bound by Courier Kendallville, Inc. The cover was printed by Phoenix Color Corp.

Pearson Education Ltd.
Pearson Education Australia Pty. Limited
Pearson Education Singapore Pte. Ltd.
Pearson Education North Asia Ltd.
Pearson Education Canada, Ltd.
Pearson Educacion de Mexico, S.A. de C.V.
Pearson Education—Japan
Pearson Education Malaysia Pte. Ltd.
Pearson Education, *Upper Saddle River, New Jersey*

Merrill
Prentice Hall

10 9 8 7 6 5 4 3 2
ISBN 0-13-030451-4

PREFACE

Word Recognition Activities: Patterns and Strategies for Developing Fluency has over 150 classroom-tested, hands-on activities for teaching word recognition and fluency in kindergarten through fifth grade. This book is unique in that it takes a developmental view of fluency that brings together theory, research, and practice. My perspective is that fluency develops sequentially and predictably during the elementary school years, and is a consequence of good teaching, experiences in reading and writing, and the acquisition of new knowledge, skills, and strategies. Fluent readers use all the cues available to them—graphophonic, syntactic, and semantic. A book that represents only code-cracking information and activities would fall woefully short of explaining fluency development. I have, therefore, extended beyond the traditional word recognition topics of phonemic awareness, phonics, and structural analysis, and included explanations and activities for teaching word meaning, rapid word recognition, and fluency in oral and silent reading.

A DEVELOPMENTAL ORGANIZATION ■ ■ ■ ■ ▬▬

The journey toward fluency begins in kindergarten as children read and write, and as they develop phonological awareness of rhymes, syllables, and sounds, learn letter names and sounds, and connect meaning with print. In the first chapter, future and practicing teachers learn about fluency, how children use context cues and sound-based cues to identify words, the stages of word fluency, and how children gradually move from one stage to the next. Chapter 2 describes teaching activities to develop phonological awareness of words, rhymes, and syllables; presents activities to develop phonemic awareness of sounds in words and the ability to blend. As children enter into reading, they combine phonological awareness with the understanding that written words consist of letters and that letters represent sounds. Children generally develop this knowledge in kindergarten, so Chapter 3 explains how to teach letter names and sounds, and presents teaching activities to stimulate, engage, and challenge these emergent readers.

At first, children use only part of the letter and sound cues to identify and learn new words. But as children develop letter knowledge and awareness of the sounds in words, they begin to pay attention to all the graphophonic cues in the new words they meet in text. Word family words are one of the first ways that children and their teachers begin to explore the letters and sounds in words.

Chapter 4 includes a variety of activities for teaching word families, such as the *at* in *cat* and *hat*. Word families are a useful gateway into decoding, but word family knowledge alone is not enough to support identifying and learning many different words in text. If children are to become accomplished fluent readers, they must understand the more useful letter patterns in English. Therefore, Chapter 4 includes useful teaching resources: a table of letter patterns to use as a ready reference, guidelines for teaching phonics, and phonics activities.

With reading and writing experiences, children's attention gravitates to the large and often meaningful letter groups that make up the basic structural units in words. Consequently, Chapter 5 focuses on structural analysis, which is the process of identifying and learning new words by paying attention to large, pronounceable units, such as prefixes (the *pre-* in *preheat*), suffixes (the *-ful* in *bountiful*), syllables, and root words borrowed from Greek and Latin (the *micro-* in *microscope*). In reading this chapter, future and practicing teachers learn the structural units of words, and activities for teaching these word parts—from simple suffixes to syllables and root words.

It would be foolish to assume that teaching the alphabet, phonemic awareness, phonics, and word structure is all that is necessary to build fluency. Fluent readers are experts at using context cues while reading, and they understand the meaning of the words they read in text. Consequently, a comprehensive and balanced language arts program must include the teaching of context cues and word meaning. For this reason, Chapter 6 explains guidelines for teaching vocabulary, activities to develop skill at using the reading context, and activities to develop rapid, accurate, and effortless word recognition. While rapid, accurate, and effortless word recognition is necessary for fluent oral and silent reading, it certainly is not sufficient. Fluent reading sounds like talk, conveys meaning through attention to punctuation, and is smooth and expressive. Fluency like this requires practice, and so Chapter 7 describes the different levels of oral reading fluency, and activities for developing fluent oral and silent reading.

The first seven chapters give future and practicing teachers a plethora of teaching ideas grounded in a comprehensive theoretical framework and solid research. When children speak English at home and at school, teachers have a spoken language base upon which to build the knowledge and insights into spoken and written language that underpin fluency. However, many teachers have children in their classrooms for whom English is not the mother tongue. These teachers will find Chapter 8 especially useful. Chapter 8 explains the levels of bilingualism and the four stages of second language learning. The text describes teaching activities for each second language learning stage and eleven ways to create a supportive classroom learning environment.

A VARIETY OF FLUENCY ACTIVITIES

The reader will find a select group of activities in Chapters 2 through 6 that are specifically designed to develop fluency. When children are fluent, they recognize words rapidly, accurately, and effortlessly, and they read text smoothly at the pace of speech and with expression. Fast, accurate, and effortless word recognition and smooth, expressive text reading develop through good instruction and many experiences in reading and writing. Future and practicing teachers will find 43 fluency activities: 28 that lead to or develop fast, accurate, and effortless word level recognition, and 15 that develop fluent text reading. Word-level fluency activities are timed, have a game-like format, and ask children to read or write quickly and accurately. Developing text reading fluency involves activities such as reading to an audience, rereading text, and learning how to read in meaningful phrases. Inside the front cover is a convenient list, with page numbers, of all activities to be found in the book.

Planning Guides for Grades K–5

In taking a developmental perspective toward fluency development, some word study components are going to increase, decrease, or disappear altogether as children move toward accomplished fluent reading. This text provides weekly teaching guides that spell out how much to emphasize certain knowledge and skills, ranging from a significant emphasis to a moderate emphasis to no emphasis at all as children become accomplished readers. Because children's needs change so dramatically in the kindergarten and first grade, weekly teaching guides for the first and second half of the kindergarten and first grade years are presented. The second and third grades each have a separate weekly teaching guide, and the fourth and fifth grades have a single guide. The guides are integrated into chapters throughout the book. In this way, future and practicing teachers may, if they choose, consult only those chapters that are specifically relevant to the age, grade, and abilities of the children whom they teach.

Teacher Contributions

This book is enriched by the contributions of many teachers who used activities in their classrooms, who made suggestions for ways to make activities effective and easy to implement, and who critiqued the manner in which different activities were matched to the sequence in which fluency develops. Teachers brought to this project an unbridled enthusiasm for meeting the needs of the children whom they teach, a boundless commitment to excellence, and a deep desire to share their insight and wisdom of practice with others in our profession. I am honored to have worked collaboratively with such gifted professionals, and am pleased to share with you, the reader of this book, the knowledge these teachers bring to their classrooms. The photographs (P-1) show the teachers who shared their insights and who encouraged me to make this book classroom based, teacher friendly, and child oriented.

Elizabeth Beecher has taught every elementary grade during her more than 37 years in the classroom. She excels at taking children who lag far behind their peers at the beginning of the year and bringing them up to grade level in reading and writing. She brings to teaching the wisdom of practice and a knowledge of curriculum that are the consequences of good teaching, carefully planned and delivered instruction, and many years of classroom experience. In her free time, Elizabeth enjoys reading mystery novels and caring for her cats, KeeKee and KC.

Heather M. Bosela is an exceptionally talented teacher who is in her fifth year of teaching kindergarten. Heather nurtures literacy with a flood of books, writing, reading, language, and multisensory activities. Her children begin kindergarten knowing little, if anything, about literacy and most leave for first grade reading on a three–four level or above. She creates learning from any situation, and the exceptional reading and writing her kindergarten children display are testaments to her teaching skills. Heather completed a bachelor's degree in New York and then moved to North Carolina, where she now lives with her silky terrier, Sammy.

Malissa Bailey Carr, who is training as a school psychologist, earned an undergraduate degree in child development in Pennsylvania. She became interested in education through teaching Sunday school in the youth ministry in her church, and has 3 1/2 years of teaching experience. She now combines her understanding of test data with an appreciation of how children learn to read. Malissa brings to education a dedication to excellence, an undaunted spirit, and a willingness to put in extra time and extra effort. She is a joy to everyone with whom she works, and she tells many funny stories about her mischievous cat, Scooter.

Krista Hockey lives in New York, where she teaches reading to children in the third and fourth grade. I first met Krista when she was living in Carrboro, North Carolina, and teaching special education to learning disabled children in a rural county. Krista has a keen sense of activities that work for children, and uses methods and materials that children both enjoy and learn from. She continually finds approaches and methods to improve the literacy of children who lag behind their classmates in learning to read. Krista approaches everything with a positive attitude and an open mind, and she willingly shares her talents with other teachers.

Ron Honeycutt has been teaching for 17 years. He has a wide range of experience, perhaps the widest range of anyone I know. When I first met Ron, he was working for the Department of Corrections, teaching inmates to read and write. Later Ron began teaching writing to third, fourth, and fifth graders who, based on statewide tests, were below proficiency. Ron is without question the best writing teacher with whom I have had the pleasure to work. I have seen children begin instruction barely able to write a simple sentence and leave Ron's intervention program able to write complex sentences and craft interesting stories. Ron says that one Irish coffee a day keeps him going in the classroom, but I think it is his talent, intelligence, and commitment to learning that are the real sources of his success.

Before teaching in the elementary school full time, Allison J. Lewis taught preschool and received a bachelor's degree in Pennsylvania. She has taught first and second grade for the last four years. Allison is teaching second grade this year, and some of the writing samples in this book were written by her children in the early fall. After teaching for 4 years, Allison decided to attend graduate school in the evenings and summer sessions to improve her ability to teach language arts. She is a wonderful teacher who continually works to become even better. The children in her classroom and all her friends and colleagues benefit from Allison's insight and understanding of how children develop fluency.

Vanessa Masterpolo earned a bachelor's degree in New York state and then moved to Raleigh where she has been teaching special education to kindergarten through third graders for 5 years. Vanessa is energetic, committed to teaching, and will soon have a master's degree in the teaching of reading. She has boundless energy, is convinced that every child can learn, and makes sure that each child in her classroom reaches his or her full potential. We have all benefited from her professional knowledge, sense of commitment, and exceptional teaching ideas. I should also mention that Vanessa is entertaining and funny; she keeps everyone laughing with her sense of humor and her amusing way of describing life's everyday events.

Kerry McCarthy Oliveri is a reading recovery teacher who began her career teaching middle school language arts. Altogether, Kerry has been teaching for 6 years. She received a bachelor's degree in Connecticut before moving to North Carolina. Kerry is an exceptional teacher who is always ready to try something new, learn different techniques, and share her talents with her friends and fellow teachers. She smiles constantly, believes in the ability of the children whom she teaches, and conveys to children a sense of optimism about themselves as readers. No one can tell a funny story like Kerry and no one can put a smile on someone's face faster. In her spare time, Kerry likes to read, write, do crafts, and shop. She lives with her husband, Joe, who has just finished law school.

Zoa Murray teaches second grade in a rural school that serves a cross section of children. This is Zoa's first year teaching second grade; prior to this she taught middle school language arts. Zoa brings to her second-grade classroom knowledge, skill, and dedication. She drives over 60 miles each day just to get to the rural school in which she teaches, yet she never tires of looking for the best way to teach each and every child. Zoa is committed, energetic, empathetic toward her students, and always finds ways to meet individual needs. She is an excellent teacher who goes that extra mile to support learning, to share with friends and colleagues, and to ensure that the children in her classroom become fluent readers.

Kara Stewart teaches reading to diverse groups of third, fourth, and fifth graders in a rural school. She is sensitive to the strengths and abilities of children and challenges them to improve as readers. Life is never dull in Kara's classroom. Kara makes reading fun by planning mind-engaging lessons in which everyone succeeds. Therefore, it is no surprise that children look forward to the time they spend with her. Even though two elementary age children at home and a busy school schedule keep Kara constantly on the move, she still spends extra time learning new teaching techniques, using new materials, and delivering instruction that challenges every child to be a better reader.

Krista R. VanAntwerp is in her sixth year of teaching first grade. She received a bachelor's degree in New York state and then moved to North Carolina, where she has stayed ever since. Krista is innovative, enthusiastic, and committed to teaching excellence. She understands how children develop literacy and what to do to make sure that each child becomes a successful reader. Krista tries anything and everything, and she modifies ideas to suit her own teaching style and the needs and temperament of the children whom she teaches. Krista is organized, goal focused, and spontaneous. She has a logical mind with a creative spirit, and we have all benefited from her ideas, insights, and approaches. Krista lives with her husband, Matt. She likes to work out in her spare time and, when she is not working out, she practices yoga.

Tamara R. Von Matt moved to North Carolina after earning a bachelor's degree in psychology with teacher certification in the state of New York. She has taught third grade for 4 years, is certified to teach both regular and special education, and will soon be certified to teach reading as a specialty area. Tamara is especially creative and knowledgeable, and she excels in creatively linking vocabulary, concept development, and reading comprehension in ways that third graders understand. She differentiates instruction, challenges the children in her classroom to achieve to the best of their abilities, and selects activities that ensure that everyone is successful. Her classroom is an exciting and creative place where children are saturated with literature and language.

Tonya Weitzel taught fourth and first grade before moving to the second grade. All total, she has been a classroom teacher for 7 years. Tonya has a keen mind and a sense of focus that sets her apart. She has at her fingertips a cache of successful teaching ideas, and she knows how to make every child feel successful. Tonya knows how to teach children from diverse backgrounds and cultures, and how to select just the right instruction to meet the needs of each child. She combines careful observation and insight with a quick mind and a cheerful spirit. Tonya seizes ideas and translates them into effective practice. She is an exceptional teacher who understands how children become fluent readers and who knows how to teach for fluency.

Missing from this group is Mary Jane Mitchell, who was a reading recovery teacher in a rural school. Mary Jane taught in the primary grades for over 5 years and taught reading recovery for the last few years of her teaching career. She was tireless, intelligent, an exceptional teacher, a good writer, a fine student, and a good friend. Mary Jane passed away May 2001. I like to think that her influence permeates this book and the child-focused activities that are described here.

Acknowledgments

I would like to acknowledge the help, support, and contributions of all the talented teachers with whom I have had the pleasure of working over the years. Special thanks go to the many schools that lent support to this manuscript, including Bethesda Elementary, Bugg Elementary, Carthage Elementary, Green Year Round Elementary, Jones Dairy Year Round Elementary, New Hope Elementary, Salem Elementary, Triangle Day School, Weatherstone Elementary, and Wildwood Elementary. I would also like to express my appreciation for the reviewers who read and commented on this text: Priscilla Leggett, Fayetteville State University; Mary Ann Dzama, George Mason University; Gerald Calais, McNeese State University; Diane C. Greene, Mississippi State University; and Dee Caldwell, California State University–Northridge.

I thank you one and all.

—Barbara

CONTENTS

CHAPTER 3

DEVELOPING FLUENCY WITH HANDS-ON ACTIVITIES FOR TEACHING LETTER NAMES AND SINGLE LETTER SOUNDS   58

CHAPTER 4

DEVELOPING FLUENCY WITH HANDS-ON ACTIVITIES FOR TEACHING WORD FAMILIES AND LETTER PATTERNS   93

CHAPTER 5

DEVELOPING FLUENCY WITH HANDS-ON ACTIVITIES FOR TEACHING STRUCTURAL ANALYSIS   141

CHAPTER 6 . . . . .

DEVELOPING FLUENCY WITH ACTIVITIES FOR WORD MEANING AND RAPID RECOGNITION   188

CHAPTER 7 . . . .

DEVELOPING READING FLUENCY   217

How to Teach Word Recognition and Fluency

Chicka Chicka Boom Boom (Martin & Archambault, 1989) is a story about the twenty-six letters of the alphabet climbing a coconut tree and falling to the ground. After Caroline's kindergarten teacher read *Chicka Chicka Boom Boom*, Caroline pasted her own coconut tree on a large piece of construction paper (Figure 1–1). As Caroline learns a new letter, her teacher writes it on a colorful sticky dot, which then goes under Caroline's tree. The coconut letters under Caroline's tree show that she quickly, accurately, and effortlessly recognizes G, A, W, P, T, M, F, R, O, S, L, and C. Soon Caroline will have all twenty-six letters under her coconut tree. Caroline has successfully begun a long, exciting journey toward reading independence.

In a mere five years, Caroline will change from a kindergartner learning the letters of the alphabet to a fifth grader who reads challenging chapter books, learns from content area textbooks, and reads for pleasure anytime and anywhere she wishes. In fifth grade, Caroline will not pay attention to the individual letters, nor will she focus on letter-sounds or struggle with new words. She will pay foremost attention to reading for meaning. She will read for specific purposes, to verify predictions, and to draw conclusions. In addition, Caroline will fluently read texts written on a fifth-grade level.

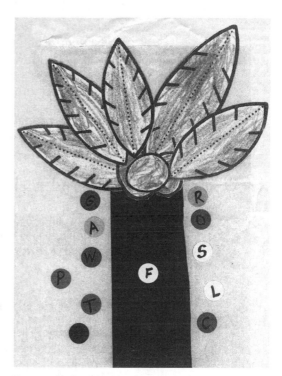

Figure 1–1 *Chicka Chicka Boom Boom* Coconut Tree with Letters

WHAT IS FLUENCY AND WHY IS IT IMPORTANT? ■ ■ ■ ■ ▬▬

Fluent reading is smooth, accurate, and expressive. Fluent readers preserve the natural flow of language, read in meaningful phrases, and emphasize certain words to communicate meaning. Fluent reading can be observed firsthand by watching the news on television. News anchors are accomplished fluent readers. During each news broadcast, anchors read a prepared text as it scrolls across the screen on a teleprompter in front of them. They read accurately, with expression, and at just the right pace for the listening audience. Anchors must accurately read the news. When anchors do misread words, however, their mistakes generally do not affect the overall meaning of the news.

Anchors are careful to add just the right amount of expression to keep our interest and to help us understand the news. For example, the sentence "Who let the dog out?" changes meaning slightly when readers emphasize different words. "**Who** let the dog out?" suggests that the person asking the question is looking for the culprit who left the door or gate open. "Who let the **dog** out?" suggests that the speaker is exasperated because the dog is not where the dog is supposed to be. News commentators emphasize **who** if the speaker in the news story is cross, and emphasize **dog** if the speaker in the news story is merely exasperated about a loose dog. Added to this, commentators read at just the right rate for the listening audience. If the news is read too slowly, we lose interest. If it is read too fast, we cannot keep up with its meaning. Commentators know this and take care to read at a comfortable pace.

Fluent Reading

When Caroline becomes a fluent reader, her oral reading will sound like conversation; she will preserve sentence patterns; and she will read aloud at the pace of normal conversation. By fourth grade, Caroline will be a fluent reader who comprehends more, reads faster, and makes fewer mistakes than her non-fluent classmates (National Center for Education Statistics, 1995). The mechanics, or skills, that support fluency are learned so well that readers do not have to pay attention to them. Fluent readers effortlessly and accurately read words, use comprehension strategies, call on their background knowledge, pay attention to punctuation, and interpret what they read.

In observing a fluent reader, the whole process of reading seems to be seamless and effortless. In many ways, this is true. Fluent reading *is* effortless. Readers' minds are on interpretation and comprehension, and reading is smooth and expressive. However, accomplished fluent reading, like most things in life, is not quite as simple as it looks. Fluency is built on a strong foundation of good spoken language, extensive reading and writing experiences, elaborate concepts and background knowledge, and on a large fluent reading vocabulary. While background experiences and concepts may differ from person to person, *all* fluent readers recognize words rapidly, accurately, and effortlessly.

A Fluent Reading Vocabulary

Fluent word recognition is important for understanding text (Snow, Burns, & Griffin, 1998) and necessary for reading smoothly and expressively. Fluent word recognition, just like fluent text reading, is fast, accurate, and effortless. A fluent reading vocabulary consists of all the words that a reader recognizes quickly, accurately, and effortlessly in context and in isolation. Fluent words are on "the tip of the tongue." They pop off the pages and into a reader's mind, apparently without any effort at all. Children recognize words in their fluent reading vocabulary by sight, by sound, and by meaning, and they do this in just one second (Figure 1–2).

Word fluency allows readers to pay complete attention to meaning. We cannot pay conscious attention to more than one thing at a time. For example, we can watch television or talk on the phone, but we cannot watch television *and* talk on the phone simultaneously. If we get a phone call in the middle of a television program that we wish to watch, we have to shift our attention back and forth from television watching to talking. Shifting attention back and forth takes away from what we get out of the television program and affects how well we participate in the conversation. Likewise, readers can either pay attention to word recognition or to comprehension. When word recognition is fluent, readers do not need to shift their attention back and forth between word recognition and comprehension. Children pay complete attention to comprehension, which is exactly what good readers do.

As you observe children in your classroom you will notice that they read some words quickly, accurately, and effortlessly, while other words are read slowly and with effort. The words children read in a mere second are in children's fluent reading vocabulary. The words that are read after some hesitation or that require self-correcting are not in children's fluent reading vocabulary. Let us use the word *town* as an example. A child might stare at *town* for a few seconds and then say "town." Or a child might first say "toe" and then self-correct to say "town." Words read after a slight hesitation or self-corrections are known words, but they are not known well enough to be fluent words. Fluent word recognition is always quick and always effortless. As teachers, we want to bring all the known-but-not-fluent words into children's fluent reading vocabulary.

Getting to Word Meaning through Fluent Word Recognition

See a New Word in Text
↓
Instantly Recognize the Word by How It Looks, How It Sounds, and What It Means

Getting to Word Meaning through Sound

See a New Word in Text
↓
Associate Letters with Sounds to Pronounce the New Word
↓
Recognize the New Written Word Is a Familiar Spoken Word
↓
Recognize the Word by How it Looks, How It Sounds, and What It Means
↓
Recognize the Words by Sight

FIGURE 1–2 Getting to Word Meaning through Fluent Word Recognition or through Sound

GETTING TO WORD MEANING THROUGH SOUND ■ ■ ■ ■ ▬▬▬

Associating sounds with letters to pronounce unfamiliar written words is called *decoding*. Good decoders have a good working knowledge of the way that letters represent sounds (Adams, 1990; Byrne, Freebody, & Gates, 1992; National Institute of Child Health and Human Development, 2000; Rupley & Wilson, 1997). Children use this knowledge to sound out words that they do not immediately recognize. On hearing themselves say the word, children recognize that it is a familiar spoken word. This route to word meaning is from (1) print (2) through the sound of a familiar spoken word (3) to the meaning of the familiar spoken word (Figure 1–2).

Caroline learns letter names and letter sounds in kindergarten. She learns that the letter *b* represents the /b/ sound in *bunny*, that *a* represents the /a/ sound in *apple*, and that *t* represents the /t/ sound in *table*. Toward the end of kindergarten or the beginning of first grade, Caroline will be able to use one or more of these single letter-sounds to read *bat*, but she will not be able to read words like *bait*, *bake*, *beat*, or *bay*. Caroline will learn about letter patterns in the first and second grade. *Letter patterns* are two or more letters that represent sound. For example, Caroline will learn that *ch* represents /ch/, and that *ea* represents the sound heard in *mean* and *bead*. She will use her knowledge of letter patterns to read and learn many different words, such as *cheat*, *beach*, and *beat*. In third, fourth, and fifth grade, Caroline will learn the pronunciation and meaning of large structures in words, such as the *pre-* in *prepay* and the *-less* and *-ness* in *lawlessness*. She will also learn to pronounce long words by dividing them into large units, which we call syllables. She will be able to read and spell words like *manipulate* by dividing them into syllables, as in *ma - nip´ - u - late*.

Good decoders are mindful of word and text meaning. Good decoders always double-check to make sure that the words he or she decodes make sense. For example, if a word is not important, such as a difficult-to-pronounce name of a minor character in a novel, Caroline may decide not to labor over the precise pronunciation. Caroline will use decoding to add useful words to her reading vocabulary, and she will also use her knowledge of letter and sound relationships to spell. *Graphophonic cues* are the letter and sound relationships, meaningful letter groups inside words (the *un-* in *unhappy* or the *port* in *airport*), syllables (*com / pu / ter* in *computer*), and punctuation in sentences. When she uses graphophonic cues, she will ask herself, "Does this word look and sound right?" The good readers in your classroom are meaning-focused decoders. That is, they focus on identifying words that make sense. They use their knowledge of sentence meaning to decide when a decoded word is correct. When words make sense, children immediately turn their attention to comprehension. When decoded words do not make sense, children give decoding another try. The children whom you teach almost always meet new words in sentences. And sentences have clues that go beyond the letters that make up individual words.

■■■ ■ ■ ■ ■ GETTING TO WORD MEANING THROUGH CONTEXT CLUES

Context clues consist of semantic and syntactic cues. *Semantic cues* are the meaningful connections in sentences, paragraphs, and whole passages. Readers combine meaning cues with their own background knowledge to decide if the message is logical, makes sense, and is consistent with the real world. When using semantic cues, children ask themselves, "Does this make sense?"

Children use *syntactic cues* to decide whether word order reflects conventional English grammar. When children use syntactic cues (grammatical cues), they ask themselves, "Does this seem like language?" For example, "Let dog the out who?" has the same five words as the sentence, "Who let the dog out?" but the word order is so scrambled that we cannot make sense of the message. The strongest and most valuable strategy for children to take is to use all three cues—semantic, syntactic, and graphophonic.

To illustrate the use of all three cues, we will consider Kathy's writing (Figure 1–3), *All About Bats!!* We know from the semantic cues that this is a short narrative report on bats. We expect Kathy to tell us something about bats, and therefore we look for information pertaining to these flying mammals. Kathy uses good English syntax. She

FIGURE 1–3
All About Bats!!

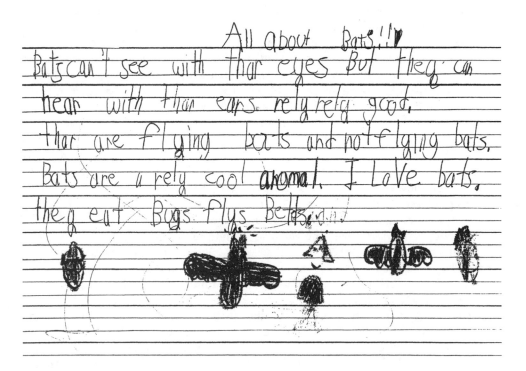

puts subjects before verbs, uses nouns and pronouns appropriately, and puts periods at the end of sentences. Most words are conventionally spelled, but a few are not. T*har*, *rely*, *anomal*, and *betets* are not English words, with the exception of *rely*. When we look at the sentence context in which *rely* appears, "Bats can't see with thar eyes but they can hear with thar ears rely rely good," we realize that *rely* does not make sense. R*ely* may look like an English word, but it does not sound right in this context.

At this point we turn our attention to graphophonic cues. A*nomal*, we surmise, means *animal*. We may sound out *anomal* by associating speech with print. So, while *anomal* is not conventionally spelled, it is readable, provided, of course, that we use our graphophonic cues to identify this word. Syntactic cues suggest that *betets* is a noun, and semantic cues suggest that *betets* is something bats eat. B*etets* is spelled with one B, two *es*, and two *ts*. These three graphophonic cues, together with semantic and syntactic cues, imply that Kathy was spelling *beetles*. And, in fact, when Kathy shared her story, that is exactly what she read.

DEVELOPING A LARGE FLUENT READING VOCABULARY ■ ■ ■ ■ ▬▬

Children develop a large fluent reading vocabulary through their experiences reading and writing, and with word recognition instruction that meets their needs. A large fluent reading vocabulary develops gradually over time and follows a predictable learning sequence. This sequence consists of five learning stages: pre-alphabetic, partial alphabetic, alphabetic, consolidated, and automatic (Ehri, 1997; Ehri & McCormick, 1998; Gaskins, Ehri, Cress, O'Hara, & Donnelly, 1997). The stages begin when children do not understand how letters represent sounds and end when children have a large and powerful fluent reading vocabulary. Each stage is associated with different knowledge, skills, and word recognition strategies. Consequently, the children in your classroom will differ in their ability to identify new words, depending on the stage of word fluency they are in at the time. The five word fluency stages are as follows:

1. The *pre-alphabetic stage*: Preschool and early kindergarten
2. The *partial alphabetic stage*: Early kindergarten to early first grade
3. The *alphabetic stage*: Late kindergarten, first and second grade
4. The *consolidated stage*: Late second grade through fifth grade
5. The *automatic stage*: Beyond elementary school (for most children)

Instruction that meets children's needs in one stage is not particularly beneficial when the same children are in another stage. We will now consider what children know and can do in each of the five stages, beginning with preschool and early kindergarten.

Stage 1. Pre-alphabetic Word Fluency: Preschool and Early Kindergarten

Many kindergarten children begin their journey toward word fluency in the pre-alphabetic stage (Ehri, 1997; Ehri, 1998; Ehri & McCormick, 1998; Gaskins, Ehri, Cress, O'Hara, & Donnelly, 1997). These children do not know that the letters in written words represent the sounds in spoken words. Children want to read, but are confused about how to go about reading.

Children in the pre-alphabetic stage do not understand that some spoken words rhyme, and all words consist of individual sounds. Understanding that some words rhyme and that all words consist of individual sounds is a special kind of insight into language. This insight, which we call *phonemic awareness*, is much more than talking and listening. It is the ability to literally divide words into individual, meaningless speech

FIGURE 1–4   Pre-alphabetic Writing Sample (Showing a Giraffe)

sounds. An example of a phonemic awareness skill is dividing the spoken word /pig/ into three individual sounds: the beginning sound /p/, the middle sound /i/, and the last sound /g/. This insight is not at all necessary to speak, to listen to, or to understand English. It is, however, absolutely necessary to learn to read. English is based on the principle that the letters in written words represent sounds in spoken words. Children who do not realize that words have individual sounds cannot match the letters in written words with the sounds in spoken words. To these children, our English alphabetic writing system is an unsolved puzzle.

Let us imagine that alphabetic writing is a large puzzle with many interlocking pieces. Each word is a puzzle unto itself that has letter-sound puzzle pieces and sound puzzle pieces. The letter-sound pieces are phonics, and the sound pieces match the individual sounds in words. With good instruction children may learn some of the letter-sound puzzle pieces. For example, children might learn that the letter *p* represents the sound /p/, the *i* represents /i/, and the *g* stands for /g/. Children who know that pig consists of the three sounds /p/, /i/, and /g/ match the sound represented by the letter *p* with the beginning sound in /pig/, the *i* with the middle sound and the *g* with the last sound. But if children do not understand that words consist of individual sounds, they do not have the sound-based puzzle pieces to interlock with the letter-sound pieces. With only part of the puzzle of alphabetic writing, children cannot fit together the letter-sound pieces with the individual sound pieces and cannot, therefore, get to word meaning through sound.

Brandon (Figure 1–4) is a kindergartner in the pre-alphabetic word fluency stage. Brandon does not understand sound-letter relationships and, therefore, writes letters and letter-like shapes one after the other across the page. Letters do not correspond to sounds, so Brandon's teacher cannot read what he writes. This type of spelling is called *precommunicative* because these children cannot communicate through writing (Gentry, 2000; Gentry & Gillett, 1993). Interestingly, when Brandon's teacher asks Brandon to tell what he writes, he is able to tell about the message immediately after writing. However, after a few hours he has forgotten what he wrote. So long as the letters on the page do not have any relationship with sound, children (and their teachers) cannot recreate meaningful spoken messages from children's writing.

Before Brandon began using letters, he made squiggly lines across the page to simulate adult longhand (cursive) writing. Later, Brandon wrote letters all over the page in no particular direction, and sometimes included letters in the pictures he drew on the page. Now that Brandon is aware of left-to-right direction, he writes letter strings across the bottom or the top of the page. Brandon does not put white spaces among letters because he does not realize that one written word corresponds to one spoken word. Since white spaces do not serve a real function from Brandon's point of view, he ignores them in writing. Even though Brandon doesn't connect spoken words with written words, he does sometimes copy words from the print in his classroom.

Brandon realizes that writing is meaningful and that writing has letters, but does not know how print-to-speech connections work. He uses five strategies to read:

1. Brandon associates words with cues in his everyday environment.
2. He makes up a story from the pictures.
3. He memorizes text.
4. He associates words with their unique shapes.
5. He focuses on one or two letters in a special word, and then thinks that any word with those letters is the special word he has memorized.

In using environmental cues, Brandon pays attention to familiar signs, logos, and buildings in his everyday environment (Masonheimer, Drum, & Ehri, 1984).

Brandon then associates the signs, logos, and buildings with whole words. For example, he might connect the word McDonalds© with the golden arches and say "McDonalds" whenever the golden arches come into view.

When Brandon uses the picture strategy, he looks for meaning in pictures and then "reads" the illustrations. Brandon also memorizes familiar stories. He holds a familiar book and recites, from memory, the text while turning the pages one by one. Children like Brandon, who are in the pre-alphabetic stage, understand that reading is meaningful, know that special words are connected to books, but cannot figure out how adult readers decipher the words they see in print.

Later in the pre-alphabetic word fluency stage, Brandon may use word shape to recognize words. For example, he might remember *elephant* because it is a very long word. Then, when Brandon sees other long words, like *octopus*, *rhinoceros*, and *dinosaur*, he says "elephant." Children like Brandon may also use one or two letters to remember a word. For instance, children might associate the *oo* (two eyes) with the word *food*. Therefore, every time that Brandon sees a word with an *oo*, like *look*, *goose*, *moon*, and *balloon*, he says "food."

Children in the pre-alphabetic word fluency stage may know how to write their own names, may know a few letter names or letter-sounds, and may even read a couple of words. You may find this to be particularly true for children who have had a strong pre-kindergarten experience or a lot of help at home. You can expect these children to know up to as many as ten letter names, especially the names of the letters in their own names (Snow, Burns, & Griffin, 1998). But none of this knowledge is transferable. Children cannot generalize this information to recognizing new words because children do not yet know how print represents speech.

Brandon is busy learning the letter names and shapes in his kindergarten classroom, which is critical to his success in kindergarten (Snow, Burns, & Griffin, 1998; Whitehurst & Lonigan, 2001). Kindergartners with more letter knowledge are better readers later in the elementary grades than kindergartners with less letter knowledge (Stevenson & Newman, 1986). In order to move to the next word fluency stage, Brandon needs to learn three things: (1) he needs to realize that some spoken words share sounds (the /at/ in /cat/, /bat/, and /fat/); (2) he needs to be able to say just the beginning sound in a spoken word (the /b/ in /bike/ or the /s/ in /sad/); and (3) he needs to know the beginning letter-sound associations in words (the letter *b* in *bug* represents the /b/ sound in /bug/) (Byrne & Fielding-Barnsley, 1990).

Stage 2. Partial Alphabetic Word Fluency: Early Kindergarten to Early First Grade

Most children move into the partial alphabetic stage sometime during kindergarten, although children may begin kindergarten while in this stage. Ideally, children should complete the partial alphabetic stage before the end of the kindergarten year. Children who begin first grade in the partial alphabetic stage must transition into the next stage, the alphabetic stage, very quickly if they are to be successful in first grade. Children in the partial alphabetic stage know some, but not all, the sounds associated with letters.

Kevin is a kindergartner in the partial alphabetic stage (Figure 1–5). Kevin uses the following strategies to recognize the new words that he sees in storybooks:

1. Kevin first looks at the picture for a clue.
2. He looks at the beginning letter-sound, and possibly the ending letter-sound.
3. He combines picture clues and story context cues with beginning and/or ending letter-sound cues to read words that make sense in the story.

Figure 1–5 Partial Alphabetic Writing Sample (Dog)

4. Kevin remembers some words by sight. In doing this, he associates a whole spoken word, /cat/, with a whole written word, *cat*. The few words that he recognizes effortlessly are already in his fluent reading vocabulary.

When Kevin meets a new word in an easy book, he first looks at the picture for a clue to the word's identity. If Kevin sees a picture that seems to make sense in the story, he says the picture name. For example, if Kevin is reading a story about his favorite food and sees a picture of an ice cream cone, he says "ice cream cone".

Kevin may also choose to look at the beginning letter-sound and, possibly, the ending letter-sound. In so doing, Kevin concentrates on using graphophonic cues. For example, on seeing *soup* in the book about favorite foods, Kevin associates an /s/ sound with the letter *s* and, possibly, a /p/ sound with the letter *p*. He then uses the /s/ and the /p/ sounds to narrow down possible word choices to just words that begin and end with these two sounds.

The third option is to think about a combination of picture clues, the story context, and the beginning and ending letter-sounds. Should the story have a picture of a *taco*, Kevin looks at the picture, thinks of the story context, and notices that *taco* begins with a /t/ and ends with an /o/. Kevin uses this information to confidently say "taco".

Kevin realizes that different words begin and end with different sounds. For example, he knows that the spoken word /dog/ begins with a /d/ sound and ends with a /g/ sound. When Kevin's teacher asks him to "Say the beginning sound in *dog*," Kevin replies "d". When Kevin's teacher asks him to "Say the ending sound in *dog*," he says "g."

Kevin knows the beginning and ending letter sounds in words. For instance, he knows that the /d/ sound is represented by the letter *d* and the /g/ sound is represented by the letter *g*. Kevin uses this knowledge to identify new words and to spell; therefore, we see that Kevin writes *dog* with a *d* and a *g*. If we did not have Kevin's drawing to help us, we could not figure out that *dg* means *dog*. However, when combined with the picture clue, we are quite confident that Kevin intended to write *dog* and not something else altogether.

Kevin uses his letter-sound knowledge to spell. In spelling, Kevin says a word to himself, associates letters with some of the sounds he hears, and then writes letters that represent the sounds. There are two reasons that Kevin uses only beginning and ending letter-sounds: (1) he does not know all the sounds associated with all the letters, so he is missing phonics knowledge, and (2) Kevin does not realize that there are middle sounds in words. Kevin cannot yet separate spoken words into each and every sound. For example, while he tells his teacher that /dog/ has a /d/ and a /g/, he cannot identify the middle sound, the /o/, in /dog/. Consequently, Kevin writes letters for some, but not all, the sounds in words. Gentry calls this *semi-phonetic spelling* (2000; Gentry & Gillett, 1993). While words do not look like English, teachers can read children's writing when the pictures help tell the story and when teachers are familiar with the context in which the stories are written.

Children like Kevin develop six essential literacy-related abilities and skills while in the partial alphabetic stage:

1. Children learn to identify and say rhyming words.
2. Children develop skill at identifying and saying the beginning, middle, and ending sounds in words.
3. Children learn all the letter names.
4. Children learn one sound for each letter.
5. Children develop skill at using beginning and ending letter-sounds to identify new words.
6. Children develop the ability to combine picture, semantic, syntactic, and beginning and ending letter-sound cues to identify new words.

In order to move to the next word fluency stage, Kevin needs to learn more about letter-sounds and more about the way that spoken words are built of individual speech sounds. Teaching letter-sounds is a cornerstone of the kindergarten language arts program (Snow, Burns, & Griffin, 1998). What's more, teaching phonics in kindergarten and first grade is more effective than waiting to teach phonics until children are already reading (National Institute of Child Health and Human Development, 2000). Because Kevin uses only beginning and ending letter-sounds, he usually does not recognize unfamiliar words without the help of his teacher. If the picture does not give a strong clue and if the story context is weak, Kevin cannot narrow his choices further than the beginning and ending letter-sounds in words. Vocabulary growth is slow because Kevin uses only part of the letter and sound clues to identify and remember words. In order for Kevin to dramatically increase his fluent reading vocabulary, he must learn more about letter and sound relationships (Adams, 1990).

Stage 3. Alphabetic Word Fluency: Late Kindergarten, First, and Second Grade

Most children enter the alphabetic stage toward the end of kindergarten or at the beginning of first grade. Stephen is a first grader in the alphabetic stage (Figure 1–6). He wrote a story during the first month of school, which reads: I like my dog because it is the cutest dog I've seen on earth. Stephen conventionally spells I, *my*, *dog* (with a reversed *b/d*), *it*, *is*, *the*, and *on*. These words are in his fluent reading vocabulary. Stephen reads these words quickly, accurately, and effortlessly.

Stephen is learning how patterns of two or more letters represent sound. Stephen sounds his way through words. In reading, he pays attention to the beginning, middle, and ending letter-sounds. Stephen spells known words conventionally and invents ways to spell other words. Stephen invents his own unique spellings by saying words to himself, listening for all the sounds in words, associating a letter with each sound, and then writing the letters. As a consequence, Stephen spells words the way they sound, not necessarily the way they look. For example, Stephen spells *seen* as *sen* and *like* as *lik*. *Because* looks just like it sounds (*be kus*) except, of course, *because* is one word, not two. As Stephen slowly said *because* to himself, he heard a known word, *be*, and then wrote *kus*.

As he invents spelling, Stephen explores and extends his understandings of letter and sound relationships. Spelling *osum* for *awesome* and *crec* for *creek* is called

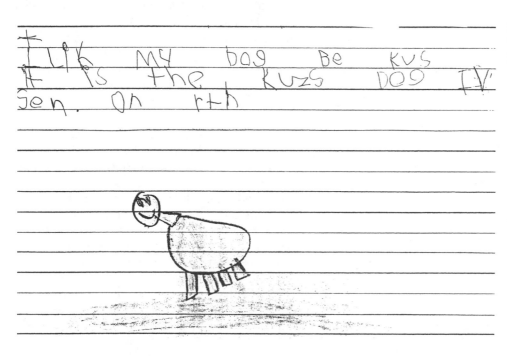

FIGURE 1–6 Alphabetic Writing Sample (Cutest Dog Story)

FIGURE 1–7 Moving Through the Stages of Word Fluency

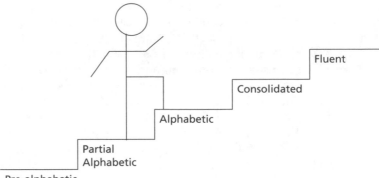

Children move through the stages of word fluency just like we climb stairs, gradually and with a fluid motion so that one stage flows smoothly and continuously into another stage.

either invented spelling or phonetic spelling (Gentry, 2000; Gentry & Gillett, 1993). Let us take a closer look at *rth* (*earth*). *Rth* does not have a vowel letter (*a, e, i, o, u*). But if we say "earth" aloud, we hear the /r/ and /th/, which is exactly what Stephen wrote. *Rth* is more typical of the partial alphabetic stage.

Children gradually move from one stage to another. We can liken moving through the stages of word fluency to climbing stairs. Imagine that we are climbing five stairs. We put our first foot on the first stair while placing our second foot on the second stair. Then we shift our weight to the second foot (second stair) while we move our first foot to the third stair, and so on. At any given point in time we may be on one particular stair, but most of the time we are transitioning from one stair to the next. Children move through the stages of word fluency like we climb stairs, gradually and with a fluid motion so that one stage flows into another (Figure 1–7). We sometimes see vestiges of an earlier stage when children are completing a transition into a higher stage. When children are in a particular stage, we observe that they predominantly use knowledge, skills, and strategies characteristic of that stage. And then as children gradually begin to transition into the next higher stage, they start to use new knowledge, skills, and strategies. Eventually children use the new knowledge, skills, and strategies all of the time. When this happens, we are confident that children have transitioned into the next stage.

Decoding is slow at the beginning of the alphabetic stage, and Stephen is a rather slow, plodding decoder. Because decoding takes a good bit of time and energy, we sometimes describe children like Stephen as being "glued to print." However, this is only a short-lived phase within the alphabetic stage of word fluency. By no later than the second half of the first grade year, and throughout the second grade, decoding becomes faster, more accurate, and more effortless. As Stephen moves further into the alphabetic stage, he will pay more and more attention to vowel letters and he will eventually learn how the same sound can be represented by several letter patterns.

Semaji (Figure 1–8) is a beginning second grader who is further into the alphabetic stage. She realizes that the same sounds can be spelled with different letters. Semaji looks for different letter patterns that represent the same sound, such as the sound of *o* we hear in *stove, boat, go,* and *snow*. Semaji's reading vocabulary is growing by leaps and bounds. She reads

FIGURE 1–8 Alphabetic Writing Sample (Robot)

many words quickly, accurately, and effortlessly, and she uses her knowledge of phonics and the reading context to figure out the identity of many new words in stories. Semaji looks for vowels in words when she reads, and includes vowels in words when she spells. When Semaji reads, she focuses on meaning and uses word identification only when she meets words that are not already in her fluent reading vocabulary.

1. Semaji associates sounds with all the letters in words.
2. She completely sounds out new words.
3. She decodes and learns new words on her own without help from her teacher.
4. She corrects her own decoding mistakes.
5. Semaji actively works at identifying words that make sense in the reading context.

Unlike Stephen, who does not yet know how different letter patterns represent the same sound, Semaji is well aware of the letter patterns in words. For example, Semaji confuses *wear* with the similar-sounding word *where*, and uses an *s* in *certain* (spelled *serten*) instead of a *c*. She writes *pere* for *pair*. Interestingly, the *ere* in *where* and *there* represent the /air/ in *pair*. Most of the words in Semaji's letter are conventionally spelled. One explanation is that Semaji is developing a good working knowledge of phonics. However, this is not a completely satisfactory explanation. Semaji has a great deal of experience reading and writing, good reading instruction, and understands that words consist of individual speech sounds. In other words, Semaji knows a good deal about spoken and written language, and learns words through direct instruction, and through experiences reading and writing.

Semaji reads independently and teaches herself new words. The more Semaji reads and writes, the more words she adds to her fluent reading vocabulary. As Semaji adds more words to her fluent reading vocabulary, she is able to tackle longer words in harder books. While in the alphabetic stage, children like Stephen and Semaji develop and refine the following knowledge, skills, and strategies:

1. Children further develop phonemic awareness. By second grade, phonemic awareness is developed well enough so that children no longer need instruction in this area.
2. Children learn how letter patterns represent sounds in words, such as the *aw* in *awful*, the *oi* in *point*, and the *ee* in *street*.
3. Children learn simple compound words (*foot* + *ball* = *football*).
4. Children learn frequently used contractions, which are shortcuts for writing words such as *isn't* and *doesn't*.
5. Children learn a few frequently used prefixes (meaningful multi-letter structures added to the beginning of a word), such as the *un-* in *unhappy* and the *re-* in *reuse*.
6. Children learn a few frequently used suffixes (meaningful multi-letter structures added to the end of words), such as the *-ed* in *played* and the *-er* in *bigger*.

As a second grader, Semaji uses letter and sound relationships to recognize and learn words. By the time she is in the third grade, Semaji will be a far better reader than her classmates who are not skilled at using letter and sound relationships (Byrne, Freebody, & Gates, 1992). Semaji is well on her way toward becoming a reader with a large fluent reading vocabulary. By the end of the second grade Semaji will have left the alphabetic stage behind. As children understand more about the way that letters represent sound, children like Semaji begin to notice large groups of meaningful and non-meaningful letters in words. When children do this, they gradually move into the consolidated word fluency stage.

Stage 4. Consolidated Word Fluency: Late Second Grade, and Third, Fourth, and Fifth Grades

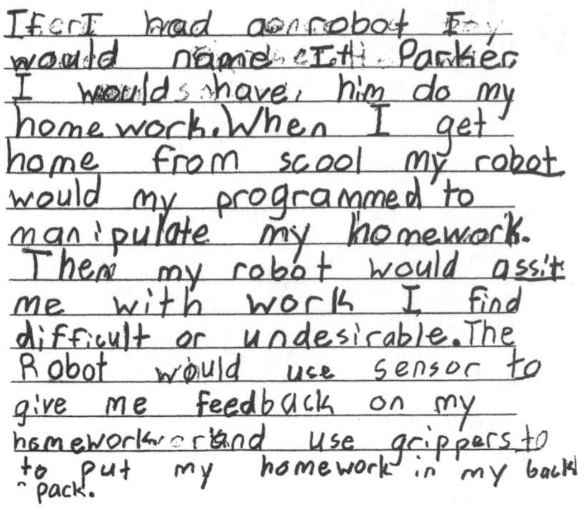

> If or I had an robot I
> would named it Parkier
> I woulds have him do my
> homework. When I get
> home from scool my robot
> would my programmed to
> manipulate my homework.
> Then my robot would assit
> me with work I find
> difficult or undesirable. The
> Robot would use sensor to
> give me feedback on my
> homework work and use grippers to
> to put my homework in my back
> pack.

FIGURE 1–9   Consolidated Writing Sample (Robot)

The consolidated stage may begin in the late second grade or in the early third grade. It is important for children to reach the consolidated stage before they go to the fourth grade. Children in this stage work their way through new words in large bites as they look for meaningful and non-meaningful letter groups. Jeremy (Figure 1–9) is in the consolidated stage. Jeremy conventionally spelled all the words in his story, although he wrote *my* instead of *be* in one sentence.

Jeremy thinks of long words as consisting of several large, and often meaningful, structures. Look at the way he spelled *manipulate*. The way he wrote this word suggests that he was figuring out how to spell the word as he was writing it. The first portion, *man*, is separated somewhat from the *i*, which is also a bit of a distance from *pulate: man i pulate*. This is, no doubt, the way that Jeremy sounded through this word. Jeremy also adds an *-ed* to *programmed*. He has a good working knowledge of phonics, so he knows to double the last letter, the *m*, before adding the *-ed* word ending. He adds two meaningful structures to the word *desire*. He puts an *un-* on the beginning and an *-able* on the end to spell *undesireable*.

Jeremy is comprehension focused. He is an independent reader whose word recognition and comprehension are almost seamless. In addition to the knowledge, skills, and strategies learned in earlier word fluency stages, Jeremy does the following:

1. He uses the reading context along with large meaningful and non-meaningful multi-letter groups to learn and to recognize new words.
2. Jeremy corrects his own word recognition mistakes.
3. Jeremy's fluent reading vocabulary is growing rapidly and steadily.

Children in the consolidated word fluency stage are independent readers. These children add words to their fluent reading vocabulary through reading and writing experiences. They read long words with ease, and their fluent reading vocabulary is growing rapidly. Jeremy, and other children like him, are now using reading as a tool to help them learn the material in their content subject textbooks.

When Jeremy meets words that are not in his fluent reading vocabulary, he is quick to find the largest possible multi-letter groups in words. As Jeremy moves through the consolidated stage, he will learn a great deal about the multi-letter groups in words.

1. Jeremy will learn to read and write many different prefixes, such as the *pre-* in *prepay* and the *il-* in *illegal*.
2. He will learn to read and write many different suffixes, like the *-es* in *peaches* and the *-ful* in *beautiful* (Nagy, Diakidoy, & Anderson, 1993; Singleson, Mahony, & Mann, 2000).
3. He will learn to recognize more challenging contractions than were learned in the alphabetic stage (*there's* and *would've*).
4. He will learn to recognize more unusual compound words than were learned in the alphabetic stage.
5. He will learn to read and write long words by dividing them into large structures, which we call syllables. M*anipulate*, for example, has four syllables: *ma / nip / u / late*.
6. Jeremy will learn to recognize and understand the meaning of root words borrowed from Latin and Greek (the *port* in *transport* and *report*).

Concentrating on a few structures streamlines word recognition and supports learning long words. This brings the long words in content area textbooks within the grasp of third, fourth, and fifth graders. Eventually, children have enough reading and writing experiences, and enough classroom instruction, to be able to recognize 99 percent of the words in any text they wish to read. When this happens, children move into the automatic stage.

Stage 5. Automatic Word Fluency: Middle School and Above

Children reach the automatic stage when they quickly and effortlessly recognize all the words in the books they wish to read. Readers pay special attention to the context and they expect the writing in books to make sense. These children use many different strategies to understand words, sentences, passages, and entire chapters. Children are fully independent readers who use reading as a learning tool, who read books that are appropriate for their age and interests, and who have sufficient reading ability to sustain them through higher education, employment, and a lifetime of leisure reading.

DECIDING WHAT TO TEACH AND WHEN TO TEACH IT ■ ■ ■ ■ ▬▬

Children in a certain word-fluency stage need very different instruction than children in another stage. For instance, the knowledge, skills, and strategies that meet the needs of children in the pre-alphabetic stage are not at all appropriate for children in the alphabetic stage. We want to select just the right instruction for what children know, what children can do, and what children need to learn. To do this, we need to know: (1) what to teach; (2) when in the elementary grades to teach it; and (3) how much time to spend teaching. The answer to what to teach, when to teach it, and how much time to spend teaching knowledge and skills depends on the children's stage of word fluency. Figure 1–10 is a summary of when children enter each word fluency stage, what children in each stage know and can do, and what children need to know to move to the next higher stage. Figure 1–10 also indicates where to look for chapters with teaching activities that are tailor-made to meet the needs of children in the different stages.

We have worked out weekly teaching guides for children at different word-fluency stages, beginning in kindergarten and ending in fifth grade. Each weekly teaching guide is specifically crafted to help you know what to teach, when to teach, and how often to teach. Children change immensely from the first to the second half of kindergarten and from the first to the second half of first grade. Therefore, there are two guides for kindergarten (first half and second half of the year) and two guides for first grade (first and second half of the year). There is one guide for second grade, one for third grade, and one for a combination of fourth and fifth grades.

Each guide is specifically designed for children at a specific stage of word fluency:

1. The teaching guide for the first half of kindergarten is for children in the pre-alphabetic stage.
2. The teaching guide for the second half of kindergarten is for children in the partial alphabetic stage.
3. The teaching guide for the first half of first grade is for children who have just moved into the alphabetic stage.
4. The teaching guide for the second half of the first grade is for children in the alphabetic stage who are developing a working knowledge of phonics.
5. The teaching guide for the second grade is for children in the alphabetic stage who are refining their knowledge of phonics.
6. The teaching guide for the third grade is for children who have just moved into the consolidated stage.
7. The teaching guide for the fourth and fifth grades is for children who are refining knowledge of the large structures in words and who are reading longer words in harder text.

FIGURE 1–10 The Five Stages of Word Fluency

Stage	Chapter	Begins	Ends	Knowledge and Strategies
Stage 1 Pre-alphabetic	Chapters 2 and 3	Preschool or Early Kindergarten	Mid-Kindergarten	**What Children Know** May know a few letter names or letter sounds. May know how to read a few words. May be able to write own name. **What Children Do** Use an environmental print strategy (associate words with signs and logos). Use a picture reading strategy to tell a story from the pictures. Read from memory by reciting the story. Recognize words by their unique shapes. Associate a word with a special letter and read every word with that letter as the same word. **What Children Need to Know and Do to Move to the Next Stage** Know that some words rhyme. Identify and say beginning sounds in words (/bug/ begins with /b/). Learn beginning letter-sound associations. Understand that beginning letters represent the beginning sounds in words.
Stage 2 Partial Alphabetic	Chapters 2 and 3	Kindergarten Early First Grade	Late Kindergarten Early First Grade	The fluent reading vocabulary slowly increases. **What Children Know** Understand that readers construct meaning from print. Understand that some words rhyme. Understand that words have beginning and ending sounds. Know the names of all the letters. Know single letter-sounds. Understand concepts of print, such as left-to-right direction. Know how to find separate words on the page. Know how to find individual letters in words. Know how to match the beginning and ending letters in words with the beginning and ending sounds in words. May have a few words in the fluent reading vocabulary. Reading is meaningful. **What Children Can Do** Use semantic, syntactic, and picture cues to recognize words. Use beginning letter-sound cues to recognize words. Use ending letter-sound cues to recognize words. Remember some words by sight (associate *boy* with spoken word /boy/). Effortlessly recognize the words in their fluent reading vocabulary. Read for meaning.

| Stage 3 Alphabetic | Chapters 2 and 3 in in late kindergarten and the first half of first grade | Late Kindergarten Early First Grade |
| | Chapters 4 through 7 | Late Second Grade Third Grade |

<u>What Children Need to Know and Do to Move to the Next Stage</u>
Blend sounds together to pronounce words (/c/ + /a/ + /t/ = /cat/).
Improve the ability to identify the individual sounds in words.
Learn how two or more letters represent sounds (the long o in go, phone, and boat).
Associate sounds with all the letters in words to pronounce new words.
Learn common word families (at in cat, fat, bat, and rat, or ig in pig, big, and dig).
Use word family patterns in known words (the at in cat) to recognize new words (bat, hat).

The fluent reading vocabulary expands rapidly. Decoding is slow at the beginning of this stage. Later in the alphabetic stage decoding is faster and more efficient.

<u>What Children Know</u>
Understand that words consist of individual speech sounds.
Realize that individual sounds can be blended together to make words.
Know that compound words are two words that make a new word (cow + boy = cowboy).
Know how word family patterns like at and ind represent the same sounds in different words (sat, rat, slat, and mind, kind, and blind).
Know how groups of letters represent sounds (the oi in soil; the vowel-consonant-e pattern in bike, face, hope, and mule).
Recognize frequently used suffixes (-ed in played).
Recognize a few frequently used prefixes (un- in unhappy).
Have many words in their fluent reading vocabulary.

<u>What Children Can Do</u>
Separate words into sounds (/dog/ consists of /d/, /o/, and /g/).
Blend sounds into words (/d/ + /o/ + /g/ = /dog/).
Remember whole words by sight.
Decode by analogy. Use letter patterns in familiar words to infer the pronunciation of unfamiliar words with the same letter patterns.
Decode by sounding out. Associate sounds with all the letters in words to pronounce new words.
Read compound words (snowman).
Identify often-used contractions (is + not = isn't).
Effortlessly recognize many words in their fluent reading vocabulary.
Learn words on their own, without help from the teacher.
Self-correct word recognition mistakes.
Read for meaning.

<u>What Children Need to Know and Do to Move to the Next Stage</u>
Learn different prefixes (the il- in illegal).
Learn different suffixes (the -ful in beautiful).
Learn to identify syllables in long words (per/haps).
Learn the meaning of root words borrowed from Latin and Greek (the port in transport and report)

FIGURE 1–10 Continued.

Stage	Chapter	Begins	Ends	Knowledge and Strategies
Stage 4 Consolidated	Chapters 4 through 7	Late Second Grade Early Third Grade	Fifth Grade	The fluent reading vocabulary is rapidly expanding. _What Children Know_ Know how prefixes (re- in _replay_) affect word meaning. Know how suffixes (-ed in _played_) affect word meaning. Know all contractions (abbreviated words) such as _they'll_ and _we're_. Understand how written words are divided into syllables (per/haps). Know the meaning of root words borrowed from Latin and Greek (the _port_ in _transport_ and _report_). Have a large fluent reading vocabulary. _What Children Can Do_ Decode by dividing words into large multi-letter syllables. Decode by identifying prefixes (re- in _reuse_) and suffixes (-est in _biggest_). Associate meaning with common root words borrowed from Latin and Greek, such as the _port_ in _transport_ and _report_. Decode by analogy. Use letter patterns in familiar words to infer the pronunciation of unfamiliar words that have the same letter patterns. Decode by sounding out. Associate sounds with letters to pronounce new words. Effortlessly recognize words in the fluent reading vocabulary. Read long words with ease. Self-correct word recognition mistakes. Learn words on their own, without help from the teacher. Read for meaning. _What Children Need to Know and Do to Move to the Next Stage_ Continue to add words to their fluent reading vocabulary. Refine understanding of the structural elements in words (prefixes, suffixes, root words borrowed from Latin and Greek).
Stage 5 Automatic		Middle School or Later		Ninety-nine percent of the words children read are in their fluent reading vocabulary. _What Children Know_ Fully understand how our alphabet represents sound and how to comprehend, enjoy reading, learn from text.

Match the guide you use with the children's stage of word fluency. You may use guides for children in grades below or above your current grade level, so long as the guide and children's word fluency levels are the same. Each guide indicates certain days for teaching certain aspects of word study. You do not need to teach on these days of the week. Adjust the guide to your own weekly routine. Switch days and re-arrange the schedule, but do follow the recommendations of what, when, and how much to teach children at each stage of word fluency.

PUTTING IT ALL IN PERSPECTIVE ■ ■ ■ ■ ■ ▬▬▬

A solid working knowledge of how letters represent speech is absolutely basic to becoming a successful reader (National Institute of Child Health and Human Development, 2000; Tunmer & Hoover, 1992). However, we cannot teach phonics and nothing but phonics, although we cannot neglect phonics, either. On the one hand, word recognition in and of itself is not enough to ensure comprehension. On the other hand, children cannot understand text if they cannot read the words.

In a sense, the reason children learn written words is quite similar to the reason they learn spoken words when they are very young. Young children cannot effectively interact with their environment if they cannot speak. In order to speak, children must learn how to say words, how words label objects and ideas, and how to use words to express their feelings, desires, and reactions. Likewise, children learn how to read written words so that they can interact with print. When you teach children how to recognize words and help children learn how words sound, what words look like, and what written words mean, this supports comprehension by allowing children to pay full attention to understanding the text.

Each chapter has ideas and activities for developing some aspect of word fluency. Chapter 2 has activities to develop phonemic awareness for kindergartners and beginning first graders in the pre-alphabetic, partial alphabetic, and alphabetic stages. Chapter 3 has activities to teach letter names and single letter-sounds to kindergartners in the pre-alphabetic and partial alphabetic stages. Chapter 4 includes activities for teaching late kindergartners, and first and second graders in the alphabetic stage, how two or more letters represent sound (the *at* in *cat*, *hat*, and *fat*; the sound of /a/ in *cake*, *paid*, and *may*). Chapter 5 includes activities for teaching the structural units in words, such as *un-* in *unhappy* and *-ing* in *joking*, to children in the alphabetic and consolidated stages. Chapter 6 has activities for teaching word meaning and rapid word recognition. Chapter 7 includes activities for improving oral and silent reading fluency, and Chapter 8 is especially for teachers who teach children who speak languages other than English at home.

All in all, there are activities for each and every stage of word fluency, and each grade in the elementary school from kindergarten through fifth. The teaching activities are classroom tested with children just like the ones whom you teach. Select activities that meet children's needs and that are the best fit for your own personal classroom teaching situation, and enjoy, as we do, sharing literacy and literacy learning with children in the elementary school.

REFERENCES ■ ■ ■ ■ ▬▬▬

Adams, M. J. (1990). *Beginning to read: Thinking and learning about print.* Cambridge, MA: The MIT Press.

Byrne, B., & Fielding-Barnsley, R. (1990). Acquiring the alphabetic principle: A case for teaching recognition of phoneme identity. *Journal of Educational Psychology, 82,* 805–812.

Byrne, B., Freebody, P., & Gates, A. (1992). Longitudinal data on the relations of word-reading strategies to comprehension, reading time, and phonemic awareness. *Reading Research Quarterly, 27,* 140–151.

Ehri, L. C. (1997). Sight word learning in normal readers and dyslexics. In B. Blachman (Ed.), *Foundations of reading acquisition and dyslexia: Implications for early intervention* (pp. 163–189). Mahwah, NJ: Lawrence Erlbaum Associates.

Ehri, L. C. (1998). Grapheme-phoneme knowledge is essential for learning to read words in English. In J. L. Metsala & L. C. Ehri (Eds.), *Word recognition in beginning literacy* (pp. 3–40). Mahwah, NJ: Lawrence Erlbaum Associates.

Ehri, L. C., & McCormick, S. (1998). Phases of word learning: Implications for instruction with delayed and disabled readers. *Reading & Writing Quarterly: Overcoming Learning Difficulties, 14*, 135–163.

Gaskins, I. W., Ehri, L. C., Cress, C., O'Hara, C., & Donnelly, K. (1997). Procedures for word learning: Making discoveries about words. *The Reading Teacher, 50*, 312–327.

Gentry, R. J. (2000). *The literacy map: Guiding children to where they need to be (K-3).* New York: MONDO Publishing.

Gentry, R. J., & Gillett, J. W. (1993). *Teaching kids to spell.* Portsmouth, NH: Heinemann.

Heilman, A. W., Blair, T. A., & Rupley, W. H. (2002). *Principle and practices of teaching reading, 10th edition.* Columbus, OH: Merrill Prentice Hall.

Martin, B., & Archambault, J. (1989). *Chicka chicka boom boom.* New York: Aladdin Books.

Masonheimer, P. E., Drum, P. A., & Ehri, L. C. (1984). Does environmental print identification lead children to reading? *Journal of Reading Behavior, 16*, 257–271.

Nagy, W. E., Diakidoy, I. N., & Anderson, R. C. (1993). The acquisition of morphology: Learning the contribution of suffixes to the meaning of derivatives. *Journal of Reading Behavior, 25*, 155–170.

National Center for Education Statistics (1995). Listening to children read aloud: Oral fluency. *NAEP Facts,* (1). Available FTP: National Center for Education Statistics: http:/nces.ed.gov/pubs/95762.html

National Institute of Child Health and Human Development. (2000). *Report of the National Reading Panel: Teaching children to read: An evidence-based assessment of the scientific research literature on reading and its implications for reading instruction: Reports of the subgroups* (NIH Publication No. 00-4754). Washington, DC: U.S. Government Printing Office.

Richgels, D. (2001). Invented spelling, phonemic awareness, and reading and writing instruction. In S. B. Neuman & D. K. Dickinson (Eds.), *Handbook of early literacy research* (pp. 142–155). New York: Guilford Press.

Rupley, W. H., & Wilson, V. L. (1997). Relationship between comprehension and components of word recognition: Support for developmental shifts. *Journal of Research and Development in Education, 30*, 255–260.

Singleson, M., Mahoney, D., & Mann, V. (2000). The relation between reading ability and morphological skills: Evidence from derivational suffixes. *Reading and Writing: An Interdisciplinary Journal, 12*, 219–252.

Snow, C. E., Burns, M. S., & Griffin, P. (Eds.) (1998). *Preventing reading difficulties in young children.* Washington, DC: National Academy Press.

Stevenson, H. W., & Newman, R. S. (1986). Long-term prediction of achievement and attitudes in mathematics and reading. *Child Development, 57*, 646–659.

Tunmer, W. E., & Hoover, W. A. (1992). Cognitive and linguistic factors in learning to read. In P. B. Gough, L. C. Ehri, & R. Treiman (Eds.), *Reading acquisition* (pp. 175–214). Hillsdale, NY: Lawrence Erlbaum Associates.

Whitehurst, G. J., & Lonigan, C. J. (2001). Emergent literacy: Development from prereaders to readers. In S. B. Neuman & D. K. Dickinson (Eds.), *Handbook of early literacy research* (pp. 11–29). New York: Guilford Press.

Developing Fluency with Hands-on Activities for Teaching Phonemic Awareness

Use these phonemic awareness activities with kindergartners and first graders in:

▷ **The Pre-alphabetic Word Fluency Stage**

▷ **The Partial Alphabetic Word Fluency Stage**

▷ **The Alphabetic Word Fluency Stage in Early First Grade**

The four kindergartners sitting cross-legged on the floor prick up their ears as their teacher holds up a long-eared, cheery-faced puppet. The puppet begins asking children questions, starting with, "What sound do you hear at the beginning of *mother*?" "M," Susan replies. "How many sounds are in *cat*?" "Three," says Paul. "Say *stop* without the /s/." "Top," shouts Paul. "What's the middle sound in *gate*?" "A," Chyna replies. "What sounds do you hear in *fish*?" "F - i - sh," replies Carlos. "What word does /p/ - /a/ - /n/ make?" "Pan," says the group in chorus. Susan, Paul, Carlos, and Chyna can identify the beginning, middle, and ending sounds (or phonemes) in words, and can blend separate sounds (or phonemes) into whole words (/p/ + /a/ + /n/ = /pan/).

A *phoneme* is the smallest sound that differentiates one word from another. For example, if we were to exchange the /a/ in *fat* for an /i/, we would pronounce a different word, *fit*. The /a/ and the /i/ are two English phonemes because these sounds make one word different from another. Each phoneme consists of many slight variations in sounds, which we call *allophones*. We do not worry about distinguishing each allophone in a phoneme because we treat the allophones as though they are the same sound. Try this experiment: Say *fat*; then say *mast*. Listen carefully to the /a/. The /a/ in each word is a slightly different sound. The /a/ in *fat* and the /a/ in *mast* are allophones of the phoneme /a/. The surrounding phonemes (or sounds) affect the sound of a particular phoneme. Therefore, the /a/ in *fat* is slightly different from the /a/ in *mast*. We take allophones in stride. We become familiar with the allophones and phonemes of English and naturally adjust our pronunciation when we speak and when we decode.

WHAT IS PHONEMIC AWARENESS? ■ ■ ■ ■ ▬▬

Phonemic awareness is the understanding that spoken words consist of individual sounds. Phonemic awareness refers to the insight that each spoken word is built from different sounds or phonemes. Phonemic awareness is specific to insight into the sounds of English. Children who are phonemically aware can tell you that *map* consists of three sounds: /m/ - /a/ - /p/. *Phonological awareness* is a more global term.

The *phon-* in phonological awareness comes from the Greek language and means *sound* or *voice*, as in *telephone* and *microphone*. *Logy* also comes to us from the Greek language, and means *the study of*, while *-ic* and *-al* are Greek for *pertaining to*. Therefore, we can say that phonological pertains to the study of sound. Phonological awareness is insight into the words, syllables, rhymes, and sounds in spoken language, as well as insight into the way we change voice emphasis in speech. For instance, we pronounce pumpkin with a different voice emphasis in the following sentences: "I made a *pumpkin* pie." "Look at that 500-pound prize-winning *pumpkin*!" "Is this a *pumpkin* pie?" (Richgels, 2001). We will use the more global term phonological awareness to refer to developing insight into words, syllables, and rhymes. We will use phonemic awareness to refer to developing insight into the sounds (phonemes) in language.

The four kindergartners demonstrated phonemic awareness as they quickly and easily answered the questions the puppet asked. Carlos demonstrated phonemic awareness when he separated *fish* into three speech sounds (phonemes): /f/ - /i/ - /sh/. Paul showed that he can delete sounds from words when he said *stop* without the /s/. Everyone demonstrated blending skill when they combined the individual sounds, /p/ - /a/ - /n/, into *pan*. Susan, Paul, Carlos, and Chyna are aware of the individual sounds in words. They think about the sounds individually, pronounce just one sound from a word, and blend sounds together. They understand that meaningful words consist of essentially meaningless sounds, and they use this knowledge when they sound out new words and when they associate sounds with letters to spell new words.

■■■■■■ ■ ■ ■ ■ WHY IS PHONEMIC AWARENESS IMPORTANT?

Phonemic awareness helps children to understand and use the alphabetic principle. The alphabetic principle is the concept that the letters in written words represent the speech sounds in spoken words. English, like all other alphabetic languages, uses only a small set of visual symbols, just twenty-six letters in English, twenty in German, twenty-six in French, and twenty-six (or twenty-eight) in Spanish. Phonemic awareness is necessary for making sense of the alphabetic principle (Compton, 2000).

To grasp the principle of alphabetic writing, children must understand that words consist of sounds that have no real meaning in and of themselves. Beginning readers must understand that the sounds that letters represent are the same sounds that they hear in words. Once children are aware of individual speech sounds, they understand that the letters they see in new words can be used to figure out the sounds of those words. It is not surprising, then, that phonemic awareness during kindergarten predicts decoding, word recognition, comprehension, and overall reading achievement in later grades (Adams, 1990; Dufva, Niemi, & Voeten, 2001; National Institute of Child Health and Human Development, 2000).

When children develop phonemic awareness, they step away from word meaning and concentrate instead on small, meaningless sounds. Phonemic awareness, unlike any other spoken language skill, does not help children communicate with you, their classmates, or their parents. Children can be quite competent language users without being aware that the words they use in everyday conversations consist of individual sounds. Though phonemic awareness is not necessary for carrying on everyday conversations, it is necessary for learning to read English.

Phonemic awareness and phonics are different. Phonemic awareness is a spoken language-based skill. In phonemic awareness, children listen for, pronounce, rearrange, and blend the sounds they hear in words. Susan, Paul, Carlos, and Chyna answered the puppet's questions without ever seeing a written word. When we teach children to identify the beginning, middle, and ending sounds in words, and when we teach children how to blend, we are teaching phonemic awareness.

Phonics, however, is the study of how letters represent sounds. The letter-sound associations of phonics connect written language with spoken language. Children therefore must see words, letters, and letter patterns in order to use phonics. When we teach Chyna that *s* represents /s/, *u* stands for /u/, and *n* represents /n/, or that *un* stands for /un/, we are teaching phonics. And when we show Chyna, through direct instruction in reading and writing, how to use this information to read and spell *sun*, *fun*, and *run*, we are also teaching phonics.

While phonemic awareness and phonics are different from one another, they are mutually reciprocal in that children who are good at one (phonemic awareness) get better at the other (phonics), and vice versa. Without phonemic awareness, children are bewildered by the way that the same letters, when arranged in different sequences, represent different spoken words. However, with phonemic awareness, children understand how and why letter patterns are transformed into familiar spoken words. The more children understand about phonemic awareness, the greater their capacity to use phonics; and the more phonics children learn, the greater their insight into the individual sounds in words. To be effective teachers of phonemic awareness, we first need to know the full range of phonological awareness skills, and then we need to decide which of the skills are the best ones to teach the children in our classes. These are the topics of the next two sections.

WHAT ARE THE SEVEN PHONOLOGICAL AWARENESS SKILLS? ■ ■ ■ ■ ▬▬▬

Phonological awareness skills consist of: (1) word awareness, (2) syllable awareness, (3) rhyme awareness, (4) beginning sound matching, (5) sound awareness, (6) blending, and (7) sound manipulation.

Awareness follows a relatively predictable developmental sequence, moving from awareness of large language units to awareness of the smallest language units. Children first become phonologically aware of words in sentences and eventually become phonemically aware of individual sounds in words. Children may become aware of words as early as three or four years of age. Most children are aware of individual sounds before they go to first grade. The seven skills are described in roughly the same sequence in which they develop in the majority of children.

1. *Word Awareness: Separating Sentences into Individual Words*

Children who are aware of words can separate a sentence like "We like to swing" into the words /we/, /like/, /to/, and /swing/. Generally speaking, you can expect kindergartners to come to school with word awareness. However, we teach some kindergartners who do not have an awareness of the individual words in sentences and, therefore, I have included a few activities that call children's attention to words through song and through arranging words in sentences from familiar books.

2. *Syllable Awareness: Identifying the Syllables in Long Words*

Children demonstrate syllable awareness by tapping for each syllable in a word. Children might, for example, tap once for /pig/, twice for /tiger/ (ti-ger), and three times for /elephant/ (el-e-phant). Syllable awareness develops earlier than sound awareness, probably because multi-sound syllables are easier to pull out of words (/ti/ in /tiger/) than individual sounds (/t/ in /tiger/). Most children enter your classroom already aware of the syllables in words. Syllable awareness usually develops after word awareness and before awareness of individual sounds (the ability to say /p/ - /a/ - /n/ make up the word *pan*).

3. *Rhyme Awareness: Identifying and Saying Rhyming Words*

Children who are aware of rhyme can tell you that /pan/ and /man/ rhyme but that /pan/ and /pig/ do not. If you are saying a familiar rhyming poem and hesitate when pronouncing a rhyming word, children will quickly supply that word. When asked to think of a word that rhymes with /cat/, children say words like /hat/, /mat/, and /fat/. Jingles and rhyming poetry are often used to teach children about rhyming language. Many children become aware of rhyme in preschool and hence come to kindergarten with this understanding. While teaching children to identify rhyme and alliteration (words that begin with the same sound, such as big bad bumpy bean) has positive effects on reading and spelling (Bradley & Bryant, 1991), rhyme awareness is a poorer predictor of reading achievement than sound awareness (Nation & Hulme, 1997). Use rhyme activities with the children in your classroom who are unaware of rhyming language, but also teach these children how to separate words into sounds and how to blend sounds together to make real words.

4. *Beginning Sound Matching: Identifying Words that Begin with the Same Sound*

Children who are skilled at sound matching are aware of the beginning sounds in words and can: (1) sort pictures into stacks of words that begin with the same sound; (2) tell which two words belong together, /man/, /moon/, or /bad/; (3) tell which word does *not* belong, /hat/, /pig/, or /hip/; and (4) say a word that begins like /fat/, such as /fit/ or /food/. Sound matching tasks do not call for completely separating words into individual sounds, only for recognizing that words have beginning sounds and that some words have the same beginning sounds. Beginning sound matching is a first step toward identifying all the sounds in words.

5. *Sound Awareness: Separating Words into Individual Sounds*

Children understand that words consists of individual sounds. These children can, therefore, separate a word like /pig/ into its three unique sounds: /p/, /i/, and /g/. While there are many ways to teach awareness of sounds, most activities fall into one of three categories: sound counting, sound isolation, or sound segmentation. In sound-counting teaching activities, children listen for sounds in a word and then count those sounds. For example, children would say that /mad/ has three sounds while /mats/ has four. Sound-isolation activities ask children to separate one sound from a word and to say that targeted phoneme. An example of sound isolation is having children say the beginning sound in /sad/ (/s/), the middle sound in /hat/ (/a/), or the ending sound in /can/ (/n/). In sound-segmentation activities, children say all of the sounds in a word. For instance, you might ask a child to tell you all the sounds in /cat/. The sound-aware child then replies by saying three separate sounds: /c/ - /a/ - /t/. Children who are skilled at sound segmentation quickly and effortlessly pronounce all the sounds in a word. The sound-awareness teaching activities in this chapter use the techniques of sound counting, sound isolation, or sound segmentation, or are an adaptation of these activities.

6. *Blending: Combining Individual Sounds or Syllables into Words*

Blending is the ability to combine separate sounds or syllables into meaningful words. Children demonstrate blending when they combine the three sounds of /b/, /a/, and /t/ into the whole word /bat/. Successful blending calls on children to make slight changes in the way they say individual sounds. For instance, the sounds /b/, /a/, and /t/, when pronounced all by themselves, do not sound exactly the same as they do when they are pronounced in the whole word /bat/. The sounds in words overlap a bit, somewhat like the shingles on a roof. Each sound flows into the next, changing the way the sounds are pronounced. As an illustration, say out loud the three sounds /b/, /a/, and /g/. Now, say the same sounds in exactly the same way, only say them faster. When you do this, you hear something like /buh-a-guh/. You only hear /bag/ when you adjust, ever so slightly, the way you pronounce the sounds. Blending is not just saying sounds fast; it is consciously and purposefully adjusting sounds so that they join together to make a real, meaningful word. Blending requires that children remember sounds, recall the sequence of sounds, and fold sounds together.

7. *Sound Manipulation: Adding, Deleting, and Substituting Sounds in Words*

When children add sounds, they attach sounds to the beginning or end of words. For example, children might add an /s/ to /at/ to say /sat/ or add an /s/ to the end of /cat/ to pronounce /cats/. Adding sounds requires that children remember, sequence, and blend sounds. Sound deletion involves removing one or more sounds from a word or syllable. For example, children might take the /s/ away from the beginning of /sat/ to pronounce /at/ or remove the /s/ from /cats/ to say /cat/. Deleting a beginning or ending sound, as when the /s/ is taken away from /sat/ and /cats/, calls for identifying, remembering, and removing sounds, but not for blending sounds.

Deleting middle sounds is much harder than changing sounds at the beginning or end of words. For instance, taking the /s/ away from /cast/ requires reblending the /ca/ and /t/ to pronounce /cat/. This skill is sometimes called *elision*, and refers to taking a sound out of the middle of a word and then pronouncing what is left. When children delete middle sounds, they identify the sounds in a word, remember the order in which the sound occurs, remove a sound, and then reblend to pronounce what is left (/cat/ instead of /cast/).

When children substitute sounds, they remove a sound and replace it with another. For example, children might replace the /a/ in /cat/ for an /o/ to pronounce /cot/, substitute the /c/ in /cat/ for an /h/ to say /hat/, or exchange the /t/ in /cat/ for a /p/ to pronounce /cap/. We often ask children to substitute beginning consonants, such as replacing the /c/ for an /s/ to pronounce /sat/. You might hear teachers talk about initial consonant substitution as a way of identifying new words. Initial consonant substitution is a form of sound substitution in which only the beginning sound is exchanged. For example, children who know the sounds associated with single consonant letters and who also know that *at* represents /at/ substitute the beginning letter-sound to read *bat, cat, mat, hat, rat,* and *sat*. Substituting sounds requires that the child identify the sounds in a word, remember the order in which the sounds occur, replace one particular sound with another sound, and then reblend to pronounce a different word.

WHICH PHONEMIC AWARENESS SKILLS SHOULD ■ ■ ■ ■ ▬▬▬▬ YOU TEACH AND WHY?

Not all phonemic awareness skills are equally useful for decoding and spelling in the early grades. While there are many different phonemic awareness skills you might teach, separating words into sounds and blending sounds into words are the most closely related to literacy and, therefore, have the greatest impact on reading and spelling achievement (Ehri et al., 2001).

Blending

Blending is directly involved in decoding (Ehri et al., 2001). In order to decode, children must know the letter and sound associations of phonics, but they must also be able to blend the sounds they pronounce after they make the letter-sound connections. To decode the word *man*, children must associate the letter *m* with /m/, the letter *a* with /a/, and the letter *n* with /n/. As children associate sounds with letters, they pronounce each sound separately: /m/ - /a/ - /n/. Now, in order to figure out the word, children must blend /m/ + /a/ + /n/ into /man/. Successful blenders quickly identify the written word *man* as the spoken word /man/.

Rather than decoding *man* letter-sound by letter-sound, children could associate /m/ with the letter *m* and /an/ with the letters *an*. This leaves children with only two things to blend, the /m/ and the /an/, rather than three sounds, /m/ - /a/ - /n/. Blending /m/ + /an/ into /man/ is easier than blending each and every individual sound /m/ + /a/ + /n/ (Schatschneider, Francis, Foorman, Fletcher, & Mehta, 1999). If the children whom you teach struggle when blending individual sounds, start with larger chunks, such as /m/ + /ad/ and /p/ + /ig/, and then progress to blending individual sounds: /m/ + /a/ + /d/ = /mad/ and /p/ + /i/ + /g/ = /pig/.

Finally, blending /p/ + /i/ + /g/ into /pig/ is much easier than blending /p/ + /o/ + /g/ into the nonsense word /pog/. In fact, blending sounds into nonsense words (/p/ + /o/ + /g/ = /pog/) is one of the most difficult phonemic awareness tasks (Schatschneider, Francis, Foorman, Fletcher, & Mehta, 1999). You may use the blending activities in this chapter with real (/p/ + /i/ + /g/) or nonsense (/p/ + /o/ + /g/) words. We prefer real words. Not only is blending real words easier for children, but in blending real words children learn to cross-check to see if they said a word that they know and a word that makes sense. We want children to realize when they successfully blend (/p/ + /i/ + /g/ = /pig/) and also to realize when they make a mistake (/p/ + /i/ + /g/ = /pag/).

Separating Words into Sounds

Spelling requires an altogether different phonemic awareness skill from that which is needed to decode. The ability to separate words into sounds is most closely connected with spelling (Ehri et al., 2001). Let us consider what happens when a child figures out how to spell *man*. The child first says the word to herself, "man." She then separates the beginning sound, /m/, from /man/, associates the letter *m* with this sound, and writes an *m* on her paper. Then she thinks about the /a/, associates the letter *a* with /a/, and writes the letter *a* beside the *m* to produce *ma*. Last, she associates the letter *n* with the /n/ and writes *n* next to the *ma*, thus spelling *man*. Nowhere in the spelling process does the child do any blending whatsoever. The reason, of course, is that the child starts out with a blended word that she wants to spell, in this example the whole word /man/. The trick for spellers is to figure out the way that the sounds in the whole word /man/ are represented by letters. This, of course, requires that spellers separate words into individual sounds. Phoneme segmentation is one of the more difficult phonemic awareness skills (Schatschneider, Francis, Foorman, Fletcher, & Mehta, 1999), so do not be discouraged or surprised if it takes quite a bit of teaching and practice for children to become skilled at separating words into sounds.

CONNECTING BLENDING AND SOUND AWARENESS ■ ■ ■ ■ ▬▬▬
WITH PHONICS AND SPELLING

We have learned that decoding depends more on blending, while spelling relies more on the ability to separate words into sounds. We teach sound blending and sound awareness to help children develop skill at decoding and spelling. It stands to reason, then, that we can support decoding and spelling by connecting these phonemic awareness skills with the sounds that letters represent in words. Because we want to demonstrate how to separate and blend sounds, and how to connect letters and sounds to decoding and spelling, we want to select only decodable words. Decodable words are spelled just like they sound, such as *bun, lamp,* and *hit.* You also want to focus on the words children are learning in your classroom. Children spell when they make words with letter cards; children decode when they associate sounds with letters and then blend to say a whole word. At every step you model and explain the process, and at every step children repeatedly practice spelling and sounding out short words. We will use the words *sat, mat,* and *man* in this example:

1. Give children letter cards; for example, cards with *s, a, t, m,* and *n.* Ask children to put the *s, a,* and *t* cards from left-to-right on their table. Write the letters *s, a, t* on the board.

| s | a | t |

2. Hold up the *s* letter card and tell the children that the letter *s* represents /s/. Have children put their fingers under the *s* in front of them. Have the children repeat the sound, /s/, drawing it out so that it sounds like /sssss/. Hold up the *a* letter card and tell children that the *a* represents /a/. Ask children to put their fingers under the *a* letter card. Have the children repeat the /a/, drawing this sound out so that it sounds like /aaaa/.

3. Demonstrate how to blend /s/ + /a/. Stretch out the sounds and say them together as /ssssaaaaa/. Sweep your hand under the two letters on the board as you pronounce "ssssaaaa." Have the children imitate your voice, pointing to the letters on their tables as they blend /ssssaaaa/. If children try to simply say /s/ and /a/ fast (that is, together but without actually blending), demonstrate how to slightly overlap the sounds to blend them into /ssssaaaa/. Ask the children to repeat blending several times, following your example.

4. Now hold up the *t* letter card. Tell children the *t* represents the /t/ sound. While we cannot effectively draw out, or stretch, the /t/ sound, we can emphasize this sound as we say it. Have the children point to the letter *t* and pronounce /t/. Turning to the letters on the board, blend /ssssaaaat/, sweeping your hand under each letter as you blend the sounds together. Have the children repeat blending /ssssaaaat/.

Some phonemes are easier to sound stretch than others. Sounds we pronounce until we run out of breath are relatively easy to stretch. Examples of easily stretched sounds are the consonants /f/, /v/, /z/, /l/, /m/, /n/, /s/, /r/, /y/, and the short and long vowels /a/, /e/, /i/, /o/, and /u/. Sounds we pronounce by stopping the air flow are less easily stretched. Examples of these sounds are /p/, /b/, /t/, /g/, /j/, /k/, and /d/. Sounds like these are difficult to stretch because we add an extra vowel, an *uh,* to the end of sounds when we pronounce them alone. Hence, our voices sound something like *duh,* or *buh,* or *puh* when we try to stretch these sounds. It may take just a little longer to help children feel comfortable blending these consonant sounds. Children must learn how to drop the *uh* when blending. We often take extra time modeling how to blend consonants with the added *uh,* and we give children extra practice following our examples. We try our best to "clip" the *uh* off these sounds whenever possible. To do this, we pronounce the sound but then stop our voice immediately thereafter. This is easier to do with ending consonant sounds than with beginning sounds.

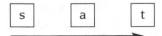

5. Erase the letter *s* and write the letter *m* on the board. Ask children to take away the *s* and put an *m* in its place. Review the sounds of each letter card by holding up the *m* and telling children the *m* represents /mmmm/. Have the children point to *m* and say /mmmm/. Then demonstrate how to blend /mmmmaaa/, followed by blending the whole word, /mmmmaaaat/. Sweep your hand under each letter as you pronounce and blend the sounds. Ask the children to repeat blending two or three times.

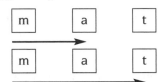

6. Erase the *t* and write an *n* on the board. Have the children take away the *t* and put an *n* in its place. Tell the children that the *n* represents /nnnn/. Have the children point to the *n* letter card and say /nnnn/. Demonstrate blending and have the children repeat blending, following your example.

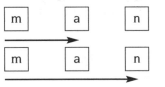

In this teaching strategy, we first stretch the beginning sound, /mmmm/, then blend it with the middle sound, /mmmmaaaa/, and finally blend the last sound to pronounce the whole word, /mmmmaaaan/. We can make blending easier by asking children to blend /m/ + /an/. The idea is to divide the beginning sound in a short word so as to blend only two units, /m/ + /an/. Other examples include /c/ + /an/, /f/ + /an/, and /p/ + /an/, or /s/ + /un/, /f/ + /un/, and /b/ + /un/. You would give children cards with an *m* and the *an*, as shown. Say the sound associated with the letter *m*, /mmmm/, and the sounds associated with the *an*, /aaaan/. Have the children repeat your example, saying the sounds and pointing to the letters. Then sweep your hand under the letters as you blend /mmmman/. Ask the children to repeat blending /mmmman/ several times.

Replace the *m* card with an *f* and have the children associate the /f/ with the letter *f* and the /an/ with the *an* card. Then demonstrate and practice blending.

Exchange the *an* card for *un* and repeat the process of associating sounds with the *un* and then blending /f/ + /un/ into /fun/, as shown.

When you connect letters with sounds and demonstrate blending, you explicitly show children how to spell, how to decode, how to focus on individual sounds (/f/) or groups of sounds (/un/), and how to blend. The letters give children a physical reference point, or a visual representation of sounds. This helps children remember the sounds they are to blend when decoding and also helps children develop awareness of the individual sounds in words when spelling.

TEACHING PHONEMIC AWARENESS ■ ■ ■ ■ ▬▬▬

Sounds are ephemeral; they last only a very short time and they change based on the sounds next to them in words. When we blend sounds into words, the sounds flow and fold into one another. This makes separating sounds and blending sounds, the skills required for reading, very tricky. Fortunately, we know a good deal about how to teach phonemic awareness and how to make the most of classroom hands-on teaching strategies and activities.

Teach Both Sound Separation and Blending

In blending, children connect sounds together; in segmenting, children separate words into sounds. It is not likely that the children in your classroom, if given instruction in only one of these skills (blending or segmenting), will automatically and dramatically improve in the other. Most children need direct instruction in both separating and blending.

Teach Phonemic Awareness and Phonics Together

If you teach phonemic awareness along with the letter-sounds of phonics, you will be a far more effective teacher than if you teach phonemic awareness alone (Chew, 1997; Ehri et al., 2001; National Institute of Child Health and Human Development, 2000). Separating words into sounds requires that children quickly perceive individual sounds, remember the sounds, and later pronounce them. For example, when we ask children to listen for the /t/ in /top/, we expect children to be quick enough at identifying sounds to latch on the /t/ as it swiftly flows into the /o/ in /top/. This is very difficult for some children because they must depend solely on their auditory memory for individual sounds.

When we link phonemic awareness to phonics, we give children a concrete visual representation, the letter T, for the /t/ sound. Let us assume, for the purpose of illustration, that you are reading an alphabet book and ask children, "What sound does the letter T represent?" In asking this question, you show children a letter that stands for the /t/ sound and, additionally, say the individual /t/ sound. When you ask children to find pictures on the alphabet book page that begin with /t/, you give children practice listening for, identifying, and pronouncing the /t/ in the context of familiar words. All this makes listening for and identifying /t/ somewhat simpler. Now the ephemeral /t/ is represented by a static, identifiable letter. Children can point to T and say /t/. They can listen for /t/ in words, and they can link this to their speaking vocabularies and to the letter T.

Help children benefit from the reciprocal relationship between phonemic awareness and phonics, in which improving in one skill results in becoming more skilled in the other. Show children how beginning, middle, and ending letters in written words represent the beginning, middle, and ending sounds in spoken words. Model how to sound out words and how to blend sounds when decoding. Use activities like writing words on the word wall and making charts of words that begin with the same letter-sound. In teaching phonemic awareness and phonics together, you ask children to join you in associating sounds with letters to read and spell words, and you show children how phonemic awareness and phonics are related.

You can expect the children whom you teach to increase sound awareness when they listen for the sounds that letters represent in words, learn letter-sounds through reading alphabet books (Murray, Stahl, & Ivey, 1996), and use letter-sound cues to identify words. Consequently, as children develop letter-sound knowledge, they also increase their awareness of the sounds in spoken words.

Teach Phonemic Awareness Early

Teaching phonemic awareness early, in kindergarten, is more effective than teaching phonemic awareness in any other grade (National Institute of Child Health and Human Development, 2000). Teaching phonemic awareness in kindergarten and first grade helps children: (1) move from the pre-alphabetic to the partial alphabet and on to the alphabetic stage in time to meet or exceed grade level expectations, (2) become better spellers, (3) dramatically increase their reading vocabulary, and (4) succeed as readers and spellers throughout the elementary grades.

Teach Phonemic Awareness in Small Groups

You will be a more effective teacher if you teach phonemic awareness to small groups (Ehri et al., 2001; National Institute of Child Health and Human Development, 2000). Children in small groups have more opportunities to personally respond to their teachers, and teachers have more opportunities to observe the effects of instruction. Phonemic awareness is, after all, a group of language-based skills and it stands to reason that children need opportunities to use language as they listen for sounds and blend sounds. Small groups are more likely than large groups to nurture and encourage children to respond, practice, and experiment with language. Therefore, the phonemic awareness activities in this chapter are for teaching small groups.

Differentiate Phonemic Awareness Instruction

Two ways to improve your effectiveness in teaching phonemic awareness are: (1) spend at least eighteen hours teaching phonemic awareness to small groups who are baffled by phonemic awareness, and (2) move high-awareness children on to other language arts activities before, or at completion of, eighteen hours of phonemic awareness instruction (Ehri et al., 2001).

The children in your classroom will differ in how much phonemic instruction they require and in the phonemic awareness skills they need to develop. Some children come to school with relatively well-developed phonemic awareness, while others are unaware of the sounds of language. By and large, between five and eighteen hours seems to be the optimum amount of time to devote to teaching phonemic awareness to small groups of English-speaking children (Ehri et al., 2001). However, we may need to spend more than eighteen hours teaching children who struggle with phonemic awareness skills.

Focus on Only One or Two Critical Phonemic Awareness Skills at a Time

Teaching one or two phonemic awareness skills has twice the impact as teaching multiple skills (Ehri et al., 2001; National Institute of Child Health and Human Development, 2000). Perhaps children do not really master skills when many different skills are taught at once, or perhaps children become confused about how to apply the skills. Knowing that it is less effective to target multiple skills is useful so long as we know which skills to teach. From the perspective of transfer to reading and spelling, separating words into sounds and blending sounds into words are the two most important skills. These two abilities are directly involved in reading and spelling, and therefore are the skills most likely to promote literacy (Ehri et al., 2001; National Institute of Child Health and Human Development, 2000).

LEARNING ABOUT PHONEMIC AWARENESS IN THE PRE-ALPHABETIC, PARTIAL ALPHABETIC, AND ALPHABETIC WORD FLUENCY STAGES

Stage 1. Pre-alphabetic Word Fluency: Preschool and Early Kindergarten

Table 2–1 shows the weekly teaching guide for the first half of kindergarten when children are in the pre-alphabetic word fluency stage. Children do not realize that some words rhyme and that all words consist of individual speech sounds. A few kindergartners may not realize that sentences consist of words. The guide calls for developing awareness of rhyming words and the beginning sounds in words. It is beneficial to teach rhyming word and beginning sound awareness in combination with letter names and letter-sound instruction, and to teach rhyme and beginning sound awareness in small groups. During the first half of kindergarten, children need to begin to understand that: (1) some words rhyme (the /at/ in /cat/, /bat/, and /hat/), (2) words begin with sounds (the /b/ in /boat/ and /bug/), (3) beginning sounds can be pronounced separately from the words themselves (/b/ for /bug/), and (4) the beginning letters in written words represent the beginning sounds in spoken words (the letter *b* in *bug* represents the /b/ sound in the spoken word /bug/). When children begin to recognize new words by combining beginning sound awareness with knowledge of a few beginning letter-sound associations, they move into the partial alphabetic stage.

Stage 2. Partial Alphabetic Word Fluency: Early-to-Early First Grade

Kelly (Figure 2–1) is a kindergartner in the partial alphabetic stage. Kelly knows that written words match spoken words. She is aware of most of the sounds in words, as we see from the manner in which she spelled *family* (*fmle*). Kelly identifies four sounds in *family*, and associates letters with these sounds. She is aware of punctuation and is meaning focused. In order to sound out new words, Kelly needs to be able to blend separate sounds into meaningful words and to separate spoken words into each and every sound.

Table 2–2 shows the weekly teaching guide for children in the partial alphabetic stage of word fluency. This teaching guide is designed to help children like Kelly develop skill at identifying all the sounds in words, especially the middle sounds. The weekly guide calls for teaching phonemic awareness everyday, teaching in conjunction with letter name and letter-sound instruction, and teaching to small groups. If children are not proficient at identifying rhymes, beginning sounds in words, and ending sounds in words, focus instruction on these phonemic awareness skills before concentrating on middle sounds. Introduce blending when children (1) can identify beginning and ending sounds in words, and (2) are learning to identify middle sounds. Though children will probably not become fluent blenders at this stage, it is important to begin to model blending and to give children practice blending short words so that they are prepared to move into the alphabetic stage.

TABLE 2–1 Kindergarten Weekly Teaching Guide: First Half of the Year for Children in the Pre-alphabetic Word Fluency Stage*

MONDAY	TUESDAY	WEDNESDAY	THURSDAY	FRIDAY
Phonemic Awareness Rhyming In centers and in small groups	**Phonemic Awareness** Beginning Sounds In centers and in small groups	**Phonemic Awareness** Rhyming In centers and in small groups	**Phonemic Awareness** Beginning Sounds In centers and in small groups	**Phonemic Awareness** Rhyming In centers and in small groups
Single Letter-Sounds **Letter Names** Single consonant and short vowel letter-sounds (until proficient) Teach in context and with focused study	**Single Letter-Sounds** **Letter Names** Single consonant and short vowel letter-sounds (until proficient) Teach in context and with focused study	**Single Letter-Sounds** **Letter Names** Single consonant and short vowel letter-sounds (until proficient) Teach in context and with focused study	**Single Letter-Sounds** **Letter Names** Single consonant and short vowel letter-sounds (until proficient) Teach in context and with focused study	**Single Letter-Sounds** **Letter Names** Single consonant and short vowel letter-sounds (until proficient) Teach in context and with focused study
	Fluency Letter-names or single letter-sounds			
Word Meaning Teach in context and with focused study		**Word Meaning** Teach in context and with focused study		**Word Meaning** Teach in context and with focused study

Teach phonemic awareness along with phonics, when appropriate.
*For children who do not have developmental or learning disabilities.

FIGURE 2–1   Partial Alphabetic Writing Sample (I Love My Fmle)

Stage 3. Alphabetic Word Fluency: Late Kindergarten, First, and Second Grade

Evelyn (Figure 2–2) wrote *All About Rles* during the first half of her first grade year. Evelyn can separate words into sounds, although she is not fully proficient at this process. While she can blend, blending is sometimes slow and may require several attempts. The weekly teaching guide calls for teaching phonemic awareness three days a week, always in combination with phonics (Table 2–3). The goal is to improve skill at separating words into sounds and blending sounds into words so that children become more effective decoders and spellers.

Table 2–4 presents the weekly teaching guide for children in the second half of first grade. This guide suggests teaching phonemic awareness once a week in combination with phonics, and makes provision for teaching phonemic awareness (with phonics) on a second day, if children need extra practice. By the second half of the year, first graders should have enough skill at blending and at separating words into sounds to support decoding and spelling. Consequently, phonemic awareness improves through experiences in decoding and spelling. As children continue to gain skill at decoding, teachers spend less and less time teaching phonemic awareness.

Table 2–5 shows the weekly teaching guide for second graders. There is only one *optional* lesson in phonemic awareness each week that is taught along with phonics. This optional lesson is for second graders who are not quite fluent at blending and separating words into sounds. These children lag slightly behind their classmates and, therefore, benefit from a little extra practice. It is not necessary to teach phonemic awareness to the average second graders who decode, spell, and read on a second-grade level.

TABLE 2–2 Kindergarten Weekly Teaching Guide: Second Half of the Year for Children in the Partial Alphabetic Word Fluency Stage*

MONDAY	TUESDAY	WEDNESDAY	THURSDAY	FRIDAY
Phonemic Awareness** Ending Sounds In centers and in small groups	**Phonemic Awareness** Rhyming and Blending*** In centers and in small groups	**Phonemic Awareness** Ending Sounds In centers and in small groups	**Phonemic Awareness** Rhyming and Blending*** In centers and in small groups	**Phonemic Awareness** Ending Sounds In centers and in small groups
Single Letter-Sounds Letter Names Single consonant and short vowel letter-sounds (until proficient) Teach in context and with focused study	**Single Letter-Sounds Letter Names** Single consonant and short vowel letter-sounds (until proficient) Teach in context and with focused study	**Single Letter-Sounds Letter Names** Single consonant and short vowel letter-sounds (until proficient) Teach in context and with focused study	**Single Letter-Sounds Letter Names** Single consonant and short vowel letter-sounds (until proficient) Teach in context and with focused study	**Single Letter-Sounds Letter Names** Single consonant and short vowel letter-sounds (until proficient) Teach in context and with focused study
	Word Family Words	**Word Family Words**	**Word Family Words**	
			Fluency Letter-names or single letter-sounds	
Word Meaning Teach in context and with focused study		**Word Meaning** Teach in context and with focused study	**Word Meaning** Teach in context and with focused study	**Word Meaning** Teach in context and with focused study

Teach phonemic awareness along with phonics, when appropriate.
*For children who do not have developmental or learning disabilities.
**Beginning sounds, if needed.
***Blending for children who are aware of syllables, beginning sounds, ending sounds, and rimes.

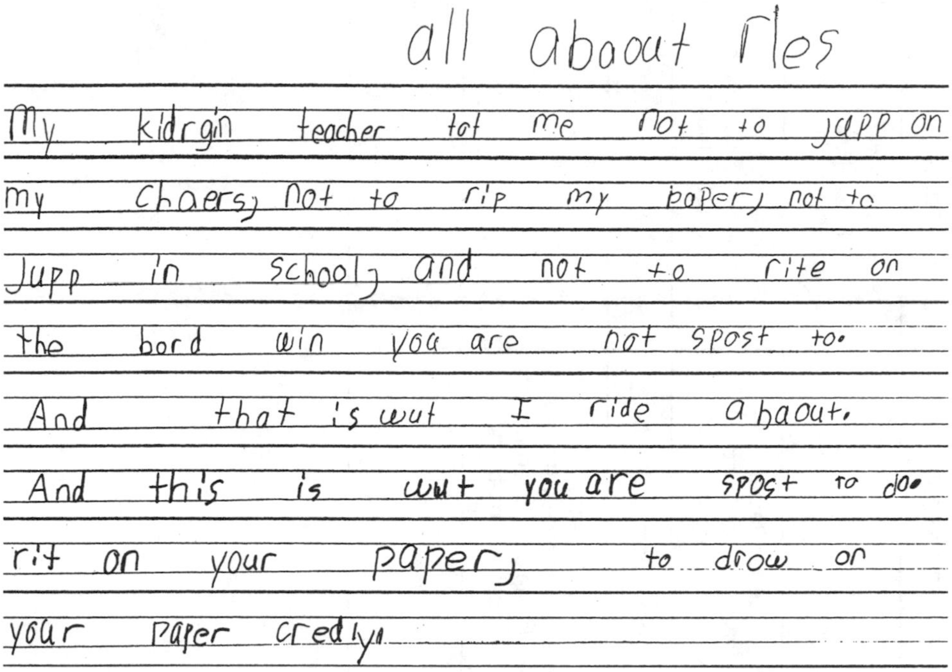

all aboout rles

My kidrgin teacher tot me not to jupp on
my chaers, not to rip my paper, not to
jupp in school, and not to rite on
the bord win you are not spost to.
And that is wut I ride ahaout.
And this is wut you are spost to doo
rit on your paper, to drow or
your paper credly.

FIGURE 2–2 Alphabetic Writing Sample (All About Rules)

HANDS-ON ACTIVITIES FOR TEACHING PHONEMIC AWARENESS ■ ■ ■ ■ ▬▬

Phonemic awareness improves the reading achievement of children who are average readers, learning disabled, at-risk, or who speak languages other than English at home (Blachman, Tangel, Ball, Black, & McGraw, 1999; Ehri et al., 2001; National Institute of Child Health and Human Development, 2000; Snow, Burns, & Griffin, 1998). You can expect the beginning readers in your classroom to have higher achievement when you teach them how to separate words into sounds and how to blend sounds into words. Teach phonemic awareness early, teach it well, and teach it in small groups. Focus on sound awareness and blending, and show children how phonemic awareness relates to reading and spelling by combining phonemic awareness activities with teaching phonics and spelling, as appropriate for the learning and achievement of the children in your classroom.

HANDS-ON ACTIVITIES FOR TEACHING WORD AWARENESS ■ ■ ■ ■ ▬▬

CLAPPING SPECIAL WORDS IN FAMILIAR SONGS, POEMS, AND CHANTS

▷ SMALL GROUP
WORD AWARENESS

In this word awareness activity, children listen for a special word in a familiar poem, chant, or song, and then clap when they hear that word. Clapping is a good way to introduce the concept that speech consists of spoken words. Clapping is highly motivational, which helps get everyone involved in the activity, and the physical act of clapping helps children focus on the special word they separate from speech. Use this phonological awareness teaching activity with children in the pre-alphabetic stage.

MATERIALS: Familiar poems, chants, and songs. Select poems, chants, and songs that the children already know. If the children are not familiar with a particular poem, chant, or song, teach it before using this activity.

TABLE 2–3 First Grade Weekly Teaching Guide: First Half of the Year for Children in the Alphabetic Word Fluency Stage*

MONDAY	TUESDAY	WEDNESDAY	THURSDAY	FRIDAY
	Phonemic Awareness Beginning, middle, and ending sounds and blending	**Phonemic Awareness** Beginning, middle, and ending sounds and blending		**Phonemic Awareness** Beginning, middle, and ending sounds and blending
Letter Patterns Teach in context and with focused study	**Letter Patterns** Teach in context and with focused study	**Letter Patterns** Teach in context and with focused study	**Letter Patterns** Teach in context and with focused study	**Letter Patterns** Teach in context and with focused study
Word Family Words			**Word Family Words**	
			Fluency In letter patterns, word family words, rapid word recognition or oral reading fluency	
Word Meaning Teach in context and with focused study	**Word Meaning** Teach in context and with focused study			

Teach phonemic awareness along with phonics, when appropriate.
*For children who do not have developmental or learning disabilities.

TABLE 2–4 First Grade Weekly Teaching Guide: Second Half of the Year for Children in the Alphabetic Word Fluency Stage*

MONDAY	TUESDAY	WEDNESDAY	THURSDAY	FRIDAY
			Phonemic Awareness Beginning, middle, and ending sounds and blending	**Phonemic Awareness** Beginning, middle, and ending sounds and blending (as needed)
		Letter Patterns Teach in context and with focused study	**Letter Patterns** Teach in context and with focused study	**Letter Patterns** Teach in context and with focused study
Word Family Words (as needed)	**Word Family Words** (as needed)		**Word Family Words** (as needed)	
Structural Analysis High utility prefixes, suffixes, and compound words Teach in context and with focused study	**Structural Analysis** High utility prefixes, suffixes, and compound words Teach in context and with focused study			
	Fluency In letter patterns, word family words, rapid word recognition, or oral reading fluency			**Fluency** In letter patterns, word family words, rapid word recognition, or oral reading fluency
Word Meaning Teach in context and with focused study	**Word Meaning** Teach in context and with focused study	**Word Meaning** Teach in context and with focused study		

Teach phonemic awareness along with phonics, when appropriate.
*For children who do not have developmental or learning disabilities.

TABLE 2–5 Second Grade Weekly Teaching Guide for Children in the Alphabetic Word Fluency Stage*

MONDAY	TUESDAY	WEDNESDAY	THURSDAY	FRIDAY
		Phonemic Awareness* (Optional)		
		Letter Patterns Teach in context and with focused study	**Letter Patterns** Teach in context and with focused study	**Letter Patterns** Teach in context and with focused study
Structural Analysis High utility prefixes, suffixes, compound words, and contractions Teach in context and with focused study		**Structural Analysis** High utility prefixes, suffixes, compound words, and contractions Teach in context and with focused study		
	Fluency In letter patterns (if needed), word structure, rapid word recognition, oral and silent reading fluency			**Fluency** In letter patterns (if needed), word structure, rapid word recognition, oral and silent reading fluency
Word Meaning Teach in context and with focused study	**Word Meaning** Teach in context and with focused study			**Word Meaning** Teach in context and with focused study

Teach phonemic awareness along with phonics, when appropriate.
*For children who do not have developmental or learning disabilities.
**For children who cannot consciously manipulate the sounds in words.

DIRECTIONS: Children clap every time they hear a specific word in a poem, chant, or song. Ask children to only clap for one-syllable words. Do not have them clap for multi-syllable words. The syllable is the natural beat of English and hence children have a natural tendency to clap for every syllable in language. Asking children to clap for two- or more syllable words is likely to be confusing because the beat, as measured in syllables, calls for more than one clap. Try it yourself. Say, "me," then say, "lizard." It is easy to clap just once for *me,* while the two-syllable word *lizard* begs for two claps—*liz* (one clap), *ard* (one clap). For example, in singing "Mary Had a Little Lamb" children might clap when they hear *lamb;* in "This Old Man" they might clap for *man;* in "The Wheels on the Bus" they may clap for *wheels, bus,* or *round.* In singing the text for *Twelve Lizards Leaping* (Stevens, 1999), children may clap for words like tree, true, love, give, or me.

CLAPPING WORDS IN OTHER LANGUAGES   Carefully consider the lyrics in songs in Spanish and in other languages, such as "Las Ruedas Del Camion," which is Spanish for "The Wheels on the Bus" (Orozco, 1997). One-syllable English words are often multi-syllable words in other languages. *Bus* in Spanish, for example, is *camion,* a multi-syllable word.

Examples of Literature Connections

Orozco, J.-L. (1997). *Diez deditos: Ten little fingers and other play rhymes and action songs from Latin America.* New York: Dutton Children's Books.

   Written in Spanish and English, this collection of finger plays and songs from Latin America is appropriate for kindergartners and early first graders.

Orozco, J.-L. (1999). *De colores and other Latin-American folk songs for children.* New York: Puffin.

   Colorful illustrations, background notes on songs, and suggestions for games make this anthology of twenty-seven songs from Latin America especially useful for classroom teachers.

Stevens, J. R. (1999). *Twelve lizards leaping: A new twelve days of Christmas.* Flagstaff, AZ: Rising Moon.

   The southwestern flare and cheery illustrations in this book are particularly meaningful to Latino children whose native culture includes holiday piñatas, tamales, and luminarias. Multicultural: Hispanic cultural traditions.

FILLING-IN MISSING WORDS IN FAMILIAR SONGS, POEMS, AND CHANTS

▷ SMALL GROUP
WORD AWARENESS

Children complete familiar lyrics, poems, and chants by filling in missing words and, in so doing, develop phonological awareness of spoken and written words. Filling-in missing words is appropriate for kindergartners in the beginning of the year who are in the pre-alphabetic word fluency stage.

MATERIALS: Familiar songs (see "Clapping Words" for suggested books), poems, and chants; sticky notes; marker; chart paper. Write familiar poems, chants, and song lyrics on large charts.

DIRECTIONS:

FILLING-IN SPOKEN WORDS WHEN LISTENING   Ask children to listen to you sing a familiar song or recite a familiar poem or chant. Explain that you are going to leave out a special word and that children should say the word you leave out. For example, you might sing, "Mary had a little lamb" and leave out "lamb": "Mary had a little ____." Children chime in by saying the word *lamb.*

FILLING-IN SPOKEN WORDS AND WRITTEN WORDS ON A CHART   Write familiar poems, chants, and lyrics on a chart. Read the poem, chant, or lyrics while moving your hand under each word as you read it. Then have children join you by reading in chorus as you move your hand under each word. Put a sticky note over a familiar word. Ask children to join you in rereading the chart and saying the missing word. Have a volunteer pull off the sticky note to reveal the word. Talk about the match between spoken and written words. Put sticky notes over other words on the chart. Have the children repeatedly join you in reading or singing, filling-in the missing words, and then taking off the sticky notes to show the written word.

COUNTING WORDS IN FAMILIAR SONGS AND CHANTS

▷ SMALL GROUP
WORD AWARENESS

Children listen for a special word and keep track of how many times that word is sung or chanted. This phonological awareness teaching activity is just right for children in the pre-alphabetic word fluency stage.

MATERIALS: Songs (see "Clapping Words" for suggested books) and chants; chart paper; marker; word window. A word window is a strip of tagboard with a word-size window cut out so as to make just one word visible when the tagboard is placed over a chart or big book. Write lyrics and chants on large pieces of chart paper.

DIRECTIONS:

COUNTING WORDS   Use songs and chants that repeat the same words several times. Divide the class in half. While one half sings or chants, the other half listens for a special word and keeps track of the number of times that word is sung or chanted. Then switch roles. Ask the other half of the class to listen for a different word.

COUNTING WRITTEN WORDS   Extend spoken word awareness to written language by writing the lyrics or chants on chart paper. Ask the children to sing or chant, while you point to the words as they are sung or chanted. Then focus on a particular word that the children have already identified through counting. Use a word window to draw attention to the word or frame the word (cup your hands around it). Ask children to point to the repeated word; use colored marker to underline the word; count the number of times the word occurs in the lyrics or chant. Put the word on the word wall.

To combine counting the number of repeated words in a song or chant with learning to count from one to ten, sing songs with lyrics that include number words, such as "This Old Man." For good counting songs in Spanish and English, look at "Diez Deditos (Ten Little Fingers)" and "Las Horas (The Hours)" in *Diez Deditos: Ten Little Fingers and Other Play Rhymes and Action Songs from Latin America* (Orozco, 1997). In counting from one to ten, ask children to hold up their fingers to show the number.

▷ **SMALL GROUP WORD AWARENESS**

MOVING WORDS

Children wear words around their necks and line up to make sentences from a familiar story. Moving words is a good phonological awareness activity for children in the pre-alphabetic and the partial alphabetic stages of word fluency.

MATERIALS: A marker; two sentence strips; hole punch; colored yarn; scissors. Books you have read and shared many times with children. Cut yarn into approximately two-foot lengths. Write a sentence from a familiar book on a sentence strip. Set it aside.

DIRECTIONS: After reading and rereading a favorite book, write a sentence from that book on a sentence strip. You might, for example, select the sentence *She hangs up the dresses* (p. 5) from *Mrs. McNosh Hangs Up Her Wash* (Weeks, 1998). Read and reread the sentence in chorus with the children, tracking the words with your hand or a pointer. Tracking is physically pointing to each word as it is read. This helps children stay focused on the appropriate words and also demonstrates left-to-right movement. Have the children watch as you cut the sentence strip into individual words; leave periods and commas connected to words.

Demonstrate how to arrange the words into the original sentence. Put the cards on a table. Give children practice arranging the cards into the familiar sentence, then punch a hole in either side of each sentence strip word. Loop the yarn through the holes to create a word necklace. Ask the children to wear one word each. Now bring out the second sentence strip you made before the activity began, and put it up where everyone can see it. Have the children line up to recreate the original sentence. Ask children to look at the second sentence strip and to read the sentence in chorus. As the children read, children wearing a certain word take two steps forward when their word is read.

Replace one of the words with another word. In this example, you might replace *dresses* with other words from the book, such as *shirts, underwear,* or *skirts.* You might select only words from the book, or children might dictate a sentence to you while you write it on a sentence strip. Follow the same procedure in which you read the sentence to children, they read in chorus, you cut the sentence into words, and children arrange the words into the original sentence. Making new sentences calls attention to the manner in which different words change the sentence's meaning.

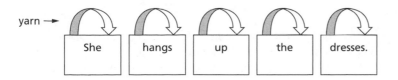

yarn → | She | hangs | up | the | dresses.

HANDS-ON ACTIVITIES FOR TEACHING SYLLABLE ■ ■ ■ ■ ▬▬ AWARENESS WITH RHYTHM STICKS

These phonological awareness activities use rhythm sticks to develop syllable awareness. PVC pipe, pencils, or dowels make good, inexpensive rhythm sticks.

HOW TO MAKE YOUR OWN RHYTHM STICKS

1. *PVC pipe rhythm sticks.* You need two PVC pipe sections that are twelve inches long by one inch in diameter for every child. Purchase PVC pipe at your local home improvement store and ask store personnel to cut the PVC pipe into ten- to twelve-inch sections. Give each child two pipes, and, Voila!, you have homemade rhythm sticks! Not only are these rhythm sticks inexpensive, but they last a lifetime.
2. *Pencil rhythm sticks.* Children tap two fat pencils together.
3. *Dowel rhythm sticks.* Purchase wooden rods from a home improvement store. Have the rods cut into ten- to twelve-inch pieces. Purchase two ten- to twelve-inch pieces for each child. Brush fine grain sandpaper over the ends if the wood is prickly. You will then have nice wooden rhythm sticks!

TAPPING THE SYLLABLES IN CHILDREN'S NAMES

▷ SMALL GROUP
SYLLABLE AWARENESS

Children listen for syllables in their own names and the names of their classmates and then tap for each syllable they hear. Use syllable tapping with children who are aware of the words in sentences, but are not yet aware of the syllables in words. These children are in the pre-alphabetic word fluency stage.

MATERIALS: Rhythm sticks; chart paper; marker.

DIRECTIONS: Pass out two rhythm sticks to each child. Explain that each child's name has a special rhythm, which we call syllables. Demonstrate by saying a child's name and tapping the rhythm sticks for each syllable. For the purposes of demonstration, pick a child with a two-syllable name. You might, for example, say, "Chyna" while tapping the sticks for each syllable: Chy-na. Make the syllables visible by writing children's names on the chalkboard. Write the names syllable-by-syllable, leaving a little extra space between each syllable and underlining the syllables. For example, you might write:

Ebony	Mario	Ann	Brandon	Tyrone	Juno	Chu
<u>Eb</u> <u>on</u> <u>y</u>	<u>Mar</u> <u>i</u> <u>o</u>	<u>Ann</u>	<u>Bran</u> <u>don</u>	<u>Ty</u> <u>rone</u>	<u>Ju</u> <u>no</u>	<u>Chu</u>

Explain that children tap the rhythm sticks once for each underlined part. Ask the children to use the underlined parts to count the syllables in their own names. Make a chart of children's names, written syllable-by-syllable. Count the number of syllables in children's names. Have the children repeatedly read the names and tap for each syllable. This sounds like a chant when children read and tap in chorus.

As a follow-up, have children tap the syllables in the days of the week, months of the year, and words from their favorite storybooks, science books, and social studies books.

MYSTERY NAMES

▷ SMALL GROUP
SYLLABLE AWARENESS

In this activity, children guess the names of their classmates by listening to you tap the syllables with a set of rhythm sticks. Mystery names is an engaging activity that is appropriate for developing syllable awareness for children in the pre-alphabetic word fluency stage.

MATERIALS: Rhythm sticks.

DIRECTIONS: Ask two or three children to stand. Choose children whose names have different numbers of syllables, such as *Ebony* (Three syllables) and *Ann* (one syllable). Tell the group to listen carefully as you tap the syllables in one of the names. For example, you might tap three times for Ebony. Ask children to tell the name you tapped: Ebony or Ann. Children say the mystery name. Invite children who are able to tap syllables to be the mystery name tappers.

▷ SMALL GROUP
SYLLABLE AWARENESS

SINGING, TAPPING, AND COUNTING SYLLABLES

Children sing, tap, and count the syllables in familiar songs. Like the other activities in this section, use counting syllables with pre-alphabetic readers who are aware of the words in sentences, and who are developing an awareness of the syllables in words.

MATERIALS: One set of rhythm sticks for each child; familiar songs; chart paper; marker.

DIRECTIONS: Write the lyrics of a song children already know on a large chart. Leave lots of space between the lines. Explain that children are going to tap for the syllables in words. Have children say each word and tap for each syllable. Write a slash under each word to show the number of taps (syllables). For instance, if children are going to tap rhythm sticks to "Are You Sleeping?" the first line would look like this:

Are you sleeping?
/   /   /   /

Have the children sing and tap for each syllable. Use the chart as a guide when singing and tapping. Ask children to count the slashes to find the longest word or words with only one syllable. Help the children conclude that words with only one syllable are short, words with more than one syllable are usually long, and words with many syllables are usually the longest words of all.

Examples of Literature Connections
Bryan, A., & Manning, D. (1991). *All night, all day: A child's first book of African-American spirituals.* New York: Atheneum Books for Young Readers.

The twenty African-American spirituals in this book include guitar and piano arrangements. Multicultural: African-American Songs

■■■■ ■ ■ ■ ■ HANDS-ON ACTIVITIES FOR TEACHING SOUND AWARENESS

▷ SMALL GROUP
SOUND AWARENESS

RUBBER BANDING AND SOUND STRETCHING

In this phonemic awareness teaching strategy, you call attention to the individual sounds in words by pronouncing words slowly so as to elongate the pronunciation of each sound, while at the same time keeping the sounds themselves in the context of whole words. Use this activity with children who are in the partial alphabetic stage of word fluency. This activity is also beneficial for kindergartners or first graders who have just entered the alphabetic word fluency stage. Such children are aware of sounds, but are not yet proficient at separating longer words into sounds and sometimes have to reblend several times before pronouncing a recognizable word.

MATERIALS: Decodable words; that is, words which sound like they are spelled.

DIRECTIONS: The technique of pronouncing words slowly and elongating sounds is called either rubber banding or sound stretching. Rubber banding or sound stretching the word *man* would sound something like /mmmmaaaaannnn/. While rubber banding is an effective teaching strategy all by itself, it is even more effective when children see the letters that represent the rubber-banded sounds in words.

RUBBER BANDING SOUNDS WHILE WRITING WORDS LETTER-BY-LETTER   Rubber banding while writing words letter-by-letter makes the sounds visible by linking them to letters and, not coincidentally, gives children letter-sound information. We will use /man/ as an example of rubber banding while writing words letter-by-letter. You would write *m* as you say /mmmm/, *a* when you say /aaaa/, and *n* while pronouncing /nnnn/. Repeat the whole word, /man/. Finally, invite the children to join you in rubber banding /mmmmaaaannnnn/ in chorus while you point to each letter as the sound is rubber banded.

RUBBER BANDING THE SOUNDS REPRESENTED BY LETTERS IN WORDS   To rubber band the sounds associated with letters in words, you would point to the first, middle, and last letters as you pronounce each stretched sound: "*mmmm* (point to *m*), *aaaa* (point to *a*), *nnnn* (point to *n*)." Ask children to count the letters. Rubber band and point to each letter again, asking, "What is the first sound in *mmmmaaaannnn*? The middle sound in *mmmmaaaannn*? The last sound in *mmmmaaaannnn*?" Use two- and three-sound decodable words, such as *be, me, go, no, run, fan, man, mat, met, fin,* and *sun*. Avoid long words and words with silent letters, as in *knock, knee, write,* and *wrong*.

SOUND PULLING

▷ SMALL GROUP
SOUND AWARENESS
LETTER-SOUNDS

If you have watched children pull long strings of bubble gum from their mouths, you have a mental picture of sound pulling. We have used sound pulling effectively for many years and find that it works especially well for younger and less-mature children. Use this activity to move partial alphabetic readers into the alphabetic stage, and to improve the ability of alphabetic readers to efficiently separate words into sounds.

MATERIALS: None.

DIRECTIONS.   Imagine that you are pulling a long string of bubble gum out of your mouth, only instead of gum you are pulling sounds in words. Bring your hand to your mouth, with your thumb and forefinger pressed together. Pull your hand slowly away from your mouth as you slowly say each sound in a word. Have the children join you in pulling the sounds from their mouths.

To help children remember the exact position of sounds in words:

1. Pull the sounds of a short word, such as /me/.
2. Ask the children to sound pull /me/ with you, together in chorus.
3. Once children can sound pull with you in chorus, have children stop when they pull /m/ and stop again when they pull /e/.

Once children are comfortable with sound pulling, demonstrate and illustrate where sounds are when they are pulled, and ask children to point to the letters that show the sounds. The picture in Figure 2–3 illustrates how you can combine sound pulling with associating letters with sounds in words. Have children join in sound pulling as they point to letters on the sound-pulling picture which gets children involved visually, auditorially, and kinesthetically. We find this combination to be especially beneficial for children who struggle with sound awareness. There is a reproducible sound-pulling pattern in Appendix I (A-1). Copy the pattern and write in any letters you wish, or ask children to listen to sounds and to write the letters that represent those sounds in the proper place on the pattern.

FIGURE 2–3   Sound Pulling

▷ SMALL GROUP OR
INDIVIDUAL SOUND
AWARENESS
LETTER-SOUNDS

SOUND BOXES

Elkonin, a Soviet researcher, developed a sound-awareness teaching strategy called Elkonin boxes, sound boxes, or sound pushing, in which children develop sound awareness by pushing a token into a box for each sound heard in a word. When you write letters in the boxes, children also learn how letters represent sounds in words. Sound boxes teach partial alphabetic readers about the individual sounds in words. This activity is also beneficial for improving the sound awareness and letter-sound knowledge of children in the alphabetic stage.

MATERIALS: Sound boxes (reproducible pattern Appendix I, A-2); several tokens for each child; pencil; pictures with two-, three-, and four-sound names (optional). Sound boxes are connected boxes. They usually range from two to four boxes, depending on the number of sounds in the words.

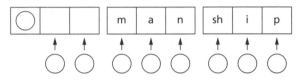

FIGURE 2–4   Sound Boxes

DIRECTIONS: Pronounce a word and ask children to push a token into a box for every sound heard (Figure 2–4). In addition to pronouncing words, show children pictures of words. Pictures help clarify word meaning, which is especially helpful for children who speak languages other than English at home. Follow these steps to rubber band words as children push tokens into sound boxes:

1. Rubber band a word (/mmmmaaannnn/).
2. Ask children to move a token into the first box for /mmmm/ in /mmmmaaannnn/.
3. Repeat rubber banding, asking children to move a token for the /a/ and the /n/ in /mmmmaaaannnn/.
4. Ask children to point to the first box and say the sound /m/, to the second box while saying /a/, and to the last box when saying /n/.
5. Blend /m/ + /a/ + /n/ into /man/. You may blend while tracking the letters with a finger or the children may blend together with you in chorus.

   Extend awareness of the spoken sounds of individual letter-sounds by writing the letters in the boxes (Figure 2–4). Rubber band a word and have children push a token into each box for every sound heard. Then take the tokens away and write *m* in the first box, *a* in the second, and *n* in the third. Have children point to each letter as they say the sounds with you, and then blend the sounds into /man/. Writing letters in boxes makes the sounds visible by showing children the letters that stand for sounds, demonstrates the alphabetic principle, and helps children develop an understanding of letter and sound relationships in words. When two letters represent one sound, as in the *sh* in *ship* or the *oa* in *boat,* write the two letters in the same box. The number of boxes then equals the number of sounds in a word, as shown in Figure 2–4.

▷ SMALL GROUP
SOUND AWARENESS
LETTER-SOUNDS

SPELLING FOR SOUNDS

You can assist children in spelling new words letter-sound by letter-sound. Spelling for sounds demonstrates the individual sounds in spoken words and also shows children how letters represent sounds in spoken words. Use spelling for sounds with partial alphabetic learners who are getting ready to move into the alphabetic stage, and with alphabetic learners who need more practice listening for sounds in words and associating letters with sounds.

MATERIALS: Chalk board or white board; chalk or dry erase markers. Decodable words.

DIRECTIONS: Assist children in spelling new words by showing children how to identify the sounds in words and then to associate those sounds with letters. For instance, suppose children want to spell the word *sad.* Go to the board and rubber band sad: /ssssaaaadddd/. Ask children to listen for the first sound. Once children identify the beginning sound, /s/, ask them to name the letter that the /ssss/ represents. Write *s* on the board. Next say /saaaa/, rubber banding the

/a/ phoneme. Ask children to say the letter that represents the /aaaa/ sound and write *a* beside *s*. The writing now looks like: *sa*. We cannot rubber band /d/ for a long period because the air flow is obstructed while saying this phoneme. Pronounce the /d/ with a strong voice emphasis so as to draw children's attention to this sound: /ssssaaaa**d**/. Ask children to say the sound that /d/ represents; write *d* on the board, thus completing the spelling of *sad*. Rubber band /sad/ again, tracking sounds with your finger.

If children do not yet know all the letter-sounds, assist them by writing in the letters for sounds the children have not yet learned. In this instance, children spell all the sounds they are able to connect with letters. For example, if children know only the letter-sound relationships for *s* and *d*, you could still use spelling for sounds. You would assist them in identifying the /s/ and associating the letter *s* with this sound. Having written *s* on the board, you would then rubber band /ssssaaaa/ and *tell* children that the letter *a* represents /aaaa/. Write *sa* on the board. Then, once the children have come to /d/, a sound they associate with a letter, you return to the strategy of rubber banding, asking children to identify the sound, and saying the letter that represents that sound. We find spelling for sounds so helpful that we even use it when our children are not completely sure of all the letter-sound associations in a word. Coincidentally, when used in conjunction with other activities, we find that spelling for sounds helps our children identify sounds in words, use phonics, and learn more about letter-sound relationships.

SOUND TUNNELS

▷ SMALL GROUP OR
INDIVIDUAL
SOUND AWARENESS
BLENDING

Sound tunnels are devices that create a slight delay in the time children say a word or sound and the time that children hear the word or sound. The slight delay helps children focus on individual sounds in words, and the blending feedback helps children improve blending based on the sound of their own voices. Use this activity with children who are in the partial alphabetic stage and getting ready to move into the alphabetic stage, and with children in the alphabetic stage who need more practice separating sounds and blending sounds.

MATERIALS: Purchase a Sound-Around: A Speech Amplifier© from educAn (toll free 877–471–7210) or make your own sound tunnel. To make your own sound tunnel, purchase the following plumbing supplies: two 1 1/2 inch, 45 degree PVC street elbows, two 1 1/2 inch, 90 degree PVC street elbows, and one 1 1/2 inch, 20 degree PVC elbow. Look in the plumbing section of any home improvement store for the PVC fittings. Make a sound tunnel by fitting together two 45 degree street elbows, two 90 degree street elbows, and one 20 degree elbow (Figure 2–5). Another way to make a sound tunnel is to get a section of large hose (or other tube-shaped object).

DIRECTIONS: Show children how to place one end of the sound tunnel next to their ear and the other end near their mouth. To avoid spreading colds and other diseases, make sure that the children avoid touching their mouths to the PVC sound tunnel.

USING SOUND TUNNELS FOR SOUND AWARENESS To help children become aware of the individual sounds in words, ask children to pronounce a word in the sound tunnel and to listen for a designated sound, then have the children say the sound they listened for in the tunnel. The slight delay in hearing the word has the effect of amplifying the sounds, including the sound children are listening for. Saying the sound in isolation reinforces children's awareness of that sound.

USING SOUND TUNNELS FOR BLENDING Demonstrate how to blend sounds into a two-sound word, such as /me/. Have the children hold the sound tunnel to their ear and imitate the way you blend /me/. Then ask children to listen to you blend /me/ again. Have children blend /me/ in the sound tunnel, checking to hear if their blending sounds like the way you blended. When children are able to blend two-sound words, move to three- and four-sound words. Children for whom blending is very difficult benefit from using sound tunnels along with an illustration of a slide (Figure 2–14 in this chapter). The slide gives children a visual representation of blending, while the sound tunnel gives children immediate feedback on their own personal blending success. You may also use the sound tunnels, Sound-Around Speech Amplifiers©, or soft large hoses to encourage children to explore their favorite songs (Silberg, 1998).

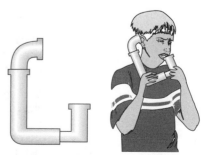

FIGURE 2–5 Sound Tunnel

CHEERIOS© SOUND COUNTING

Children count sounds with tasty Cheerios©. Cheerios© sound counting, like all other sound-counting teaching strategies, asks children to separate spoken words into each and every individual sound, and then to count the sounds one-by-one. Sound counting is beneficial for partial alphabetic readers who are moving into the alphabetic stage, or alphabetic readers who need more practice separating words into sounds.

MATERIALS: Several boxes of Cheerios©; paper plates; marker; soap, moist towelettes or antiseptic gel for washing hands. Sketch two or three connected sound boxes on as many inexpensive paper plates as there are children in a small group. (Figure 2–4 illustrates connected boxes.)

DIRECTIONS: After reading *The Cheerios*© Counting Book (McGrath, 1998a), sprinkle a few Cheerios© on a paper plate and explain that you will say a word and move one Cheerio© into a connected box for every sound and count the Cheerios©. Model sound counting with a few two- and three-sound familiar words. Rubber band a word and show children how to move one Cheerio© into each box for every sound heard.

    When children understand how to sound count with Cheerios©, give each child one paper plate and pour a few Cheerios© on it. Pronounce two- and three-sound words, asking the children to move just one Cheerio© into a box for every sound they hear. Once the Cheerios© are lined up, ask children to count the Cheerios© to find out how many sounds they heard in the word. Follow-up by asking children to tell the beginning sound, the middle sound, and the ending sound. After sounds are counted and identified, children should eat the Cheerios© in the boxes. Pronounce another two- or three-sound word and repeat the process.

Examples of Literature Connections
McGrath, B. B. (1998a). *The Cheerios*© *counting book.* New York: Scholastic.
  The bright illustrations and simple language in this counting book make it an excellent link for sound counting.
McGrath, B. B. (1998b). *A contrar Cheerios.* New York: Scholastic.
  This is the Spanish language version of *The Cheerios*© counting book.
Curriculum Connections
Learning Numbers   Integrate this activity with counting and number identification.
Counting in Spanish   Use the Spanish language version to teach children how to count in Spanish. If you use the two books side-by-side, children observe connections between the number words in Spanish and English.
Multicultural   Spanish language.

SOUND GRAPHING

Children count the sounds in words and then make a graph that shows how many words have two, three, or even four sounds. Use graphing sounds with small groups of children who know how to count sounds in words. Sound graphing helps partial alphabetic readers move toward the alphabetic stage, and helps children in the alphabetic stage improve their ability to separate words into sounds.

MATERIALS: Pictures from old workbooks and magazines; tape; a very large sheet of chart paper or newsprint. Draw two, three, and four connected sound boxes at the top of chart paper. Leave a large space between each set of sound boxes.

DIRECTIONS: Children may cut out pictures or you may wish to give children pictures. Ask children to name each picture and to count the sounds in the picture name. Have children tape the pictures under the correct number of sound boxes. The result is a giant display of pictures and boxes showing the number of sounds in picture names (Figure 2–6). For extra practice, rubber band the picture names; count sounds; and ask children to identify the first, middle, and last sound in each word.

FIGURE 2–6 Sound Graphing

SOUND SORTING

Children sort by putting pictures with the same beginning, middle, or ending sounds into sacks that have pictures that represent the same sounds in the same beginning, middle, or ending positions. Children may also sort by putting words with the same number of sounds into the same sacks. Sorting by beginning or ending sounds is appropriate for partial alphabetic readers who are getting ready to move into the alphabetic stage. Sorting by middle sounds and by the number of sounds in words is appropriate for kindergarten children and early first graders who are in the alphabetic word fluency stage.

MATERIALS: Two or three paper lunch sacks for each group; marker; easy-to-identify pictures; chart paper. If children are to sort according to the beginning, middle, or ending sounds in words, put a picture on each sack and write the target letter above the picture. If children are to sort by the number of sounds in words, write a numeral or the number of connected boxes on each sack to show the number of sounds in a picture name.

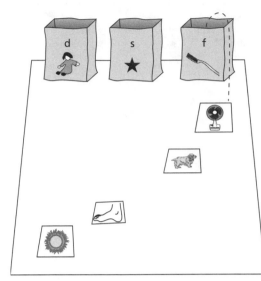

FIGURE 2–7   Sorting for Beginning, Middle, or Ending Sounds in Words

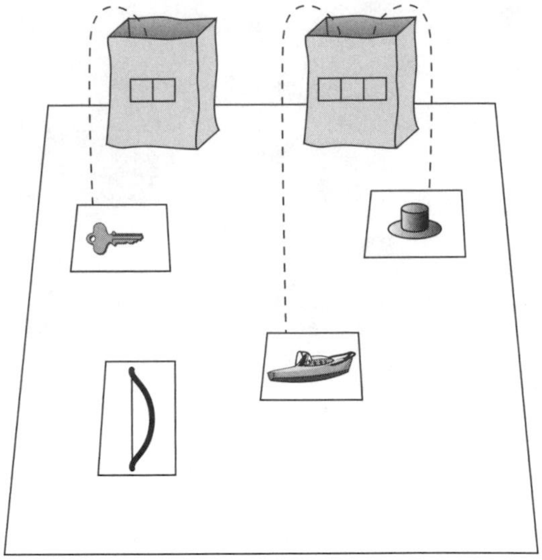

FIGURE 2–8   Sorting for the Number of Sounds in Words

DIRECTIONS:

SORTING ACCORDING TO THE BEGINNING, MIDDLE, OR ENDING SOUNDS IN WORDS   Show children the sacks with letters and pictures. Explain that children are to sort pictures with certain beginning (middle or ending) sounds into sacks with a matching picture, word, or letter (Figure 2–7). For example, in sorting for the beginning sounds /d/, /s/, and /f/, children might sort pictures of a *dog, dish, desk, duck,* and *dinosaur* into a sack with a picture of a *doll,* the letter *d,* or the word <u>d</u>oll. Children put pictures of *sack, sun, seal,* and *sail* into a sack with a picture of a *star,* the letter *s,* or the word <u>s</u>tar. Pictures that begin with /f/, such as *feather, fan, fire,* and *foot,* are put into a sack with a picture of a *fork,* the letter *f,* or the word <u>f</u>ork. After sorting, talk with children about the letter and the word written on each sack. Write the words for the picture names on a large chart. Write the words in three columns: a *d* column, an *s* column, and an *f* column. Read the list in chorus. Have children identify the /d/, /s/, or /f/ sound in each word and underline the letter in each word. Put some of the words on the word wall. Add this sorting activity to a learning center.

SORTING BY THE NUMBER OF SOUNDS IN WORDS   Show children the numeral or connected boxes on each sack. Explain that the numeral or connected boxes represent the number of sounds heard in words. Have children work with a partner or individually to sort pictures by the number of sounds (Figure 2–8). When children finish sorting, take the pictures out of the sacks and pronounce each picture by name. Ask children to hold up two fingers for two-sound picture names and three fingers for three-sound picture names. Place this sorting activity in a learning center. You may add different pictures to the mix or give children extra practice with the same set of pictures. In asking children to sort the same picture set, children have an opportunity to develop fluency. That is, by repeating the same picture set, sorting becomes fast, accurate, and effortless. In sorting a slightly different picture mix, children have opportunities to extend their insight into the sound structure in words.

BEGINNING SOUND ROLL

Children roll a small ball to one another while sitting in a circle. In front of each child is a card with a picture and a letter that represents the beginning sound in the picture name. The child who catches the ball says a word that begins with the same sound and letter as shown on the card in front of that child. Use this activity to help partial alphabetic word readers further develop their ability to identify beginning sounds and to associate beginning sounds with letters.

MATERIALS: One medium-size soft ball; 5 × 8 cards with pictures and letters on them; masking tape. Tape cards to the floor, in a circle, with masking tape loops.

DIRECTIONS: Have a small group sit cross-legged on the floor in a circle. Ask each child to sit in front of a card with a picture and a letter on it. Explain that children will roll the ball to one another. Children who catch the ball say the picture name, the beginning sound, and the letter name on the card in front of them. Make this activity more challenging by asking children to think of a different word that begins with the same sound and letter as shown on the card. After the children have rolled the ball around the circle once, have children scoot over one place. This gives children practice with different words, beginning sounds, and letter-sounds.

▷ SMALL GROUP
SOUND AWARENESS
LETTER NAMES AND
LETTER-SOUNDS

HAND-CRAFTED SOUND AND LETTER CHANTS

Children combine beginning sound awareness with letter-sounds as they craft their own chants. Use this activity with partial alphabetic readers who need more practice identifying beginning sounds in words, and connecting beginning sounds with letters.

MATERIALS: Colored markers or crayons; construction paper.

DIRECTIONS: After reading *Alphabet Soup* (Banks, 1994) or another book that features letters and sounds, write a letter the children are learning. For instance, if children are learning the name and sound of the letter *b,* you might write *b* three times—*b b b*—horizontally across the chalk board or chart paper. Point to the *b* and ask children to name the letter and join you in saying the letter-sound. Put your hand under the first *b,* and pronounce the sound, /b/, followed by the second and the third sounds in succession. This forms the first part of the letter-sound chant, "/b/ - /b/ - /b/." Now ask children to think of a word that begins with the /b/ sound. Draw a picture of the word. Should children say "boat," you would draw a *boat.* Now there are three letter *b*s followed by a *boat.* Turn this into a chant by saying each /b/ in succession, while pointing to each letter, and then immediately saying "boat." Try it with the group in chorus, "/b/ /b/ /b/   boat." Examples of letters and words from *Alphabet Soup* include: *h h h house; h h h hat; r r r rain; m m m man; m m m mountain.*

Give each child a large piece of construction paper. Put several crayons in the center of the children's work space. Ask children to make their own chants for letters, sounds, and pictures. Encourage children to use examples from the books they are sharing in your classroom, from the word wall, and from their own imaginations. Ask them to make up three chants. Display the chants and, at various times during the day, share the chants with everyone in the class. Making and saying their own chants gives children ample opportunities to identify beginning sounds and to connect these sounds with letters. The children enjoy the chant-like language, and reading from copies of their own work gives the children a special stake in this choral activity. Figure 2–9 shows two groups of chants: One group is: *b b b bunny* (/b/ - /b/ - /b/ - bunny); *d d d dragon* (/d/ - /d/ - /d/ - dragon); and *j j j jewel* (/j/ - /j/ - /j/ - jewel). The other group is: *s s s snake* (/s/ - /s/ - /s/ - snake); *c c c car* (/c/ - /c/ - /c/ - car); and *t t t turtle* (/t/ - /t/ - /t/ - turtle).

Examples of Literature Connections

Banks, K. (1994). *Alphabet soup.* New York: Alfred A. Knopf.

   As a daydreaming boy pulls words from his alphabet soup, the words magically come to life, and the ensuing adventure sets the stage for creating chants.

Tabor, M. N. G. (1993). *Albertina anda arrriba: el abecedario/ Albertina goes up: An alphabet.* Watertown, MA: Charlesbridge Publishing.

   Written in Spanish with an English translation, this book presents each letter in the Spanish alphabet.

▷ SMALL GROUP
SOUND AWARENESS
LETTER-SOUNDS

FIGURE 2–9a
Hand-crafted Letter and
Sound Chant

FIGURE 2–9b
Hand-crafted Letter and
Sound Chant

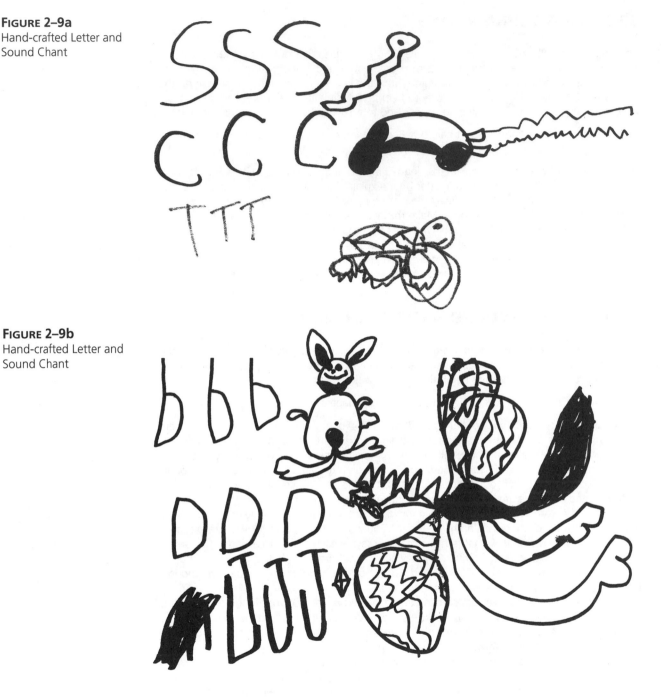

▷ **SMALL GROUP OR**
INDIVIDUAL
SOUND AWARENESS
LETTER-SOUNDS

PICTURE AND LETTER TOSS

Children toss a cube with a picture and letter on each side. Children say another word that begins (or ends) with the sound associated with the picture and accompanying letter, or children
say the picture name sound-by-sound. Ask partial alphabetic readers to identify beginning
sounds, and have alphabetic readers separate the picture name into individual sounds.

MATERIALS: Cubes with pictures and letters. Duplicate the cube pattern in Appendix I (A-3).
Put six key words, key pictures, and letter combinations on the six-sided cube (Figure 2–10).
Create many different cubes with different picture and letter combinations. For larger, sturdier
cubes than those constructed with the pattern in Appendix I, cover an empty square tissue box
(not an oblong box) with white contact paper. Voila! You have a big, sturdy cube.

DIRECTIONS:

BEGINNING SOUND IDENTIFICATION
Have a small group of partial alphabetic readers take turns tossing the cube. Children say a word that begins with the same sound as the face-up picture and the sound represented by the letter.

SEPARATING PICTURE NAMES INTO SOUNDS Ask more phonemically aware children to completely separate the picture name into sounds. For example, if the pictures show a sun and an *s,* children would say: /s/ - /u/ - /n/.

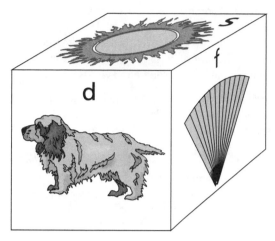

FIGURE 2–10 Picture and Letter Toss

COLORED SOUNDS

Children use colorful construction paper squares to add sounds, substitute beginning sounds, or separate words into sounds. Adding and substituting beginning sounds is appropriate for partial alphabetic readers who have some awareness of beginning and ending sounds. Separating words into individual sounds is beneficial for partial alphabetic readers who are moving into the alphabetic stage and for alphabetic readers who need more practice identifying the individual sounds in words.

MATERIALS: A variety of one-inch colored construction paper squares; markers; glue sticks.

DIRECTIONS:

SEPARATING WORDS INTO SOUNDS Working with a small group or an individual, place several colored construction paper squares on a table. Explain that the squares stand for sounds in words. Explain further that children will use the squares to show the individual sounds in words. Say a short word, such as /bed/, then demonstrate how to move a colored square for each sound in the word. For instance, you might move a blue square for the /b/, a green square for the /e/, and a white square for the final /d/. Rubber band /bed/ and ask a volunteer to point to the squares that represent the sounds as you rubber band. Then have children select a colored square to represent each sound in /pig/. Count the squares. Rubber band /pig/, asking each child to point to the colored square that represents the sound as you rubber band /ppppiiiigggg/. Then say individual sounds and have children point to the squares that represent those sounds.

Extend this activity to letter-sounds by writing the letter on each colored square. For example, you might write *p* on one square, *i* on another, and *g* on still another. Children now have three colored squares with the letters *p, i,* and *g.* Have children point to the squares as you rubber band /pig/. You should say the sounds one at a time, such as /i/, and ask children to point to the square that represents this sound. Use this same procedure with other familiar two- and three-sound words. Writing letters on the squares demonstrates the connection between phonemic awareness and literacy, and simultaneously calls attention to the sounds and letters in words. Children may take the squares home with them. We like to have children use glue sticks to glue squares to paper. This preserves the order of spelling and ensures that papers make it home intact.

ADDING BEGINNING SOUNDS Begin by showing children how to line up two different squares, one to represent /a/ and one for /t/. Let us assume that we have a red square for /a/ and a blue square for /t/. Ask children to point to /a/ and to /t/. Demonstrate how to blend /a/ and /t/ into /at/, and then have the children imitate the way that you blended. Next, show children how to turn /at/ into /mat/ by putting a yellow square in front of the red and blue squares. Now the three squares (yellow, red, and blue) represent /mat/. Have the children point to the square that represents the /m/, /a/, and /t/. Write a letter on each square, thus spelling *mat.* Have children take the /m/ away (the yellow square, in this example). Ask children what is left (/at/). Then

> *SMALL GROUP OR*
> *INDIVIDUAL*
> *SOUND AWARENESS*
> *LETTER-SOUNDS*

instruct children to select a square that would show /fat/. Should a child select an orange square, the sequence would look like: orange, red, and blue. The red and blue squares have *a* and *t* on them, respectively. After children point to squares that represent different sounds in /fat/, write an *f* on the first square (the orange square, in this example). Follow this same procedure, making and separating words into sounds and associating sounds with letters.

SUBSTITUTING SOUNDS Alternatively, you may wish to make an extra long square that represents /at/. In this instance, children would place the large /at/ square in the center of their work space. Let us assume that the /at/ square is red. Then, in order to spell *mat,* children would put a different color square in front of the *at* square, perhaps blue, to represent /m/. Have children point to the /m/ and to the /at/, then ask children to take away the /m/ and replace it with a square to stand for /p/. Children may select any color they wish to represent beginning sounds. Continue substituting beginning consonants to make many different /at/ words, including *bat, cat, fat, hat, mat, pat, rat, sat,* and *vat.*

STICKER HAND COVERS

In this activity, a plain sheet of paper is folded to make a hand cover with a sticker of a familiar object and, if desired, a letter that represents the beginning sound in the picture name. Use sticker hand covers with partial alphabetic readers who need more experience listening for, and identifying, sounds in words in order to become more phonemically aware.

MATERIALS: 8 1/2 × 11-inch blank sheets of light-colored construction paper, one for each child; tape; stickers of familiar objects; markers. Paper hand covers are easy to fold and tape; just follow the directions in Figure 2–11. Make as many folded paper hand covers as there are children in a small group.

DIRECTIONS: Show the children a completed hand cover. Explain that children are to put on a hand cover and select three stickers for their cover. One sticker goes on the top of the hand cover, the second sticker goes on the upper inside, and the third goes on the lower inside (Figure 2–11). Talk about the picture names of the stickers and the beginning sounds in the picture names. Ask each child, individually, to tell the beginning sound in the name of the pictures. Write the beginning letter-sound for each sticker picture. Each finished hand cover has three stickers with a letter that begins with the sticker (picture) names. Ask children in the small group to share by showing their hand-cover stickers and letters, saying the sticker (picture) name, the letter name, and, if you wish, the letter-sound. Have children take their hand covers home to share with their family.

1. Using an 8½ X 11 inch sheet of construction paper, fold the paper three times, lengthwise. This makes a long piece one-third the width of the paper.

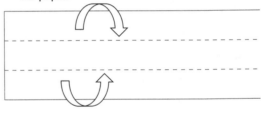

2. Fold the paper in half.

3. Fold each end back to the center, forming a zigzag pattern.

4. You now have a slot for the thumb and a slot for four fingers. Tape any loose pieces of paper. Children select three stickers and say the beginning letter-sounds. Put the stickers on the hand cover, one on the top, one on the upper inside, and one on the lower inside. Write the beginning letter-sound.

FIGURE 2–11 Sticker Hand Covers

BEGINNING SOUND CLOTHES LINE

Children use clothespins to hang words with the same beginning sounds in rows on a clothesline.

MATERIALS: Scissors; word cards or the clothes patterns in Appendix I; clothespins; rope for clothesline; letter cards. When you use the reproducible patterns in Appendix I, copy them onto sturdy construction paper. String a thin rope across the classroom. Fasten it firmly with tape. As an alternative to suspending a string across a portion of your classroom, you might want to zigzag a lightweight rope or heavy string down a bulletin board, fastening it securely with thumbtacks.

DIRECTIONS: Read alliterative (words that begin with the same sound) alphabet books or other alliterative books that children enjoy. Discuss alliterative language. Find words on the word wall that begin with the same sound and the same letter and challenge children to look for other alliterative words. Make lists of the alliterative words and then ask a small group of children to join you at a table. Put one to three cards containing letters the children are learning on the table. Talk about letter names, letter-sounds, and words that begin with the letter-sounds. For example, if the children are learning about beginning sounds and are also learning the name and sound of the letter d, you might ask children to draw one picture on each card that shows a word that begins with d. As children complete their sketches, ask them what word you should write on the card, and what sound and letter the word begins with. Each completed card has a sketch and a word. For example, one card may have a picture of a dog with the word *dog,* another a picture of a doll with the word *doll,* and still another picture of a dragon with the word *dragon.*

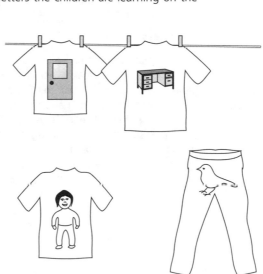

Use clothespins to hang the letter cards on the clothesline (Figure 2–12). When all the words (clothes) are hung on the clothesline, ask the children to read the words together. Review the beginning sound and letter. Leave the beginning sound clothesline up in your room. Also leave a few cards nearby so that children can add other words to the clothesline.

FIGURE 2–12   Alliteration Clothesline

Examples of Literature Connections

Base, G. (1996). *Animalia.* New York: Puffin.
   This is an alliterative alphabet book with intricate pictures showing a plethora of alliterative words.
Kellogg, S. (1987). *Aster aardvark's alphabet adventures.* New York: Mulberry Books.
   This alliterative alphabet book has lots of examples of words beginning with the same letter and sound.
Sendak, M. (1991). *Alligators all around: An alphabet.* New York: Harper-Trophy.
   Sendak's illustrations adorn this amusing, alliterative alphabet book.

HANDS-ON ACTIVITIES FOR TEACHING BLENDING ■ ■ ■ ■ ▬▬

ARM BLENDING

Children blend by placing imaginary sounds on their arms and then sweeping their hands down their arms as they blend sounds into words. Use this activity with children in the alphabetic stage who need more practice blending.

MATERIALS: None.

DIRECTIONS: Begin by demonstrating arm blending. Suppose, for example, that you wish to demonstrate arm blending with the word /cat/. Show children how to "place" the /c/ on their shoulder, the /a/ on their elbow, and the /t/ on their wrist. Place the imaginary sound on the arm that is opposite of the child's preferred hand, then show children how to blend by saying sounds as they move their hand from their shoulder to wrist. As children sweep their hands from the shoulder, the children say /c/. Moving on down to the elbow, children say /a/, and finally complete blending by saying /t/. The fluid sweeping motion from shoulder to wrist encourages children to blend the sounds together in a natural flow. The idea of imagining the sounds placed from shoulder to wrist helps children fix the order of sounds in their minds, and moving the hand in a sweeping motion from the shoulder to the wrist is a kinesthetic analog for the blending voice. Once children learn the arm blending technique, they use it on their own to support blending.

▷ SMALL GROUP OR
INDIVIDUAL
BLENDING

PENCIL BLENDING

Children imagine that sounds are placed on the edge of a table and use their pencils to sweep across the imaginary sounds as the children blend. This analog for arm blending is less obvious and equally easy for children to use on their own. Use pencil blending with alphabetic readers who stumble when blending. We find that older children enjoy, benefit from, and independently use pencil blending.

MATERIALS: Pencils.

DIRECTIONS: Ask a small group to bring a pencil and join you at a table. Pronounce a three-sound word, such as /cake/. Ask children to join you in using their pencils to tap the edge of the table for each sound. Children would join you in tapping the table edge once while saying /c/. Move over about an inch and tap the table while saying a long /a/. Then move over another inch and tap the table edge as you say /k/. By tapping all three sounds, /c/, long /a/, and /k/, children have separated /cake/ into sounds. Each individual sound now has an imaginary place on the table edge. Imagining that sounds are placed on the table edge helps children fix the sounds in memory and, therefore, reduces the instances of forgetting sounds, adding sounds, or reversing sounds. To blend, children sweep their pencils across each imaginary sound, blending the sounds together as they say them. Sweeping the pencil across the imagined sounds gives children a physical analog of how to pronounce sounds by naturally allowing one sound to flow into the next. Pencil blending is easy for children to use on their own. Pencil blending is not obvious, which is important for older children. The older children whom we teach independently use this strategy when reading books in the library or other public places.

▷ SMALL GROUP OR
INDIVIDUAL
BLENDING

FINGER AND KNUCKLE BLENDING

Children use their fingers or knuckles to help them remember the sequence of sounds and to guide them while blending. These two blending activities are beneficial for alphabetic readers who struggle with blending.

MATERIALS: None.

DIRECTIONS:

FIVE FINGER BLENDING   Let's assume that children are going to learn five finger blending using the word *lamp* as a blending example. Have the children join you in touching their forefingers against their thumbs when saying /l/. Then have children touch their middle fingers when saying /a/, their ring fingers when saying /m/, and their little fingers when saying /p/. Children blend by rapidly touching each finger, in succession, to their thumbs. Five finger blending is easy for children to use and works with words up to four sounds long. Five finger blending is a successful way to practice blending with small groups of children.

SINGLE FINGER BLENDING   To use single finger blending, children imagine that four sounds are placed on their forefinger, beginning with the first knuckle and extending to the tip of the finger. Right-handed children touch the first knuckle of the left hand for /l/, halfway to the middle knuckle on the forefinger while saying /a/, halfway between the middle knuckle and the finger tip while saying /m/, and the finger tip while saying /p/. Then children blend by sweeping the right forefinger over the first knuckle all the way to the finger tip while folding sounds together into /lamp/. Single finger blending, like five finger and knuckle blending, is suitable for practicing blending in small groups and is portable; that is, children use this blending technique on their own and in any place whatsoever.

Knuckle Blending   As an alternative to finger blending, we teach many older, struggling readers to use the knuckles on their hand to support blending. This technique is very much like five finger blending and single finger blending, in that sounds are mentally "placed" on knuckles. The children use their forefingers to tap the first knuckle while saying /l/, the second knuckle for /a/, the third for /m/, and the fourth for /p/. Then children blend by sweeping the forefinger over each knuckle while saying the sounds in sequence. Like the other blending techniques in this section, placing sounds on knuckles helps children remember the sounds and the order of the sounds they are to blend.

BLENDING CHANTS

▷ SMALL GROUP OR INDIVIDUAL BLENDING

Children say and blend beginning and rhyming sounds, or say and blend individual phonemes in a rhythmic cadence. Clapping and knee slapping add a kinesthetic element to chants. Blending beginning and rhyming sounds is helpful for partial alphabetic readers who need to learn more about blending in order to move into the alphabetic stage. Sound-by-sound blending is useful for alphabetic readers who need more blending practice.

MATERIALS: A teacher-created blending chant tailor-made for the children in your class.

DIRECTIONS:

Beginning Sound and Rhyming Sound Chants   There are two ways to blend beginning sounds and rhyming sounds with homemade chants. In the first variation, children say the beginning sound, the rhyming sound, and the whole word as they chant. In the second version, children say the beginning sound and rhyme and then fill in the word on their own. The easier of the two goes likes this:

I know a word.
It starts with /c/.
It ends with /at/.
What is the word?
/c/ /at/ makes cat!

Teach children to clap for the first two words and slap their knees for the second two words.

Slapping and clapping goes like this:

I (clap) know (clap) a (slap) word (slap).
It (clap) starts (clap) with (slap) /c/ (slap).
It (clap) ends (clap) with (slap) /at/ (slap).
What (clap) is (clap) the (slap) word (slap)?
/c/ (clap) /at/ (clap) makes (slap) cat (slap)!

The words in this chant are only one syllable long. Children naturally want to clap and slap for syllables. We have discussed the syllable as the basic pronunciation unit in language. If you are careful to use only one-syllable words, children will not be misled by trying to clap or slap for extra syllables.

The second variation is somewhat more challenging because children must blend a beginning sound and a rhyming sound, and then pronounce the word on their own. Explain that children are going to say a chant and blend the word on their own at the end of the chant. It goes like this:

I know a word.
It starts with /c/.
It ends with /at/.
Blend it, blend it.
And you get ____!

Children fill in the word *cat* on their own. The whole group may say /cat/ or you may call on a volunteer to be the special child to complete the chant. The child who finishes the chant then gets to call on someone else to be the next "chant finisher." Clapping and slapping are the same: Clap for the first two words and slap for the second two words.

SOUND-BY-SOUND BLENDING CHANTS   Children say each individual sound, and then blend the sounds to pronounce a word. We begin by chanting children's names and then go on to chant other words. This chant sounds like a football rally. Imagine yourself at a college sporting event, and you have the picture! Here is how it goes. We will use Brian to illustrate how this chant works with a child's name:

Teacher:	Give me a /b/!	Children:	/b/!
Teacher:	Give me an /r/!	Children:	/r/!
Teacher:	Give me an /i/!	Children:	/i/!
Teacher:	Give me an /a/!	Children:	/a/!
Teacher:	Give me an /n/!	Children:	/n/!
Teacher:	What does it say?	Children:	/brian/!

Add variety by asking the children to clap as they echo each sound—/b/ clap; /r/ clap/; /i/ clap; /a/ clap; /n/ clap; /brian/ clap. You may also ask a child to lead the chant.

▷ SMALL GROUP OR
INDIVIDUAL
BLENDING

PICTURE BLENDING

Picture blending uses pictures of familiar objects to demonstrate the concept of blending. Illustrations are cut into one or two pieces. Sounds from the picture name are associated with the pieces and then the sounds are blended as the pieces of the picture are slid together (Catts & Vartiainen, 1993). The difficulty of blending is determined by how many picture pieces children blend. We use from two to four pieces, depending on children's needs and the length of words we are blending. Use this teaching strategy with partial alphabetic readers who need to learn about blending.

MATERIALS: Large pictures of familiar objects; scissors. We laminate the picture sections for longevity and, coincidentally, we have found that laminated picture pieces slide together more easily.

DIRECTIONS: Begin by showing children a picture and saying its name. If you are using laminated pieces of a picture, put the pieces together to show the entire object. If you have an intact illustration, name the picture and cut it into two, three, or four pieces as children watch. For example, /boat/ may be cut into two pieces by dividing the beginning sound and the rhyming sounds, /b/ + /oat/; or it may be cut into three pieces that correspond to each phoneme, /b/ + long /o/ + /t/ (Figure 2–13).

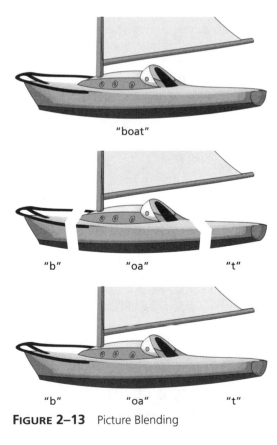

"boat"

"b"   "oa"   "t"

"b"   "oa"   "t"

FIGURE 2–13 Picture Blending

PIÑATA WORDS

Children listen to the sounds in words and then blend the sounds together to identify the objects hidden in a piñata. Use this activity with partial alphabetic readers who need to learn to blend and with alphabetic readers who need more blending practice.

MATERIALS: A piñata; small objects to put inside the piñata; letter cards. Place an assortment of small objects inside a piñata. Suggested objects include a small car; ball; spoon; fork; pencil; button; plastic egg; crayon; eraser; marker; block; and miniatures from bags of small toys, like a cow, horse, pig, wagon, lamb, fence, and tree.

DIRECTIONS: After reading *Fiesta!* (Guy, 1996), show children a piñata; shake the piñata; listen to the objects rattling around. Explain that instead of breaking the piñata the children will guess the hidden things inside by listening to the sounds in the words. Put your hand in the piñata; grasp an object but do not show the children what you have. As the children carefully listen, say each sound of the word. For example, if you select a small plastic *cow* from a farm animal set, you would ask something like, "What is hiding in the piñata? Its sounds are /c/ /ow/." The closer together you pronounce sounds, the less effort it takes to blend; the farther apart the sounds, the more difficult blending becomes. Say sounds fairly close together when teaching a group which is just beginning to develop blending skill. Say sounds with longer spaces between them when teaching a small group of alphabetic learners. We find that children find the idea of hidden objects inside a piñata to be especially intriguing. If you have children in your classroom who do not speak English at home, and if you are able to pronounce a few words in the children's home languages, you might add these words to the mix. If you cannot find plastic objects or small toys to put inside the piñata, you may substitute pictures.

Example of Literature Connections
Guy, G. F. (1996). *Fiesta!* New York: Greenwillow Books.
   Using a birthday party theme, this counting book shows numbers and number words in Spanish and English, such as dos trompetas (two horns) and cinco trompos (five tops).
Multicultural Connection: Spanish Language

BLENDING SLIDE

A picture of a playground slide helps children visualize the blending process and guides children as they blend. This teaching strategy is beneficial for partial alphabetic readers who need to learn to blend, and for alphabetic readers who need more blending practice.

MATERIALS: Picture of a slide. (Copy the pattern in Appendix I.)

DIRECTIONS: Show a small group a picture of a slide (see pattern in Appendix I) or draw a slide on the board. Explain that when we blend sounds we slide them together. For example, you might blend the word *fat* by saying the sounds separately: /f/ - /a/ - /t/. Put your hand at the top of the slide when you pronounce /f/, in the middle of the slide when you say /a/, and toward the bottom as you pronounce /t/. Then, beginning at the top of the slide, blend the /f/, /a/, and long /t/ together as you slide your hand to the bottom. Pronounce /fat/ when you get to the bottom of the slide.

   Connect sounds with letters by writing letters on the slide. In the example of /fat/, you would write *f* at the top of the slide, *a* toward the middle, and *t* at the bottom (Figure 2–14). Call children's attention to the sounds to be blended and to the letters that represent those sounds. When children finish blending, ask a volunteer to write the whole word at the bottom of the slide. Once children understand what they are to do, invite volunteers to be the slider—the person who moves his or her hand down the slide. Have the whole group join in blending the sounds as the

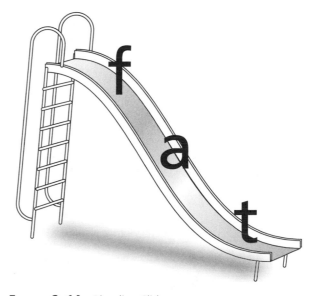

FIGURE 2–14   Blending Slide

"slider" slides toward the bottom. Ask the slider to pronounce the whole word when he or she gets to the bottom, and ask the slider to write the whole word at the bottom of the slide.

We teach phonemic awareness to develop language concepts that children need to make sense of the alphabetic principle. Phonemic awareness is both a cause and a consequence of learning to read. On the one hand, children draw on phonemic awareness skills when decoding and spelling. On the other hand, children gain greater insight into the sounds in words as they decode and spell. Children use blending when they decode words and separate words into sounds when they spell.

In addition to phonemic awareness, children need to know the sounds of individual letters, letter patterns, and words that are spelled with the same vowel and ending consonants (bed, red, and fed). Chapter 3 describes specific activities for teaching letter names and letter-sounds to pre-alphabetic and partial alphabetic readers, while Chapter 4 describes activities for teaching letter patterns and words with the same vowels and ending consonants to alphabetic word readers. The overarching instructional goal is to move kindergarten and first grade children toward word fluency by helping them transition from pre-alphabetic to partial alphabetic, and finally to the alphabetic stage. Eventually, of course, we want children to reach word fluency by moving through the consolidated stage and into the automatic word fluency stage.

REFERENCES

Adams, M. J. (1990). *Beginning to read: Thinking and learning about print.* Cambridge, MA: The MIT Press.

Base, G. (1996). *Animalia.* New York: Puffin.

Banks, K. (1994). *Alphabet soup.* New York: Alfred A. Knopf.

Blachman, B. A., Tangel, D. M., Ball, E. W., Black, R., & McGraw, C. K. (1999). Developing phonological awareness and word recognition skills: A two-year intervention with low-income, inner-city children. *Reading and Writing: An Interdisciplinary Journal, 11,* 239–273.

Bradley, L., & Bryant, P. (1991). Phonological skills before and after learning to read. In S. A. Brady & D. P. Shankweiler (Eds.), *Phonological processes in literacy: A tribute to Isabelle Y. Liberman* (pp. 37–45). Hillsdale, NJ: Lawrence Erlbaum Associates.

Bryan, A., & Manning, D. (1991). *All night, all day: A child's first book of African-American spirituals.* New York: Atheneum Books for Young Readers.

Catts, H. W., a Vartiainen, T. (1993). *Sounds abound: Listening, rhyming and reading,* East Moline, IL: Lingui Systems.

Chew, J. (1997). Traditional phonics: What it is and what it is not. *Journal of Research in Reading, 20,* 171–183.

Compton, D. L. (2000). Modeling the growth of decoding skills in first-grade children. *Scientific Studies of Reading, 4,* 219–259.

Dufva, M., Niemi, P., & Voeten, M. J. M. (2001). The role of phonological memory, word recognition, and comprehension skills in reading development: From preschool to grade 2. *Reading and Writing: An Interdisciplinary Journal, 14,* 91–117.

Ehri, L. C., Nunes, S. R., Willows, D. M., Schuster, B. V., Yaghoub-Zadeh, Z., & Shanahan, T. (2001). Phonemic awareness instruction helps children learn to read: Evidence from the National Reading Panel's meta-analysis. *Reading Research Quarterly, 36,* 250–287.

Guy, G. F. (1996). *Fiesta!* New York: Greenwillow Books.

Kellogg, S. (1987). *Aster aardvark's alphabet adventures.* New York: Mulberry Books.

McGrath, B. B. (1998a). *The Cheerios© counting book.* New York: Scholastic.

McGrath, B. B. (1998b). *A contrar Cheerios©.* New York: Scholastic.

Murray, B. A., Stahl, S. A., & Ivey, M. G. (1996). Developing phoneme awareness through alphabet books. *Reading and Writing: An Interdisciplinary Journal, 8,* 307–322.

Nation, K., & Hulme, C. (1997). Phonemic segmentation, not onset-rime segmentation, predicts early reading and spelling skills. *Reading Research Quarterly, 32,* 154–167.

National Institute of Child Health and Human Development. (2000). *Report of the National Reading Panel. Teaching children to read: An evidence-based assessment of the scientific research literature on reading and its implications for reading instruction: Reports of the subgroups* (NIH Publication No. 00–4754). Washington, DC: U.S. Government Printing Office.

Orozco, J. L. (1997). *Diez deditos: Ten little fingers and other play rhymes and action songs from Latin*

America. New York: Dutton Children's Books.

Orozco, J.-L. (1999). *De colores and other Latin-American folk songs for children*. New York: Puffin.

Richgels, D. J. (2001). Phonemic awareness. *The Reading Teacher, 55*, 274–278.

Schatschneider, C., Francis, D., Foorman, B., Fletcher, J., & Mehta, P. (1999). The dimensionality of phonological awareness: An application of item response theory. *Journal of Experimental Child Psychology, 66*, 311–340.

Sendak, M. (1991). *Alligators all around: An alphabet*. New York: Harper-Trophy.

Silberg, J. (1998). *I can't sing book*. Beltsville, MD: Gryphon House.

Snow, C. E., Burns, M. S., & Griffin, P. (Eds.) (1998). *Preventing reading difficulties in young children*. Washington, DC: National Academy Press.

Sound-around: A speech amplifier. Kenansville, NC: educAn. Toll free (877–471–7210).

Stevens, J. R. (1999). *Twelve lizards leaping: A new twelve days of Christmas*. Flagstaff, AZ: Rising Moon.

Tabor, M. N. G. (1993). *Albertina anda arrriba: El abecedario/ Albertina goes up: An alphabet*. Watertown, MA: Charlesbridge Publishing.

Weeks, S. (1998). *Mrs. McNosh hangs up her wash*. New York: Harper Collins Juvenile Books.

Use these letter name and letter-sound activities with kindergartners in:

▷ **The Pre-alphabetic Word Fluency Stage**

▷ **The Partial Alphabetic Word Fluency Stage**

3 DEVELOPING FLUENCY WITH HANDS-ON ACTIVITIES FOR TEACHING LETTER NAMES AND SINGLE LETTER SOUNDS

How many letters do beginning readers learn? Twenty-Six? Fifty-Two? Nineteen? Forty-Five? Children learn fifty-two letters, twenty-six uppercase letters and twenty-six lowercase letters. If you said forty-five, this, too, could be considered a correct answer, because seven of the lowercase letters are smaller versions of their uppercase forms: Cc, Oo, Ss, Vv, Ww, Xx, and Zz. Children who begin kindergarten with more letter knowledge are better readers later in the elementary grades than children who begin school with less letter knowledge (Stevenson & Newman, 1986). Teaching kindergartners letter names and letter sounds is vital to the success of your kindergarten classroom language arts program (Snow, Burns, & Griffin, 1998). Because each and every word consists of a different group of letters, the kindergartners in your classroom must identify individual letters to successfully learn, and eventually fluently recognize, many different words (Whitehurst & Lonigan, 2001).

All things considered, there is just a handful of letters to learn, and the letters themselves do not have particularly intricate shapes. There are two things to keep in mind when teaching children to differentiate one letter from another. First, letter orientation is critical and particularly vexing because letter identity changes with a mere 180 degree rotation. Second, because all fifty-two letters are built from the same small group of features, some of the letters look quite a bit alike. Children must learn to pay attention to the specific characteristics, or distinctive features, that distinguish one letter from another. Orientation is one of several important distinctive features. We will use a flip trick to show how important orientation is to a letter's identity. Try this with the children whom you teach; they will not only be amazed, but will also learn something about letter orientation.

Step 1 Write a lowercase *p* on one side of a small piece of paper and a *q* on the other side.

Step 2 Show the child the letter *p*. p

Step 3 Flip the card over. What do you see? The letter *q*!

Step 4 Flip the *q* over and up. Now you see the letter *d*!

Step 5 Turn the *d* over. Now there is a *b*!

The flip trick is so easy that you can grab a scrap of paper and use it on the spot to show a child how *p*, *q*, *d*, and *b* differ.

Letter orientation is troublesome in light of children's experiences with objects in their everyday environment. Before children meet the alphabet, all their life experiences convince them that objects in the real world stay the same regardless of object orientation. Let's take a common *chair* as an example. A *chair* is a *chair* whether it is right side up, upside down, or on its side (Figure 3–1).

Likewise, dogs have four legs, a tail, and they bark. A dog is a dog whether it is a chihuahua or a beagle, but this is not true for letters. A *b* turns into a *d* when its direction is reversed. A *d* is a *p* when rotated 180 degrees. An uppercase P jumps above the line while a lowercase *p* falls below it. Having a circle and a stick does not distinguish an uppercase P from a lowercase *p*, a lowercase *d*, or an uppercase *b*. If we were to apply the same principle to real objects we use to identify letters, a chair turned upside down would not be a chair; a chihuahua might be a dog, but a beagle would be something else altogether.

We teach these children to think about the lines on the page as consisting of three different spaces: the space on the line, the space above the line, and the space below the line. Sometimes teachers use a house as a metaphor to describe these three spaces.

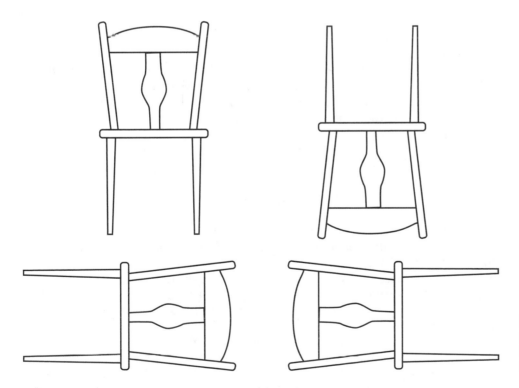

Figure 3–1 Illustration of a Chair Right Side Up, Upside Down, and Facing Left and Right on Its Side

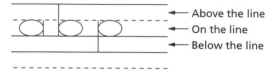

← Above the line
← On the line
← Below the line

Letters on the line are in the first floor of the house; letters above the line go upstairs, while letters that drop below the line go down to the basement.

There are six features, beyond orientation, that affect a letter's identity. Kindergartners, first, and second graders learn to use circles, straight lines, and curved lines to form letters. Features that differentiate one letter from another include whether the letters have a: (1) circle (a, b, d, g, o, p, q, Q); (2) curve (c, e, m, n, s, u, B, C, D, G, P, R, U); (3) straight line (a, b, d, f, h, i, k, l, p, q, r, t, v, w, x, y, z, A, B, D, E, F, H, I, K, L, M, N, P, Q, R, T, V, W, X, Y, Z); (4) portion that extends below the line (g, j, p, q, y); (5) portion that extends above the line (b, d, f, h, k, l, t, plus all uppercase letters); or (6) letters that stay on the line (a, c, e, m, n, o, r, s, u, v, w, x, z). Children use these six features to distinguish one letter from another. You may see the term *distinctive feature* in some of the reading that you do. Distinctive features consist of these six different components we use to build letters plus the orientation of letters.

The more features two letters have in common, the more difficult it is to distinguish one letter from another. For example, while it is not particularly difficult to distinguish *s* from *q*, children have great difficulty distinguishing *b* from *d*. Whereas *s* and *q* have no features in common, *b* and *d* each consist of a ball and a stick (circle and line). The only difference between these two letters is their different orientation on the page. Avoid teaching letters that look a lot alike at the same time. Teach, instead, letters that look dissimilar from one another. Therefore, teaching *n* and *l* is a good choice, but teaching *l* and *t* at the same time is not. In addition to understanding letter orientation and perceiving the distinctive features, children must understand that words and letters are different, and that words consist of letters (Purcell-Gates, 1998). If this were not enough, children must also know why there are white spaces on the page, what these spaces tell us, and how to use this information when engaging with print.

Letters are divided into two groups: consonants and vowels. The twenty-one consonant letters consist of: Bb, Cc, Dd, Ff, Gg, Hh, Jj, Kk, Ll, Mm, Nn, Pp, Qq, Rr, Ss, Tt, Vv, Ww (when *w* begins a word or syllable), Xx, Yy (when *y* begins a word or syllable), and Zz. All the other letters (Aa, Ee, Ii, Oo, Uu, and sometimes Yy and Ww) are vowels. The two primary classifications for vowels are short and long. The short vowel sounds are heard in *apple, hen, igloo, ostrich,* and *umbrella.* The long vowel sounds are heard in *apron, eraser, ice, overalls,* and *unicorn.* Learning letter names in kindergarten is one of several important components of kindergartners' language arts programs (Shanker & Ekwall, 1998). Letter name knowledge in kindergarten by itself is nearly as good a predictor of reading achievement as scores from an entire reading readiness battery (Snow, Burns, & Griffin, 1998).

Letter names have several advantages. First, learning letter names gives children and their teachers a convenient handle to use when referring to individual letters. When we talk to children about the alphabet, it is easier to say letter names than to pronounce single letter-sounds. Consequently, we often use letter names when we refer to letters in our classroom. We are more likely to say "find the M (em, letter name) on the alphabet strip" than to say "find the /mmm/." When you ask a child to find the letter S (*ess,* letter name) in an alphabet book, you use letter names to teach reading. Likewise, when you ask children to look at the word wall under the letter N (*en,* letter name), you use letter names to teach reading.

Second, to learn letter names, children have to work out in their minds how one letter differs from another. When you ask a child to write the letters *b* (bee), *m* (em), and *p* (pee, letter names), you expect that child to associate the letter names with letter shapes and to use this information to write the letters. In order for a child to point to a *b* and say *b* (bee, letter name) and then point to the letter *d* and say *d* (dee, letter name), the child absolutely must distinguish the *b* from the *d*.

Third, it is easier to teach the letter-sounds if children already know the letter names (Searfoss, Readence, & Mallette, 2001). Some of the letter names give clues to the letter-sounds. For example, the name of the letter Mm, "emm," contains a portion of the /mmm/ sound this letter represents. Furthermore, teaching letter names helps children figure out the difference between letter names and letter sounds (Adams, 1990). Even though letter names are important, children cannot sound out a word like *man* if they only know the letter names (Carnine, Silbert, & Kameenui, 1997). This brings us to the question: Which single letter-sounds should you introduce first?

When you teach the single letter-sounds, you should focus on the sound that is commonly associated with an individual letter. For example, the single letter *l* represents the /l/ we hear in *lion*, the letter *n* the /n/ in *nut*, the letter *r* the /r/ in *ring*, and the letter *i* the /i/ in *igloo*. Each picture on the alphabet strip in your classroom represents a word that contains a single letter-sound. Table 3–1 shows the twenty-six single letters and words that contain the single sound that each letter represents. We know that our alphabet has twenty-six letters, but how many of those letters represent their own unique sound? Twenty-Six? Twenty-Three? Twenty-One? A careful look at Table 3–1 reveals that we have three letters that do not represent a sound that some other single consonant already represents. The letters that do not represent their own unique sounds consist of:

1. C*c*   C has no sound of its own. C represents both /k/ and /s/, depending on the vowel that follows the *c* in a word. C followed by *e, i*, and *y* usually represents the /s/ we hear in *center, city*, and *cycle*. C followed by *a, o*, and *u* typically represents the /k/ we hear in *cat, coat*, and *cut*.
2. Q*q*   The *q* represents the /k/ in *mystique*. Q is usually followed by *u* in English words, though a few words borrowed from other languages do not have the *qu* combination, as in *Iraq*. The *qu* combination represents /kw/. Say *queen*. Listen carefully as you pronounce *queen*. You hear /kw/ in *queen, quiz*, and *quack*. Therefore, the letter *q* is an extra letter in that it stands for no special sound of its own.
3. X*x*   We could drop the letter *x* from our alphabet and use instead *gz, ks*, or *z*. The *x* stands for *gz* in *example, ks* in *six*, and *z* in X*erox*. We more often use the *gz* and *ks* pronunciations.

Introduce some single consonant letter-sounds first. There are two reasons to introduce a few consonant letter-sounds before vowel letter-sounds. First, the sounds associated with the consonant letters are more predictable and dependable than the sounds associated with the vowels. For instance, the *d* in *dog* represents the same /d/ sound most of the time, as in *doll* and *doughnut*. This is especially true when *d* is the first letter in a word. The vowel letters are another matter altogether. The letter *i* might stand for the long vowel sound in /ice/, the short vowel sound in /igloo/, or be almost lost in the /r/ in /bird/, just to mention a few variations.

Second, most English words begin with consonants. The beginning letter gives readers a valuable graphophonic clue. For instance, if children see the word *duck* and do not know how to read this word, they identify the first sound by paying attention to the beginning letter. Combining this graphophonic cue with other picture cues, semantic cues, and syntactic cues may give children a good idea as to the word's identity. For example, the child who reads, "The boy saw a _____ in the pond," may guess *fish, goose, duck, snake, frog*, or *turtle*, depending on the child's prior knowledge, story meaning, and picture cue. However, when the child pays attention to the beginning consonant letter in the word, the probability of making an accurate, informed guess is quite high. Should the sentence be, "The boy saw a d_____ in the pond," the child reads "duck," but should the sentence say, "The boy saw a f_____ in the pond," the child reads "fish." Added to this, we want children to look at words from left-to-right; that is, from the first to the last letter. Introducing a few of the powerful consonants helps plunge children into productively combining their background knowledge with all the cues available to them: picture cues, letter-sound (graphophonic) cues, semantic cues, and syntactic cues.

TABLE 3–1 Letters, Pictures, and Key Words for Single Letter-Sounds	Single Letters	Picture	Key Words with Single Letter-Sounds
	a		apple (short a)
	a		apron (long a)
	b		boat
	c		cat
	d		dog
	e		hen (short e)
	e		eraser (long e)
	f		fish
	g		goat
	h		hat
	i		igloo (short i)
	i		ice (long i)
	j		jeep
	k		kite
	l		lion
	m		moon

TABLE 3–1 Continued.

Single Letters	Picture	Key Words with Single Letter-Sounds
n	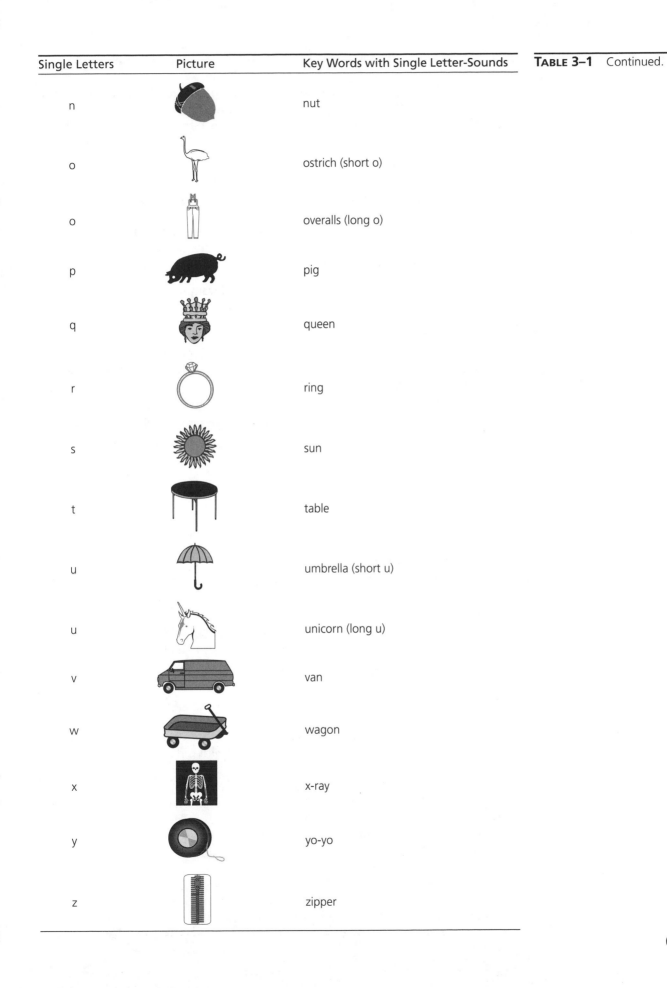	nut
o		ostrich (short o)
o		overalls (long o)
p		pig
q		queen
r		ring
s		sun
t		table
u		umbrella (short u)
u		unicorn (long u)
v		van
w		wagon
x		x-ray
y		yo-yo
z		zipper

■■■■ ■ ■ ■ ■ **TEACHING LETTER NAMES AND SINGLE LETTER-SOUNDS**

When you teach letter names and sounds, you help children learn the difference between letters and words and, not coincidentally, introduce children to the alphabetic principle. From a word learning and spelling perspective, we want kindergarten children to:

1. Know the difference between letters and words.
2. Differentiate, name, and write upper- and lowercase letters.
3. Match the beginning and ending sounds in words with beginning and ending letters.
4. Identify words by their beginning and/or ending letters and sounds.
5. Use some letter and sound knowledge to read new words.
6. Use some letter and sound knowledge to spell.

In teaching letter names and sounds, you will want to use matching and sorting activities, key words, alphabet books, word wall words, and letter-sound charts, as explained below:

1. *Matching* Matching activities help children differentiate one letter from another, learn upper- and lowercase letters, learn letter names, and learn single letter-sounds. Ask children to match:

- Uppercase letters that look exactly alike: A with A; B with B; D with D.
- Lowercase letters that look exactly alike: *a* with *a*; *b* with *b*; *d* with *d*.
- Uppercase letters with lowercase letters that have the same name: A with *a*; B with *b*; D with *d*.
- Words that begin with the same letters and sounds: *a* with *apple* and *ax*; *b* with *bat* and *ball*; *d* with *dog* and *day*.
- Words that end with the same letters and sounds: *n* with *train*; *m* with *drum*; *f* with *leaf*.

2. *Sorting* Sorting helps children differentiate one letter from another and become sensitive to the letters and letter-sounds in words. Ask children to sort by:

- *Letter name*: put all the As in one stack (A, a), all the Bs in another (B, b), and so on.
- *Upper- and lowercase*: put all the uppercase letters in one group (A, B, C), and all the lowercase letters in another group (a, b, c).
- *Shape*: put all the letters with the same shape in one group (d, d, and d) and letters with another shape in another group (b, b, and b).
- *Sound*: put all the pictures with names that begin with one sound (/l/) in one group and all the pictures that begin with another sound (/m/) in a different group.
- *Letter-sound*: put all the words that begin or end with one letter-sound in one group and words that begin or end with different letter-sounds in a different group.

3. *Finding Letters in Words* Finding letters in words helps children figure out how words and letters are different, identify letters in running text, and learn the sounds associated with single letters. You might, for example, make lists of words that begin with the same letter; have children underline letters in words; or ask children to find words with target letters on the word wall or in big book words.

4. *Key Words* Key words help children learn letters and letter-sounds. For example, *apple* may be the key word for the letter A*a* and the short *a* sound. Table 3–1 has a list of letters, key words, and key sounds. Key words help children learn letter names and letter-sounds. Each key word is already in children's speaking vocabulary. Key words either begin with a special letter and letter-sound, as in the key

word *boat* for the letter B*b* and the sound /b/. Sometimes, in the case of vowels, key words have the letter and sound in the middle of the word, such as the key word *hen* for the letter E*e* and the short /e/ sound.

Key words are usually nouns that are shown with an easy-to-recognize picture, much like the words in alphabet books. For example, the key word *nut* is shown with a picture of a *nut*. Putting letters in the context of familiar key words acts as a sort of mnemonic for remembering the letters themselves (the *n* at the beginning of *nut*) and for recalling letter-sounds (the /n/ at the beginning of /nut/). When children see the key word *nut*, they are reminded of the letter N*n* and its sound. The picture creates a mental image of a word that children have in their speaking vocabulary. Therefore, on seeing a picture of *nut*, children recall the pronunciation of the familiar word. The picture-spoken word connection reminds children of the letter N*n* and the /n/ sound it represents (Figure 3–2).

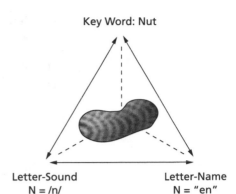

Key Word: Nut

Letter-Sound
N = /n/

Letter-Name
N = "en"

FIGURE 3–2 Key Words to Teach Letter Name and Letter-Sound Associations

Certain words on the word wall may act as key words that ground letter-sounds in real language. The alphabet strip in your classroom is an excellent key word reference for children to use when recalling and writing single letter-sounds. You may use Table 3–1 as a guide to key words and pictures. If your classroom language arts curriculum has already identified key words for letter-sounds, use those key words to help children remember letter names and sounds.

5. *Alphabet Books* Children gain insight into letter-sounds and letter names through reading alphabet books. Some alphabet books even help children develop and expand their speaking vocabularies. This happens when alphabet books illustrate *common* words that are not yet in children's speaking vocabulary. Look for alphabet books that:

- Use ball-and-stick letters made of simple circles, arcs, and straight lines.
- Present upper- and lowercase letters.
- Place letters and words in the upper-left corner or, at the very least, put them in a predictable place on each page.

We want to teach children left-to-right progression from the very start, and what better way to begin than with alphabet books that show letters in the upper left of each page? If an alphabet book does not have letters in the upper-left corner, look to see if letters are in the same place on each page. Consistency helps children know where to look for the all-important letters and words. This makes it easier to use alphabet books for teaching, as well as eliminating a potential source of confusion for children.

- Have pictures of many different words that begin with the featured letter-sound.
- Show pictures or illustrations that are easy for children to identify.
- Illustrate familiar objects and words that should be in children's speaking and listening vocabularies.

The last point, pictures of words in children's speaking and listening vocabularies, is important because we want to use alphabet books to identify letter names and letter-sounds. If alphabet books show words that are not in children's speaking and listening vocabulary, you will have to familiarize children with those words before using the words to reinforce letter name and letter-sound connections. You cannot, for example, use a book with a picture of *valise* to connect the letter V*v* with its name and sound unless children know the meaning of this word. Examples of unusual and unfamiliar words in current alphabet books include *aptitude, coloratura, entreated,* and *gamboled.* If you see words like these, rest assured that the alphabet book is geared for older, more sophisticated children.

6. *Word Walls* Word walls help children learn letter names when the word wall has an upper- and lowercase letter above each word list. For example, a word wall

might have B*b* above words like *bat*, *boy*, and *bubble* or Q*q* above *queen*, *quack*, and *quit*. Word wall words also help children learn letter-sounds when the teacher draws attention to the common letter-sound connection among words, such as the /b/ sound in the B*b* words *bat*, *boy*, and *bubble*. Word wall words are the words that children meet in reading and need for spelling, as well as words that the children suggest. Read a word wall list by first asking children to name the letter and say the letter-sound, and then read, in chorus, all the words that have that letter-sound combination.

7. *Letter-sound Charts* Make charts of words that begin with the letters and letter-sounds children are learning. Write a letter in both upper- and lowercase at the top of the chart, and then write words that begin with the consonant or are spelled with the vowel letter. Begin by explaining that D*d* represents the /d/ sound in *dog* (the key word). Ask children to suggest words that begin with the sound at the beginning of *dog*. Children may think of words on their own or may refer to words under the D*d* on the word wall. Take the opportunity to talk about uppercase and lowercase letters. In this example, someone in the small group suggested the name David. This introduces an opportunity to compare and contrast words that do and do not begin with a capital letter. When the chart is finished, ask children to read the words in chorus. As children read, track the words with your hand; that is, move your hand under each word as it is read. Keep the word list on display as a reference, and ask children to suggest a word or two from the chart to add to the classroom word wall.

Use matching, sorting, finding letters, key words, alphabet books, word walls, and letter-sound charts to teach letter names and letter-sounds. Additionally, use the hands-on activities that are described in the next section.

Dd	
dog	desk
doll	dime
dig	dish
do	donut
dad	David
dark	down
door	dress

LEARNING ABOUT LETTER NAMES AND SINGLE LETTER-SOUNDS IN THE PRE-ALPHABETIC AND PARTIAL ALPHABETIC WORD FLUENCY STAGES

Stage 1. Pre-alphabetic Word Fluency: Preschool and Early Kindergarten

In the first half of kindergarten, Brett (Figure 3–3) writes letter strings across the bottom of his paper. He understands that letters go from left-to-right and is developing an awareness of punctuation. Table 3–2 shows a weekly teaching guide for the first half of kindergarten. The weekly plan calls for teaching letter names or teaching beginning letter-sounds everyday. Teaching letter-sounds may be in context or through focused study on individual letters. If focused instruction removes letter-sounds from the reading context, find opportunities for children to use beginning letter-sounds when reading and writing. The plan suggests that instruction in letter-sounds and phonemic awareness be combined in the same activity on most days. Teaching phonemic awareness along with letter-sounds is more effective than teaching these two separately, so you will save instructional time and children will learn more.

It is important for kindergartners like Brett to develop fluency in naming letters and associating sounds with single letters. Consequently, time is set aside once each week to develop fluency in letter names and sounds. Look for fluency activities at the end of this chapter. Children must understand the meaning of the words they read, and so word meaning is built into the plan, as well. When Brett has some insight into the letters that represent beginning sounds in words, he will have the information he needs to move into the partial alphabetic stage.

FIGURE 3–3   Pre-alphabetic Writing Sample (Car)

TABLE 3–2 Kindergarten Weekly Teaching Guide: First Half of the Year for Children in the Pre-alphabetic Word Fluency Stage*

MONDAY	TUESDAY	WEDNESDAY	THURSDAY	FRIDAY
Phonemic Awareness Rhyming in centers and in small groups	**Phonemic Awareness** Beginning Sounds in centers and in small groups	**Phonemic Awareness** Rhyming in centers and in small groups	**Phonemic Awareness** Beginning Sounds in centers and in small groups	**Phonemic Awareness** Rhyming in centers and in small groups
⟷	⟷	⟷	⟷	⟷
Single Letter-sounds Letter Names Single consonant and short vowel letter-sounds (until proficient) Teach in context and with focused study	**Single Letter-sounds Letter Names** Single consonant and short vowel letter-sounds (until proficient) Teach in context and with focused study	**Single Letter-sounds Letter Names** Single consonant and short vowel letter-sounds (until proficient) Teach in context and with focused study	**Single Letter-sounds Letter Names** Single consonant and short vowel letter-sounds (until proficient) Teach in context and with focused study	**Single Letter-sounds Letter Names** Single consonant and short vowel letter-sounds (until proficient) Teach in context and with focused study
	Fluency Letter-names or single letter-sounds			
Word Meaning Teach in context and with focused study		**Word Meaning** Teach in context and with focused study		**Word Meaning** Teach in context and with focused study

Teach phonemic awareness along with phonics, when appropriate.
*For children who do not have developmental or learning disabilities.

FIGURE 3–4 Partial Alphabetic Writing Sample (Dress)

Stage 2. Partial Alphabetic Word Fluency: Early Kindergarten to Early First Grade

Anna (Figure 3–4) knows some, but not all, of the letter-sounds. Anna recognizes enough letter-sounds to identify new words by their beginning and ending letters, picture cues, and story context. When Anna first entered into the partial alphabetic stage, she used beginning letter-sounds, picture cues, and context to identify new words. Later, Anna began to use the beginning and ending letter-sound cues in words. When Anna spells, she uses two or three letters to write an entire word (*drs* for *dress*). She usually does not use vowel letters because she does not understand how different letter patterns represent different vowel sounds (*mad* versus *made*).

Brian (Figure 3–5) is also in the partial alphabetic stage. He writes M FL*ee* (My Family) to describe the picture he drew, M for Morgan (an older sister), D for dad, M for mom, and his own name, B*rian*, under his self portrait. As is typical of children in the partial alphabetic stage, Brian uses one letter to represent most words. However, when we look at FL*ee* for *family*, we see that Brian has used four letters to spell *family*. Interestingly, he heard the /f/, the /l/, and the last sound, which he represented with a double *e* (*ee*). Brian has begun to develop the idea that vowel letters represent vowel sounds. This is an excellent sign, for it suggests that Brian is beginning to gradually move toward the alphabetic stage of word fluency.

Table 3–3 is the weekly teaching plan for the second half of kindergarten. The plan calls for teaching children like Anna and Brian phonemic awareness, letter-sounds, and letter names everyday. Children should know the letter names, then focus on teaching only the letter-sounds. By the second half of kindergarten, children in the partial alphabetic stage are already aware of some of the beginning sounds in words. Therefore, it is time to discuss both beginning and ending letter-sounds in words. Introduce the short vowel sounds, if you have not already done so (Table 3–1).

Teach word families toward the end of the school year (i.e., in the last couple of months of school). Word family words are groups of words that share a common vowel and ending consonant, such as the *ig* in *big, pig,* and *dig* or the *ad* in *bad, had,*

FIGURE 3–5 Partial Alphabetic Writing Sample (My Family)

TABLE 3–3 Kindergarten Weekly Teaching Guide: Second Half of the Year for Children in the Partial Alphabetic Word Fluency Stage*

MONDAY	TUESDAY	WEDNESDAY	THURSDAY	FRIDAY
Phonemic Awareness** Ending Sounds in centers and in small groups	**Phonemic Awareness** Rhyming Blending*** In centers and in small groups Teach in context and with focused study	**Phonemic Awareness** Ending Sounds In centers and in small groups	**Phonemic Awareness** Rhyming Blending*** In centers and in small groups	**Phonemic Awareness** Ending Sounds In centers and in small groups
Single Letter-sounds Letter Names Single consonant and short vowel letter-sounds (until proficient) Teach in context and with focused study	**Single Letter-sounds Letter Names** Single consonant and short vowel letter-sounds (until proficient) Teach in context and with focused study	**Single Letter-sounds Letter Names** Single consonant and short vowel letter-sounds (until proficient) Teach in context and with focused study	**Single Letter-sounds Letter Names** Single consonant and short vowel letter-sounds (until proficient) Teach in context and with focused study	**Single Letter-sounds Letter Names** Single consonant and short vowel letter-sounds (until proficient) Teach in context and with focused study
	Word Family Words	**Word Family Words**	**Word Family Words**	
			Fluency Letter-names or single letter-sounds	
Word Meaning Teach in context and with focused study		**Word Meaning** Teach in context and with focused study	**Word Meaning** Teach in context and with focused study	**Word Meaning** Teach in context and with focused study

Teach phonemic awareness along with phonics, when appropriate.
*For children who do not have developmental or learning disabilities.
**Beginning Sounds, if needed.
***Blending for children who are aware of syllables, beginning sounds, ending sounds, and word families.

and *mad* (Chapter 4). Many word families consist of short vowels (as in *ig* and *ad*). Word family words with short vowel sounds give children an immediate opportunity to use their vowel letter-sound knowledge to identify and spell new words. Children move into the alphabetic stage when they are aware of the middle sounds in words (the /i/ from /big/) and know letter-sound relationships for those middle sounds.

■■■■■■ HANDS-ON ACTIVITIES AND STRATEGIES FOR LETTER NAMES AND SINGLE LETTER-SOUNDS

Match these teaching strategies and activities to the knowledge, skills, and needs of the children whom you teach. Use the strategies and activities to complement the ongoing language arts activities in your classroom. Modify them to fit your teaching situation, and tailor them to children's specific needs. The goal is to use teaching strategies and activities that give children the knowledge and skills they need to transition into the partial alphabetic word fluency stage by the end of kindergarten or, at the very least, shortly after starting first grade.

▷ SMALL GROUP
LETTER NAMES
LETTER-SOUNDS
SOUND AWARENESS

HIDDEN LETTER RUBBING

Hidden letters are revealed when children rub crayons over a sheet of paper that covers letters. Halfway through rubbing, children predict the identity of the partially revealed letters.

MATERIALS: Large oaktag upper- and lowercase letters; tape; colorful construction paper; an assortment of peeled crayons. If your school has a dye cut machine, use it to make sturdy oaktag letters. Laminate the letters. Not only do laminated letters last a long time, but crayons also glide more smoothly over construction paper with laminated letters underneath.

DIRECTIONS: Read and share a book like *26 of the Most Interesting Letters in the Alphabet* (Sandhaus, 1999). This book is particularly well suited for letter rubbing because the book and the letter rubbing activity both ask children to think about the unique shape of each letter. In sharing this and other alphabet books, draw children's attention to letter shapes, the beginning sounds in words, and the letters that represent those sounds.

Tape oaktag letters on a table. Arrange the letters so that one large piece of construction paper covers two to four letters. Put a colorful piece of construction paper over the letters and tape each corner to the table. Place a jar of peeled crayons in the center of the table; ask a small group to join you. Explain that letters are hidden under the construction paper. Demonstrate how to rub a peeled crayon over the construction paper to reveal the hidden letters underneath. Discuss letter shapes, then demonstrate letter rubbing a second time. Pause halfway through rubbing and encourage children to predict the letter based on a portion of its shape.

As children rub, occasionally ask the group to "freeze" and to look at a particular child's rubbing. Point to a partially revealed letter and challenge children to predict the identity of it. Pausing to predict the identity of partially revealed letters helps children draw on their mental images of letter shapes and encourages children to pay attention to the unique shape of each letter. Make sure children rub whole letters and do not stop in the middle of letters, unless you ask everyone to "freeze." Figure 3–6 shows a letter rubbing done by a kindergartner. The colorful letter rubbings make cheerful place mats for classroom celebrations and nice additions to bulletin boards, or you might use the letter rubbings to decorate children's tables for open house and holidays. Send the letter rubbings home for children to share their letter knowledge with their families.

Examples of Literature Connections
Sandhaus, E. (1999). *26 of the most interesting letters in the alphabet.* New York: Paul Sandhaus Associates, Inc.

  Written in English and Spanish, this alphabet book presents letters in short rhymes accompanied by illustrations.
Multicultural   Spanish Language

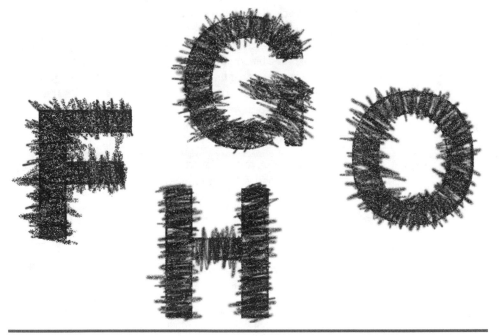

FIGURE 3–6   Hidden Letter Rubbing

LETTER SANDWICHES

This activity combines letter name and letter-sound learning with a cooking activity in which children use Alpha-bits© cereal to make sandwiches.

MATERIALS: *Alphabet Soup: A Feast of Letters* (Gustafson, 1996), *The Giant Jam Sandwich* (Lord & Burroway, 1972), or other books about peanut butter or sandwiches. You may use this activity to: (1) make sandwiches with real bread, peanut butter, and Alpha-bits© cereal, or (2) make paper and pencil sandwiches by writing letters on an outline of a slice of bread sketched on a paper plate.

TO MAKE REAL SANDWICHES YOU NEED   Two slices of bread for each child; peanut butter; three to four boxes of Alpha-bits© cereal; two paper plates for each child; a dull plastic knife to spread the peanut butter; napkins; pictures; upper- and lowercase letters.

TO MAKE PAPER AND PENCIL SANDWICHES YOU NEED   One paper plate with an outline of a slice of bread for each child or one piece of construction paper with an outline of a slice of bread; a second clean paper plate for each child; colored markers, crayons, or pencils; pictures; upper- and lowercase letters.

DIRECTIONS: Read and share alphabet books like *Alphabet Soup: A Feast of Letters* (Gustafson, 1996). Talk about letter shapes, letter names, and words that begin with single letter-sounds. Read aloud *The Giant Jam Sandwich* (Lord & Burroway, 1972). Talk about the problem in which wasps invade a small village and the villagers' solution to lure the wasps to a giant jam sandwich. Explain that children are going to make their own sandwiches and that the sandwiches have letters instead of jam.

REAL SANDWICHES   Before making sandwiches, smear peanut butter on slices of bread and put the bread on paper plates. Give each child a paper plate with a generous handful of Alpha-bits© cereal. Encourage children to observe that all the Alpha-bits© cereal letters are uppercase. Show children a picture; for example, a *sun*. Rubber band the /s/ in *sun* (/sssssssun/) to help children identify the beginning sound. Have children look at their own Alpha-bits© cereal to see if they have an *S*. Give each child a second paper plate with a slice of bread. Children who have an *S* gently place it on the peanut butter. Repeat with other picture-letter combinations. Should individual children need a greater variety of cereal letters, pour a few more letters onto their paper plates.

▷ SMALL GROUP
LETTER NAMES
LETTER-SOUNDS
SOUND AWARENESS

FIGURE 3–7   Letter Sandwich

PAPER AND PENCIL SANDWICHES   Give each child a paper plate or a piece of construction paper with a sketch of a slice of bread on it. Explain that children are going to make paper sandwiches by writing letters either inside the bread outline or on the paper plate or construction paper. Follow the same picture-letter matching procedure above, only instead of finding Alpha-bits© cereal letters children write the letters themselves. We use both real sandwiches and paper and pencil sandwiches successfully with kindergartners. Figure 3–7 is a letter sandwich written by a kindergartner.

ALPHABET SONG   For some extra reinforcement, not to mention fun, sing the alphabet song with this modification:
A B C D E F G
H I J K L M N O P
Q R S T U V
W X Y Z   Now I've eaten my ABCs.   May I have more cereal, please?

Examples of Literature Connections

Gustafson, S. (1996). *Alphabet soup: A feast of letters.* New York: Greenwich Workshop Press.

   The alliterative text fosters phonological awareness of beginning sounds and the clear illustrations reinforce the connections between letters with the beginning sounds in words.

Lord, J. V., & Burroway, J. (1972). *The giant jam sandwich.* New York: Houghton Mifflin.

   This long-time favorite describes a clever plan to rid a village of unwanted wasps.

Westcott, N. B. (1987). *Peanut butter and jelly: A play rhyme.* New York: Dutton Children's Books.

   This rhyming book, which tells how to make a peanut butter and jelly sandwich, has a chant-like quality.

▷ SMALL GROUP
LETTER-SOUNDS
SOUND AWARENESS

TAKE-HOME MAGNETS

Children make their own sets of letter magnets and then use those magnets to identify and name letters. When children know the letter names, children take their magnets home to put on the refrigerator.

MATERIALS: A 1 1/2- to 2-inches wide magnetic strip with adhesive on one side; colored poster board cut into strips the same width and length as the magnetic strips; markers; letter cards; cookie sheets or pizza pans. Look for magnet strips in discount, craft, or business supply stores. Magnetic strips are packaged in coils and have an adhesive on one side. One coil will, in all probability, last the entire school year or longer. Colored poster board should be the same weight as the cardboard inserts in new men's shirts. Cut the magnetic and poster board into strips of equal length and width.

DIRECTIONS:

MAKING MAGNETS   Read and share a book like *Mr. Fixit's Magnet Machine* (Scarry & Herman, 1998). Bring in magnets; play with them; and experiment with them. Encourage children to explore the magnetic properties of features in your classroom—furniture, windowpanes, chalk boards, magnetic white boards, and door knobs.

   Place magnetic strips, poster board strips, and markers on a table. Demonstrate how to write letters on the poster board strips. Put the poster board strips on the adhesive side of the magnetic strips. Voila! Homemade letter magnets. Homemade magnets stick to chalk boards and to some white boards. If you have a metal teacher's desk or a file cabinet, the magnets stick to them, too.

RECOGNIZING LETTERS BY NAME AND BY SOUND   Ask a small group to put several of their homemade magnets on the tray of a magnetic black board or a magnetic white board, or ask children to put letter magnets along the edge of a cookie sheet or pizza pan. Draw a circle on the black board (or white board) in front of each child, or draw a circle on each cookie sheet (or pizza pan). Say a letter name or letter-sound. Have children pick up the magnet for the letter you designated and put it in the circle. Figure 3–8 shows an activity with all twenty-six letters. You may want to

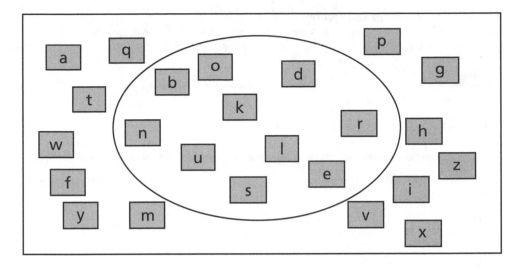

FIGURE 3–8 Whereas this Take-home Letter Magnet activity uses all twenty-six lowercase letters, you may want to use fewer letters so as to concentrate on the letters children are currently learning in your classroom

use fewer letters, concentrating on only those letters that children are currently learning in your classroom. Children are ready to learn and practice different letters when they find the specific letters you name or sound accurately, quickly, and effortlessly. Children who hesitate or copy their neighbor's work need more practice. As children learn the names or sounds of letters, send the magnets home along with a note suggesting that parents or caregivers put magnets on the re-frigerator and review letter names or sounds with their children.

Examples of Literature Connections

Scarry, R. & Herman, G. (1998). *Mr. Fixit's magnet machine.* New York: Simon Spotlight.
   This read-aloud story is a lighthearted look at magnetism.

FINGER PAINT WRITING

Children think about letter shapes, identify beginning sounds in words, and explore color as they use large sweeping motions to write finger paint letters.

MATERIALS: Finger paint; one large sheet of finger paint paper for each child; books that ex-plore color; shallow bowls to hold the paint; moist sponges; soap, water, and towels for clean-ing hands.

DIRECTIONS: Read books about color and art, such as *Paintbox Penguins: A Book About Col-ors* (Leonard, 1990). Review letter names and sounds; have children name letters or think of words that begin with the single letter sounds. Display color circles and color words. Prop the color circles on the chalk tray or tape them to the chalk board. To review color names, tape the color words randomly to the chalk board. Ask children to identify each color by name, to find the word, and to put it by the color circle.

   Pour finger paint into shallow bowls, and place the bowls on a table. Ask a small group to don their paint smocks and sit around a table. Give each child a large piece of finger paint pa-per and explain that children are going to write letters in finger paint. Demonstrate by dipping your finger in the paint and writing a colorful letter on the paper. Ask partial alphabetic readers to write the specific letters they are learning or need to practice. Children may write letters that you name or letters that represent the beginning sounds in words you pronounce. Show pre-alphabetic learners a letter, discuss the letter name, and find the letter in words in your class-room. Then ask children to copy the letter, using finger paint as the writing medium.

   Set the papers aside until dry. Pin them to a bulletin board. Refer to the papers from time-to-time by asking the children to "Point to a red Rr, a green Oo, or a blue Mm." Another follow-up is to have the children count the number of letters in one color, write the numbers on the chalk board, and make a simple bar graph showing these data. In looking at the bar graph, encourage children to think about which colors are the most preferred, and which col-ors are the least often chosen.

▷ SMALL GROUP
   LETTER NAMES
   LETTER-SOUNDS
   SOUND AWARENESS

Examples of Literature Connections
Leonard, M. (1990). *Paintbox penguins: A book about colors.* Mahwah, NJ: Troll Communications.
This book explains color mixing through the shenanigans of two penguins as they paint their fence a variety of colors.
Multicultural Link Haiti

▷ LARGE GROUP
SMALL GROUP
LETTER NAMES
LETTER-SOUNDS
SOUND AWARENESS

CAT FOLD-TOGETHERS

In this activity, children write letters on a paper cat with arms that fold over to hide the text.

MATERIALS: Cat fold-together pattern copied on white construction paper (Appendix A-6); pencils; crayons.

DIRECTIONS: Read and share stories about cats, such as *Clifford's Kitten* (Bridwell, 1984). Talk about letter names and sounds, and have children take turns matching letters with picture names that begin with the single letter-sounds. Ask children to get out crayons and pencils, and to think of letters to write on the blank center part of the cat fold-together. You can also dictate letters by name or by sound and have children write the letters in the center of the fold-together. Children then color the fold-togethers and decorate them, if desired, by adding extra touches, such as spots, hair ribbons, eyelashes, and so forth. Children share the finished fold-togethers with their classmates and then take them home to share with their families. For a sample, see Figure 3–9.

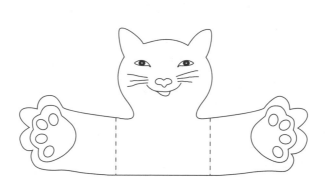

Cat Fold Pattern   Partially folded

FIGURE 3–9   Cat Fold-togethers

Examples of Literature Connections
Bridwell, N. (1984). *Clifford's kitten.* New York: Scholastic.
A Clifford story in which Emily shelters a stray kitten and Clifford's attempts to imitate the kitten lead to all sorts of havoc.

▷ SMALL GROUP
LETTER NAMES
LETTER-SOUNDS
SOUND AWARENESS

BIG LETTER STENCILING

Children stencil big, colorful letters on bright construction paper, and write or dictate words that begin with the stenciled letters.

MATERIALS: Your favorite alphabet books; one large sheet of construction paper for every child; letter stencils; tempera paint; shallow bowls to hold the paint; one or two small sponges for each paint bowl; soap, water, and towels for cleaning hands after stenciling. If your school has a dye cut machine, use it to punch the big letter stencils out of heavy oaktag, or purchase stencils at discount, office supply, and craft stores. Look for stencils with ball and stick letters. Laminate the stencils.

DIRECTIONS: Read and share alphabet books such as *Gathering the Sun: An Alphabet in Spanish and English* (Alda, 1994) and *Farm Alphabet Book* (Miller, 1981). Make lists of words that

FIGURE 3–10 Big Letter Stenciling

begin with the same letters; ask children to match and sort letters. When children have some familiarity with letters, pour tempera paint into shallow bowls, and give each child in a small group a large piece of construction paper. Put three or four bowls with paint in the center of the shared work space. Moisten as many small sponges as there are shallow paint bowls. Review letter names and sounds. Target letters children are learning; discuss letter shapes; find words with the letters; have children listen for the sounds of letters in words. Identify the letters children are to stencil. Show them how to place the stencil on the construction paper, dip a small sponge in the paint, and dab the paint-laden sponge on the paper. When the stencil is removed, a big, beautiful colored letter remains!

Set the paper aside to dry. Return the papers when the letters are dry. Ask children to think of a word that begins with each of the stenciled big letters, or to look at the word wall for words that begin with the letters. Children, who cannot yet write the words, tell words to an adult, who writes the words beside the big stenciled letters. Children who know how to write may write their own words with your help in spelling. Put the stenciled big letter papers on the bulletin board. Ask children to point to letters by name or by sound; have children count all the letters in one color, or make a simple bar graph showing how many letters are in each color. Figure 3–10 is an example of a big letter paper made by a kindergartner.

Examples of Literature Connections

Alda, F. A. (1994). *Gathering the sun: An alphabet in Spanish and English.* New York: Lothrop, Lee & Shepard Books.

   This is a beautifully illustrated alphabet book that celebrates migrant farm workers, as well as their Spanish language and culture.

Miller, J. (1981). *Farm alphabet book.* New York: Scholastic.

   The informative text, easy-to-recognize pictures, and upper- and lowercase ball-and-stick letters make this book a good match for kindergartners who enjoy studying farm animals.

Multicultural   Spanish Language

BIG BAKED DOUGH LETTERS

▷ SMALL GROUP
LETTER NAMES
LETTER-SOUNDS
SOUND AWARENESS

In making impressive baked dough letters, children identify letter shapes, letter names, and single letter-sounds. Children share dough letters with their classmates, which gets the whole class involved in naming letters and in associating sounds with them.

MATERIALS: Large mixing bowl; spoon to stir the dough mix; measuring cup; cookie sheet; rolling pin; as many small cutting boards as there are children in a small group; colorful poster paint; brushes; plastic letters or letter cards to serve as models; colorful strands of yarn to string through a hole at the top of the baked dough letters; scissors; several toothpicks.

Baked Dough Ingredients:
2 cups all purpose flour*, plus a few sprinkles to prevent sticking when shaping the letters
1 cup salt
2 tablespoons vegetable oil
3/4 to 1 cup water
* Do *not* substitute self-rising flour for all-purpose flour.

Try your hand at making baked dough letters at home before using this activity at school, as altitude and humidity affect the consistency of the dough. Dough keeps, when wrapped in plastic, for several days or weeks in the refrigerator. We prefer to bake the letters at home, returning to school the next day with a batch of cool, fully baked letters.

DIRECTIONS:

PREPARING DOUGH AHEAD OF TIME   Follow these steps to make dough in advance.

Step 1   Mix flour and salt in a large bowl.
Step 2   Add the vegetable oil to 3/4 cup of water. Add liquid slowly, stirring with a large spoon.
Step 3   Check consistency. If the dough is too dry, add water. Dough is ready when it is clay-like and does not stick to your hands.

FASHION DOUGH INTO LETTERS   Read one or more alphabet books, discuss letter shapes, letter names, and letter-sounds. Use one or more familiar alphabet books as inspiration when introducing this activity. Children are ready for this activity when they are familiar with a handful or more of letters. Ask a small group to join you at the table. Put a small cutting board in front of each child; put plastic letters (ball-and-stick letters) or letter cards in the center of the table. Show children a sample dough letter and explain that they are going to make their own big letters.

As children watch, sprinkle a little flour on a cutting board to prevent the dough from sticking. Work lumps of dough into smooth balls. Make sure that there are no gaps or lines in the dough balls you fashion. Dough balls must be nice and smooth because any lines in the dough show up in the finished letters.

Talk about the lines and circles that make up letter shapes. Ask each child to select a letter, say its name, its sound, and a word that begins with that sound. Before making dough letters, ask the children to pretend to write that letter by tracing it on the surface of the table. Give one dough ball to each child. Show the children how to roll the dough balls into snakes and how to form the snakes into letters. Use plastic ball-and-stick letters or letter cards as guides. Ask children to form their own dough snakes into dough letters. Put the finished letters on a cookie sheet.

BAKE LETTERS   Bake letters for one hour at 250 degrees (longer for thick letters). Baked letters are going to be slightly thicker than they were before baking. This recipe works best when all the items are approximately the same thickness.

DECORATING LETTERS   When the letters are cool, ask a small group to don their paint smocks and join you at a table. Put paints and brushes in the middle of the table. Ask children to paint their letters. Shaking glitter on the letters before the paint is dry creates very glamorous, eye-catching letters that are popular among kindergartners (Figure 3–11).

Invite children to show their letters to their classmates, to tell the name of the letter they made, and, if possible, to name something that begins with the letter-sound. When sharing is over, generously wrap each letter in newspaper for a safe journey home.

MOTHER'S DAY LETTER NECKLACE   Children make a big baked dough letter for the first letter in their mothers' names. If making a necklace, use a toothpick to poke a hole in the top of each *unbaked* letter. Make the hole wide enough for a colorful piece of yarn to be threaded through it. Decorate baked letters with paint and sparkling glitter. A colorful piece of yarn strung through the hole in the top of the letter makes a handmade necklace every mother will surely treasure.

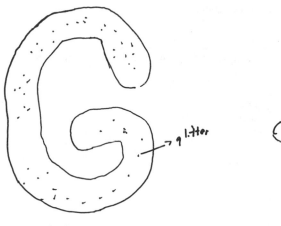 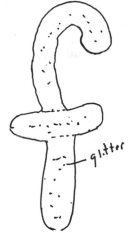

FIGURE 3–11 Big Baked Dough Letters

Examples of Literature Connections

Hirsch, L. A. (1991). *Have you met the alphabet?* New York: Derrydale Books.

  This book reinforces uppercase letter recognition. Since capital letters are easy to make out of dough, the focus on uppercase letters is appropriate for this activity.

Seuss, Dr. (1991). *Dr. Seuss's ABC*. New York: Random House.

  This alphabet book challenges children to think of things that begin with a target letter.

DELICIOUS CROCK POT ALPHABET SOUP

▷ **LARGE GROUP**
LETTER NAMES
LETTER-SOUNDS

This alphabet soup cooking activity strengthens children's letter knowledge and involves everyone in making soup with alphabet macaroni, listening to books about soup, and enjoying a healthy snack. Children read the soup ingredients in chorus. After making soup, the class members write a language experience story about their experience. Children read their story in chorus, and find letters and words in the story. Children then sort letters into soup can containers.

MATERIALS:

TO MAKE CROCK POT ALPHABET SOUP YOU NEED   Measuring cups for dry and liquid ingredients; measuring spoons; large pan; large crock pot; ladle; knife; celery; salt; carrots; tomatoes; corn; potatoes; green beans; alphabet macaroni. Purchase alphabet macaroni in grocery stores or online. *End of the Commons* sells alphabet macaroni over the Internet and by phone, and ships nationwide. Look for them online at:

      http://www.endofthecommons.com/pasta.html.

  If you would prefer, substitute Campbell's© soup for crock pot homemade soup.

FOR CAMPBELL'S© VEGETABLE ALPHABET SOUP YOU NEED   Several cans of alphabet soup; something to heat soup in; large spoon for serving soup.

MATERIALS NEEDED BEFORE AND AFTER MAKING SOUP   Dark color construction paper; alphabet macaroni; bowls, spoons, and napkins. You also need an assortment of alphabet books and books about food and soup. Some of our favorites are *Growing Vegetable Soup* (Ehlert, 1987), *A Sembrar Sopa de Verduras* (Ehlert, Ada, & Campoy, 1987), *Sip, Slurp, Soup, Soup – Caldo, Caldo, Caldo* (Bertrand, 1996), and *Stone Soup* (McGovern, 1987).

DIRECTIONS:

BEFORE MAKING SOUP   Write soup ingredients on a large chart. Ingredients for crock pot homemade soup and the ingredients in a can of Campbell's© vegetable alphabet soup are listed below. Campbell's© makes more than one type of alphabet soup. Only the ingredients for the vegetable soup are listed here.

Crock Pot Alphabet Soup	Campbell's© Vegetable Alphabet Soup*
water	potatoes
celery	carrots
salt	peas
carrots	green beans
tomatoes	alphabet macaroni
corn	
potatoes	*Only vegetable and pasta ingredients
green beans	are listed.
alphabet macaroni	

Announce that the class is going to make alphabet soup. Read the soup ingredients, pointing to words as you read them. Have children read the ingredients together in chorus. Ask children to find words that begin with certain letters and also ask children to point to different soup ingredients. Follow the directions below for homemade soup, or heat up several cans of Campbell's.© When the soup is ready, pass out bowls of delicious soup, along with plastic spoons and napkins.

Directions for Crock Pot Alphabet Soup

Soup Recipe

8 cups of water	1 tablespoon salt
3 ribs of celery, sliced	2 tablespoons minced onion
6 beef bouillon cubes	1 large potato, cubed
1 carrot, sliced	1 cup green beans
1 can corn	1 1/2 cup alphabet macaroni
1 15-oz can chopped tomatoes	

Put all ingredients in a large crock pot. Turn on high, and cook for 55 minutes or until the potato cubes and alphabet macaroni are done.

Challenge the children to carefully look at their spoonfuls of soup and tell the letters that they see. Make a list, in alphabetical order, of the letters the children find. Did the children find all twenty-six letters? If not, which ones are missing? Ask the children to think of words that begin with the sounds of the macaroni letters. Make an alphabet food chart, listing as many foods as the children think of that begin with the letter names and sounds you are teaching. For a list of foods for each of the twenty-six letters, look at the alphabet soup website at:

http://virtual.clemson.edu/groups/FieldOps/Cgs/ef_alph.htm.

MAKING A BIG BOOK Discuss soup making; encourage children to talk about soup ingredients, how they made soup, and how the soup tasted. Use shared writing to write about the soup-making experience. You may want to make a big book. To make a big book, talk about the soup-making experience and reread alphabet soup books. Then write sentences the children dictate to you at the bottom of very large sheets of white construction paper. Write one sentence per page. Figure 3–12 shows the sentences on seven pages of the big book that a group of kindergartners wrote: We put green beans in our soup (page one). We put carrots in our soup (page two). We put peas in our soup (page three). We put potatoes in our soup (page four). We put onions in our soup (page five). We put tomatoes in our soup (page six). Our soup was good (page seven). Different small groups were asked to draw pictures to illustrate the sentence on each large page. The kindergarten teacher made a

We Made Alphabet Soup

We put green beans in our soup.
We put carrots in our soup.
We put peas in our soup.
We put potatoes in our soup.
We put onions in our soup.
We put tomatoes in our soup.
Our soup was good!

FIGURE 3–12 Delicious Crock Pot Alphabet Soup Big Book Story cover out of very large green construction paper. She wrote the title, We Made Alphabet Soup, on the cover. A small group illustrated the title page. The whole book (one title page and seven large pages of text and pictures) was then stapled together. The teacher and children read and reread their big book, and the teacher left the book on display for children to read on their own.

WRITING A STORY ON A PIECE OF CHART PAPER   You may prefer to write a story on one or two pieces of lined chart paper. To do this, reread books about alphabet soup. Talk about the sequence for making alphabet soup. Talk about what went into the soup, how the soup was cooked in the crock pot (or heated if using canned soup), and how the soup tasted. Then have the children think of a title. Write the title at the top of the chart paper. Write the sentences the children dictate. Read and reread the story in chorus, moving your hand under each word as it is read. Have individual children read selected sentences or phrases. Frame and read words that begin with letters the children are currently learning. Have volunteers find these words. Ask children to find specific letters in words. Talk about the beginning letters, and ask children to listen to the words to identify the beginning sounds. Put the story on a large chart and display it in your classroom.

SOUP CAN LETTER SORT   Collect empty soup cans. Write letters on colored index cards or construction paper, and tape one letter card to each empty soup can.

SORTING LETTERS   Children sort letters by putting them into the soup cans with matching letters.

SORTING PICTURES BY BEGINNING LETTER-SOUNDS   Children sort pictures by putting them into soup cans with letters that represent the beginning sounds in picture names.

Examples of Literature Connections

Bertrand, D. G. (1996). *Sip, slurp, soup, soup – caldo, caldo, caldo.* Houston, TX: Piñata Books.
   This book, written in English and Spanish, includes a soup recipe and sprinkles Spanish words throughout English text.
Ehlert, L. (1987). *Growing vegetable soup.* New York: Harcourt Brace.
   Simple language and colorful pictures explain how to grow vegetables and how to make them into vegetable soup.
Ehlert, L., Ada, A. F., (translator) & Campoy, I. (translator). (1987). *A sembrar sopa de verduras.* New York: Harcourt Brace.
   This is the Spanish edition of *Growing Vegetable Soup.* There are no English words, so you need both books to create parallelism between the English and Spanish versions.
McGovern, A. (1987). *Stone Soup.* New York: Scholastic.
   The favorite tale of how a young man tricks a woman into preparing a kettle of tasty soup.
Multicultural   Spanish Language

ABC PLACE MATS

▷ SMALL GROUP
LETTER NAMES
SOUND AWARENESS

Woven paper place mats show off children's burgeoning knowledge of the letters of the alphabet. Through sharing literature with children and talking about weaving, children learn weaving terms and the traditions of Navajo weavers.

MATERIALS: Large (12 × 18) construction paper in *two* different colors (colors should be light enough to show letters written in crayon or marker); white construction paper; glue; paper cutter; markers or crayons; stapler; plastic letters or letter cards to serve as models.

EACH WEAVER NEEDS THE FOLLOWING   Three 18-inch-long construction paper strips in one color; three 18-inch-long construction paper strips in a contrasting color; two white construction paper strips 12-inches long; one 12 × 18 base sheet (warp), which may be any color as this sheet does not show in the finished mat. Figure 3–13 shows how to prepare the mats for weaving.

DIRECTIONS: Read and share books about weaving, such as *The Goat in the Rug* (Blood & Link, 1990) and *Charlie Needs a Cloak* (dePaola, 1973). Talk about the words weavers use to describe their craft. Call attention to the alphabet strip in your classroom, to words on the word wall, and to letters displayed in your room. Put some magnetic letters or letter cards on a table, and

FIGURE 3–13 ABC Place Mat Weaving Directions

To prepare mats for weaving:

Step 1. Staple the 18-inch strips to the base sheet of 12 x 18 paper (warp).

Step 2. Alternate 18-inch-long colored strips; staple them to the 12-inch side of the base sheet (warp).

Step 3. To weave, hold up one set of color strips and place a white strip under them. Then hold up the other color strips and place a white strip under those strips. Continue until all strips are used.

Step 4. Staple strips to the base sheet to secure the weaving.

ask the children to pick out the letters by name. When the children can write all twenty-six letters, in either upper- or lowercase, they are ready to weave an ABC place mat.

Each woven place mat has more than twenty-six squares, so there is plenty of room to write every letter of the alphabet. For purposes of illustration, we will assume that the children are weaving a place mat in red, green, and white. To weave ABC place mats, children alternately hold up red and green strips that are stapled to the base sheet (warp), while putting a white strip on the base (Figure 3–13).

WEAVING ABC PLACE MATS   To weave place mats, children must:

1. Hold up the *green* strips with one hand.
2. Pick up a white strip with the other hand.
3. Put the white strip on the base under the green strips. Push each white strip snugly against the top of the mat under the green strips.
4. Hold up the *red* strips.
5. Pick up a white strip.

6. Put the white strip under the red strips. Push the white strip snugly against the other strips on your mat.
7. Repeat this process until all eight white strips are in place.
8. Staple the strips to the base. The completed mats sport a cheerful red, green, and white checkered pattern.

WRITING LETTERS ON WOVEN PLACE MATS
Now it's time to write letters on the mats. Children use a marker or a crayon to write one letter in each square. Finished mats show all twenty-six letters in alphabetical order from top to bottom (Figure 3–14). The children may write the letters in squares horizontally or vertically, whichever pattern suits your sense of aesthetics or fits into the way you plan to use the mats in the future. For an activity book of ABC place settings in which children color, write letters, and illustrate replicas of table settings, look for *ABC Place Mats* (Chirinian, 1996). This book is a fine complement to the ABC mat weaving activity.

FIGURE 3–14   ABC Place Mat

Examples of Literature Connections
Blood, C. L., & Link, M. (1990). *The goat in the rug.* New York: Aladdin Paperbacks.
  Set in Window Rock, Arizona, this book describes how a Navajo weaver follows age-old rug weaving traditions.
dePaola, T. (1973). *Charlie needs a cloak.* New York: Aladdin Paperbacks.
  Delightful illustrations embellish this story of a shepherd who makes a red winter coat.
Multicultural   Native Americans; Navajo Weavers

LETTER PANCAKES

LARGE GROUP
SMALL GROUP
LETTER NAMES
LETTER-SOUNDS
SOUND AWARENESS

In this phonics, phonemic awareness, and cooking activity, everyone in your classroom makes and eats pancakes shaped like letters the children are learning.

MATERIALS: Chart paper; marker; pancake mix and the ingredients specified on the box; mixing bowl; measuring cup; whisk; spoon; pancake turner; turkey baster with a *wide* opening; electric frying pan; butter, oil, or non-stick spray; spatula; plates; forks. Add butter, syrup, and fruit to the list if desired. The turkey baster should have a wide opening so that the thick pancake mix flows easily into the frying pan.

DIRECTIONS: Read books about pancakes and talk about pancakes, then write letters the children are learning, or need to practice, on chart paper. Children name the letters and think of words that begin with the letter-sounds. Pronounce words, rubber banding the beginning sounds. Ask children what sounds they hear at the beginning of words, such as /nnnut/. To further reinforce phonemic awareness, have children listen to words you pronounce and put their thumbs up when they hear a targeted sound at the beginning of words.
    Have paper plates and forks ready, as well as syrup, butter, and fruit, if you plan to add toppings to the letter pancakes. Prepare the pancake batter according to the directions on the box. Turn on the electric frying pan and add a little non-stick spray or butter. When the frying pan is hot, draw some pancake mix into the turkey baster. Make sure that the turkey baster has a wide opening to allow the pancake batter to flow smoothly.
    Tell the children that the baster is a *pancake pencil* for writing pancake letters. Ask children to name letters or to think of words that begin with particular sounds. Make pancakes in the shapes of the letters children identify by name and/or by sound. Turn the pancake letters over when bubbles form on the tops. Put the cooked letter pancakes on paper plates, as illustrated in Figure 3–15.

FIGURE 3–15   Letter Pancakes

If some of the children in your classroom speak languages other than English at home, you might select a word from the children's home language, ask the children what sound the word begins with, and what letter you should make with the pancake pencil, such as an *f* for *fiesta*. Since the letter-sound associations differ from English, look for examples that match English at the letter and sound level, if possible, such as the /f/ in *fiesta*. Another way to honor other languages is to refer to English words borrowed from children's home languages. For example, if you have a child who speaks German in your class, you might point out that *butter* is a word we borrowed from the German language.

As a follow-up, use shared writing to compose a story about making and eating pancakes. Take opportunities during shared writing to point out words that begin with letters and sounds the children are learning, need to practice, or words that were featured in the letter pancake-making activity. An alternative to creating a shared writing story is to ask the children to draw pictures about making the letter pancakes and to tell you about their pictures while you write their words at the bottom of the page. Still another follow-up idea is to reread the wordless picture book *Pancakes for Breakfast* (dePaola, 1990), and then to use shared writing to create a text story to accompany the pictures.

Examples of Literature Connections
dePaola, T. (1990). *Pancakes for breakfast.* New York: Harcourt Brace.
  This wordless picture book tells a picture story of making and sharing pancakes on a snowy winter morning.
Foster, K. C. (1995). *The pancake day.* Houppauge, NY: Barron's.
  Written in decodable text, this book uses many different long vowel words to tell the rhyming story of animals in a pancake-eating contest.
Numeroff, L. (1998). *If you give a pig a pancake.* New York: Harpercollins Juvenile Books.
  This circle story begins when a little girl gives a pig a pancake and then, through a series of humorous events, the story cycles back to another pancake.
Numeroff, L., & Mlawer, T. (translator). (1999). *Si le das UN panqueque a una cerdita.* New York: Harpercollins Juvenile Books.
  The same delightful pictures and wacky circle story as above, only told in Spanish.
Rey, M., & Rey, H. A. (1998). *Curious George makes pancakes.* Boston, MA: Houghton Mifflin.
George saves the day by making pancakes and gets covered with sticky syrup.
Multicultural   Spanish Language

▷ SMALL GROUP
LETTER NAMES
LETTER-SOUNDS
SOUND AWARENESS

ABC SAILOR HATS

Kindergartners decorate paper hats with the letters they are learning in your classroom, share hats with their classmates, and take hats home to share their letter knowledge with their families.

MATERIALS: As many large pieces of colorful construction paper as there are hat makers in your classroom; scissors; colored markers; a selection of pictures; several copies of colorful construction paper letters; a stapler; several glue sticks; brightly colored feathers or construction paper cut into feather shapes. Optional items include glitter and colored glue. Fold and staple the children's hats the day before. Figure 3–16 shows you how to fold a piece of paper into a sailor hat.

DIRECTIONS: Read and share the predictable book *Red Hat! Green Hat!* (Gikow, 2000). The small lion in this book wears a sailor hat of red on one side and green on the other. The sailor hat looks like the one the children make, only the children's sailor hats have letters on them. Discuss the small lion's hat, its red and green sides, and why the animals in the library are confused. If children are learning to identify colors, ask them to find things in your classroom that

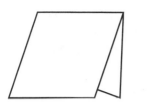

Step 1. Fold the construction paper in half, lengthwise.

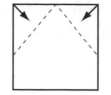

Step 2. Fold the corners so that the paper touches in the middle.

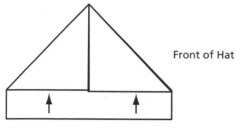

Front of Hat

Step 3. Fold the bottom flap up. Staple.

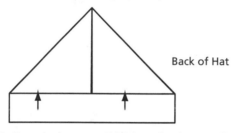

Back of Hat

Step 4. Turn the hat over. Fold the other bottom flap up. Staple.

FIGURE 3–16   Directions for Folding ABC Sailor Hats

are red and green. You may also want to read aloud and share the photographs in *Hats, Hats, Hats* (Morris, 1989).

Show the children the folded and stapled hats you made the day before. Explain that children are going to make ABC sailor hats like the hat the small lion wears in the book (Figure 3–16). The small lion's hat has a feather. Explain that children's hats have a feather, too, as well as letters the children identify by name or by sound.

Place an assortment of colorful construction paper letters and several pictures on the table. Children take turns picking up a paper letter, saying the letter name and/or finding a picture that begins with the letter sound. The letters that each child identifies are candidates for that child's ABC sailor hat. Children choose the color of the letters to go on their ABC sailor hats. Staple selected letters to the brims of the hats, and glue them on the tops of the hats. On the very top-most peak, staple or glue a construction paper feather or a real colored feather (Figure 3–17). The finished hats look like the small lion's hat in *Red Hat! Green Hat!* (Gikow, 2000). Children share their ABC sailor hats by telling the names of the letters. Give children opportunities to wear their hats around the school. A hat parade to another kindergarten classroom is loads of fun. Finally, have the children take their hats home and share their letter knowledge with everyone in the family by naming the letters and saying a word that begins with each letter-sound.

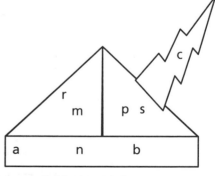

Finished ABC Sailor Hat.

FIGURE 3–17   ABC Sailor Hat

Examples of Literature Connections

Gikow, L. (2000). *Red hat! Green hat!*. New York: Golden Books.

A small lion wearing a two-color sailor hat creates all sorts of havoc among animals in a library.

Morris, A. (1989). *Hats, Hats, Hats*. New York: Mulberry Books.

This book is chock full of photographs of people wearing hats around the world.
Multicultural   Hats Around the World

▷ SMALL GROUP
LETTER NAMES
LETTER-SOUNDS
SOUND AWARENESS

BIRD FEEDER LETTERS

Children make bird feeders from the letters they know by name or by sound. Homemade bird feeders integrate nicely with science and nature study.

MATERIALS: Sturdy foam paper plates; scissors; hand-held hole punch; plain peanut butter; bird seed; four 24-inch strands of colored yarn for each child; multiple copies of letter cards or plastic letters; newspaper; plastic bowls; spoons. Punch four holes in each sturdy foam paper plate, equally distributed about an inch or two from the outside edge.

DIRECTIONS: Ask a small group to join you at a table. Give each child several letter cards or plastic letters. Ask children to name the letters or say words that begin with the letter-sounds. When children are familiar with the letter names and/or sounds, ask each child to select one letter that the child can name and/or associate with a beginning sound in a word.

Spread newspaper on the table and give each child a foam paper plate. Use a plastic knife to make a known letter on a paper plate for each child. Put a container of bird seed on the table. Children then sprinkle the bird seed over the peanut butter, which sticks to the peanut butter. Shake off any extra seed. (Bird seed can be a bit messy, so if it is a nice day you might want to take the children outside to make bird feeders.) Thread one strand of colored yarn through each hole and tie a knot just above the plate edge. Do this for all four strands. Gather the four yarn strands together about a foot above the plate; tie the strands in a sturdy knot. Twist the rest of the strands all the way to the end and tie a second knot (Figure 3–18). Children tie their bird feeders to trees, posts, or some other places where birds are likely to see the feeder.

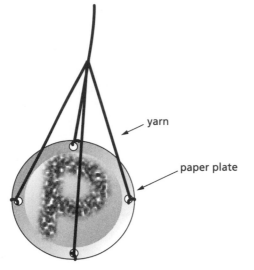

FIGURE 3–18   Bird Feeder Letter

Examples of Literature Connections

Caldone, P. (1984). *Henny penny.* New York: Clarion Books.

A traditional tale is retold in language that makes it a good read aloud story.

Oppenheim, J. (1990). *Have you seen birds?* New York: Scholastic.

This book tells about a multitude of birds in all seasons, including birds at feeders.

▷ SMALL GROUP
LETTER NAMES
LETTER-SOUNDS
SOUND AWARENESS

BLACKTOP LETTER WALK

Children walk on a path of chalk letters, saying letter names or sounds as their feet land on letters.

MATERIALS: Sidewalk chalk; cement or pavement outdoors.

DIRECTIONS: Use colored sidewalk chalk to make a letter walk pattern on blacktop or cement, as shown in Figure 3–19. Write letters in upper- or lowercase about a foot or so apart. Wind the letters in a snake-like pattern so children do not walk in a boring straight line. If there is a lot of room to spread out, make the letter walk as elaborate as you wish. Children step on a letter and say

FIGURE 3–19   Blacktop Letter Walk

the letter name, letter-sound, or a word that begins with the letter-sound. Children cannot go to the next letter until they give the letter name, letter-sound, or a word that begins with the sound of the letter on which they are standing. If children have trouble, they may get help from you, your teacher assistant, or a parent volunteer. Repeat the letter walk until children are confident naming letters or associating sounds with letters.

Examples of Literature Connections

Hutchins, P. (1983). *Rosie's walk*. New York: Aladdin Books.
  Rosie strolls through the farmyard unaware of the fox on her trail.
Williams, S. (1992). *I went walking*. New York: Harcourt Brace.
  Text and pictures invite listeners and readers to guess what a child sees on a walk.

WATER WRITING

Children use water-soaked sponges to write letters on the blackboard or cement sidewalks.

MATERIALS: Sponges; water; bowls.

DIRECTIONS: Read *Mr. Putter and Tabby Paint the Porch* (Rylant, 2001). Explain that children are going to write letters with water. Just like Mr. Putter, who painted his porch several times, the children write letters several times. To write with water, children simply dip small sponges in water and write the letters that you dictate by name, correspond to sounds you pronounce, or represent the beginning sound in words you pronounce. Water letters show up on the chalk board and cement, and then magically disappear as the water evaporates.

Turn water writing into a game by calling it mouse painting after the book *Mouse Paint* (Walsh, 1995). The children pretend that the cat is coming and they want to make as many letters as they can before any one letter disappears. Writing letters in water uses large muscles, which is a relatively unique feature for letter learning and writing activities.

Examples of Literature Connections

Rey, H. A. (1989). *Curious George goes to school*. New York: Houghton Mifflin.
  Curious George is up to mischief in the art room as he tries his hand at being an artist.
Rylant, C. (2001). *Mr. Putter and Tabby paint the porch*. New York: Harcourt Brace.
  Part of the Mr. Putter and Tabby series, this story relates humorous mishaps as Mr. Putter paints his porch.
Walsh, E. S. (1995). *Mouse paint*. New York: Harcourt Brace.
  This is a concept book about color that tells of mice who make a design on a paper while hiding from a cat.

▷ SMALL GROUP
LETTER NAMES
LETTER-SOUNDS
SOUND AWARENESS

LETTER LID MEDALLIONS

The letters children name or associate with sounds are written on the back of plastic lids, which are then worn as medallions around children's necks.

MATERIALS: Round plastic lids from food containers; brightly colored permanent markers; hand-held hole punch; colored yarn; an alphabet book with ball-and-stick letters in upper- and lowercase; letter cards. Poke a hole at the top of each lid.

DIRECTIONS: Read *Curious George and the Rocket* (Rey, 2001). Talk about medals and medallions, and what people do to earn them. Show children an alphabet book like *From Acorn to Zoo and Everything in between in Alphabetical Order* (Kitamura, 1992). Review the letters in the alphabet book; talk about words that begin with the letter-sounds. Show children letter cards. Ask children to name as many letters as they can. Put all known letters in a pile and count them. Tell children how many letters they know.

Put lids on the table with the blank side face-up. Having learned so many letters, children earn a letter medal, just like George got a medal for going into space. Use a colored permanent marker to write on the lid: (1) the children's favorite letter; (2) the most recently introduced letter; (3) the first letter of children's names (appropriate for pre-alphabetic word learners); or (4) the letter you have just introduced that day. Also write the number of letters children can name. In the beginning of the school year, the spread in children's letter knowledge is the least, so the start of the year might be a good time to reward children by putting the number of

▷ SMALL GROUP
LETTER NAMES

known letters on the lids. String the yarn through the hole. Tie the yarn around children's necks. Voila! Children have colorful letter medallions to wear home (Figure 3–20).

Examples of Literature Connections

Rey, R. A. (2001). *Curious George and the rocket.* Boston, MA: Houghton Mifflin.

   Space-traveling George gets a medal for his efforts.

Kitamura, S. (1992). *From acorn to zoo and everything in between in alphabetical order.* New York: Farrar, Straus and Giroux.

   Easy-to-recognize ball-and-stick letters and clear illustrations are presented in a format that simplifies teaching and learning.

FIGURE 3–20 Letter Lid Medallion

▷ **INDIVIDUAL LETTER NAMES**

PIG LETTER WHEELS

As children turn a wheel, letters appear in a pig's mouth; children say letter names, letter-sounds, or words that begin with the letter-sound.

MATERIALS: Two tagboard circles nine inches in diameter for each child; brads for fastening the two circles together; crayons; scissors; pig pattern (Appendix A-7). If using paper plates, find plates that are relatively flat. Duplicate the pattern (Appendix A-7). Draw lines across one circle, dividing it into eight equal parts. Write one letter in each part, toward the edge. Duplicate the pig face pattern on the tagboard or onto sturdy construction paper. Cut out the mouth, as shown in Figure 3–21.

DIRECTIONS: Give each child a pig face pattern. Ask the children to color their own pig patterns, and fasten the pig pattern to the tagboard circle with a brad. When children turn the pig face, different letters appear in the pig's mouth (Figure 3–21). Children name the letters as they appear. Make a pig letter wheel for each child; write letters on these wheels that children routinely confuse or have difficulty remembering. You may want to change the pig face to something that corresponds to the curriculum, like the face of a cow or some other farm animal.

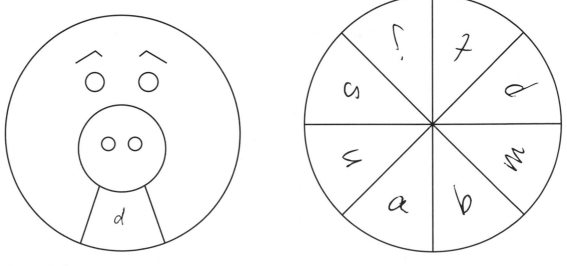

FIGURE 3–21 Pig Letter Wheel

SHAVING CREAM LETTERS

Children write in shaving cream the letters that you dictate by name or letters that represent beginning sounds in words you pronounce.

MATERIALS: Shaving cream; paper towels.

DIRECTIONS: Review letters before writing in shaving cream. Ask children to name the letters, to find letters in words, and to put their thumbs up when they hear you pronounce words that begin with the targeted letter-sounds. Put a little shaving cream on the table in front of each child. Have the children spread the shaving cream around so that it makes a nice writing surface. Pronounce a letter by name or by sound, or say a word that begins with a targeted letter-sound. Children write the letter in shaving cream. This is a nice multi-sensory activity that does not take too much time, is an excellent review, and, coincidentally, is a great way to clean table surfaces. Use this dual purpose activity just before open house or other special days when you expect guests. Tables will be spotless and children will have had an opportunity to write letters in a different medium and to reinforce letter name and letter-sound knowledge at the same time.

> ▷ SMALL GROUP
> LETTER NAMES
> LETTER-SOUNDS
> SOUND AWARENESS

LETTER CUBES

Children roll letter cubes, and say the letter name, letter-sound, or a word that begins with the sound of the face-up letter.

MATERIALS: Cube pattern (Appendix A-3); sturdy unlined paper; tape; black marker. Copy the cube pattern; write a different letter on each of the six sides. Tape together. Make several cubes showing different letters. Letters may be upper- or lowercase (Figure 3–22).

DIRECTIONS: Children sit cross-legged in a circle on the floor and take turns tossing letter cubes. Children say the name or sound of the letter that lands face-up. In identifying letters by sound, children may pronounce the sound, /l/, or say a word that begins with the letter-sound, /lady/. Use at least two different letter cubes. Alternate cubes so that one child tosses a cube and then another child tosses a different cube. For example, if one child tosses a cube with the letters *a, m, t, s, u,* and *p,* the next child would toss a different letter cube, perhaps a cube with *b, d, e, c, i,* and *f.* Children earn one point for each letter they name or associate with a sound. The first child to earn six points wins.

> ▷ SMALL GROUP
> LETTER NAMES
> LETTER-SOUNDS
> SOUND AWARENESS

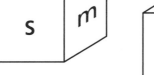

FIGURE 3–22   Letter Cubes

LETTER NAME CONCENTRATION

Children select two face-down cards from several cards on a table and, if the letters match when the cards are turned face-up, children say the letter name and keep the matched letter cards.

MATERIALS: Up to fifty-two sturdy cards with letters on one side and blank space on the other. Write the letters twice. You may write all lowercase (a, a), all uppercase (A, A), or one upper- and one lowercase form for each letter (A, a). Once you have made the fifty-two cards, you may have children play with all fifty-two, or you may divide the deck into twenty-six cards with thirteen duplicate letters in each deck.

DIRECTIONS: Children play this game just like regular Concentration©. Place all cards face-down. Children take turns turning up two cards. If the two letters match, the child says the letter name and keeps the cards. If the two letters do not match, the child flips the cards back over. The child with the most cards at the end of the game wins.

> ▷ SMALL GROUP
> LETTER NAMES

▷ SMALL GROUP
LETTER NAMES
LETTER-SOUNDS
SOUND AWARENESS

SIMON SAYS LETTERS

Children follow verbal instructions to identify letters in novel ways.

MATERIALS: Multiple copies of the same set of ten (or more) upper- and lowercase letters for each child in a small group.

DIRECTIONS: Give each child sitting around a table a set of letter cards. Put the letter cards face-up in front of each child. Explain that whenever you say "Simon says," children are to follow the directions. If they do not hear "Simon says," they should not follow the directions. Examples of "Simon Says" directions are: put your thumb on the *s;* touch the uppercase *B;* touch the *p* with your pinky finger; put two fingers on the *m;* pick up the *r;* touch the *n* to your nose; touch the letter *e* to your elbow; put three fingers on the *u.*

▷ SMALL GROUP
LETTER NAMES
LETTER-SOUNDS

ABC VEST

Children make vests from brown grocery bags, and adorn their vests with letters they can write and know by name and by sound.

MATERIALS: As many brown grocery bags as there are children in a small group; crayons or markers; scissors; glue; construction paper letters; glitter. Prepare the vests ahead of time, according to the directions in Figure 3–23.

DIRECTIONS: Ask a small group to join you at a table. Review the letters the children have been learning. Ask children to name the letters and to think of words that begin with the letter-sounds.

Step 1: Place a paper bag on table.

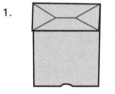

Step 2. Pull out the sides of a bag and also pull up the bottom (closed portion where the groceries sit—when right side up this would be the bottom). Pulling out the the sides and pulling up the bottom where the groceries sit makes the bag flat.

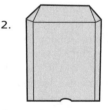

Step 3. Cut arm holes by snipping the two corners where the pulled-out sides meet the bottom of the bag.

Step 4. Cut a neck opening.

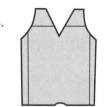

Step 5. Cut a slit from the open portion of the bag to the neck hole. This opens up the bag and creates a vest.

Step 6. Turn the bag inside out. Ask children to write letters they know and to decorate them with illustrations and , if desired, glitter and other art supplies, like feathers or shiny stars.

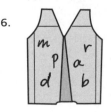

FIGURE 3–23   ABC Vest

Place glue, construction paper letters, and glitter on the table. Write down all the letters that each child knows. Give children construction paper letters that they know; have children glue letters on their vests and decorate with glitter. If children have good fine motor skills, they might write the letters on their vests. After letters are glued or written on the vests, you may wish to have children dictate words that begin with the letter-sounds and write those words next to the letters. Children may also adorn their vests with smallish pictures of some of the words that begin with letter-sounds. Have children wear their vests. Ask them to share their ABC vests with everyone in the class. Children may stand, one at a time, and have other children name the letters on their vests, or you may take an ABC vest walk around the school, perhaps stopping by other kindergarten classrooms or the principal's office to show off how many letters children know. Send children home in their letter vests so that they may share their letter knowledge with their families.

TEN MINUTE FLUENCY ACTIVITIES FOR LETTER NAMES AND SINGLE LETTER-SOUNDS

Use these fluency activities to develop speed and accuracy in naming letters or saying sounds associated with letters you have already taught. Fluency activities are appropriate for children who are accurate but slow in using letter name and sound information. The goal is to increase speed and accuracy so as to bring letter name and letter-sound knowledge to fluency; that is, to enable children to develop sufficient skill to use letter names and sounds accurately, rapidly, and effortlessly when reading and writing.

WRITE IT FAST

▷ SMALL GROUP
LETTER NAME
FLUENCY
LETTER-SOUND
FLUENCY

Write it fast develops fluency in remembering and writing letters you have already taught.

MATERIALS: Chalk board and chalk, or a white board and erasable pens.

DIRECTIONS: Ask a small group of children who need to bring letter names or letter-sounds to fluency to come to the chalk board. Have the children pick up a piece of chalk (or a marker). Ask them to face you; that is, to stand with their backs to the blackboard.

LETTER NAME FLUENCY   Tell children to listen for a letter name. When children hear you say a letter name, they turn around and write the letter as fast as they can.

LETTER-SOUND FLUENCY   Explain that you will say a word. When children hear the word they turn around and write the letter that represents the beginning sound.

    Children who "write it fast" and who write correctly earn one point. Remind the children to work independently and not look at their neighbor's work. If some children write so fast that their handwriting cannot be read, caution that in order to earn a point you have to be able to read what the children write. As children write on the board, you get a bird's eye view of how close individual children are to fluency in writing letters by name or by sound.

PICTURE LETTER-SOUND SPEED SORT

▷ SMALL GROUP
LETTER NAME
FLUENCY

Use this timed sort to help kindergarten readers bring to fluency the letter-sounds you have already taught.

MATERIALS: Three or more letter cards for each child; as many sets of picture cards for letter sorting as there are children in a small group.

DIRECTIONS: Ask a small group to join you at a table. Show the pictures and ask children to name each one, then give each child a handful of pictures. Tell children to put the pictures in a stack on the table. Give each child three letters. Ask the children to put the letters in a row on the table. Explain that you will set the timer for two, three, or four minutes. When the timer starts, the children sort the pictures by putting them under the letter that stands for the beginning sound in each picture name. For example, if the children are sorting pictures that begin with the sounds of /m/, /b/, and /f/, they place the three letters in a row: m, b, and f. Set the timer, and begin the timed sort saying, "Ready. Set. Go!"

Sorting stops when the timer goes off. Ask children to check their work by putting letters in a column under each picture. Check the beginning sound in each picture name by asking children to say the picture word and the beginning sound. Repeat this fluency matching activity until the children sort quickly and accurately. When the children are fluent sorting one set of letters with the beginning sounds in picture names, introduce other letters that the children need to bring to fluency.

▷ SMALL GROUP
LETTER NAME
FLUENCY
LETTER-SOUND
FLUENCY

SAY IT FAST MARCHING LETTERS

This small-group fluency activity emphasizes quick, accurate letter-name or letter-sound associations.

MATERIALS: Tape recorder; marching music tape; dessert-size paper plates with one letter on each; markers; masking tape. 5 × 8 cards may be substituted for paper plates. Write one letter on each paper plate. Tape the plates to a table about two feet apart. Move chairs away from the table; set up the tape recorder with the marching music tape.

DIRECTIONS: Each child stands beside a paper plate letter. The children march around the table as the music plays. When the music stops, each child stands in front of a paper plate letter and rapidly says the letter name, the letter-sound, or a word that begins with the letter-sound. Designate a different child to go first on each round. Should a child take more than three seconds to respond, tell that child the letter-name, the letter-sound, or a word that begins with the letter-sound. Encourage the children to keep a fast pace as they take turns identifying paper plate letters. Restart the marching music when every paper plate letter has been identified. After one round, restart the music and stop it when children are standing in front of different paper plate letters. Make sure that the *first* paper plate letter identified by name or sound is different in each round. Starting with a different paper plate letter in each round assures that children will not simply memorize the letter order.

▷ SMALL GROUP
LETTER NAME
FLUENCY

QUICK COOKIE SHEET LETTERS

Children rapidly sort magnetic letters according to the letter names. Not only do children use their tactile and kinesthetic senses when sorting the three-dimensional magnetic letters, but sorting on cookie sheets also makes this fluency activity highly portable and easy to modify.

MATERIALS: One large cookie sheet (or pizza tin) for every child in the group; an assortment of magnetic letters with three or four duplicate letters for each child; two to four different color erasable markers; a timer.

DIRECTIONS: Decide on two to four letters for timed sorting. Select as many cookie sheets as there are children in the group. Draw cloud shapes on each cookie sheet (or pizza tin), one cloud for each letter to be sorted. Use a different color marker to draw each cloud. Have the children sit in a circle on the floor. Give each child a tin cookie sheet (or large pizza tin) on which you have already drawn the same number of different colored clouds as there are letters for sorting. Give each child magnetic letters. Ask children to put the letters in the middle of the cookie sheet, outside the clouds. We use this timed sort with lowercase letters, uppercase letters, or a combination of both upper- and lowercase letters (Figure 3–24).

For purposes of illustration, we will suppose that children are sorting b, s, and p. Explain that everyone has a cookie sheet with colored clouds on it. Ask the children to hold up as many fingers as there are clouds on their cookie sheets. Have children point to the different color clouds. Have children raise their hands if they see the letter b, the letter s, and the letter p, respectively. Tell children which color cloud each letter goes in. For example, all the *b*s go in the blue cloud, the *p*s in the green cloud, and the *t*s in the red cloud.

Explain that you are going to set the timer for one minute (shorter or longer, depending on the group). The children put the letters into the colored clouds as fast as they can. When the timer goes off, it is time to stop sorting. Start the timed sort saying, "Ready! Set! Go!" Check the sort when the timer goes off. Are all the *b*s in the blue cloud? The *p*s in the green one? The *t*s in the red?

QUICK COOKIE SHEET NUMBERS   Use this same fluency activity to bring number names to fluency. Exchange magnetic letters for numerals and follow the same procedure as previously described.

FIGURE 3–24   Quick Cookie Sheet Letters

POWER LETTERS

Power Letters develop letter-name or letter-sound fluency with a rapid-fire say-it show-it group response.

MATERIALS: Letter cards.

DIRECTIONS: Pass out several letter cards to each child. Ask the children to put the letter cards on their tables. It does not matter what order the letters are in, so long as they are right-side-up. To develop letter name fluency, tell children you will say a letter name and they are to quickly find the letter and hold it in the air. For letter-sound fluency, say a sound or a word that begins with a letter-sound, and ask children to hold up the letter that represents the sound. Say the letter names or sounds quickly, one every three to five seconds. Children who quickly hold up letters are fluent, while those who hesitate benefit from more fluency practice.

After using the whole group response over several days, you will have a good idea of which letters individual children have brought to fluency and which letters need more practice to become fluent. The whole group response encourages the children to work as fast as they can, which in turn helps children develop fluency. If your school asks that you document fluency in letter recognition, you may want to use power letters as one means of documentation. In this way, power letters serve the dual purpose of helping children bring letter knowledge to fluency and help you verify which letters individual children know fluently and with which letters children are approaching fluency.

As children gain fluency in naming letters and associating sounds with letters, children move to the alphabetic word fluency stage. In order to decode new words, children must: (1) understand how vowel and consonant letter patterns function within word contexts, (2) understand how the vowels and consonants at the end of word family words (*at, ig*) make many different words (*cat, hat, bat; big, pig, wig*), and (3) use all this knowledge to pronounce new words in a variety of reading contexts and to spell words when writing. Chapter 4 describes teaching activities to develop, enhance, refine, and bring to fluency letter pattern and word family (*at, ig*) knowledge.

▷ **LARGE GROUP**
SMALL GROUP
LETTER NAME
FLUENCY
LETTER-SOUND
FLUENCY

REFERENCES ■ ■ ■ ■ ▬▬

Adams, M. J. (1990). *Beginning to read: Thinking and learning about print.* Cambridge, MA: The MIT Press.

Alda, F. A. (1994). *Gathering the sun: An alphabet in Spanish and English.* New York: Lothrop, Lee & Shepard Books.

Baer, G. (1979). *Paste, pencils, scissors and crayons.* West Nyack, NY: Parker Publishing Company.

Bertrand, D. G. (1996). *Sip, slurp, soup, soup – caldo, caldo, caldo.* Houston, TX: Piñata Books.

Blood, C. L., & Link, M. (1990). *The goat in the rug.* New York: Aladdin Paperbacks.

Bridwell, N. (1984). *Clifford's kitten.* New York: Scholastic.

Caldone, P. (1984). *Henny penny.* New York: Clarion Books.

Carnine, D. W., Silbert, J., & Kameenui, E. J. (1997). *Direct instruction reading, 3rd edition.* Columbus, OH: Merrill.

Chirinian, H. (1996). *ABC place mats.* Los Angeles, CA: Lowell House Juvenile.

dePaola, T. (1973). *Charlie needs a cloak.* New York: Aladdin Paperbacks.

dePaola, T. (1990). *Pancakes for breakfast.* New York: Harcourt Brace.

Ehlert, L. (1987). *Growing vegetable soup.* New York: Harcourt Brace.

Ehlert, L., Ada, A. F., & Campoy, I. (translators). (1987). A *sembrar sopa de verduras.* New York: Harcourt Brace.

Foster, K. C. (1995). T*he pancake day.* Houppauge, NY: Barron's.

Gikow, L. (2000). *Red hat! Green hat!* New York: Golden Books.

Gustafson, S. (1996). *Alphabet soup: A feast of letters.* New York: Greenwich Workshop Press.

Hirsch, L. A. (1991). *Have you met the alphabet?* New York: Derrydale Books.

Hutchins, P. (1983). *Rosie's walk.* New York: Aladdin Books.

Kitamura, S. (1992). *From acorn to zoo and everything in between in alphabetical order.* New York: Farrar, Straus and Giroux.

Leonard, M. (1990). *Paintbox penguins: A book about colors.* Mahwah, NJ: Troll Communications.

Lord, J. V., & Burroway, J. (1972). T*he giant jam sandwich.* New York: Houghton Mifflin.

Miller, J. (1981). F*arm alphabet book.* New York: Scholastic.

Morris, A. (1989). *Hats, hats, hats.* New York: Mulberry Books.

Numeroff, L. (1998). *If you give a pig a pancake.* New York: Harpercollins Juvenile Books.

Numeroff, L., & Mlawer, T. (translator). (1999). *Si le das UN panqueque a una cerdita.* New York: Harpercollins Juvenile Books.

Oppenheim, J. (1990). *Have you seen birds?* New York: Scholastic.

Purcell-Gates, V. (1998). Growing successful readers: Homes, communities and schools. In J. Osborne & F. Lehr (Eds.), *Literacy for all: Issues in teaching and learning* (pp. 51–72), New York: Guilford Press.

Rey, H. A. (1989). *Curious George goes to school.* New York: Houghton Mifflin.

Rey, H. A. (2001). *Curious George and the rocket.* Boston, MA: Houghton Mifflin.

Rey, M. & Rey, H. A. (1998). *Curious George makes pancakes.* Boston, MA: Houghton Mifflin.

Rylant, C. (2001). *Mr. Putter and Tabby paint the porch.* New York: Harcourt Brace.

Sandhaus, E. (1999). *26 of the most interesting letters in the alphabet.* New York: Paul Sandhaus Associates, Inc.

Scarry, R., & Herman, G. (1998). *Mr. Fixit's magnet machine.* New York: Simon Spotlight.

Searfoss, L. W., Readence, J. E., & Mallette, M. H. (2001). *Helping children learn to read: Creating a classroom literacy environment, 4th edition.* Needham Heights, MA: Allyn and Bacon.

Seuss, Dr. (1991). *Dr. Seuss's ABC.* New York: Random House.

Shanker, J. L., & Ekwall, E. E. (1998). *Locating and correcting reading difficulties, 7th edition.* Columbus, OH: Merrill.

Snow, C. E., Burns, M. S., & Griffin, P. (Eds.) (1998). *Preventing reading difficulties in young children.* Washington, DC: National Academy Press.

Stevenson, H. W., & Newman, R. S. (1986). Long-term prediction of achievement and attitudes in mathematics and reading. *Child Development, 57,* 646–659.

Walsh, E. S. (1995). *Mouse Paint.* New York: Harcourt Brace.

Westcott, N. B. (1987). *Peanut butter and jelly: A play rhyme.* New York: Dutton Children's Books.

Whitehurst, G. J., & Lonigan, C. J. (2001). Emergent literacy: Development from prereaders to readers. In S. B. Neuman & D. K. Dickinson (Eds.), *Handbook of early literacy research* (pp. 11–29). New York: Guilford Press.

Williams, S. (1992). I *went walking.* New York: Harcourt Brace.

Developing Fluency with Hands-on Activities for Teaching Word Families and Letter Patterns

Use these word family words and letter pattern activities with first and second graders in:

▷ **The Alphabetic Word Fluency Stage**

As Shandra reads aloud, she meets a word she has never seen before. The way Shandra pronounces this new word is written above the line.

> *sa . . . sam . . . same*   *sa . . . same*
> Jolie and Jan are best friends. They play the *same* games. They like the *same*
>
> *sss . . . same*   *same*
> things and eat the *same* food. They even wear the *same* shoes.

On the first encounter, Shandra tries "*sa . . . sam*" and then self-corrects to read "*same*." On the second attempt, she begins with the familiar short vowel pronunciation, "*sa*," but quickly changes to "*same*." On the third try, she says "*sss*" to herself and then reads the whole word, "*same*." By the fourth encounter, Shandra recognizes *same* without sounding it out. Shandra knows a lot about phonics, about meaning, and about English syntax, and uses this information when she meets a word she does not recognize on sight. Children like Shandra, who know phonics and use phonics, are better readers and better spellers in the early grades (Adams, 1990; Byrne, Freebody, & Gates, 1992; National Institute of Child Health and Human Development, 2000; Rupley & Willson, 1997).

Most of the words children learn to read and write are not memorized in class, drilled by their teachers, or even frequently repeated in stories. There is not enough time to teach all the new words children meet in each school year (Adams, 1990). Perhaps if words are used over and over again children could learn them through sheer repetition. Whereas a handful of words do occur frequently, most do not, and the less-frequent words carry much of the meaning. For instance, other than in the context of the book B*iscuit* (Capucilli, 1997), which is part of a series about Biscuit the dog, children encounter *biscuit* only about three times in every one million words (Zeno, Ivens, Millard, & Duvvuri, 1995). B*ean*, from J*asper's Beanstalk* (Butterworth & Inkpen, 1997), appears in about ten of every one million words. S*weet*, from M*innie and Moo and the Musk of Zorro* (Cazet, 2000), occurs slightly over thirty times in one million words (Zeno, Ivens, Millard, & Duvvuri, 1995). While children do not regularly encounter *sweet*, they do encounter words spelled with *sw* (*sweep, swim, swift*), *ee* (*green, feel, speech*), and *eet* (*sweet, meet, feet*). Consequently, children use letter and sound cues to pronounce a great many words. The point is not so much how often a particular word appears in English text, but rather the reader's ability to use letter pattern cues to identify, learn, and remember words.

■■■■■ USING WORD FAMILIES TO DECODE BY ANALOGY

When children decode by analogy, they use letters in a familiar word, such as the *eet* in *sweet*, to infer the pronunciation of an unfamiliar word that is spelled with the same letters, as in *greet*. Children divide unfamiliar words into two chunks: (1) the beginning consonant(s), and (2) the vowel and final consonant(s). The beginning consonant(s) (*gr*) in a word or syllable is called the *onset*. The vowel and following consonants (*eet*) is called the *rime*. A rime may have more than one vowel letter (*eet*), but never more than one vowel sound. An onset may consist of up to three consonant sounds, as in the *str* in *street*. Words spelled with the same rime belong to the same word family. *Street*, *sweet*, *meet*, and *feet* all belong to the *eet* family. Words in the *an* family consist of *ban*, *can*, *clan*, *Dan*, *fan*, *man*, *Nan*, *pan*, *plan*, *ran*, *tan*, and *van*; the *ig* family includes *big*, *dig*, *fig*, *jig*, *pig*, *rig*, *wig*, *swig*, and *twig*; *ot* family members include *cot*, *dot*, *got*, *hot*, *jot*, *lot*, *not*, *pot*, *rot*, *tot*, *blot*, *plot*, *shot*, *slot*, *spot*, and *trot*. Table 4–1 shows one-syllable and two-syllable words divided in onsets and rimes. Kindergarten, first-, and second-grade teachers emphasize rimes in one-syllable words because the rimes in these words are far more obvious than the rimes in multi-syllable words. Look at Table 4–2 for a list of rimes that are part of many English words.

The rimes in words are intact multi-letter and multi-sound patterns. For example, in *ship* the *sh* = /sh/ and the *ip* = /ip/. It is much simpler to blend onsets and rimes than to blend individual letter-sounds. Children have fewer individual sound groups to remember, sequence, and fold together when blending onsets and rimes. For instance, dividing *ship* into onset and rime (*sh* and *ip*) requires that children only blend /sh/ + /ip/, while dividing *ship* into individual letter-sounds calls for blending /sh/ + /i/ + /p/. When children decode by analogy, they:

TABLE 4–1 Onsets and Rimes in One-syllable Words

Word	Onset	Rime	Word	Onset	Rime
sad	s	ad	drank	dr	ank
told	t	old	ring	r	ing
splat	spl	at	spill	sp	ill
couch	c	ouch	tweet	tw	eet
train	tr	ain	strike	str	ike
bright	br	ight	heat	h	eat
clamp	cl	amp	wild	w	ild

Onsets and Rimes in Two-syllable Words

Word	First syllable Onset	Rime	Second syllable Onset	Rime
complete	c	om	pl	ete
pencil	p	en	c	il
garden	g	ar	d	en
fifteen	f	if	t	een
finish	f	in		ish
something	s	ome	th	ing
rabbit	r	ab	b	it
surprise	s	ur	pr	ise
playtime	pl	ay	t	ime
hotdog	h	ot	d	og
lantern	l	an	t	ern
carpet	c	ar	p	et

1. Identify the rime in a word they have never seen before, such as the *ake* in *stake*.
2. Compare the new word, *stake*, with a known word family word, such as *make*.
3. Remove the /m/ from *make* and replace it with /st/ to pronounce /stake/.

The vowels in rimes have a certain consistency or dependability. For example, the *i* in *it* represents the short sound in *sit* and *fit*; likewise, the *i* in *ind* represents the long vowel sound in *mind* and *find*. Knowing the sounds associated with word family patterns, such as *it* and *ind*, allows children to develop a relatively dependable knowledge base for identifying word family words. It is not surprising, then, that beginning readers seize on the regularity of the rimes in word family words (Goswami, 2001). This said, we can depend on exceptions in English, even when word family rimes are concerned. For instance, the *aid* family, which consists of words like *laid*, *maid*, *paid*, and *raid*, does not include among its members the words *said* and *plaid*.

WHAT YOU NEED TO KNOW TO EFFECTIVELY TEACH DECODING WITH WORD FAMILIES

In teaching children to decode by analogy, you help children learn how to use what they already know (the rime in a familiar word family word) to pronounce an unfamiliar word in the same word family. Follow these guidelines when teaching children to decode word family words with analogy:

1. *Show Children How to Decode by Analogy*   Children's ability to decode by analogy is likely to develop much faster when you explicitly teach them how to use this strategy (Goswami, 2001; Savage, 2001). Some children will not begin to make analogies

Word Family	Examples	Word Family	Examples
ab	cab, grab, lab, tab	ell	bell, fell, sell, tell
ace	face, place, race, space	en	den, hen, men, pen
ack	back, black, sack, track	ent	bent, sent, tent, went
ad	bad, had, mad, sad	est	best, rest, test, west
ade	grade, made, shade, trade	et	bet, set, pet, wet
ag	bag, flag, rag, tag	ice	dice, mice, nice, twice
ail	fail, mail, sail, tail	ick	brick, lick, quick, trick
ain	gain, main, pain, train	ide	bride, side, tide, wide
air	chair, fair, pair, stair	ig	big, dig, pig, wig
ake	bake, make, take, wake	ight	fight, night, right, sight
all	ball, call, fall, tall	ill	bill, fill, hill, pill
am	clam, ham, ram, slam	in	fin, pin, thin, win
ame	came, game, name, same	ing	king, ring, sing, sting
amp	camp, damp, lamp, stamp	ink	link, pink, sink, wink
an	can, fan, man, tan	ip	dip, hip, ship, slip
and	band, hand, land, sand	it	hit, pit, sit, slit
ang	bang, hang, rang, sang	ock	block, rock, sock, stock
ank	blank, drank, rank, sank	og	dog, frog, hog, log
ap	cap, lap, map, nap	old	cold, fold, hold, told
at	cat, fat, hat, sat	op	hop, mop, pop, stop
ate	date, gate, late, rate	ot	dot, hot, got, lot
eam	beam, cream, dream, team	ug	bug, dug, hug, tug
eat	beat, meat, neat, seat	ump	bump, dump, hump, pump
ed	bed, fed, led, red	un	bun, fun, run, sun
eed	deed, feed, need, seed	ut	but, cut, nut, shut

TABLE 4–2 Fifty Common Word Families for Word Study

among word family words unless you explicitly teach them how to do this. As these children watch you demonstrate decoding by analogy, they learn how decoding by analogy works and, consequently, become better at using this decoding strategy.

2. *Teach Rhyme Awareness*   Decoding by analogy depends on the ability to separate words into onsets and rimes, and to identify, classify, and produce rhyming words (Goswami, 2001). Children who tell you that *top* begins with /t/ and rhymes with *mop*, and explain that *mop* and *top* both have /op/ in their pronunciation, are aware of onsets and rimes. If children cannot identify the beginning sound in words, then you should teach them this phonemic awareness skill. If children cannot identify, classify, and produce rhyming words, then you should teach children to listen for and identify the rhymes in word family words.

3. *Use Clue Words to Teach Decoding by Analogy*   The children in your classroom learn more words with less effort when you teach them how to use clue words to decode by analogy (Wang & Gaffney, 1998). Clue words are known words that children refer to when they see a familiar rime in a word family word. For instance, *make* might be the clue word for the *ake* word family; *pig* for *ig*; *fan* for *an*; *bug* for *ug*. When a child meets a new word, the child: (1) identifies the word family rime in the new word; (2) remembers the clue word (e.g., *make*); (3) associates rime in the word family clue word (/ake/) with the rime in the new word; and (4) uses the rime in the word family clue word (*make*) to infer the pronunciation of a new word (*bake*).

Put word family clue words on the word wall and remind children to refer to them when decoding. For example, when a child meets the new word *bake* in the sentence *Mary wanted to bake an apple pie*, you might ask questions like: "What word family word do you know that looks a lot like this one?" "What word do you know that has *ake*?" "Can you think of another *ake* word that will help you figure out this one?" "Can you see a word under the Mm on the word wall that is spelled a lot like this one?" In each of these examples, you remind the child to refer to a word family clue word (*make*) to identify a new word (*bake*) that belongs to the same family.

4. *Teach Children How the Letters in Word Families Represent Sound*   Children are better at decoding by analogy when they know how each letter in a rime represents sound (Wang & Gaffney, 1998). In fact, some knowledge of letter-sound relationships may be necessary for children to successfully decode by analogy (Ehri & Robbins, 1992; Goswami, 1999). The most effective instruction includes: (1) phonics instruction in which children learn how the letters in word families represent sounds, (2) phonemic awareness instruction in separating words into sounds, and (3) phonemic awareness instruction in blending sounds into whole words (Gaskins et al., 1996/1997; Juel & Minden-Cupp, 2000). For example, you might show children how *at* is part of many different words in the *at* family (*sat, fat, mat*). Then take instruction a step further by teaching children the letter and sound associations in *at*. Teach children how the letter *a* represents the short *a* sound, /a/, and how the letter *t* represents the /t/ sound. Learning how the letters in rimes represent sounds helps children remember word families and increases children's success using word families to decode (Gaskins et al., 1996/1997; Juel & Minden-Cupp, 2000).

5. *Increase Children's Reading Vocabulary*   Children who know how to read many words are better at decoding with analogy and make fewer decoding miscues than children who know how to read just a few words (Wang & Gaffney, 1998). Making analogies requires that children know how to read enough words to make comparisons. The more words children read, the more comparison words they draw upon when making analogies. The fewer words children read, the fewer comparisons they make. Older children have larger reading vocabularies than younger children, so it makes sense that older children use analogies more than younger children (Goswami, 2001).

While the rimes in word family words are helpful to beginning readers, there are too many rimes in English to depend completely on teaching decoding through word families. Each word family rime represents one specific group of vowel and consonant sounds, such as the *ig* in *pig* and the *ot* in *hot*. The child who knows that *ot* represents /ot/ has to learn a different set of symbol-sound correspondences to read and write *it*, *ug*, and *ed*. Word family rimes are not generalizable; that is, knowing one word family rime does not help a child figure out the pronunciation of a word that is spelled with an unknown rime. Knowing *ot*, for example, does not help children read *pig*, *hot*, and *bug*, because these words belong to totally different word families.

DECODING WITH LETTER PATTERNS ■ ■ ■ ■ ▬▬

How Letter Patterns Stretch Our Alphabet

If our alphabet was perfect, every letter would represent one, and only one, sound. However, the English language uses forty-four sounds, but we have only twenty-six letters in our alphabet. Therefore, if we were to change our alphabet to make it represent one sound with one letter, we would need to add more letters. Since we do not have enough letters to represent each sound, we combine letters in different patterns. A letter pattern consists of two or more letters that represent sound. For example, the *sh* represents /sh/ in *ship*, the *oi* represents /oi/ in *soil*, the *oa* represents the long *o* in *boat*, and the VCe pattern (vowel-consonant-e) represents a long vowel sound (*same*, *hide*, *hope*, *fuse*). Letter patterns, then, are predictable letter sequences that represent one or more sounds in words.

Letter patterns help us stretch the alphabet. They allow us to use different letter groups to represent the sounds that are not represented by single letters. By combining the *sh* together, we have a letter pattern that represents a sound that is totally different from that of the two individual letters. We stretch the alphabet by adding *sh*, *ch*, *ph*, and *th*. We also stretch the alphabet by using the letter patterns *oi*, *oy*, *ow*, and *ou*, as in *soil*, *boy*, *cow*, and *ouch*. *Au* and *aw* represent the sounds in *caught* and *saw*, while *ar*, *er*, *ir*, *or*, and *ur* represent the sounds we hear in *car*, *her*, *stir*, *for*, and *fur*. Letter patterns give us insight into the long and short vowel sound in words. When we see a short word with a single vowel in the middle, we assume that the vowel is likely to be short (*hat*, *hem*, *him*, *hop*, *hut*). When we see a vowel followed by a consonant and an e (VCe), we assume that the vowel is most likely to be long (*came*, *kite*, *hole*, *mule*). When we see certain vowels side-by-side, we expect the sound to be long (*street*, *boat*, *nail*, *play*, *leaf*). Therefore, in addition to teaching word family words, we teach letter patterns. Once a child learns letter patterns, that child will sound out and spell any word that consists of the known patterns.

Letter Patterns Are Generalizable

Letter patterns are more generalizable than word family rimes. Our alphabet represents speech at the sound level, and letter patterns give us clues as to how to pronounce sounds. For example, children who understand the VC letter pattern sound out *mat*, *beg*, *bun*, *cop*, and *miss* with equal ease. Children need only know the VC pattern to sound out *mat*, *beg*, *bun*, *cop*, and *miss*. They do not need to know five different word families (*at*, *eg*, *un*, *op*, and *iss*). *Mat*, *bet*, *bun*, *cop*, *miss*, and many more short words are spelled with the VC letter pattern. Children who know this pattern have a basis for attempting to pronounce any word that fits the pattern.

The *ar* in *star* is another example of a letter pattern. The *ar* represents the r-controlled vowel pattern. This letter pattern, expressed as Vr, is generalizable to vowel and r sequences. The *r* completely changes the way we pronounce the vowel, as in *far*, *her*, *fir*, *for*, and *fur*. Let us consider another letter pattern, the vowel-consonant-silent e pattern. Many words are spelled with the VCe pattern in which a vowel is followed by a consonant and a silent final *e*. This pattern usually means that the first vowel, the one before the consonant and final *e*, represents its long sound, as in *dive*, *state*, *rode*, and *tube*. Letter patterns may consist of vowel and consonant combinations, vowels only, or consonants only. Look in Table 4–3 for consonant letter patterns and in Table 4–4 for vowel patterns.

TABLE 4–3 Consonant Patterns for Word Study	**Double Consonants**

Double consonants can occur in the middle (*rabbit*) or at the end (*miss*) of a word. One consonant sound is heard; the other is silent.

bb	*rabbit, ebb, ribbon*
dd	*hidden, ladder, puddle*
ff	*waffle, coffee, muffin*
ll	*jelly, bell, pillow*
mm	*summer, hammer, command*
nn	*dinner, minnow, funnel*
pp	*puppet, copper, happen*
rr	*carrot, burro, narrow*
zz	*buzz, drizzle, pizza*

Consonant Clusters

Consonant clusters consist of two or three consonants which are blended together when pronounced (*clown, spray*). Some teachers' manuals use the term *blend* to refer to the consonant clusters. Consonant clusters are taught as whole letter patterns rather than as single letters (e.g., *st* as representing two blended phonemes /st/, rather than an isolated /s/ and an isolated /t/). The most common clusters occur at the beginning of words or syllables and include the letters *r, l,* and *s*.

r Clusters	Words	l Clusters	Words	s Clusters	Words	w Clusters	Words
br	*bright*	*bl*	*black*	*sc*	*scout*	*dw*	*dwell*
cr	*crayon*	*cl*	*class*	*scr*	*scream*	*sw*	*swing*
dr	*dress*	*fl*	*flower*	*sk*	*sky*	*tw*	*twin*
fr	*free*	*gl*	*glad*	*sm*	*small*		
gr	*green*	*pl*	*plan*	*sn*	*snow*		
pr	*pretty*	*sl*	*slide*	*sp*	*spot*		
shr	*shrink*			*spl*	*splash*		
thr	*three*			*spr*	*spring*		
tr	*train*			*squ*	*square*		
				st	*stop*		
				str	*string*		

Many consonant clusters occur at the end of English words or syllables. Final clusters are sometimes taught as part of word families, such as *old* (*told*), *ild* (*wild*); *ilk* (*milk*); and *alt* (*salt*).

Final Clusters	Words	Final Clusters	Words
ct	*fact*	*nch*	*bunch*
ft	*lift*	*nd*	*end*
ld	*old*	*nk*	*pink*
lk	*milk*	*nt*	*went*
lp	*help*	*pt*	*kept*
lt	*salt*	*sk*	*desk*
mp	*jump*	*sp*	*grasp*
		st	*last*

The *l* in *lk* is frequently silent: *balk, chalk, folk, stalk, talk, walk, yolk.* If you hear /l/ in these words, it is because of regional dialect.

TABLE 4–3 Continued.

Consonant Digraphs

Consonant digraphs consist of two letters that represent one sound, and that sound is different from the sound that the letters individually represent.

Digraphs	Words	Digraphs	Words
ch	chair	ck	thick*
ph	phone	dg	fudge
sh	shoe	ng	king
unvoiced th	thumb	nk	think
voiced th	that		
wh	whale		

We pronounce *th* two different ways: The unvoiced *th* is whispered, as in *think*. We use our vocal cords to pronounce the voiced *th*, as in *this*.

*ck represents /k/ at the end of words or syllables with a short vowel.

c + Vowel Patterns

The letter *C* represents two sounds: (1) a hard sound as heard in *cat*, and (2) a soft sound as in *city*. The *C* usually represents /k/ (the hard sound) when followed by *a* (*cat*), *o* (*coat*), or *u* (*cut*), when it appears at the end of a word (*comic*), and when followed by any other letter (*cloud*). *C* usually represents /s/ (the soft sound) when it is followed by *e* (*cent*), *i* (*city*), or *y* (*cycle*).

c plus a, o, u	Words	c plus e, i, y	Words
ca	cat (/k/) (hard sound)	ce (/s/)	cent (soft sound)
co	coat (k) (hard sound)	ci (/s/)	city (soft sound)
cu	cut (/k/) (hard sound)	cy (/s/)	cycle (soft sound)

g + Vowel Patterns

The letter *G* represents two sounds: (1) a hard sound, as heard in *goat*, and (2) a soft sound, as heard in *gem*. *G* usually represents /g/ (the hard sound) when it is followed by *a* (*gate*), *o* (*go*), or *u* (*gum*), when it appears at the end of a word (*leg*), and when followed by any other consonant letter (*glass*). *G* may represent /j/ (the soft sound) when it is followed by the vowels *e* (*gerbil*), *i* (*giant*), or *y* (*gypsy*), although with exceptions.

g plus a, o, u	Words	g plus e, i, y	Words
ga	gate (hard sound)	ge	gerbil (soft sound)
go	go (hard sound)	gi	giant (soft sound)
gu	gum (hard sound)	gy	gypsy (soft sound)

Silent Letters

Some letters are silent; that is, they do not represent a sound. There are eight silent letter patterns: *mb, bt, ght, gn, kn, lk, tch,* and *wr*.

Silent Pattern	Words	Explanation
bt	doubt	*B* is silent when preceding *t* in a syllable.
ght	night	*Gh* is silent following *t* in a syllable.
gn	align	*G* is silent following *n* in a syllable.
kn	knight	*K* is silent when preceding *n* at the beginning of words.
lk	chalk	*L* is silent when preceding *k* in a syllable.
mb	bomb	*B* is silent following *m* in a syllable.
tch	witch	*T* is silent when preceding *ch* in a syllable.
wr	write	*W* is silent when preceding *r* at the beginning of words.

TABLE 4–4 Vowel
Patterns for Word Study

Short Vowels	Symbols	Key Words	Long Vowels	Symbols	Key Words
a	ă	*apple*	a	ā	*apron*
e	ĕ	*egg*	e	ē	*eraser*
i	ĭ	*igloo*	i	ī	*ice*
o	ŏ	*ox*	o	ō	*overalls*
u	ŭ	*umbrella*	u	ū	*umbrella*

We use a breve (˘) to indicate short vowel sounds, and a macron (-) to indicate long vowel sounds.

VC Short Vowel Pattern

The most common vowel-consonant pattern is that of the VC (vowel-consonant) in which the V (vowel) represents its short sound. One, two, or three consonants may precede the vowel in the VC pattern.

Vowel	Words with a VC Pattern
a + Consonant	*at, pat, patch, trap, man, crab, mad, mast*
e + Consonant	*etch, pet, stretch, bed, leg, pen, step, dress*
i + Consonant	*it, hit, hitch, stick, rib, trim, spin, trip, miss*
o + Consonant	*ox, pot, soft, blob, prod, off, toss, log, nod*
u + Consonant	*up, pup, punch, drum, shut, clutch, fuss, bus*

VCCe Short Vowel Pattern

When the V (vowel) is followed by two consonants and a final e (VCCe), we usually use a short sound when pronouncing the first vowel and the final e is silent.

VCCe Pattern	Words
aCCe	*dance, romance, chance, lapse*
eCCe	*fence, ledge, sense, edge*
iCCe	*since, rinse, bridge, prince*
oCCe	*bronze, dodge, blonde, lodge*
uCCe	*smudge, plunge, judge, lunge*

VCe Long Vowel Pattern

When a V (vowel) is followed by a consonant and a final e (VCe), the e is silent and the first vowel usually represents the long sound.

VCe Pattern	Words
aVe	*ape, ate, name, face, made, cage, cake, drape, wave*
iVe	*hide, ice, like, smile, dime, dine, pipe, bite, hive, bride*
oVe	*hope, hole, dome, close, vote, drove, bone, code, dose*
uVe	*huge, cube, cute, mule, accuse, use, fume, fuse*

CV Long Vowel Pattern

The vowel is usually long in words and syllables that end in a vowel letter and vowel sound (CV).

CV Pattern	Words
Consonant + ay	*day, tray, sway, gay, may, play, stray*
Consonant + e	*be, me, he, we, she*
Consonant + o	*go, no, so, pro*
Consonant + y	*try, by, dry, my, cry, fly, fry, sky, pry, shy, sly, spy*

VV Long Vowel Pattern

TABLE 4–4 Continued.

In the VV pattern, two vowels appear together in a word or syllable. The first vowel usually represents the long sound and the second vowel is silent. Some vowel pairs follow the generalization more consistently than others. This pattern is also called vowel pairs or vowel teams.

VV	Words
ai	rain, nail, wait, fail, drain, mail, maid, pail, paid, train
ay	play, day, may, clay, tray, gay, hay, lay, pay, say, way
oa	boat, coal, coat, foam, goal, load, loaf, loan, road, soak
ea	each, bean, deal, heat, heap, lead, leaf, leak, meal, mean
ee	keep, sleep, beef, beet, feed, feel, feet, keep, meet, peek
ie	pie, die, tie, lie

Vowel Diphthongs

A diphthong is a single vowel phoneme, represented by two letters, which resembles a glide from one sound to another. We teach children about two diphthong sounds. Two different letter combinations represent each sound. (1) Both *ou* and *ow* represent the same sound. When this sound is heard at the beginning (*ouch*) and middle (*couch*) of a word, it is represented by the letters *ou;* when this sound appears at the end of a word (*cow*) or syllable (*power*), the sound is represented by the letters *ow*. (2) Both *oi* and *oy* represent the same sound. When this sound is heard at the beginning (*oink*) or in the middle (*coin*) of a word, it is represented by the letters *oi*. When this sound is heard at the end of a word (*boy*) or syllable (*foyer*), it is represented by the letters *oy*.

Diphthong Pairs	Words	Diphthong Pairs	Words
ou	mouse, cloud, couch, count	oi	coin, boil, soil, joint
ow	town, fowl, brown	oy	boy, toy, joy

OO V Pattern

oo Pattern	Words
oo	food, moon, spoon, broom, boot
oo	hook, took, good, hoof, root, wood

You may see the sound of *oo* in *food* represented by $\overline{oo}$ in teachers' manuals. This is the same sound we use to identify the long *u* (*tune* and *blue*).

Vr (R-controlled) Vowel Pattern

When the only vowel letter in a word or syllable is followed by *r*, the vowel will be affected by that *r*, and the vowel sound is almost lost in the consonant.

Vr	Words
ar	car, alarm, start, hard
er	her, gerbil, over, after
ir	bird, circle, fir, stir, shirt
or	corn, more, for, store, sort
ur	fur, burden, spur, turn, hurt

a Followed by l, ll, w, and u

The letter *a* often represents the sound in *salt* (al), *tall* (all), *saw* (aw), and *haul* (au) when followed by l, ll, w, and u.

al	Words	all	Words	aw	Words	au	Words
al	almost	all	tall	aw	saw	au	haul
	bald		call		draw		fraud
	calm		mall		jaw		clause
	halt		fall		law		fault

TABLE 4–4   Continued.   Vowels in Unaccented Syllables

The vowel in an unaccented syllable usually represents a soft "uh," or the sound we associate with short *i*. The dictionary uses a schwa (ə) to indicate the soft "uh" sound in many unaccented syllables. The vowel in unaccented syllables represents the soft "uh" more often than the short *i*.

Schwa ("uh")	Examples
a (ə)	comm<u>a</u> (soft "uh")
e (ə)	chick<u>e</u>n (soft "uh")
i (ə)	fam<u>i</u>ly (soft "uh")
o (ə)	butt<u>o</u>n (soft "uh")
u (ə)	circ<u>u</u>s (soft "uh")

How Children Decode with Letter Patterns

When children decode with letter patterns, they:

1. Consider the left-to-right letter sequence in an unfamiliar word.
2. Identify the letter patterns in the word.
3. Associate sounds with the letter patterns.
4. Blend sounds together to pronounce a familiar, contextually appropriate word.

Children consider the letters from left-to-right because the letters to the right of the vowel affect the vowel pronunciation. For instance, if we were to sound out *star* single letter-sound by single letter-sound, we would pronounce something like /s/ /t/ /a/ (short *a* as in *apple*) /r/ (as in *ring*). Blended together, these sounds would not even come close to /star/. In order to solve the pronunciation of *star*, we absolutely must stand back from single letters and think about how to group letters into patterns. In so doing, we observe that *star* consists of two letter patterns: (1) the *st* consonant blend, and (2) the *ar*, which is an r-controlled vowel. Once we associate sounds with the letter patterns, /st/ and /ar/, all we need to do is blend the sounds together to pronounce a textually meaningful word.

■■■■ ■ ■ ■ ■   ## WHAT YOU NEED TO KNOW TO EFFECTIVELY TEACH DECODING WITH LETTER PATTERNS

Good readers are more sensitive to letter patterns than less-skilled readers (Gottardo, Chiappe, Siegel, & Stanovich, 1999). Understanding how print represents speech is an effective, and indeed necessary, pathway to reading fluency. We need to help children become aware of letter patterns and the sounds they represent, and we also need to teach children how to apply letter patterns to decoding. Teach letter patterns in the real words children read and spell everyday in your classroom, and follow these five teaching guidelines for effective teaching:

1. *Show Children How to Decode with Letter Patterns*   We cannot assume that children automatically infer how to use letter patterns to identify new words. Show children how to associate sounds with the letter patterns in words and how to blend sounds together to pronounce words. Children who are just learning how to decode pattern-by-pattern, and this includes low-progress first graders, benefit from watching you use pattern-by-pattern decoding while using semantic and syntactic cues to streamline decoding (Juel & Minden-Cupp, 2000). Select real words children are reading in your classroom and think aloud as you decode. Describe the process you go through in decoding, and then give children practice using the

patterns in words along with semantic and syntactic cues to figure out words they have never seen before.

2. *Teach Phonemic Awareness, When Needed*   Average first graders have good sound awareness by the spring of the year. While these children have enough phonemic awareness to support decoding, they continue to refine and extend phonemic awareness as they read and write. If children have enough phonemic awareness to support decoding, you do not have to spend much, if any, time on phonemic awareness. However, some children continue to need instruction in phonemic awareness because, by the end of the first grade, they still have not become skilled at separating words into sounds and blending sounds into words. Teach phonemic awareness to children who need to develop this skill; do not teach it to children who have enough awareness to decode successfully.

3. *Balance Teaching Decoding with Letter Patterns with Decoding by Analogy*   You will be a more effective phonics teacher if you teach letter patterns and word family words. Children have larger reading vocabularies when their teachers teach both letter patterns and word family rimes (Juel & Minden-Cupp, 2000). Interestingly, children who know many letter patterns make fewer miscues when decoding by analogy than children who know few patterns (Wang & Gaffney, 1998). Therefore, we can say that your classroom language arts program benefits from a balanced approach to decoding that gives children instruction in, and opportunities to use, both decoding by analogy and decoding by letter patterns.

4. *Teach on Instructional Level*   Instructional level is the level at which children read with a typical amount of help from their teachers. Word recognition ranges from 90 to 95 percent correct and comprehension from 70 to 89 percent (McCormick, 1999). Since instructional level books have a few words that children do not rapidly recognize, there is room for children to apply decoding strategies. However, there are not so many new words that children lose meaning or get bogged down in decoding. Limiting the number of hard words gives you the opportunity to help children by modeling and demonstrating decoding. Additionally, text that has only a few hard words gives children opportunities to use their knowledge of letter patterns to decode words in meaningful contexts. Since the focus is on understanding the text, children are encouraged to self-monitor and cross-check when decoding.

5. *Develop Decoding Flexibility*   Flexible decoders try the most logical sounds first and then, if those sounds do not produce a recognizable word, decoders try other possible sounds. Flexible decoders have a backup plan; that is, one or more sounds to try if the first attempt fails. For example, the *oo* pattern (see Table 4–4) almost always represents two sounds: the /oo/ in *food* and the /oo/ in *hook*. There are no clues as to which of these two sounds the *oo* represents in a new word. The flexible decoder knows to try one sound, say the /oo/ in *food* and, if that does not produce a meaningful word, to try the other *oo* sound, the sound heard in *hook*. The flexible decoder knows that one of these two sounds is going to work.

The flexible decoder knows to automatically go to a backup plan when decoding does not work on the first try. Let's use the word *have* as an example. *Have* is spelled with a VCe pattern (Table 4–4) and therefore the *a* should be pronounced as a long sound (as heard in *cave*; Table 4–4). But *have* is not consistent with the VCe pattern. Does this mean that the child is completely stumped? No. The *h* and *v* each represent predictable sounds, /h/ and /v/, respectively. This leaves the pesky vowel, the *a*. The wise and flexible decoder tries the long sound first. When this does not work, the flexible decoder automatically tries the short vowel sound (as heard in *apple*, Table 4–4).

Flexibility is built on a solid knowledge of letter patterns and the mindset to try decoding more than once. The child who knows only a few letter patterns does not have the knowledge needed to guide second attempts. However, a knowledgeable child who does not go beyond one attempt is puzzled by exception words (*have*), and words with patterns that represent more than one sound (the *oo* in *food* and *hook*; the *ow* in *row* and *clown*). Neither child is an independent decoder, because each child has to rely on someone else for help if the first try is not successful. While our alphabetic writing system is certainly not perfect, choices (when they exist) are finite and limited. In particular, help children develop the following flexible habits:

1. When children see an unfamiliar word with a VCe pattern, help them develop the habit of trying the long vowel sound first and, if that does not work, advise them to try the short vowel sound.
2. When children see a VC pattern, help them learn to try a short vowel sound first. Then, if the short vowel sound does not make a meaningful word, advise them to try the long sound.
3. Teach children that when they see *oo* in words like *food* and *hook*, they may try either the sound in *food* or the sound in *hook*. If one sound does not work, the other one will.
4. Teach children that when they see a Vr pattern, the vowel is neither long nor short. Advise children to try /or/ when they see *or* (*more*). If this does not result in a pronounceable, meaningful word, help children learn to try the /er/ sound (*worm*). Help children learn to try the /er/ when they see *er*, *ir*, or *ur* (*her, sir*, sure) and to try the /ar/ when they see *ar*/ (*star*).
5. Help children learn to try the /s/ for the letter *c* when they see *ce, ci*, and *cy* (*cent, city, cycle*). If this does not result in a meaningful word, help children learn to try the /k/ sound as a *backup*.
6. Teach children that, if they see *ca, co*, or *cu*, they should try the /k/ sound (*cat, coat, cut*). If this does not make a meaningful word that fits the context, help children learn to try the /s/ sound.
7. Help children learn to try the /g/ sound when they see *ga, go*, and *gu* (*gay, goat, guy*). If the /g/ sound does not work, teach children to try the /j/ sound.
8. Teach children to try the /j/ sound when they see *ge, gi*, and *gy* (*gem, giant, gypsy*). If the /j/ sound does result in a word that makes sense in the reading context, teach children to try the /g/ sound next.
9. When children see *ow* in a word, help them learn to try the long *o* as in *snow* or the /ow/ as in *cow*. If one sound does not make a contextually meaningful word, the other probably will.

■■■ ■ ■ ■ USING DECODABLE BOOKS

Decodable words sound like they are spelled. These words follow the spelling-to-sound conventions of phonics, and hence readers use their knowledge of letter patterns to figure out pronunciation. Decodable books derive their name from the unusually high number of decodable words that make up the text. The high density of decodable words gives children much needed opportunities to apply phonics knowledge while reading connected text. Focused practice using letter patterns not only helps children develop phonics knowledge, but also encourages them to use this knowledge to identify unfamiliar words (Juel & Roper-Schneider, 1985).

Because the text in decodable books may be somewhat artificial, these books should not replace good quality literature or limit reading choices. Select decodable books that match your classroom curriculum, have the best plots, and use the most natural language patterns. Use decodable books when children are learning letter patterns, usually in the first grade. Children who are already skilled at decoding do not need to read decodable books. Decodable books are useful under three circumstances: (1) when children in the partial alphabetic stage are moving into the alphabetic word fluency stage (Mesmer, 2001); (2) when children in the alphabetic stage lack fluency using particular letter patterns; and (3) when children have letter pattern knowledge but do not use it. In this last circumstance, reading decodable books demonstrates to children that using patterns is a useful reading tool. If you remember that decodable books serve a very specific purpose and use decodable books to serve this purpose, then the books will be used the way they are intended and children will benefit from practice using the letter patterns they are learning in your classroom.

LEARNING ABOUT WORD FAMILIES AND LETTER PATTERNS ■ ■ ■ ■ ▬ IN THE ALPHABETIC WORD FLUENCY STAGE

Stage 3. Alphabetic Word Fluency: Late Kindergarten, First and Second Grade

Cheyenne (Figure 4–1) is a first grader who has just entered the alphabetic stage of word fluency. Cheyenne conventionally spells I, *won, a, fish, my, mom, win, it, like, the,* and *was.* All other words are spelled phonetically, or invently. We can read these words because Cheyenne writes a letter for each sound, as we see in *golld* for *gold*

FIGURE 4–1 Alphabetic Writing Sample (Gold Fish)

hilpt for *helped*, and *fier* for *fair*. As a beginning first grader, Cheyenne sounds out and spells short words. She pays attention to vowels in words and puts a vowel in most syllables she spells.

Table 4–5 shows the weekly teaching guide for children like Cheyenne, who are in the first half of the first grade year. Cheyenne can sound out VC words and is learning to sound out VCe words. Decoding is often slow and time-consuming. However, by the end of the first grade, Cheyenne will be a faster and more accurate decoder. At this point in her progress toward fluency, Cheyenne benefits from learning about word family words and letter patterns. The weekly guide calls for teaching letter patterns daily, and for teaching word family words and phonemic awareness three times a week. Teaching phonemic awareness and letter patterns in the same lesson is more effective than teaching these two areas separately. The purpose of teaching word meaning twice each week is to develop language and to ensure that children have the words in their speaking vocabulary that they meet in text. The guide calls for setting aside time once a week to develop speed and accuracy in recognizing letter patterns, word family words, and whole words. While children like Cheyenne cannot read silently, they can read orally, and hence benefit from developing oral reading fluency (explained in Chapter 7).

Maryanne, a first grader (Figure 4–2) who is just beginning the second half of first grade, uses her knowledge of word family words and letter patterns to read and to spell. Maryanne enjoys playing on the monkey bars (*mucey bras*) at school. She still spells phonetically, or inventedly. However, she knows more words than Cheyenne and, not coincidentally, is faster at decoding. Table 4–6 shows the weekly teaching guide for the second half of the first grade. The guide suggests teaching word family words as needed. By the second half of first grade some children have

FIGURE 4–2 Alphabetic Writing Sample (Monkey Bars)

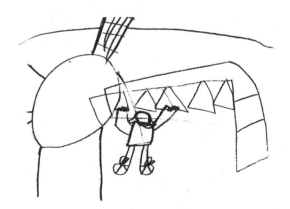

TABLE 4–5 First Grade Weekly Teaching Guide: First Half of the Year for Children in the Alphabetic Word Fluency Stage*

MONDAY	TUESDAY	WEDNESDAY	THURSDAY	FRIDAY
	Phonemic Awareness Beginning, middle, and ending sounds and, blending ⟺	**Phonemic Awareness** Beginning, middle, and ending sounds and, blending ⟺		**Phonemic Awareness** Beginning, middle, and ending sounds and, blending ⟺
Letter Patterns Teach in context and with focused study	**Letter Patterns** Teach in context and with focused study	**Letter Patterns** Teach in context and with focused study	**Letter Patterns** Teach in context and with focused study	**Letter Patterns** Teach in context and with focused study
Word Family Words			**Word Family Words**	
			Fluency Letter patterns, word family words, rapid word recognition, or oral reading fluency	
Word Meaning Teach in context and with focused study	**Word Meaning** Teach in context and with focused study			

Teach phonemic awareness along with phonics, when appropriate.
*For children who do not have developmental or learning disabilities.

TABLE 4–6 First Grade Weekly Teaching Guide: Second Half of the Year for Children in the Alphabetic Word Fluency Stage*

MONDAY	TUESDAY	WEDNESDAY	THURSDAY	FRIDAY
			Phonemic Awareness Beginning, middle, and ending sounds blending	**Phonemic Awareness** Beginning, middle, and ending sounds blending (as needed)
		Letter Patterns Teach in context and with focused study	**Letter Patterns** Teach in context and with focused study	**Letter Patterns** Teach in context and with focused study
Word Family Words (as needed)	**Word Family Words** (as needed)		**Word Family Words** (as needed)	
Structural Analysis High utility prefixes, suffixes, and compound words Teach in context and with focused study	**Structural Analysis** High utility prefixes, suffixes, and compound words Teach in context and with focused study			
	Fluency Letter patterns, word family words, rapid word recognition, or oral reading fluency			**Fluency** Letter patterns, word family words, rapid word recognition, or oral reading fluency
Word Meaning Teach in context and with focused study	**Word Meaning** Teach in context and with focused study	**Word Meaning** Teach in context and with focused study		

Teach phonemic awareness along with phonics, when appropriate.
*For children who do not have developmental or learning disabilities.

learned the highly useful word family words and are ready to move on to a more detailed study of letter patterns. Maryanne has not yet reached this point, so her teacher will teach word family words twice a week until Maryanne is more proficient at reading and spelling word families.

Children in the second half of first grade are beginning to notice and use word structures (suffixes like the -ing in playing and the -ed in played). Therefore, the guide calls for teaching structural analysis, which we will discuss in Chapter 6. Because children read more varied text, they are more likely to meet words whose definitions they do not completely understand. Therefore word meaning is taught at least three times a week in the second half of first grade. Fluency is also important. It is suggested that time be set aside to teach fluency twice each week with a focus on letter patterns, word family words, rapid whole word recognition, or oral reading (Chapter 7). Fluency activities are usually timed and require only a short amount of class time. The children whom we teach consider fluency activities to be more game-like than any other activity we use.

Peter (Figure 4–3) is in the first half of second grade. He knows word family words and the basic long and short vowel patterns. He is now refining his knowledge of diphthongs, as well as r-controlled and other patterns, like aw and au. Table 4–7 shows the weekly teaching guide for second graders like Peter. The optional phonemic awareness lesson is useful for children who are not yet completely proficient at blending and separating words into sounds. Word family words are not taught in the second grade because children already know the high utility word families. At this point in their progress toward word fluency, children benefit from refining their knowledge of letter patterns and exploring the large structures in words (explained in Chapter 5). Peter reads independently and his fluent reading vocabulary is growing rapidly. Fluency and word meaning continue to be significant and hence are part of the weekly teaching guide. As a consequence of good instruction and experiences in reading and writing, Peter is a successful second grade reader. By all indications he will be through the alphabetic stage and into the consolidated word fluency stage before the end of second grade.

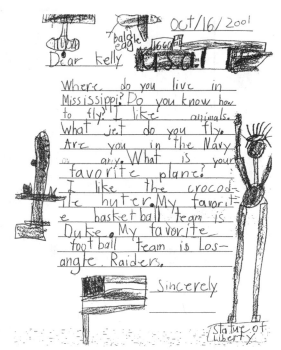

FIGURE 4–3 Consolidated Writing Sample (Letter to the Troops)

HANDS-ON TEACHING ACTIVITIES FOR TEACHING WORD FAMILIES AND LETTER PATTERNS

Children need to know the letter-sound associations in word families to decode by analogy, and need to know letter patterns to decode pattern-by-pattern (Palmer, 2000). The specific word families and letter patterns any individual child knows at any point in time depends on the classroom curriculum, the child's ability to learn word families and use letter patterns, and the amount of print exposure gained through reading and writing. Use these teaching strategies and activities to develop and reinforce knowledge of letter patterns and word families. However, just knowing word families and letter patterns is not enough; children must also be fluent using word families and letter patterns to decode new words. Therefore, some of the strategies and activities also develop fluency with letter patterns and word family words.

When using these and other teaching activities, keep in mind that sounding out words does not give children word meaning unless they: (1) already know the word in speech or (2) can infer meaning from the sentence context. Give children

TABLE 4–7 First Grade Weekly Teaching Guide: Second Half of the Year for Children in the Alphabetic Word Fluency Stage*

MONDAY	TUESDAY	WEDNESDAY	THURSDAY	FRIDAY
		Phonemic Awareness** (optional) ⟺		
		Letter Patterns Teach in context and with focused study	**Letter Patterns** Teach in context and with focused study	**Letter Patterns** Teach in context and with focused study
Structural Analysis High utility prefixes, suffixes, compound words, and contractions Teach in context and with focused study		**Structural Analysis** High utility prefixes, suffixes, compound words, and contractions Teach in context and with focused study		
	Fluency Letter patterns (if needed), word structure, rapid word recognition, oral and silent reading fluency			**Fluency** Letter patterns (if needed), word structure, rapid word recognition, oral and silent reading fluency
Word Meaning Teach in context and with focused study	**Word Meaning** Teach in context and with focused study			**Word Meaning** Teach in context and with focused study

Teach phonemic awareness along with phonics, when appropriate.
*For children who do not have developmental or learning disabilities.
**For children who cannot consciously manipulate the sounds in words.

practice decoding words they already know in spoken language, and pre-teach the new words in sentences that have weak context clues and new words that are far afield from children's life experiences.

Use these activities to develop a fully articulated knowledge of alphabetic writing, including word families and letter patterns. Tailor activities to children's preferences, language, and cultural backgrounds. Teach only those word families and letter patterns that children either do not yet know or lack fluency in using. And, of course, teach the word families and letter patterns that children need in order to read and write in your classroom. In refining and elaborating knowledge of the rimes in word family words and letter patterns, children at the alphabetic phase move toward, and eventually enter into, the consolidated word learning.

LETTER PATTERN DECODING

▷ LARGE GROUP
SMALL GROUP
LETTER PATTERNS

We have found that four different teaching strategies are effective in teaching children to decode letter pattern-by-letter pattern: (1) marking letter patterns with slashes; (2) indicating letter patterns with a highlighter; (3) color coding patterns; and (4) dissecting words into letter patterns. The relative effectiveness of one strategy over another depends on children's learning preferences (color – no color; tactile involvement), the words children are decoding, and your own teaching preferences. We prefer to use one teaching strategy for a while, and then sift to another strategy. In this way, children do not get bored with the same teaching routine and, additionally, children have opportunities to learn pattern-by-pattern decoding through a variety of teaching strategies.

MATERIALS: Highlighters in different colors; text on which children write; dissect practice sheet (Figure 4–4); decodable words.

1. MARKING LETTER PATTERNS WITH SLASHES Look in the books children are reading for words that have one or more letter patterns children are learning. Let us suppose that children are learning the *ou* and *ow* vowel diphthongs and the word *doubt* is in the children's books. Demonstrate how to partition *doubt* into letter patterns by putting slashes between the patterns: *d/ ou/ bt.* Talk about the sound the *ou* pattern represents, and also talk about the *bt* silent consonant pattern. Then show children how to say the sounds the patterns represent and blend these sounds to pronounce *doubt.* Give children opportunities to practice putting slashes between letter patterns in other words with vowel diphthong patterns, talk about how to find letter patterns in words, and practice blending sounds into meaningful words. Have children read books with words spelled with this pattern. The vowel diphthong pattern is used so frequently that children are bound to encounter *ou* and *ow* words in context. Later, ask children to search text for words with this pattern. Write these words on the board. Ask children to put slashes between letter patterns in the words they themselves found in text.

2. HIGHLIGHTING LETTER PATTERNS This small group teaching strategy uses different color highlighters to show the letter patterns in words. Write a word on a chart. Use different color highlighters to mark each letter pattern. For example, to demonstrate how to decode *marsh* letter pattern-by-letter pattern, you might use a pink highlighter to show the *m,* a yellow to show the *ar,* and an orange to highlight *sh,* thus dividing marsh into *m-ar-sh.* Demonstrate highlighter pattern-by-pattern decoding with several words. Show children how to find letter patterns in words, associate sounds with patterns, and blend sounds into meaningful words. Then give children a chance to highlight the letter patterns in other words on the chart.

3. COLOR CODING LETTER PATTERNS Ask children to use a pencil to write several words with the same letter patterns, such as *boat, groan, roast, foam, road, loaf,* and *cloak,* then have children use a colored pencil to trace over the common letter pattern in the words. In examining whole, intact words, children get practice in finding a particular letter pattern inside words. Tracing over the pattern with a colored pencil helps reinforce, both kinesthetically and visually, the letters in the pattern. Look at the letter pattern word circle activity, described in this chapter, for an example of how to integrate color coded patterns into other activities.

FIGURE 4–4 Pattern-by-pattern Dissecting

Name: _____

Date: _____

Directions: Find the letter patterns in each word. Write the patterns on the lines. The first word is done for you.

1. play	_pl_	_ay_		
2. street	_____	_____	_____	
3. quaint	_____	_____	_____	
4. sway	_____	_____		
5. teeth	_____	_____	_____	
6. sneaker	_____	_____	_____	_____
7. smile	_____	_____		
8. toast	_____	_____	_____	
9. phone	_____	_____		
10. coach	_____	_____	_____	

Answers

2. street	str	ee	t	
3. quaint	qu	ai	nt	
4. sway	sw	ay		
5. teeth	t	ee	th	
6. sneaker	sn	ea	k	er
7. smile	sm	ile		
8. toast	t	oa	st	
9. phone	ph	one		
10. coach	c	oa	ch	

4. DISSECTING WORDS INTO LETTER PATTERNS In dissecting a word, children write each pattern in a word. Whole words are followed by as many lines as there are letter patterns in the words. For example, you might write *play* _____ _____. Show children how to find the letter patterns in *play* and write the patterns on the lines: *play pl ay.* Then associate sounds with *pl* and *ay,* and blend the sounds together to pronounce "play." Select words for dissecting from the books children are reading. Give children practice on the chalk board or on chart paper, then have children dissect on their own, preferably in a learning center. An example of a practice sheet is shown in Figure 4–4.

▷ SMALL GROUP
LETTER PATTERNS
WORD FAMILIES
WORD MEANING

STAINED GLASS WINDOWS

Children use colorful markers to write words with letter patterns or word families they are learning in your classroom. The plastic wrap naturally clings to windows, giving the window a kaleidoscopic glow.

MATERIALS: Plastic wrap (the kind that does not stick to itself while you are holding it); four magnets for every child in a small group; unlined paper; cookie sheets; pizza pans or some other flat metal object; permanent colored markers.

DIRECTIONS: Stained glass windows can be used with any words that consist of the letter patterns or word families children are learning. Have children work collaboratively to find words with the letter patterns or word families you specify in content area textbooks, storybooks, or chapter books. Engage children in sorting words according to letter patterns or word families, and in brainstorming ideas for pictures children might draw to illustrate word meaning. Invite small groups of children to gather around a table. Follow these steps to make stained glass windows:

1. Turn over a cookie sheet and tape a piece of white paper on it.
2. Tear off a piece of sturdy plastic wrap; put it on the cookie sheet.
3. Put one magnet on each corner of the cookie sheet to keep the plastic wrap in place.

4. Use a colored marker to write a word with a letter pattern or a word family.
5. Use a variety of colored markers to draw a picture to show word meaning.
6. Take off the magnets, and put the plastic wrap against the window.
7. Smooth out any wrinkles.

The wrap is invisible and hence the words and illustrations seem to be painted directly on the glass. Other suggestions for stained glass windows include making stained glass postcards, stained glass postal stamps, stained glass recycling ads, and stained glass ABC windows with a letter and a picture beginning with the letter (for readers in earlier stages).

CHILDREN WHO SPEAK LANGUAGES OTHER THAN ENGLISH AT HOME   Use stained glass windows to show the same words in two different languages and to introduce children's home languages to the rest of the class. A book like *Carlos and the Squash Plant; Carlos y la planta de calabaza* (Stevens, 1993), which is written in both English and Spanish, is a wonderful resource for making stained glass windows in two languages. In seeing English and Spanish text, children have opportunities to compare words in two languages and to appreciate literacy in English and Spanish.

Examples of Literature Connections

Stevens, J. R. (1993). *Carlos and the squash plant; Carlos y la planta de calabaza.* Flagstaff, AZ: Rising Moon.

    Written in English and Spanish, this story tells how a young boy comes to grips with the importance of being honest.

Multicultural   Spanish Language

MARTHA WORDS

▷ LARGE GROUP
SMALL GROUP
LETTER PATTERNS
WORD FAMILIES

Children find words with letter patterns or word families in *Martha Speaks* (Meddaugh, 1992) and then write these words in word-dialog balloons, just like the dialog balloons in the book which show the dog Martha talking with friends and family.

MATERIALS: *Martha Speaks* (Meddaugh, 1992) or another book of interest to your class; colored construction paper; chalk or crayons; a long piece of butcher paper; markers.

DIRECTIONS: Read *Martha Speaks* (Meddaugh, 1992). Part of the problem in this story is that Martha's brain is so full of letters that she talks non-stop. Martha's talk is shown in dialog balloons. Let's say, for the sake of illustration, that children are learning or reviewing the r-controlled vowel pattern. Vr words in *Martha Speaks* include *Martha, dinner, smart, morning, never, understood, part, surprise, order, different, over, circuit, sure, early, born, determined, were, before, world, ever, forget, remember, under, during, after, worried, matter, answer, offered, wondered, heard, burglar, barked, ferocious, officer, carcass,* and *letter.* Children work with partners to find r-controlled words in *Martha Speaks* and write these words down. Children share the words as you write them on the chalk board. Count words with the Vr pattern; talk about the vowel sounds in the r-controlled pattern. Compare and contrast the vowel sounds in Vr *Martha Speaks* words with words that do not have a Vr pattern, such as *pat* and *part, bid* and *bird, port* and *bird, Sue* and *sure.*

    Give children a piece of construction paper, crayons, or chalk. Discuss the way the author uses dialog balloons to show that Martha and the other characters are talking. Draw a simple stick figure and a dialog balloon on the board. Invite volunteers to go to the board and write Vr words in the dialog balloon.

    Give each child a large piece of white construction paper, and ask the children to draw their own rendition of Martha. Have children draw a dialog balloon and write in the balloon as many words as they can think of that have the Vr pattern. Ask children to underline or write in color every Vr pattern in words, or you may want to ask children to write phrases or sentences using Vr pattern words. The Martha words dialog balloon in Figure 4–5 was done by a first grader in the second half of the year.

MAKING A MARTHA WORDS BULLETIN BOARD   As a follow-up, read other Martha books. Sketch Martha, or another animal, on a large piece of butcher paper. Draw several large dialog balloons. Put the paper on the floor, and ask children to write messages inside the dialog balloons. Put the

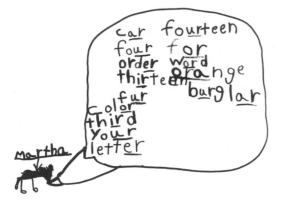

FIGURE 4–5 Martha Words for the Vr Pattern

butcher paper on the bulletin board. Leave a couple of markers close by so that children can continue to add Martha words (words spelled with a specified letter pattern). After a day or two, count the Martha words. Have children count the number of words with specific letter patterns, including the Vr pattern. Put some of the words on the word wall; have the children enter some of the words in their personal word banks or dictionaries.

Examples of Literature Connections

Meddaugh, S. (1992). *Martha speaks*. Boston, MA: Houghton Mifflin.

Martha books tell about a dog, Martha, who develops speech after gobbling a bowl of alphabet soup. This humorous story shows how written language represents spoken language. Other Martha books include:

Meddaugh, S. (1994). *Martha calling*. Boston, MA: Houghton Mifflin.

Meddaugh, S. (1996). *Martha blah, blah*. Boston, MA: Houghton Mifflin.

Meddaugh, S. (1998). *Martha walks the dog*. Boston, MA: Houghton Mifflin.

Meddaugh, S. (2000). *Martha and skits*. Boston, MA: Houghton Mifflin.

▷ SMALL GROUP
WORD FAMILIES
CROSS-CHECKING

WHITE BOARD WORD FAMILIES

Children combine onsets and rimes into word family words and then decide if the pronounced words are real or nonsense. Distinguishing real from nonsense words helps children use their speaking vocabularies to cross-check for word meaning.

MATERIALS: Several sets of colored, laminated 3 × 5 note cards with onsets and rimes; a white board, one erasable marker and one cloth (for erasing the marker) for each child in a small group. (A mini chalk board and a sock with a piece of chalk may be substituted.)

DIRECTIONS: Read and share rhyming stories or poetry. Look for books in which the majority of rhyming words belong to the same word families, such as in *red* and *bed,* but not *red* and *head*. Have children find all the word family rhyming words in a particular selection; write the words on a chart and talk about the rime in word family words. Leave the chart up in your room and invite children to add more word family words.

Ask a small group to join you at a table. Give each child a white board, one erasable marker, and a cloth for erasing the marker. Explain that you will show a card with a beginning letter and a card with a word family ending pattern. Children blend the beginning sound and the word family pattern together to pronounce a word. Children may pronounce the words to themselves, or the whole group may pronounce the word, depending on the ability of the children in the group. If the word is real, children write it on their magic slate. If the word is make believe, children do not write it down. Remind children that they are to write only real words on their white boards. For example, you might show one card with *p* and another with *ig*. Children pronounce the onset, /p/, and the rime, /ig/. Children then blend the onset and rime to pronounce /pig/ and write *pig* on their white boards. An example of a nonsense word is the onset *p* and the rime *og*. After blending /p/ and /og/, children decide that *pog* is not a real word and therefore children do not write *pog* on their white boards.

We have found practice cross-checking for real words is especially helpful for struggling readers who frequently do not stop to think about meaning when decoding. Table 4–8 has six groups of onsets and rimes that make both real and nonsense words that you might use with this and other activities. The first three groups consist of single consonant onsets and simple rimes that form VC short vowel real or nonsense words; the last three consist of onsets and rimes with consonant clusters and digraphs.

Examples of Literature Connections

Hayward, L. (1998). *Baker, baker, cookie maker*. New York: Children's Television Workshop Publishing.

This simple story, told in rhyme, is appropriate for beginning readers who benefit from experiences with rhyming language.

Lear, E. (1996). *The owl and the pussycat*. New York: Putnam.

This traditional owl and pussycat poem, in paperback version, is written in rhyme and embellished by charming illustrations.

O'Neill, M. (1961). *Hailstones and halibut bones*. New York: Doubleday.

The rhyming language in this book is suitable for children who are aware of rhyming words.

Group #1 Onsets: p , b, d, r	Rimes: ig, ug, ag, og, eg
Real words:	pig, big, dig, rig, pug, bug, dug, rug, bag, rag, bog, dog, peg, beg
Nonsense words:	pag, dag, pog, rog, deg, reg

Group #2 Onsets: h, m, l, f, p	Rimes: at, id, op, in, et
Real words:	hat, mat, fat, pat, hid, mid, lid, hop, mop, lop, pop, fin, pin, met, let, pet
Nonsense words:	lat, fid, pid, fop, hin, min, lin, het, fet

Group #3 Onsets: t, m, s, n	Rimes: ap, ip, et, ub, ot
Real words:	tap, map, sap, nap, tip, sip, nip, met, set, net, tub, sub, nub, tot, not
Nonsense words:	mip, tet, mub, mot

Group #4 Onsets: th, ch, gr, sk, sp	Rimes: in, ip, it, ill, ick
Real words:	thin, chin, grin, skin, spin, chip, grip, skip, grit, skit, spit, chill, grill, skill, spill, thick, chick
Nonsense words:	thip, thit, thill, grick, skick, spip, spick

Group #5 Onsets: thr, cl, tr, cr	Rimes: ash, amp, ust, ip, ump
Real words:	thrash, clash, trash, crash, clamp, tramp, cramp, thrust, trust, crust, clip, trip, clump, trump
Nonsense words:	thramp, clust, thrip, crip, thrump, crump

Group #6 Onsets: bl, str, scr, sm, cl	Rimes: ap, ock, ip, am, uck
Real words:	strap, scrap, slap, clap, block, clock, smock, blip, clip, strip, clam, scram, struck, cluck
Nonsense words:	blap, smap, strock, scrock, scrip, smip, stram, smam, bluck, scruck, smuck, blam

TABLE 4–8 White Board Onset-rime Combinations

PERSONAL LETTER PATTERN AND WORD FAMILY MAGNETS

▷ SMALL GROUP
LETTER PATTERNS
WORD FAMILIES

Children make a personalized set of magnets for the letter patterns and word families they are learning to read and spell. Making words with magnets that have letter patterns (*sh, thr, ow,* and *ee*) or word family rimes (*ound, ight,* and *ame*) encourages children to conceptualize letter patterns and word family rimes as complete letter and sound groups.

MATERIALS: A wide magnetic strip (1 1/2- to 2-inches wide); poster board cut into strips that are as wide as the magnetic strip; colored markers; scissors. Magnetic strips are packaged in coils, have one sticky side, and can be purchased at office supply stores. One coil will last all year, probably longer. Cut magnetic strips and poster board strips into the same lengths.

DIRECTIONS: Put scissors, the magnetic strips, poster board strips, and colored markers on a table. Ask children to write the letter patterns and word family rimes the children are learning in your classroom on the poster board strips. When children put the poster board on the adhesive side of the magnetic strip, the magnet is complete!

Give each child in a small group a cookie sheet or pizza pan. Have children build words with letter patterns or word family rime magnets. For example, children might build a word like *clown* from the *cl, ow,* and *n* patterns. Children might build a word family word like *night* from the beginning letter *n* and the rime *ight.*

Letter Pattern Magnets and Words							Word Family Rime Magnets and Words				
cl	ow	n		c	ou	ch		n	ight		br	ight

LEARNING CENTERS Put magnets with letter patterns and word family rimes which children are learning in learning centers. Ask children to build as many words as they can with specified magnets. Coordinating word building with ongoing instruction strengthens children's ability to conceptualize words as built of letter patterns and word family rimes. This, in turn, supports pattern-by-pattern decoding, as well as decoding by analogy, and spelling.

SCHOOL-HOME CONNECTION   Send the homemade magnets home. Include a note to parents asking them to put the magnets on the refrigerator, and to encourage their children to use the magnets to build different words. You might suggest which words to make with the magnets, thus helping assure that activities at home support classroom learning.

Examples of Literature Connections

Branley, F. M. (1996). *What makes a magnet?* New York: Harper Trophy.
    This book has a cornucopia of great, simple experiments with magnets that is just right for first and second graders.
Scarry, R., & Herman, G. (1998). *Mr. Fixit's magnet machine.* New York: Simon Spotlight.
    Mr. Fixit story tells about a magnet machine that attracts nearly every metal object in town.

▷ LARGE GROUP
SMALL GROUP
LETTER PATTERNS
WORD FAMILIES

GROCERY BAG FRIENDLY LETTERS

Children use their knowledge of letter patterns and word families to write friendly letters on brown paper grocery bags.

MATERIALS: One large brown grocery bag for each child; scissors; glitter and glue; crayons and markers; hole punch; and colored yarn. Cut the back off each grocery bag. Use the print-free portion of the bag for writing messages. To decorate the grocery bag messages, children may use decorative scissors (scissors that cut in patterns, rather than in straight lines), glitter and glue, crayons and markers, hole punch, and yarn.

DIRECTIONS: Read and share stories about cards and letters. Talk about special messages, how to write them, and the types of things writers tell readers. You may want to use books like *Messages in the Mailbox: How to Write a Letter* (Leedy, 1991) to show children how to write the heading, salutation, body, closing, signature, and postscript of a letter. Write a friendly letter with the whole class. The group might write to someone in your school, to a famous person, or to a character in a favorite book.

    When children are comfortable writing letters, have them write their own friendly letters, following the form previously taught. Ask children to make a tree diagram showing the structure of a friendly letter. Then, when the tree diagram is finished, have children write a first draft on plain paper. Once the first drafts are complete, ask children to work with a partner to edit the first draft. In addition, have each set of partners look for words with particular letter patterns or word families, and underline the words they find. The partners then share with the class the letter pattern and/or word family words they wrote. Talk about how to spell letter patterns or word family words, and have each child write a final draft. Set final copies aside.

    Pass out one grocery bag back panel to each child. You may ask children to use decorative scissors to cut the edges of the paper bag panel so as to create an interesting pattern. Children may also use glitter to decorate the edges of the paper. Another option is to punch holes around the edge of the paper bag panels and to string colored yarn through the holes. Any one of these options creates interesting, colorful grocery bag letters. When the paper bag panel is decorated, use glue sticks to fasten the final draft letters to the center of the panel (Figure 4–6).

    The friendly letter in Figure 4–6 is written to a friend who lives in another state. Bring the letter-writing activity closer to home by having children draw names and then write a friendly letter saying at least three nice things about the classmate. Address and deliver letters to each child. Finally, share the friendly letters and put them on display for everyone to enjoy. Writing friendly letters is a way to help children develop social skills, to focus on the positive characteristics of their classmates, and to build self-esteem.

Examples of Literature Connections

Caseley, J. (1991). *Dear Annie.* New York: Mulberry Books.
    Told almost completely through the correspondence between a little girl and her grandfather, this story illustrates a caring relationship and the pleasure of having a lifelong pen pal.
Holub, J. (1997). *Pen pals.* New York: Grosset and Dunlap.
    The easy text and a good plot line make this book a good catalyst for writing friendly letters and for a pen-pal project.
Leedy, L. (1991). *Messages in the mailbox: How to write a letter.* New York: Holiday House.

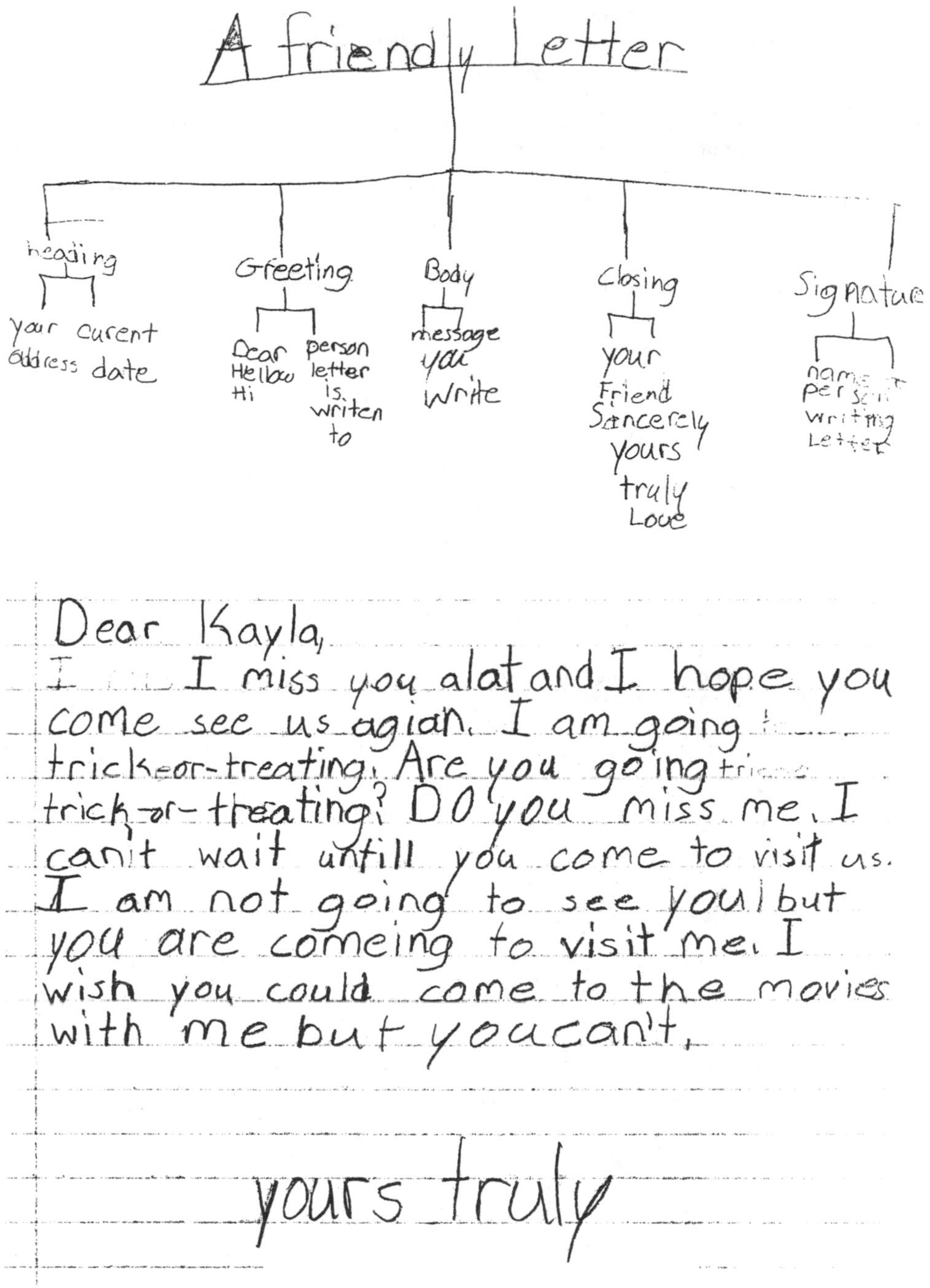

FIGURE 4–6 Example of a Grocery Bag Friendly Letter

A friendly Letter

- **heading**
  your curent address date
- **Greeting**
  - Dear Helbo Hi
  - person letter is writen to
- **Body**
  - message you write
- **Closing**
  - your Friend Sincerely yours truly Love
- **Signature**
  - name person writing Letter

Dear Kayla,
I   I miss you alat and I hope you
come see us agian. I am going
trick-or-treating. Are you going tri
trick-or-treating? DO you miss me. I
can't wait untill you come to visit us.
I am not going to see you but
you are comeing to visit me. I
wish you could come to the movies
with me but you can't.

                 yours truly

This humorous book explains how to write friendly letters, address envelopes, write postcards, write invitations, write thank-you notes, and write a host of other types of correspondence.

Spurr, E. (1997). *The long, long letter.* New York: Hyperion Paperbacks for Children.

In this humorous story, a lonely woman receives a long letter and makes new friends.

DOG FOLD-OVERS

▷ LARGE GROUP
SMALL GROUP
LETTER PATTERNS
WORD FAMILIES

Children fold a colorful piece of construction paper into a dog face, which, when open, reveals word family words or words that have the same letter pattern. After enjoying the fold-overs in your classroom, children take them home to share with their families.

MATERIALS: Light-colored construction paper; scissors; pencils; crayons.

FIGURE 4–7 How to Make
Dog Fold-overs

Use large construction paper in light colors.
Have a supply of crayons, markers, and scissors available.

Step 1. Fold the paper into a square. Cut off the extra flap to make a perfectly
square piece of construction paper.

Step 2. Fold the square diagonally to make a triangle.

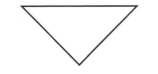

Step 3. Hold the triangle with the fold on top.
Fold each corner to make ears.

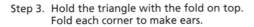
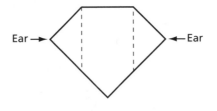

Step 4. Use crayons or colored markers to make a dog face.

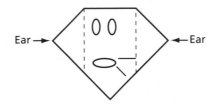

DIRECTIONS: Read and share stories about dogs. Discuss the words in books that are spelled with the letter patterns or word families children are learning. Build words with letter patterns or word family rimes. Talk about the words and write them on the board. Refer to the word wall for examples of word family words and letter pattern words.

In so far as making the fold-overs is concerned, by the second half of the first grade our children can fold paper into a dog face without teacher assistance. (See Figure 4–7 for instructions.) We present this activity in a seamless way so that the review and practice naturally flow into making the fold-overs.

Put construction paper and crayons or markers on the table. Show children a dog fold-over as an example, opening it to reveal the letter patterns or word family words inside. Demonstrate how to make a fold-over. Have the children follow your example to make their own dog fold-overs. Once fold-overs are made, children write the letter pattern or word family words inside the fold-over (Figure 4–8). Have the children share the words inside their fold-overs. Send the fold-overs home. Ask children to share their fold-overs by reading the words inside.

Examples of Literature Connections

Jones, M. T., & Dadey, D. (2001). *Top dog*. New York: Volo Books.

　Part of the Barkley's School for Dogs chapter book series, *Top Dog* recounts how Jack the dog upstages a real canine bully to act in a commercial.

Margulies, T. (2001). *Clifford the big red dog: The show-and-tell surprise*. New York: Scholastic.

　In this book for young readers, adapted from Bridwell's Clifford series, Emily brings Clifford to school for show-and-tell.

Marsh, T. J., & Ward, J. (1998). *Way out in the desert*. Flagstaff, AZ: Rising Moon.

　This rhyming book describes desert animals with a blend of narrative and informational text.

Osborne, M. P. (2000). *Dingoes at dinnertime* (Magic Tree House 20). New York: Random House.

　Set in Australia, this magic tree house book tells how Jack and Annie rescue an enchanted dog. An engaging book for skilled second-grade readers.

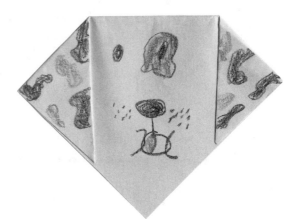

FIGURE 4–8　Dog Fold-over

LETTER PATTERN DUCKLINGS

▷ **SMALL GROUP**
LETTER PATTERNS
SOUND AWARENESS

Children count sounds in words, sequence a duckling for each sound heard in words, associate letters with the sounds, and build VC-pattern words.

MATERIALS:　Letter cards; a large picture of a duckling (Appendix A–8) laminated; *Make Way for Ducklings* (McCloskey, 1941); paper and pencils; a duckling word building guide for each child or set of partners (Reproducible Patterns A–8); ducklings reproduced on yellow construction paper (pattern A–8 in the Reproducible Pattern Appendix); marker; 3 × 5 cards; 8 1/2 × 11 envelope.

DIRECTIONS:　After reading *Make Way for Ducklings* (McCloskey, 1941), fasten a duckling to the bulletin board, put a duckling on the chalk tray, or put a duckling in a transparent pocket chart. Remind the children of how the ducklings followed their mother in a nice line. Explain that the sounds and letters in words follow each other just like the ducklings. Show children three ducklings you copied from the Reproducible Pattern Appendix (A–8). Pronounce a word. Ask children to indicate, by raising one, two, or three fingers, how many sounds they hear in the word. For example, children would hold up two fingers for /at/, and three fingers for /mat/. Ask a volunteer to come to the bulletin board (chalk tray or pocket chart) and line up as many ducklings as there are sounds in the word.

　Use a marker to write a letter on each duckling for each sound heard in the word. Ask children to pronounce the whole word. Call on volunteers to line up ducklings for several different words. Ask children to write the letters for each sound heard in words. For example, two ducklings would be lined up for /at/ and children would write the letter *a* on one duckling and the letter *t* on the other duckling. In making the word *sat*, children would add a duckling to the beginning of the word and write *s* on that duckling.

　Pass out the duckling word building guide. Explain that children are to build words with the letters at the top of the page. Each duckling represents a sound in a word. Call children's attention to the super duck at the bottom of the paper. Challenge children to use the letters to write even more words on the lines beside the super duck. The sample guide has the letters *a, i, o, n, t, b, g, d,* and *s*. Possible words include *sat, sit, bat, bit, big, bag, ban, got, gob, Nan, not, dog, dig, ant, gab, tab, nab, bib, tan,* and *tin*. Use the reproducible pattern of the word building guide (Appendix A–9) to make guides that meet the needs and abilities of the children whom you teach. Word building is easier with fewer letters, and harder with more letters.

FOLLOW-UP RIDDLES　Write a short riddle on a piece of paper. Thumbtack as many ducklings to a bulletin board as there are sounds in the word that answers the riddle. Fasten the riddle under the ducklings. Put a large envelope near the bulletin board with the riddle tacked to it. Leave a small stack of 3 × 5 cards nearby. In their free time, children write the answer to the riddle on the 3 × 5 cards, put their names on the cards, and drop them into the envelope. Change the riddle every day or so. Examples of riddles included: (1) I am a pet. I can purr. What am I? (2) I go on your head. What am I? (3) I lay the eggs you eat. What am I? (4) I am very bright. You can see me in the daytime. What am I? (5) A spider makes me. What am I? (6) I go on the top of a jar. What am I? (7) I have a tail. I bark. What am I? (8) You ride in me. What am I? (9) You sleep on me. What am I? (10) Children ride in me to school. What am I? Answers: (1) cat; (2) hat or cap; (3) hen; (4) sun; (5) web; (6) lid; (7) dog; (8) car, van, or bus; (9) bed; (10) bus, van, or car.

Examples of Literature Connections
McCloskey, R. (1941). *Make way for ducklings.* New York: Viking Press.
  In this story, ducklings follow their mother across the street and into a pond in a New York City park.

▷ SMALL GROUP
LETTER PATTERNS
WORD FAMILIES
SOUND AWARENESS

HOPSCOTCH WORD FAMILY AND LETTER PATTERN WORDS

In this outdoor game, children jump into hopscotch squares with words that they are reading in your classroom.

MATERIALS: Sidewalk chalk.

DIRECTIONS: Go outdoors. Make a giant hopscotch figure with sidewalk chalk; write one word in each hopscotch square. Each word should belong to a word family or should be spelled with a letter pattern children are learning. Children take turns jumping or hopping into the squares. Children read each word before jumping into the next hopscotch square. Figure 4–9 shows one hopscotch pattern with letter patterns that represent the long *a* sound.

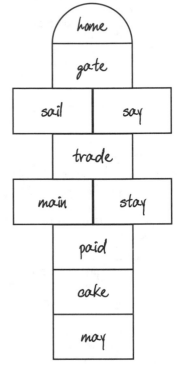

FIGURE 4–9   Word Family and Letter Pattern Hopscotch

▷ SMALL GROUP
LETTER PATTERNS

PAPER PLATE CEREAL WORDS

Children make words out of Alpha-bits© cereal, write words on paper plates, and then sort paper words in learning centers.

MATERIALS: Three to four boxes of Alpha-bits© cereal; two paper plates for each child making cereal words; directions for sorting words by letter patterns.

DIRECTIONS: Read rhyming poems like those found in *Favorite Poems by Dennis Lee: Dinosaur Dinner (With a Slice of Alligator Pie)* (Prelutsky, 1997) and *Soap Soup* (Kuskin, 1992). Have children find words in poems that are spelled with the letter patterns they are learning to read and spell. Write the words on a large chart. Pass out two paper plates to each child. Pour a handful of Alpha-bits© cereal on one paper plate. Children use the Alpha-bits© cereal to spell words with the letter patterns they are learning, and then use a pencil to write the words on the second paper plate. Review the words the children wrote on their paper plates, as shown in Figure 4–10. Put the plates on a bulletin board or send them home so that children read the words to their parents.

LEARNING CENTERS   Place a small stack of paper plates in a learning center. On one plate, write words that are spelled with two or three different letter patterns. Write words at

FIGURE 4–10   Paper Plate Cereal Words

random. On a separate paper plate, or on a sheet of paper, write each of the three pronounceable letter patterns. Children sort the words by writing them under the appropriate letter pattern on the paper plate or paper. For example, words could be sorted into VC (*pat, had, pot, cat, ban, bun,* and *cub*) and Vr r-controlled (*bird, fur, part, hard, port, cart, barn, burn,* and *curb*). A more difficult three-way sort would be to ask children to write words that belong to the VCe pattern (*phone, lone, stove, stone, joke,* and *hope*), VV pattern (*boat, toast, toad, coat, soap, roast, oatmeal,* and *coach*), and the CV pattern (*go, so, ago, hello* and *taco*), as shown in Figure 4–11.

Examples of Literature Connections

Kuskin, K. (1992). *Soap soup.* New York: Harper Trophy.

This collection of fun rhyming poems about everyday life is a good source for letter pattern words.

Prelutsky, J. (Ed.) (1997). *Favorite poems by Dennis Lee: Dinosaur dinner (with a slice of alligator pie).* New York: Dragonfly Books.

The first few poems in this book make a great introduction to paper plate cereal words.

Date: _____
Name: _____

FIGURE 4–11   Long *o* Word Sort to Accompany Paper Plate Cereal Words

Directions:
Read each of the words. Write the words in the column that has the same long *o* pattern as the word on the paper plate. Underline the long *o* pattern in each word that you write.

Trick: Some words do not have a long *o* pattern. Write these words on the plate with the Ø.

Words: home, boat, go, toast, toad, coat, oil, phone, story, lone, soap, ago, roast, stove, hopping, about, stone, road, boy, oatmeal, hello, soft, taco, joke, coach, hope, brown, so.

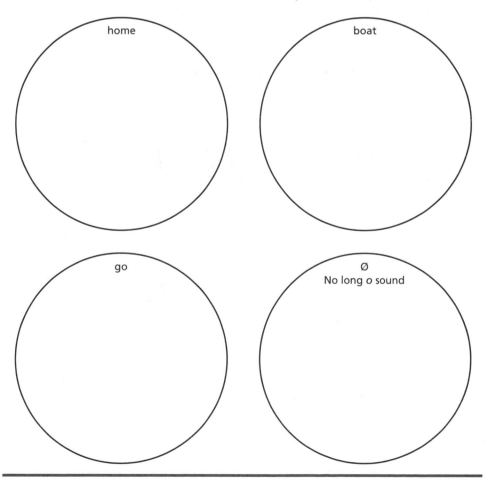

▷ LARGE GROUP
SMALL GROUP
LETTER PATTERNS
WORD FAMILIES

LETTER PATTERN WORD STARS

Children make a loop of connected stars with words that have a common letter pattern or word family, and then draw a picture illustrating the meaning of one of the words (Figure 4–12).

MATERIALS: Books children are reading in your classroom; paper and pencils.

DIRECTIONS: Read and share books in your classroom, and link some of the words in these books to the letter patterns children are learning. Talk about a letter pattern children are learning; write words with these patterns; have children look on the word wall, in classroom displays, in word banks, and in books for words with a target letter pattern or word family word. Write these words on the board or on a chart. For example, *Butterflies* (Neye, 2000) includes the following words with the *ar* pattern: *backyard, gardens, far, are, parts, hard,* and *monarch.* In *Junie B. Jones Has a Peep in Her Pocket* (Park, 2000), you will find the following words with final *y* representing long *e*: *buddy, speedy, Billy, angry, stubby, puppy, silly, huffy, fluffery, checkery, happy, funny, sorry, daddy, pony, teensy, pretty, anybody, pointy, pickery, sneaky, poundy, flaky, shiny,* and *any.* In *Booker T. Washington* (Gleiter & Thompson, 1995), look for the following words with the *Vr* pattern: *enter, under, over, other, mother, father, brother, newspaper, water, summer, winter, teacher, number, letter, speller, stepfather, better, comer,* and *later.* To make letter pattern word stars, children write words with the same letter pattern in a star, connect words with lines, and illustrate the meaning of one of the words. Figure 4–12 shows word stars a first grader made for the VC short *i* pattern.

OPTION: COLOR CODING PATTERNS   Children use a colored marker or crayon to trace over the common letter pattern in words. In so doing, the letter pattern becomes more prominent. By tracing over letters to make the patterns more obvious, children get practice identifying the pattern in words. Also importantly, children create a visually striking set of words in which patterns are prominent.

FIGURE 4–12 Letter Pattern Word Stars for the VC Short i Pattern

Name:_____

Write *in* and *it* words in the stars below. Underline the short vowel pattern in each word with a colored pencil. Connect the stars with lines. Write and draw pictures of two words in the center of the loop.

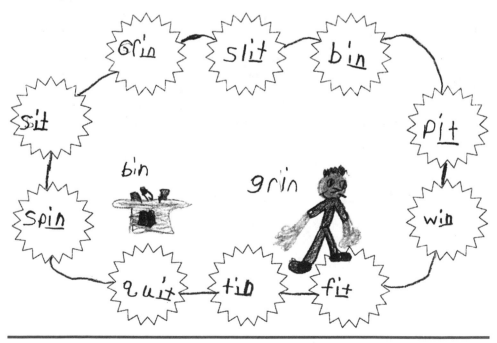

INFORMATIONAL DICTIONARY WITH LETTER PATTERN WORDS

▷ **LARGE GROUP**
SMALL GROUP
LETTER PATTERNS

Children combine their knowledge of science with their knowledge of the letter patterns in words to make a dictionary, from A to Z, that defines words, terms, plants, and animals.

MATERIALS: Reference books; crayons; twenty-six pages with lines on the bottom and a blank for an illustration on the top.

DIRECTIONS: Explore a topic in detail. Read about it; talk about it; take field trips. Stock your classroom with lots of topic-relevant books from which to choose. In the process, explain to the class that they are going to make a dictionary telling about the things they are learning. Decide on patterns children need to learn. Write on the board a list of content-related words from children's writing and from informational and narrative books, then ask volunteers to come to the board to find and underline letter patterns in words.

In making a dictionary called *A, B, Sea! A Dictionary All About Sea Life!*, the whole first grade class studied sea life using, among other resources, *Commotion in the Ocean* (Andreae & Wojtowycz, 1998). Each child chose an animal and then contributed one page to the dictionary. First graders looked for and underlined letter patterns they were learning, such as the VV pattern in *manatee, see, seals, sea, teeth,* and *reef,* and the VCe pattern in *spines, ride, white, dive, whale, survive,* and *icebergs.* Figure 4–13 shows a page about the manatee and Figure 4–14 shows a page on penguins.

Examples of Literature Connections

Andreae, G., & Wojtowycz, D. (1998). *Commotion in the ocean.* New York: Scholastic.

This highly informative book is an example of the type of information children might read and share when making a theme-based ABC book.

Doubilet, A. (1991). *Under the sea from a to z.* New York: Scholastic.

Constructed in an alphabet book format, this information-packed expository book gives readers information about life in the sea.

Ward, J., & Marsh, T. J. (2000). *Somewhere in the ocean.* Flagstaff, AZ: Rising Moon.

This beautifully illustrated, rhyming book describes mother animals and their babies living in the ocean.

FIGURE 4–13 Informational Dictionary — Manatee

FIGURE 4–14 Informational Dictionary — Penguins

FAN BOOKS

▷ **LARGE GROUP**
SMALL GROUP
LETTER PATTERNS
WORD FAMILIES

Fan books have graduated pages so that readers immediately see the topic of each page. The fan books in this activity have words that represent a targeted vowel sound, expressed in several letter patterns, or word families. The words children put in the fan books are words from the word wall, displays in your classroom, word banks, or books children are reading.

MATERIALS: Six sheets of unlined 8 1/2 × 11 construction paper per child; markers or pencils; scissors; rulers; staplers.

DIRECTIONS: Read and share books; talk about word meaning, story meaning, and the letter patterns and word families in the words that the authors use to tell stories or give information. Make charts, examine the word wall, and add words to word banks. Make fan books for letter pattern or word family words (Figure 4–15). Fan books are easy to make; just follow these five steps for making a six-page fan book:

Step 1 Measure one inch from the 8 1/2-inch side of one sheet of plain paper. Draw a vertical line along the 8 1/2-inch edge. Cut the 1-inch strip off. This leaves a page ten inches long.

FIGURE 4–15 Fan Book

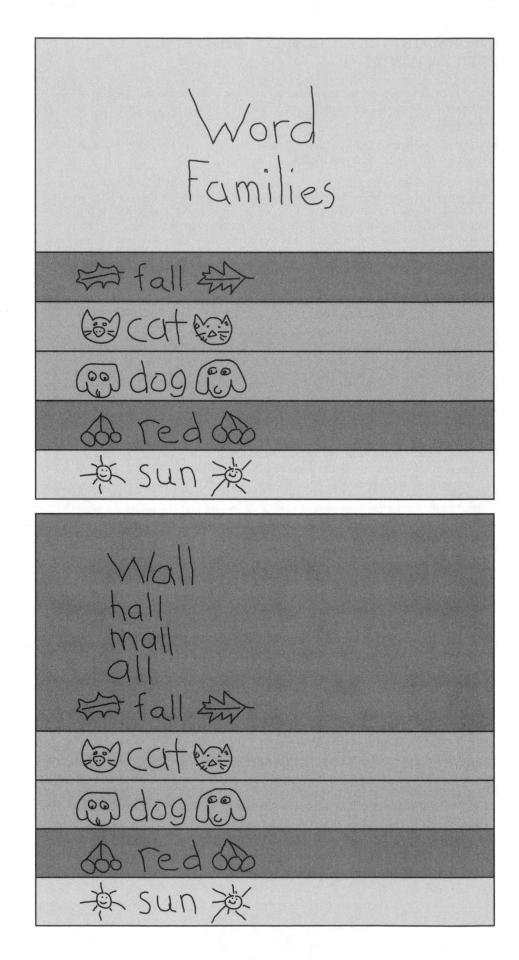

FIGURE 4–15 Continued.

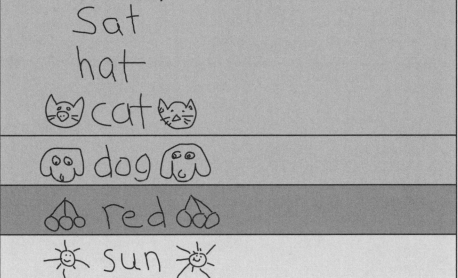

Step 2 Pick up a second sheet of plain paper. Use your ruler to measure two inches from the 8 1/2-inch edge. Draw a vertical line and cut off two inches. The second paper is now nine inches long.

Step 3 Cut three inches from the end of the third sheet (now eight inches long). Cut four inches from the fourth sheet (now seven inches long). Cut five inches from the fifth sheet (now six inches long). Cut six inches from the sixth sheet (now five inches long).

FIGURE 4–15   Continued.

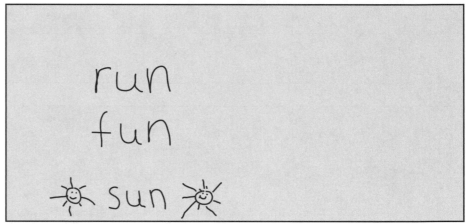

Step 4   Put your book together. Put the 10-inch sheet flat on a table. Put the 9-inch sheet on top of the 10-inch sheet, followed by the 8-inch sheet and so on. Continue stacking paper until the shortest piece of construction paper is on the top.

Step 5   Staple the edge of the fan book.

There are two different types of fan books from which to choose:

1. *Word Family Words*   This is the easiest fan book. Children write different words that belong to one word family on each page. In writing a different word family member on each fan book page, children have opportunities to generalize the specific word family rime to many different members of the word family words.

2. *Letter Patterns*   Children write words that represent one letter pattern in each page. For example, in making a fan book for the VCe pattern, children might select *wave* as a key word and then write VCe words with long *a* on the page. Children may use words from the books they are reading, the word wall, word banks, and displays in your classroom. Words from *Good Driving, Amelia Bedelia* (Parish, 1995) with a VCe long vowel pattern include: (1) long *a* — *take, made, late, name, celebrate, gave,* and *cake;* (2) long *i* — *fine, drive, nice, while, five, like, tire, smiled, slices,* and *fine;* (3) long *o* — *drove* and *home;* and (4) long *u* — *use.* A representative sample of VCe long vowel pattern words in *Earthquake in the Early Morning* (Osborne, 2001), a more difficult book, includes: (1) VCe long *a* — *take, places, save, waste, shake, wave, place, caving, scraped, shaky, awake, rage, driver, safe, take, birdcage, escape, caked,*

brave, and *slate;* (2) VCe long *i* — *time, inside, write, five, lined, fire, piling, ride, driver, smile, like, mine, hillside, write, arrive,* and *tired;* (3) VCe long *o* — *rope, note, close, stove, broken, home, wrote, smoke,* and *hope;* and (4) VCe long *u* — *huge.*

Examples of Literature Connections

Osborne, M. P. (2001). *Earthquake in the early morning.* New York: Random House.

   Jack and Annie travel back in time, arriving in San Francisco in time for the 1906 earthquake.

Parish, H. (1995). *Good driving, Amelia Bedelia.* New York: Avon Books.

   Amelia Bedelia has a humorous driving lesson in the country.

MUSICAL BUDDY WORD FAMILY WORDS

▷ LARGE GROUP
SMALL GROUP
WORD FAMILIES

Children wearing beginning consonants and word family rimes look for buddies who, when both word parts are combined, make a real word.

MATERIALS: Sheets of paper with onsets and word family rimes; hole punch; colored yarn; taped music and a recorder to play it on.

DIRECTIONS: Cut a plain sheet of paper in half, lengthwise. On one half write a word family rime, and on the other a single consonant, consonant cluster, or consonant digraph. Use the hole punch to make two holes on either end of the half sheets. String colored yarn through the holes.

   Read books, talk about onsets and word family rimes, enjoy poetry, and play language games that feature rhyming sounds. Children are ready for word buddies when they are familiar with onsets and word family rimes. Shuffle the onsets and word family rimes on the half sheets. Tie one onset or word family rime sheet around the neck of each child. Play soft music. Tell the children that they may make as many words as they can while the music is playing. When the music stops, word making stops, too.

   The children walk around the room looking for a buddy with whom they can make a real word. For example, if one child is wearing *st* and another is wearing *and,* these two word buddies would form *stand.* When a child cannot find a buddy, ask if there is anyone who could make a word with the letters the child wears. For example, should a child wearing *sh* have trouble finding a buddy, you might ask, "Who can make a word with the *sh* beginning sound?" Some combinations make nonsense words; only real words count. This gives children opportunities to cross-check for word meaning.

   Buddies who form a word tell you their words as you write them on a chart. Make a list, as shown in Figure 4–16. This list of musical buddy words was made by a first grade teacher and her class as they made buddy words. The teacher wrote the onsets in blue and the word family rimes in pink. She also wrote three nonsense words on the chart. Children talked about how to spell words and why *hin* and *git* are not real words, and why *lam* is not the way we spell *lamb.*

   Read the word list in chorus; ask individuals to find specific beginning sounds and word family ending rimes. Ask if there are other words the children could make with the beginning and ending patterns. Write these words, too. You may want to restart the music to give children opportunities to make more buddy words. We find that two or three short musical buddy word-making opportunities work well for our children.

   For more challenging word family rimes, look in books like *Binky Rules* (Krensky, 2000). Word family rimes in this book include *alk, ick, ill, ain, art, ink, eam, at, ound, ight, eel, im,* and *ind;* beginning consonants include *ch, w, p, st, br, th, t, s, f, wh,* and *tr;* word family words that can be made from these *Binky Rules* onsets and rimes include *chalk, walk, stalk, talk, chick, pick, stick, brick, thick, tick, sick, trick, chill, will, pill, still, sill, fill, chain, pain, stain, brain, train, chart, part, start, tart, chink, wink, pink, stink, brink, think, sink, fink, steam, team, seam, chat, pat, brat, that, sat, fat, wound, pound, sound, found, bright, tight, sight, fight, peel, steel, feel, wheel, brim, Tim, whim, trim, wind,* and *find.* Children who know the onsets and word family rimes will find buddies to all sorts of words, thus taking word study beyond the specific words in the story.

Examples of a Literature Connection

Krensky, S. (2000). *Binky rules.* Boston, MA: Little, Brown and Company.

   This story about misplaced blame has an interesting twist in the end.

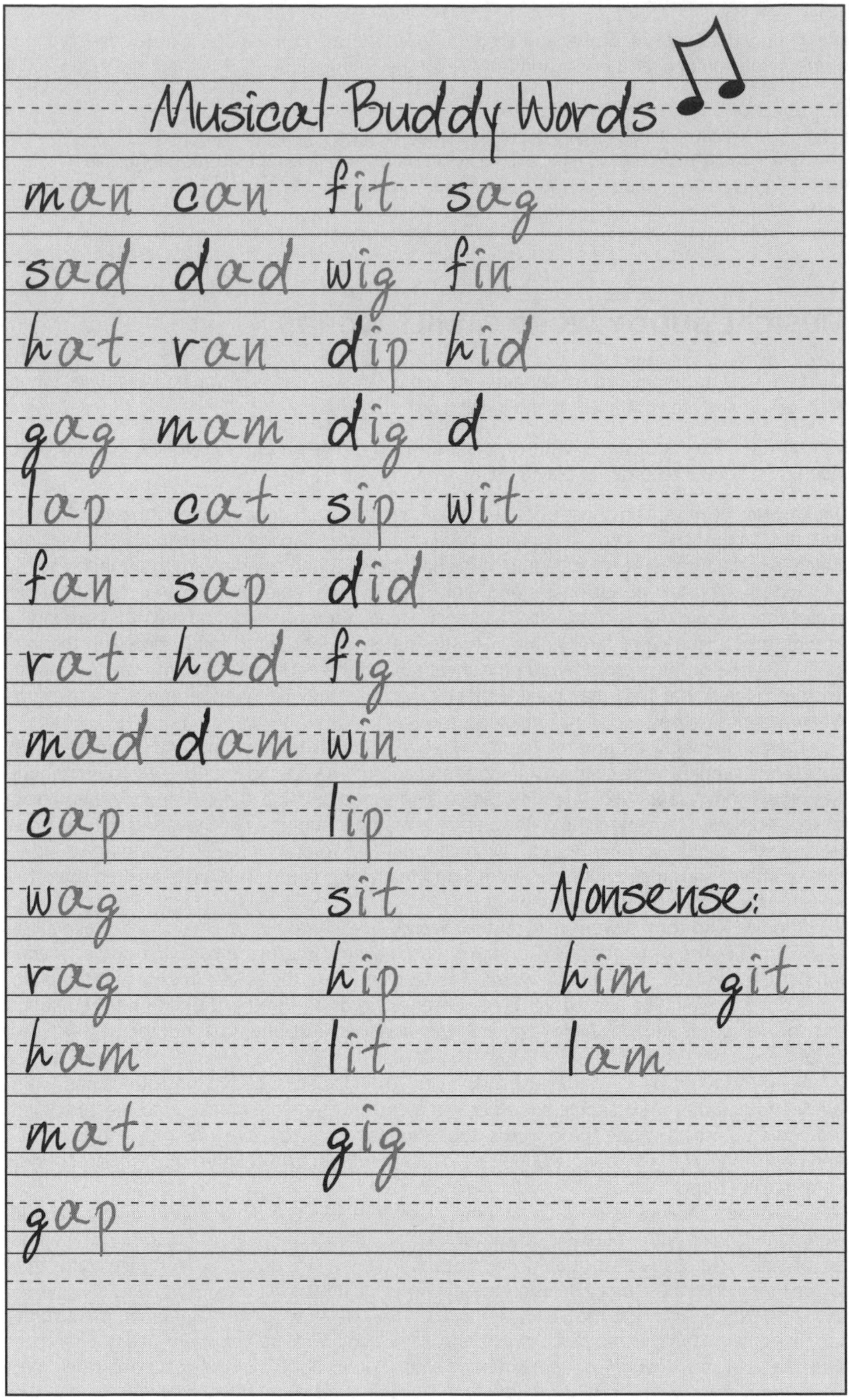

FIGURE 4–16 Musical Buddy Words Sample List Done By a Group of First Graders and Their Teacher

Musical Buddy Words

man	can	fit	sag
sad	dad	wig	fin
hat	ran	dip	hid
gag	mam	dig	d
lap	cat	sip	wit
fan	sap	did	
rat	had	fig	
mad	dam	win	
cap		lip	

			Nonsense:
wag		sit	
rag		hip	him git
ham		lit	lam
mat		gig	
gap			

128

ACCORDION WORD FAMILY AND LETTER PATTERN BOOKMARKS

SMALL GROUP
LETTER PATTERNS
WORD FAMILIES

Children find words with letter patterns or find word family words and make folded paper bookmarks that feature the patterns.

MATERIALS: Sturdy construction paper strips, three inches wide; glue sticks; scissors; colored construction paper for making a coyote or any other character in the books children are reading.

DIRECTIONS: Read and share books in your classroom; talk, too, about the letter patterns and word family words in the books. Write patterns on the chalk board; make lists of patterns; have children look on the word wall, on classroom displays, and in their word banks for words with the targeted patterns.

To make accordion bookmarks, give children one strip of colored construction paper. Children fold the strips accordion style, leaving about three inches on one end. Children write a word family word or words with the same letter pattern on each fold. When finished, the bookmark is a list of words that share a common letter pattern or words that belong to the same word family. Once the words are on the folds, decorate the accordion bookmark as an animal or with a seasonal item (a pumpkin, a shamrock, a heart).

Make bookmarks around books children are enjoying in your classroom. For example, if you are reading *Two Cool Coyotes* (Lund, 1999), children might make a coyote accordion bookmark. You might make an outline of a coyote face and have children cut and color it, or you might have children make a face out of construction paper. Construction paper faces would need a circle for the head, two triangles for ears, a small triangle for a nose, a semi-circle for a mouth, and a colorful pair of construction paper sunglasses. Glue the face (either colored or construction paper pieces) to the 3-inch top of the accordion-folded strip.

Word family ending patterns, or rimes, from *Two Cool Coyotes* (Lund, 1999) which include patterns to feature in bookmark making are: *est* in *West* and *best*; *ind* in *kind*; *old* in *told*; *ame* in *name*; *owl* in *howl*; *ast* in *fast*; *igh* in *high*; *ick* in *quick*; and *ock* in *rock*. Examples of letter patterns in words include: *sm* in *smart*; *pl* in *played*; *or* in *thorn*; *ar* in *sharp*; *ay* in *day*; *qu* in *quick*; *fr* in *friend* and *Frank*; *ow* in *follow*; and *gr* in *great*. Select a pattern children need to learn and practice in order to be successful readers and writers in your classroom. Have children look in *Two Cool Coyotes* (Lund, 1999) to find words with the pattern. Write words on the board. Talk about the pattern, and discuss the sounds the pattern represents in the words. Make a list of words with the pattern; have children add words to their word banks.

Children may use the bookmarks by straightening them out to put inside books (the folds are still visible) or you might want to put the bookmarks on the bulletin board. Figure 4–17 shows an example of an accordion bookmark.

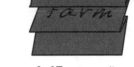

FIGURE 4–17   Accordion Bookmark

Examples of Literature Connections

Addler, D. (2001). *Cam Jansen and the barking treasure mystery* (Cam Jansen 19). New York: Puffin.
   Cam Jansen tracks down a dog collar thief.
Lund, J. (1999). *Two cool coyotes*. New York: Dutton Children's Books.
   This story of friendship lost and friendship found is a good read-aloud book.

MY WORD CARD GAME

SMALL GROUP
LETTER PATTERNS
WORD FAMILIES

Groups of two to four children play a card game in which they read words that contain letter patterns or word families the children need to practice.

MATERIALS: Unlined 3 × 5 cards (colored cards add a little something extra); marker; lots of words with letter patterns or word family words the children are learning. Select the patterns or word families you wish to feature. Write fifty-two words with the patterns, one on each card. Underline letter patterns and word family rimes to make them more visible.

DIRECTIONS: Children sit at a table and put a shuffled deck of my word cards face-down on the table. Children take turns drawing the top card from the deck, reading the word, and placing the card in front of them. If a player does not recognize the word the player drew, the child on the player's left may give it a try. If the player on the left reads the word correctly, that player gets to keep the word. The player on the left also gets to draw another word from the deck, as the next turn naturally falls to that player anyway. Each correctly read word (one card on the table in front of a player) is worth one point. The child with the most points wins the game.

▷ SMALL GROUP
LETTER PATTERNS

MELTING SNOWMAN LETTER PATTERN WORDS

Played like hangman, this game challenges a small group to identify a word from letter pattern and word shape clues.

MATERIALS: Chalk board or white board; chalk or dry erase marker.

DIRECTIONS: Select a word that has one or more letter patterns children are learning. Draw a snowman. Draw clues to the mystery word (Figure 4–18). Draw a box for each letter (Kaye, 1991). Write one, possibly two, key letters to signal one or two letter patterns.

Explain that the boxes are clues to the number and shapes of letters. The two letters in this example are clues to letter patterns in the mystery word. The goal is to guess the mystery word before the snowman melts away. Children take turns guessing the missing letters in the word. Write the correct letters in the boxes. Every incorrect guess causes the snowman to melt a little. Show melting by erasing a little of the snowman. You decide how much of the snowman to melt for every guess. Children win if they guess the identity of the mystery word before the snowman melts away. Figure 4–18 shows a melting snowman with one letter pattern clue for *turtle* and two letter pattern clues for *monkey*. Write as many, or as few, letters in the boxes as you wish.

FIGURE 4–18 Melting Snowman

Clues to the number of letters, letter shapes, and word shape. The letter in one box is a clue to one of the letter patterns in the mystery word.

Letter pattern and word shape cues for *turtle*

Letter pattern and word shape cues for *monkey*

▷ TWO CHILDREN
LETTER PATTERNS
WORD FAMILIES

WORD FAMILY AND LETTER PATTERN CHECKERS

Played like traditional checkers, this game features words with the letter patterns children are learning or word family words you are teaching.

MATERIALS: Checker pattern (Appendix A–10); twelve tokens in one color and twelve tokens in a contrasting color.

DIRECTIONS: Select sixty-four words that have letter patterns or the rimes in word family words children are learning in your classroom. Copy pattern A-10 in the Reproducible Pattern Appendix. Write words in the boxes. Write one word right side up and the other word upside down in every box. This way each player sees the words in the proper orientation.

Players can only move tokens forward. Each move must be diagonal, and players can only move into empty squares that are the same color as that assigned to them. To complete a successful move, a player reads the word in the square in which the player placed the token. An opponent's token is captured when a player jumps over it. Once a player's token reaches the last row of an opponent's side, the player gets "crowned" and the crowned token can then move backwards and forwards. The player who captures all the tokens of the opposing player wins.

100 YARD DASH LETTER PATTERN BOARD GAME

▷ TWO TO FOUR
CHILDREN
LETTER PATTERNS

100 Yard Dash is a word-building game in which players move tokens around a game board that has words in squares with a few letters replaced by blanks. There are letter patterns inside small feet around the edges of the game board. Children build words by selecting a pattern on the game board to combine with the letters in each square. To move forward, players must correctly spell and pronounce the words they build.

MATERIALS: 100 Yard Dash game board (Appendix A–11); four tokens; thirty 3 × 5 cards. Decide on the letter patterns or word families children need to practice. Duplicate the game board. Write the patterns in the feet around the edge of the game board. Write one word in each square, but leave blanks for letter patterns that are written in the feet on the edge of the game board. For example, if the VV patterns *ai, oa,* and *ee* are among the letter patterns on the game board edge, you might write in boxes r _ _ n (*rain*), b _ _ t (*boat*), and m _ _ t (*meet*). Make cards telling players how many spaces to move. On ten cards write *Move 1 Square;* on ten cards write *Move 2 Squares;* on five cards write *Lose a Turn;* and on five cards write *Go Back 1 Square.* An example of a game board ready for play is shown in Figure 4–19.

DIRECTIONS: After putting their tokens on *Start,* players take turns drawing cards and moving according to the instructions on the face-up card. Players combine any one of the letter patterns in the feet with the letters in the square to make a meaningful word. If a player does not make a word, that player goes back to the square from the previous turn. The first player who reaches *Finish* wins. Four examples of vowel patterns and words for game boards are:

VC SHORT VOWEL PATTERN — FEET: a, e, i, o, u Twenty words with missing letters: m _ d; sh _ t, tr _ ck, m _ t, l _ d, b _ d, b _ g, c _ b, c _ p, f _ n, h _ t, g _ t, h _ g, l _ t, m _ p, p _ t, b _ t, h _ m, d _ g, s _ t.

Words formed from the above patterns: mad, mid, shot, shut, track, trick, truck, mat, met, lad, led, lid, bad, bed, bid, bud, bag, beg, big, bog, bug, cab, cob, cub, cap, cop, cup, fan, fin, fun, hat, hit, hot, hut, get, got, gut, hag, hog, hug, let, lit, lot, map, mop, pat, pet, pit, pot, put, bat, bet, bit, but, ham, hem, him, hum, dig, dog, dug, sat, set, sit

VCe LONG VOWEL PATTERN — FEET: a, e, i, o, u Twenty words with missing letters: t _ me, sh _ ne, m _ le, f _ me, p _ ne, b _ ke, c _ ne, l _ ke, l _ ne, p _ le, r _ ce, r _ pe, r _ se, t _ le, br _ ke, dr _ ve, kn _ fe, m _ de, tr _ de, s _ de.

Words formed from the above pattern: tame, time, shine, shone, male, mile, mole, mule, fame, fume, pane, pine, bake, bike, cane, cone, lake, like, lane, line, lone, pale, pile, pole, race, rice, ripe, rope, rise, rose, tile, tale, brake, broke, drive, drove, knife, made, trade, side.

VV LONG VOWEL PATTERNS — FEET: ai, ay, ee, oa, ow Twenty words with missing letters: b _ _ , s _ _ , tr _ _ , b _ _ t, cl _ _ , fr _ _ , s _ _ p, r _ _ d, sh _ _ , b _ _ l, l _ _ , kn _ _ , r _ _ d, s _ _ k, fl _ _ , tr _ _ l, b _ _ t, gr _ _ , thr _ _ , gr _ _ n.

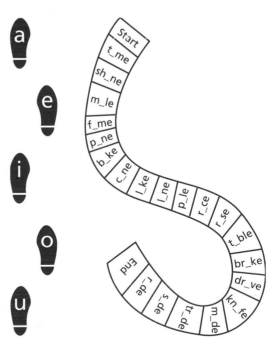

FIGURE 4–19 100 Yard Dash Game

Words formed from the above pattern: bay, bee, bow, say, see, sow, tray, tree, bait, beet, boat, clay, free, seep, soap, raid, road, show, bail, bowl, lay, low, knee, know, raid, reed, road, seek, soak, flee, flow, trail, bait, beet, boat, gray, grow, three, throw, green, grown.

LONG o PATTERNS — FEET: o, oa, old, ow   Twenty words with missing letters: gr _ _, f _ _ _, t _ _ st, n _ te, rainb _ _, b _ ne, cr _ _, g _ _ t, sc _ _ _, sm _ ke, g _ _ _, ph _ ne, st _ ve, wind _ _, g _ _ l, s _ _ p, wr _ te, c _ _ ch, r _ se, c _ _ _.

Words formed with the above pattern: grow, fold, toast, note, rainbow, bone, crow, goat, scold, smoke, gold, phone, stove, window, goal, soap, wrote, coach, rose, cold

▷ SMALL GROUP
WORD FAMILIES

WORD FAMILY CUBES

Children toss two cubes with consonants and rimes, read the word spelled by the face-up letters, and decide whether the word is real or make believe.

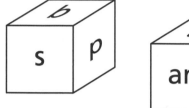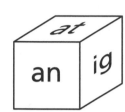

MATERIALS: Cube pattern (Appendix A–3); sturdy unlined paper; tape; black marker. Cut out the cube pattern. Write six word family rimes on each side of one cube, and six beginning consonants on each side of a second cube. Tape the cubes together (Figure 4–20).

FIGURE 4–20   Word Family Cubes

DIRECTIONS: Children sit at a table or cross-legged in a circle on the floor and take turns tossing two cubes, one with beginning consonants and one with rimes. The child who tosses the cubes pronounces a word by combining the face-up beginning sound on one cube with the face-up rime on the other cube. Some cube combinations make real words, while other combinations do not. The child tells whether the word is "real" or "nonsense." In deciding whether beginning consonant and rime combinations make real word family words or nonsense words, children get experience cross-checking for word meaning. Each child gets one point for saying the consonant-rime combination and one point for correctly indicating if the word is real or nonsense. The first child to earn twelve points wins.

■ ■ ■ ■ ■■■■
TEN-MINUTE FLUENCY ACTIVITIES FOR WORD FAMILIES AND LETTER PATTERNS

The goal of fluency activities is to help children become faster at using the letter patterns and word families. As children move through the first and second grades, their decoding should be accurate, of course, but it should also become faster and require less attention and less effort. All of these fluency activities are timed. Limiting the amount of time in which children apply knowledge improves speed without cost to accuracy (van den Bosch, van Bon, & Schreuder, 1995). Most children develop decoding fluency near the end of second grade or in the third grade (by fourth grade at the very latest). As decoding fluency develops, children increasingly use larger letter groups in word identification, which speeds up decoding even more. This, in turn, paves the way for movement into consolidated word learning.

▷ LARGE GROUP
SMALL GROUP
LETTER PATTERN
FLUENCY
WORD FAMILY
FLUENCY

RAPID BALLOON WORDS

Children use the word family rimes or letter patterns, written inside balloons, to make as many words as they can before a timer goes off and word making stops.

Name: _____
Date: _____

FIGURE 4–21 Rapid Balloons for Word Family Words

Look at the balloons below. Use the letters to make **real** words. Write your words on the lines below!

Beginning Sound   Ending Sound

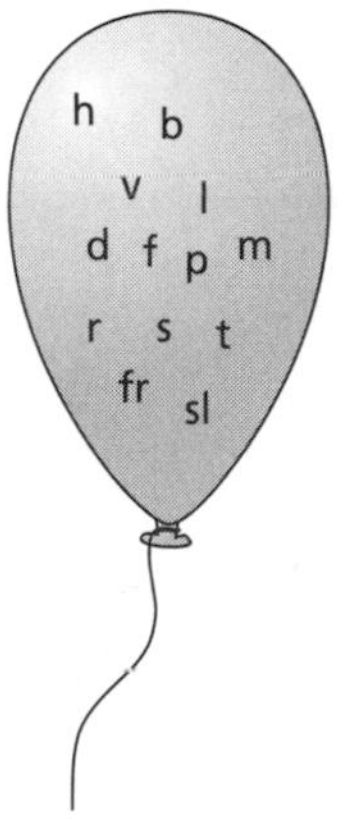

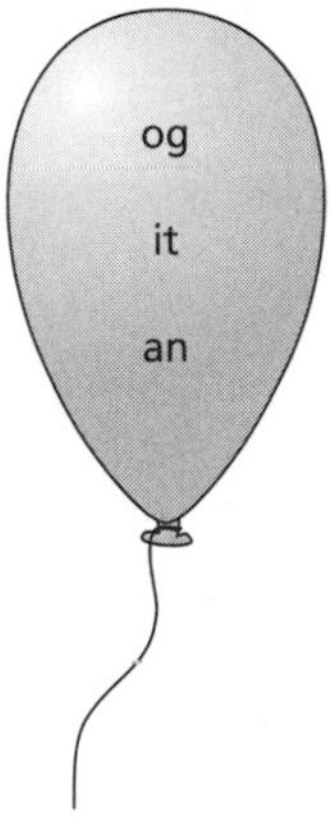

h   b
v   l
d f p m
r s t
fr sl

og

it

an

Write the words you make on the lines below.

og	it	an
hog	hit	van
dog	bit	fan
log	fit	man
fog	sit	ran
frog	lit	tan
	slit	pan

MATERIALS: A teacher-prepared rapid balloons fluency guide, one for each child (Appendixes A–12 and A–13). Each balloon has one letter pattern that, when combined with other patterns, makes words. Children should be familiar with all the patterns in the balloons.

DIRECTIONS: Read and share *Where Do Balloons Go? An Uplifting Mystery* (Curtis, 2000). Introduce rapid balloons by explaining that each balloon has an onset or rime (Figure 4–21) or a letter pattern that comes at the beginning, middle, or end of words (Figure 4–22). If using onsets and word family rimes, explain that the letters in the first balloon come at the beginning of words and the letters in the second balloon come at the end of words. Alternatively, if using balloons with letter patterns, explain that the patterns in the beginning, middle, and ending balloons form words. Show children how to build words by combining a pattern from the first balloon with patterns from other balloons, in sequence, to write a real word. Emphasize the importance of making real words. We have found that writing the patterns above the columns makes rapid balloon words easier for younger, less experienced readers (Figure 4–21). Figure 4–22 shows rapid balloon words for letter patterns.

FIGURE 4–22 Rapid
Balloons for Letter Patterns

Name: _____

Date: _____

Look at the balloons below. Use the letters to make real words. Write your words
on the lines below!

See how many **real** words you can make.

Beginning Letters	Middle Letters	Ending Letters

Balloons:
- Beginning Letters balloon: c t b h l s
- Middle Letters balloon: i a o
- Ending Letters balloon: ke ne me

Beginning Letters	Middle Letters	Ending Letters
some	sake	shame
same	take	shine
home	sane	like
hike	line	time
lake	tame	shame
bake	bike	bone
lane	cake	lime
cane	take	
choke	shake	

Pass out the balloon words guide sheets and place them face-down on children's tables. Explain that children have five minutes (more if necessary) to see how many words they can make from the patterns in the balloons. Ask the children to hold their pencils in the air, set the timer, and say, "Ready. Set. Go!" Word making stops when the timer goes off. Count the number of words each child made; write the number in the corner of the paper. As with all fluency activities, the letters you write in the balloons should be patterns the children have already learned, and the patterns that they need to bring to fluency. Appendix Figures A–12 and A–13 are blank so that you can write in two or three letter patterns. Look at Table 4–9 for examples of a few two- and three-pattern words to use in this fluency activity.

Examples of Literature Connections

Curtis, J. L. (2000). *Where do balloons go? An uplifting mystery.* New York: Joanna Cotler Books.
    Children enjoy the fanciful, rhyming answer to the question, Where do balloons go?

1. *at, it, an,* and *ig* Rime Patterns

Beginning Letters	Ending Letters
b, f, h, p, r, s	at, it, an, ig

   Words: bat, fat, hat, pat, rat, sat, bit, fit, hit, pit, sit, fan, pan, ran, big, fig, pig, rig (ban, which may not be in the children's speaking vocabulary)

2. *all, ell,* and *ill* Rime Patterns

Beginning Letters	Ending Letters
b, f, m, w	all, ell, ill

   Words: ball, fall, mall, wall, bell, fell, well, bill, fill, mill, will

3. *old, all, ind,* and *ill* Rime Patterns

Beginning Letters	Ending Letters
m, h, b, w, f	old, all, ind, ill

   Words: mold, hold, bold, fold, mall, hall, ball, wall, fall, mind, hind, bind, wind, find, mill, hill, bill, will, fill

4. *ight, ail, end,* and *ice* Rime Patterns

Beginning Letters	Ending Letters
l, n, f, s, m, r	ight, ail, end, ice

   Words: light, night, fight, sight, might, right, nail, fail, sail, mail, rail, lend, fend, send, mend, lice, nice, mice, rice (rend, which may not be in the children's speaking vocabulary)

5. CVC Short Vowel Spelling Pattern

Beginning Letters	Middle Letters	Ending Letters
p, f, b	a, e, i	t, n, g

   Words: pat, tat, bat, pet, bet, pit, tit, bit, pan, tan, ban, pen, Ben, pin, tin, bin, bag, peg, beg, pig, fig, big

6. CVC Short Vowel Spelling Pattern, Consonant Blends, and Digraphs

Beginning Letters	Middle Letters	Ending Letters
cl, st, tr, l	a, i, u, o	sh, mp, ck

   Words: clash, clamp, clack, stash, stamp, stack, trash, tramp, track, lash, lamp, lack, click, stick, trick, limp, lick, clomp, clump, cluck, stump, stuck, truck, lump, luck, *clock, stomp, stock, tromp, lock* (lush and trump, which may not be in the children's speaking vocabulary)

7. CVC Short Vowel and VCe Long Vowel Spelling Patterns

Beginning Letters	Ending Letters
h, m, sl, r	at, ate, op, ope

   Words: hat, mat, slat, rat, hate, mate, slate, rate, hop, mop, slop, hope, mope, slope, rope

TABLE 4–9 Rapid Balloon Combinations

WORD RACE

In this timed word race, children quickly move a toy car around a game board race track which has words with letter patterns or word family words the children need to bring to fluency. Each lap is timed. Children have repeated opportunities to run laps, with the goal to improve speed by reading words with letter patterns or word family words accurately, quickly, and effortlessly.

MATERIALS: Word race pattern (Appendix A–14); several toy cars or tokens; timer.

DIRECTIONS: Copy the word race pattern (Appendix A–14). Select words with letter patterns or word family words children are learning. Write one word on each square. Explain to the children in a small group that they are to race around the word track as fast as they can.

▷ SMALL GROUP
LETTER PATTERN
FLUENCY
WORD FAMILY
FLUENCY

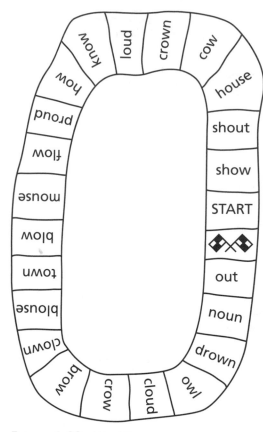

FIGURE 4–23   Word Race

▶ **LARGE GROUP**
SMALL GROUP
WORD FAMILY FLUENCY

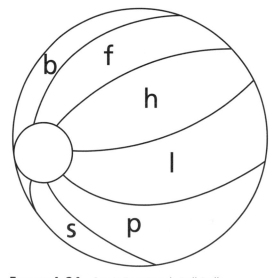

FIGURE 4–24   Say It Fast Beach Ball Roll

Children read words as their car moves over them (Figure 4–23). Each trial is timed. When you say, "Ready. Set. Go!" the child begins racing around the word track. Start the timer and stop it when the car reaches the finish line. Repeat race trials until the children are fluent at reading all the words on the track, then put different words on the track. In order for one lap around the track to count, children must read each word accurately. Errors are "yellow flag" words; that is, words that cause the race to be suspended and the lap to start over again. There is a possibility that some children might remember the word order. Should this happen, write words on another copy of the racetrack, but in a different order.

SAY IT FAST BEACH BALL ROLL

Children take turns gently rolling a beach ball with consonants written on it while quickly saying a word family word formed by the consonant closest to their right hand and one of several rimes written on the board. Children make as many words as possible within a time limit you specify. On subsequent days the group tries to beat its score by making even more words in the same time.

MATERIALS: Beach ball; permanent black marker; list of rimes; timer. (A soccer ball may be substituted.) Write single consonants, consonant clusters, or digraphs randomly on a beach ball (Figure 4–24). Write two or three familiar rimes on the board.

DIRECTIONS: Ask a small group to sit on the floor in a circle. Show the beach ball with consonant letters on it. Explain that the children are to gently roll the beach ball to each other. Children who catch the ball make a word family word by combining the beginning letter that is closest to their right hand with one of the rimes on the board. Set a time for beach ball rolling. We usually start out with four minutes, and adjust up or down depending on how the group performs. Show children the timer and tell them they have exactly four minutes to make as many words as possible. Stress that only real words count.

Keep track of the number of real words the group makes, and write that number in a corner of the board. You may simply write the total words or you may want to translate the total score into points, say one point for each real word. On subsequent days challenge the children to make even more words (or points). If working for points helps keep your children working together and goal focused, specify the number of points (words) earned in one timed session that qualifies for a special treat, such as an extra ten minutes of free time on Friday, going first to lunch, or being first in line to go to the playground. Use the same beginning consonants and rimes repeatedly until children are fluent at combining beginning consonants and rimes to pronounce words.

Select relatively easy beginning consonants and rimes for less-advanced readers, and more challenging consonants and word family rimes for more advanced readers. For example, children might begin with *b, f, h, l, p,* and *s* on the beach ball and *it* and *ag* on the board, resulting in *bit, fit, hit, lit, pit, sit, bag, hag, lag,* and *sag.* They then might move to *c, f, p, m, b, s, h, r, t, w,* and three rimes *all, ill,* and *at,* which form *call, fall, mall, ball, hall, tall, wall, fill, pill, mill, bill, sill, hill, will, cat, fat, pat, mat, bat, sat, hat,* and *rat.* Eventually they will be able to quickly, accurately, and effortlessly combine *d, p, t, g, ch, s, b, m, st,* and *sm,* plus *all, ill, art,* and *ock* into *pall, tall, gall, ball, mall, stall, small, dill, pill, gill, chill, sill, bill, mill, still, dart, part, tart, chart, Bart, mart, start, smart, dock, pock, chock, sock, mock, stock,* and *smock.*

FINGER HURDLES

Children use their fingers to jump over paper tent hurdles with words that have one or two letter patterns in common. Hurdle jumping is timed, and children try to beat their own best score on subsequent days.

MATERIALS: Unlined 3 × 5 cards; black marker; timer. To make a hurdle, fold a 3 × 5 card in half, write a word on it, and stand it on the table. For smaller hurdles, cut 3 × 5 cards in half before folding. Decide on one, two, or three letter patterns that children need practice bringing to fluency. Find from ten to twenty words with these patterns, and write one word on each paper tent. Set the hurdles on a table (Figure 4–25). Demonstrate how to jump hurdles by touching the table with fingers and saying the word. Explain that finger hurdles are timed and that children must read each word correctly. Children may self-correct, however. Should a hurdle mistakenly be knocked over, the jumper must right it before going to the next hurdle, and the time it takes to put a fallen hurdle right side up is figured into the total hurdle running time. Individual races start when you say, "On your mark. Get set. Go!" Start the timer immediately. Write down the total time in seconds. Children are competing against themselves, not other children. Challenge children to beat their own best score each time they run finger hurdles. Examples of finger hurdle words with the *ca, co, cu,* and *ce, ci, cy* patterns are:

Set I: *ca* and *co* hard *c* patterns: *candy, candle, capture, camel, cafeteria, carrot, calendar, cabinet, captain, cargo, colony, compass, count, corral, coconut, column, company, construct, contrast, couch* (twenty words)

Set II: *ge* soft *g* and *go* hard *g* patterns: *gerbil, ranger, genie, gentle, bridge, strange, village, cage, charge, goal, goose, gopher, goblin, gossip, goddess* (fifteen words)

Set III: *ge, gi,* and *gy* soft *g* patterns: *giant, gerbil, ginger, cage, gentle, huge, gypsy, gym, gigantic, giraffe, bridge, charge, village, cage, strange* (fifteen words)

Set IV: *ce, ci,* and *cy* soft *c* patterns: *dice, cellar, bicycle, lace, certain, citrus, mercy, centimeter, circle, pencil, center, cymbal, city, cell, cycle* (fifteen words)

Set V: *co* hard *c* and *ce* soft *c* patterns: *coke, comic, contain, coyote, collar, compound, confess, coin, condition, cousin, center, mice, central, concert, percent, place, face, ceiling, certain, cereal* (twenty words)

Finger hurdles take a very short time. Have children put up and take down the hurdles, and use the same set of words until children become fluent reading them. Vary the order of the word hurdles from race to race so children do not become accustomed to a particular word order. In jumping finger hurdles, children not only gain experience and practice reading words with pronounceable letter patterns, but they also develop fluency reading the words on the hurdles.

FIGURE 4–25 Finger Hurdle Races

TIMED PATTERN SEARCH

Children search on cereal boxes or in newspapers and magazines for words with specific letter patterns. Found words are written on charts and children decode pattern-by-pattern any words that are not already in the children's fluent reading vocabulary.

MATERIALS: Back panels from cereal boxes; pages from old magazines or newspapers; highlighters; timer; chart paper.

DIRECTIONS: Pass out panels from cereal boxes, a page from an old magazine or a newspaper to each child. Distribute highlighters. Write the letter pattern on the board, for example *th.* Explain that children are to find and highlight words with *th.* Tell children they have exactly four minutes (longer or shorter, depending on the group) to find as many words as they can.

Set a time limit on pattern searches because timing helps children increase their speed in locating letter patterns in words. Whereas in untimed searches children work for accuracy, in timed searches children must be both accurate and fast. Searching starts when you say, "Ready. Set. Go!" Searching stops when the timer goes off.

Have children share the words they find. Write the words on a chart. Ask children to read individual words and underline the target letter pattern. Talk about the target pattern, where it occurs in words—beginning, middle, or end—and how it represents sound. Use pattern-by-pattern decoding to pronounce any words that are not already in children's reading vocabularies. When children effortlessly read words with the letter pattern, switch to a different pattern that children need to bring to fluency.

SMALL GROUP
INDIVIDUAL
LETTER PATTERN
FLUENCY

TIMED PATTERN-BY-PATTERN WORD BUILDING

Children use magnets with letter patterns to build as many words as they can within five minutes. On subsequent days, children try to beat their own best score.

MATERIALS: Pattern magnets from the individualized letter pattern magnet activity or cards with letter patterns on them; paper and pencil; timer. Letter pattern cards may be substituted for magnets.

DIRECTIONS: This activity requires two rounds. Children work in teams of two: One team member is the word maker; the other the word writer. The team members reverse roles on the second word-building round. Explain that the word maker is to build as many words as possible in only five minutes. The word writer writes down the words the builder makes. Give teams a set of letter pattern magnets (or cards). Set the timer. Teams begin building words when they hear you say, "Ready. Set. Go!" Select team members so that the teams are fairly equal in word building and word writing ability. A super fast word builder teamed with a super slow word writer does not work. Keep a record of the number of words built in five minutes. On subsequent rounds on subsequent days, challenge teams to work faster so as to beat their own highest score.

SMALL GROUP
LARGE GROUP
LETTER PATTERN
FLUENCY
WORD FAMILY
FLUENCY

WORD FAMILY AND LETTER PATTERN RELAY

Teams compete to read accurately and rapidly word family words or words with letter patterns you have already taught.

MATERIALS: Two sets of cards with word family words or words with the letter patterns children are learning; stopwatch or watch with a second hand. Each set of cards should have about twenty words. You need another adult, in addition to yourself, to use this relay in your classroom.

DIRECTIONS: Divide the class (or group) into two teams. Make the teams relatively equal in the reading ability of team members. Shuffle each word set. Give one set to another adult and keep one set yourself. Each team forms a line in front of one adult. Set the stopwatch. Begin with, "Ready. Set. Go!"

Show the first child in each team a word card. The child reads the word and goes to the back of the line (or to the child's seat). Children may self-correct miscues. If a child cannot read a word, that child steps to the side and the next child in line reads the word. The child who had difficulty then gets to try the next word that comes up. Teams may read the sets one or more times. The first team to read all the words wins. Next time the teams read relay words, challenge the teams to read the same number of words in less time.

From a word-learning perspective, the goal of letter pattern and word family word activities is to move children in the alphabetic fluency stage into the consolidated stage and, eventually, into the automatic stage. Children in the consolidated word fluency stage use multi-letter groups to streamline word identification and to gain insight into word meaning through knowledge of prefixes, suffixes, and root words borrowed from other languages. We will consider what children need to know about multi-letter groups and teaching activities for consolidated word fluency in the next chapter.

REFERENCES

Adams, M. J. (1990). *Beginning to read: Thinking and learning about print.* Cambridge, MA: The MIT Press.
Addler, D. (2001). *Cam Jansen and the barking treasure mystery* (Cam Jansen 19). New York: Puffin.

Andreae, G., & Wojtowjcz, D. (1998). *Commotion in the ocean.* New York: Scholastic.

Branley, F. M. (1996). *What makes a magnet?* New York: Harper Trophy.

Butterworth, N., & Inkpen, M. (1997). *Jasper's beanstalk.* New York: Alladin.

Byrne, B., Freebody, P., & Gates, A. (1992). Longitudinal data on the relations of word-reading strategies to comprehension, reading time, and phonemic awareness. *Reading Research Quarterly, 27,* 140–151.

Capucilli, A. S. (1997). *Biscuit.* New York: Harper Trophy.

Caseley, J. (1991). *Dear Annie.* New York: Mulberry Books.

Cazet, D. (2000). *Minnie and Moo and the musk of Zorro.* New York: Dorling Kindersley Publishing.

Curtis, J. L. (2000). *Where do balloons go? An uplifting mystery.* New York: Joanna Cotler Books.

Doubilet, A. (1991). *Under the sea from a to z.* New York: Scholastic.

Ehri, L. C., & Robbins, C. (1992). Beginners need some decoding skill to read words by analogy. *Reading Research Quarterly, 27,* 13–26.

Gaskins, I. W., Ehri, L. C., Cress, C., O'Hara, C., & Donnelly, K. (1996/1997). Procedures for word learning: Making discoveries about words. *The Reading Teacher, 50,* 312–327.

Gleiter, J., & Thompson, K. (1995). *Booker T. Washington.* Austin, TX: Steck-Vaughn.

Goswami, U. (1999). Causal connections in beginning reading: The importance of rhyme. *Journal of Research in Reading, 22,* 217–240.

Goswami, U. (2001). Early phonological development and the acquisition of literacy. In S. B. Neuman & D. K. Dickinson (Eds.), *Handbook of early literacy research* (pp. 111–125). New York: Guilford Press.

Gottardo, A., Chiappe, P., Siegel, L. S., & Stanovich, K. E. (1999). Patterns of word and non-word processing in skilled and less-skilled readers. *Reading and writing: an interdisciplinary journal, 11,* 465–487.

Hayward, L. (1998). *Baker, baker, cookie maker.* New York: CTW Publishing.

Holub, J. (1997). *Pen pals.* New York: Grosset and Dunlap.

Jones, M. T., & Dadey, D. (2001). *Topdog.* New York: Volo Books.

Juel, C., & Minden-Cupp, C. (2000). Learning to read words: Linguistic units and instructional strategies. *Reading Research Quarterly, 35,* 458–492.

Juel, C., & Roper-Schneider, D. (1985). The influence of basal readers on first grade reading. *Reading Research Quarterly, 20,* 134–152.

Kaye, P. (1991). *Games for learning.* New York: Farrar Straus Giroux.

Krensky, S. (2000). *Binky rules.* Boston, MA: Little, Brown and Company.

Kuskin, K. (1992). *Soup soap,* New York: Harper Trophy.

Lear, E. (1996). *The owl and the pussycat.* New York: Putnam.

Leedy, L. (1991). *Messages in the mailbox: How to write a letter.* New York: Holiday House.

Lund, J. (1999). *Two cool coyotes.* New York: Dutton Children's Books.

Margulies, T. (2001). *Clifford the big red dog: The show-and-tell surprise.* New York: Scholastic.

Marsh, T. J., & Ward, J. (1998). *Way out in the desert.* Flagstaff, AZ: Rising Moon.

McCloskey, R. (1941). *Make way for ducklings.* New York: Viking Press.

McCormick, S. (1999). *Instructing students who have literacy problems, 3rd edition.* Columbus, OH: Merrill.

Meddaugh, S. (1992). *Martha speaks.* Boston, MA: Houghton Mifflin.

Meddaugh, S. (1994). *Martha calling.* Boston, MA: Houghton Mifflin.

Meddaugh, S. (1996). *Martha blah, blah.* Boston, MA: Houghton Mifflin.

Meddaugh, S. (1998). *Martha walks the dog.* Boston, MA: Houghton Mifflin.

Meddaugh, S. (2000). *Martha and skits.* Boston, MA: Houghton Mifflin.

Mesmer, H. A. E. (2001). Decodable text: A review of what we know. *Reading Research and Instruction, 40,* 121–142.

National Institute of Child Health and Human Development (2000). *Report of the national reading panel: Teaching children to read: An evidence-based assessment of the scientific research literature on reading and its implications for reading instruction: Reports of subgroups* (NIH Publication no. 00-4754). Washington, DC: U.S. Government Printing Office.

Neye, E. (2000). *Butterflies.* New York: Grosset and Dunlap.

O'Neill, M. (1961). *Hailstones and halibut bones.* New York: Doubleday.

Osborne, M. P. (2000). *Dingoes at dinnertime* (Magic Tree House 20). New York: Random House.

Osborne, M. P. (2001). *Earthquake in the early morning.* New York: Random House.

Palmer, S. (2000). Development of phonological recoding and literacy acquisition: A four-year cross sequential study. *British Journal of Developmental Psychology, 18,* 533–555.

Parish, H. (1995). *Good driving, Amelia Bedelia*. New York: Avon Books.

Park, B. (2000). *Junie B. Jones has a peep in her pocket*. New York: Random House.

Prelutsky, J. (ed.) (1997). *Favorite poems by Dennis Lee; Dinosaur dinner (with a slice of alligator pie)*. New York: Dragonfly Books.

Rupley, W. H., & Willson, V. L. (1997). Relationship between comprehension and components of word recognition: Support for developmental shifts. *Journal of Research and Development in Education, 30,* 255–260.

Savage, R. (2001). A re-evaluation of the evidence for orthographic analogies: A reply to Goswami (1999). *Journal of Research in Reading, 24,* 1–18.

Scarry, R., & Herman, G. (1998). *Mr. Fixit's magnet machine*. New York: Simon Spotlight.

Spurr, E. (1997). *The long, long letter*. New York: Hyperion Paperbacks for Children.

Stevens, J. R. (1993). *Carlos and the squash plant; Carlos y la planta de calabaza*. Flagstaff, AZ: Rising Moon.

van den Bosch, K., van Bon, W. J. J., & Schreuder, R. (1995). Poor readers' decoding skills: Effects of training with limited exposure duration. *Reading Research Quarterly, 30,* 110–125.

Wang, C. C., & Gaffney, J. S. (1998). First graders' use of analogy in word reading. *Journal of Literacy Research, 3,* 389–403.

Ward, J., & Marsh, T. J. (2000). *Somewhere in the ocean*. Flagstaff, AZ: Rising Moon.

Zeno, S. M., Ivens, S. H., Millard, R. T., & Duvvuri, R. (1995). *The educator's word frequency guide*. New York: Touchstone Applied Science Associates.

DEVELOPING FLUENCY WITH HANDS-ON ACTIVITIES FOR TEACHING STRUCTURAL ANALYSIS

5

Use these word structure activities with first through fifth grades in:

▷ **The Alphabetic Word Fluency Stage**

▷ **The Consolidated Word Fluency Stage**

prefix + use	use + suffix(es)		prefix + use + suffix(es)	
reuse	used	useful	reused	overused
disuse	user	using	reuses	overuses
multiuse	uses	useless	unused	reusable
overuse	users	usefully	misused	overusing
	usage	usability	misuses	unusable
	usable	uselessly	reusing	underused
		usefulness	misusing	

Structural analysis is the term we use for associating sound and meaning to morphemes, compound words, contractions, root words, base words, prefixes, suffixes, and syllables. Children who understand word structure know that each of the thirty words in the lists above is a form of the familiar word, *use*, and not a totally new word. Let us take *misusing* as an example. M*isusing* is a three-syllable word constructed from *mis-*, *use*, and *-ing*. To identify *misusing*, children separate the prefix (*mis-*) and then the suffix (*-ing*) from *use*. In so doing, children realize that *misusing* is the familiar word, *use*, with a prefix and a suffix. Understanding the sound and meaning of large structural elements like *mis-*, *use*, and *-ing* greatly accelerates word identification. Though children learn a handful of high utility structural elements in first and second grade, the real business of learning about word structure begins in the third grade and increases substantially in grades four and five.

MORPHEMES ■ ■ ■ ■ ▬▬

Free Morphemes

Morphemes are the basic meaning units in our English language. Morphemes can be free or bound. Free morphemes have meaning in and of themselves; they can stand alone as whole words. A free morpheme is the smallest meaningful unit that can be spoken or written without any other morpheme. For instance, *paint* is a free morpheme. *P*aint has meaning all by itself; we do not need to add any other morpheme to associate meaning with *paint*, and we cannot reduce *paint* to a smaller word. *Paint* is a complete, meaningful word all by itself.

Bound Morphemes

Bound morphemes have meaning only when they are attached to another morpheme. The *mis-* and *-ing* in *misusing* are bound morphemes. For *mis-* and *-ing* to be meaningful, they must be attached to another morpheme, as in *misplace* and *playing*. Bound morphemes do have meaning, but that meaning is only expressed when they are part of another morpheme. For example, *re-* connotes repeated action or improvement, as in *retype* or *redecorate*. However, we cannot use *re-* alone and expect to communicate in speech or print. Bound morphemes include prefixes (the *mis-* in *misusing*), suffixes (the *-ing* in *misusing*), and root words borrowed from other languages to form English words (the *aqua-* in *aquatic, aquarium*, and *aquatics*). Many English words consist of a combination of free and bound morphemes.

U*seful* consists of two morphemes: the free morpheme, *use*, and the bound morpheme, *-ful*. Combining the free morpheme *use* with one or more bound morphemes forms the thirty words in the lists at the beginning of this chapter. Combining morphemes is a common way in which we form many multi-syllable words. One way to identify an unfamiliar long word is to identify familiar free and bound morphemes in that word. Generally speaking, words that are created from free morphemes are easier to identify than those created from bound morphemes (Combs, 2002). This is particularly true of compound words.

■ ■ ■ ■ COMPOUND WORDS

Compound words are two words, or free morphemes, glued together to form a single word.

base + ball = baseball   snow + man = snowman
butter + cup = buttercup   text + book = textbook
book + shelf = bookshelf   gum + shoe = gumshoe

The meaning of some compound words is quite similar to the two words individually, as in *barefoot* and *campfire*. Because the meanings of *barefoot* and *campfire* do not stray too far afield from the meaning of the individual words, children can infer the meaning of these two compounds by analyzing the two free morphemes. For instance, a child could justifiably assume that *barefoot* means a *foot* that is *bare*; that is, a foot with no shoe or sock. Other examples of easy-to-understand compounds are *bathtub, cheerleader, firefighter*, and *tablecloth*. If a child knows the meaning of the individual words that make up the compound, then that child can infer the meaning of the compound word. The child's major task is to identify the two words that are glued together to form the compound. If the meaning of every compound could be inferred from the two words individually, then you would only have to teach children to look for free morphemes in compound words. However, the meaning of some compounds cannot be inferred from the two constituent words.

The meaning of some compounds has very little connection to the meaning of the two words that form the compounds. For instance, knowing the meaning of *butter* and *cup* does not suggest the meaning of *buttercup*. A *buttercup* looks somewhat like a cup-shaped flower filled to the brim with a yellow buttery substance. This, however, is imagery, not the meaning of *buttercup*. Children quite logically assume that they know the meaning of compound words because they see two familiar words joined into one long word. To understand compounds like *buttercup*, children must look beyond the individual words to consider sentence context and prior knowledge. Other examples of this type of compound include *eavesdrop*, *gumshoe*, and *heirloom*. In teaching these types of compounds, you need to show children how to use the sentence context to infer meaning. When the sentence context does not give enough clues, you need to directly teach the meaning of compound words.

Appendix II is a list of compound words. Compound words are so prevalent in our language that children meet them early in their journey toward literacy. Introduce beginning readers to compound words that have meaning that is easily inferred from the individual words themselves, such as *snowman* and *footprint*. Then, as children gain reading independence, introduce compounds that represent a meaning that is quite different from the meaning of the two words individually.

BASE AND ROOT WORDS ■ ■ ■ ■ ▬▬▬▬

Base Words

A base word is a free morpheme. *Buttercup* is a combination of the two base words, *butter* + *cup*. Likewise, *overuse* is created by gluing together the two base words *over* + *use*. Any word that can stand alone is a base word. Examples include verbs like *go* and *jump*, nouns such as *desk* and *book*, adjectives like *big* and *huge*, adverbs such as *slow* and *fast*, and function words like *the* and *which*. Every base word has meaning in and of itself. We can use base words individually, as in "Go!" or we can combine base words into phrases and sentences. We can find base words individually listed and defined in the dictionary.

Root Words

Root words have meaning when they are combined with another morpheme. Most root words are of Greek or Latin origin. Root words borrowed from Greek and Latin form the basis of many English words with related or connected meanings. English words that have the same root belong to a meaning family. For example, *magn-*, a root word of Latin origin, means great. Words in the *magn-* meaning family include *magnificent*, *magnify*, *magnitude*, and *magnanimous*. English is peppered with root words. Our predecessors borrowed flagrantly from Greek and Latin to coin English words, and we continue this tradition today. *Cyberspace*, *astronaut*, and *biosphere* are recent examples.

Root words are part of many long familiar words, and hence children encounter root words quite frequently. Content subjects in the upper grades introduce children to root words such as *democracy* (from the Greek *dem-*, meaning people, and *cracy*, meaning to rule) and *geologist* (from the Greek root *ge*(o)-, meaning earth, and *-ist*, meaning one who is engaged in or believes in). Knowing that *ge*(o)- means earth gives children insight into other words in the *ge*(o)- meaning family, like *geography*, *geology*, *geologic*, and *geopolitics*.

Because roots are imbedded in longer words and because the meaning of roots are borrowed from other languages, children will not necessarily be able to infer word meaning from everyday reading experiences. Added to this, each word in a meaning family has a slightly different definition. For example, the Greek root *aut*(o)-, meaning self, is present in *automobile*, *automatic*, and *autonomic*. However, these three English words have different meanings, although their meanings are related to the common root word. To identify *aut*(o)- in *automatic*, children must analyze word structure. Therefore, when fourth and fifth grade teachers teach children about root words, they are teaching both vocabulary (word meaning) and structural analysis (the essential units in words). In teaching root words, focus on root meaning and on how to identify words that belong to a meaning family. Teach the roots that children commonly encounter in reading and the roots children need for writing. Also teach root words that contribute to increasing children's speaking, listening, reading, and spelling vocabularies. Teaching root words within the context of ongoing vocabulary instruction is fitting, since the roots themselves are one of several keys to the meaning of a great many English words. Look in Appendix III for a list of root words.

■■■■ ■ ■ ■ ■ SHORT CUT WORDS

Contractions

We use two ways to shorten English words. We either abbreviate two words by making them into a single contraction or we chop off part of a long word to make it a short word. Contractions are short cuts that combine two words and then shorten one of them. For example, instead of writing two separate words for *was not*, we take a short cut and write *wasn't* instead. In shortening two words, one or more letters are removed and replaced by an apostrophe. The apostrophe signals that the word is an abbreviation. For example, *not* is abbreviated in *wasn't*. Readers know that *not* is abbreviated in *wasn't* because the apostrophe tells them which of the two words is shortened. In English we almost always abbreviate the second word in a contraction. Word meaning is the same whether words are written separately or as contractions.

wasn't = was not	who's = who is	we'd = we would
we've = we have	I'll = I will	who're = who are

All children encounter contractions and use them in writing, so teaching about contractions is an excellent large or small group activity. Table 5–1 is a list of contractions divided into groups based on the abbreviated word. Children use contractions everyday in spoken language, so the words themselves are familiar. However, in order to identify contractions in print, children must explicitly understand the basic concept behind using an apostrophe to show that a word is abbreviated. Children must also know the difference between an apostrophe that indicates an abbreviated word (*wasn't*) and an apostrophe that shows possession (*Jane's* book).

Clipped Words

Clipped words are shortened forms of long words, such as *vet* for *veterinarian*. Instead of using an apostrophe to show that a word is abbreviated, we simply chop off a large part of the word itself. This leaves us with short, one-syllable words that are easier to say and easier to write. There are many clipped words in English. Table 5–2 is a list of clipped words that fourth and fifth graders enjoy exploring.

■■■■ ■ ■ ■ ■ PREFIXES AND SUFFIXES

Prefixes are attached to the beginning of words (*re* + *play* = *replay*). Suffixes are added to the end of words (*play* + *ing* = *playing*). We use the term *affix* to refer to prefixes and suffixes together. Affixes are bound morphemes; that is, they have meaning when they are attached to another morpheme. Prefixes and suffixes lengthen words and, not coincidentally, change the way words look. Affixes also affect word meaning, which makes it doubly important for children to be able to identify, pronounce, and understand affixes. Prefixes either change meaning (*un* + *happy* = *unhappy*) or make meaning more specific (*re* + *play* = *replay*).

Inflectional Suffixes

Suffixes change meaning (*cat* + *s* = *cats*) or alter grammatical function. For example, adding *-able* to *use* changes a verb (*use*) into an adjective (*usable*). Suffixes are divided

not	is	will
aren't (are not)	he's (he is)	he'll (he will)
can't (can not)	here's (here is)	I'll (I will)
couldn't (could not)	how's (how is)	it'll (it will)
didn't (did not)	it's (it is)	she'll (she will)
doesn't (does not)	she's (she is)	they'll (they will)
don't (do not)	that's (that is)	you'll (you will)
hadn't (had not)	there's (there is)	we'll (we will)
hasn't (has not)	what's (what is)	what'll (what will)
haven't (have not)	when's (when is)	where'll (where will)
isn't (is not)	where's (where is)	
mustn't (must not)	who's (who is)	
needn't (need not)		
shouldn't (should not)		
wasn't (was not)		
weren't (were not)		
won't (will not)		
wouldn't (would not)		

have	had	would
	he'd (he had)	
could've (could have)	I'd (I had)	I'd (I would)
I've (I have)	it'd (it had)	he'd (he would)
might've (might have)	she'd (she had)	she'd (she would)
should've (should have)	they'd (they had)	they'd (they would)
they've (they have)		we'd (we would)
we've (we have)		
would've (would have)		
you've (you have)		

are	has	Other Contractions
they're (they are)	he's (he has)	I'm (I am)
we're (we are)	it's (it has)	let's (let us)
who're (who are)	she's (she has)	o'clock (of the clock)
you're (you are)		'twas (it was)

TABLE 5–1 Contractions for Word Study

into two groups: inflectional and derivational. Inflectional suffixes consist of -s (-es), -ed, -ing, -er, and -est. These suffixes change the number (one cat or two cats), affect the verb tense (walk or walked), or indicate comparison (a big house or a bigger house). Inflected endings do not change the part of speech, with the exception of -ing, which may affect grammatical function in some situations. For example, build means to construct something, while building may be either the act of constructing or an object, as in the Empire State Building or a bank building. Most children learn to read and write words with -s (-es), -ed, and -ing by the end of the first grade, and learn -er and -est by the end of the second grade.

Derivational Suffixes

Derivational suffixes affect meaning and grammatical usage. Derivational suffixes in the lists at the beginning of the chapter include -able (usable), -age (usage), -ful (useful), -less (useless), -ly (uselessly), -ability (usability), and -ness (usefulness). We usually teach

TABLE 5–2 Clipped Words

Clipped Words	Longer Words	Clipped Words	Longer Words
abs	abdominal muscles	lube	lubricant
ad	advertisement	mart	market
ag	agriculture	math	mathematics
auto	automobile	mayo	mayonnaise
bike	bicycle	memo	memorandum
bro	brother	mod	modern
burger	hamburger	movie	moving picture
champ	champion	obit	obituary
chat	chatter	oleo	oleomargarine
chute	parachute	pants	pantaloons
coed	coeducational	phone	telephone
combo	combination	photo	photograph
con	convict	pike	turnpike
con	against	plane	airplane
condo	condominium	pop	popular
co-op	cooperative	prefab	prefabricated structure
copter	helicopter	pro	professional
curio	curiosity	prom	promenade
doc	doctor	pup	puppy
dorm	dormitory	radio	radiotelegraphy
el	elevated train	ref	referee
exam	examination	rep	representative
fax	facsimile	rep	reputation
fed	federal	rhino	rhinoceros
fest	festival	roach	cockroach
flu	influenza	sax	saxophone
frank	frankfurter	semi	semitrailer
fridge	refrigerator	sis	sister
gas	gasoline	sub	submarine
gator	alligator	sub	substitute
grad	graduate	super	superintendent
gym	gymnasium	super	superior
hippo	hippopotamus	taxi	taxicab
hydro	hydroelectricity	teen	teenager
intercom	intercommunication	tie	necktie
intro	introduction	trike	tricycle
fries	French fries	tux	tuxedo
lab	laboratory	typo	typographical error
legit	legitimate	vet	veterinarian
limo	limousine	zoo	zoological garden

children about derivational suffixes during vocabulary instruction, which is appropriate because of the impact these suffixes have on meaning. Table 5–3 presents four guidelines for adding suffixes to words. Look in Appendix IV for many different prefixes and examples of words that begin with the prefixes and in Appendix V for lists of suffixes.

Children's knowledge of suffixes increases with grade level (Nagy, Diakidoy, & Anderson, 1993; Singson, Mahony, & Mann, 2000). Children learn about suffixes from their teachers and also from a plethora of reading and writing experiences. Books for children in the third grade and above have many more words with prefixes and

TABLE 5–3 Guidelines for Adding Suffixes to Words

1. Plurals Add *-s* to most words, as in *rats* and *rates*. Add *-es* to words ending in *-s* (*buses, pluses*), *-ss* (*kisses, messes*), *-ch* (*benches, lunches*), *-sh* (*washes, wishes*), and *-x* (*foxes, boxes*).

2. VC Short Vowel Words Double the last consonant before adding *-ed, -ing, -er,* or *-est* to most VC short vowel pattern words (*hopped, hopping, bigger, biggest*). Doubling the last consonant preserves the VC short vowel pattern. For example, doubling the consonant before adding a suffix to *hop* and *pin* gives the reader a clear signal that these words are spelled with a VC pattern (*hopped* and *pinned*). However, simply adding a suffix to VCe words indicates a long vowel pattern (*hoped* and *pined*). Consequently, doubling the consonant prevents children from reading VC words as if they were VCe words (*hopped, hoped; matted, mated; pinned, pined*).

3. Drop the final *e* before adding *-ed, -ing, -er,* and *-est* to VCe long vowel pattern words (*baked, baking, baker, cutest*).

4. For words that end in the letter *y*, change the final *y* to *i* before adding *-es, -ed, -er,* and *-est* (*babies, babied, busier, busiest*).

TABLE 5–4 The Most Common Prefixes and Suffixes in Grades Three Through Nine*

Prefixes and Suffixes that Occur in Up to 82 Percent of Affixed Words

Prefixes	Suffixes
un-, re-	-s (-es), -ed, -ing, -ly
in-, im-, ir-, il- (not)	-er and -or (agent)
dis-, en-, em-, non-	-ion, -tion, -ation, ition
in- and im- (meaning into)	-able and -ible
over- (meaning too much)	
mis-, sub-, pre-	

Prefixes and Suffixes that Occur in 18 Percent or Less of Affixed Words

Prefixes	Suffixes
inter-, fore-	-al and -ial (capable of)
de-, trans-, super-	-y, -ness, -ity, and -ty
semi-, anti-, mid-	-ment, -ic
under- (too little)	-ous, -eous, and -ious
	-en, -er (comparative)
	-ive, -ative, -itive, -ful
	-less, -est

* White, T. G., Sowell, J., & Yanagihara A. (1989). Teaching elementary students to use word-part clues. *The Reading Teacher, 42,* 302–308.

suffixes than do books intended for first- and second-grade readers. The number of words with prefixes and suffixes doubles from fourth to fifth grade, and doubles again by the seventh grade (White, Power, & White, 1989). Children who are aware of the base word, *use*, and who understand how this morpheme changes with the addition of different affixes are better comprehenders (Carlisle, 2000) and spellers (Leong, 2000) than their classmates.

Interestingly, fifth graders may encounter over a thousand words with the prefixes *in-, im-, ir-, il-* (meaning "not"), *un-, re-,* and *dis-* (Nagy, Diakidoy, & Anderson, 1993). Consequently, fifth-grade readers need to be quite fluent in reading words with these affixes. Table 5–4 shows the most frequently occurring prefixes and suffixes in English curriculum materials for grades three through nine, divided into those that occur in up to 82 percent of affixed words and those that occur in 18 percent or less (White, Sowell, & Yanagihara, 1989). U*n-* accounts for 26 percent of the words with prefixes, while a fourfold combination of *un-, re-, in-,* and *dis-* accounts for 58 percent of the affixed words that children are likely to read in grades three through nine (White, Sowell, & Yanagihara, 1989). The *-s* (*-es*), *-ing*, and *-ed* endings account for 65 percent of the suffixes in materials for third through ninth grade readers (White, Sowell, & Yanagihara, 1989).

How to Identify Prefixes and Suffixes in Long Words

Prefixes and suffixes make base words longer. That is, when we add a prefix or a suffix to a word, the word itself becomes long and, not coincidentally, also contains more syllables. Not surprisingly, affixes change the way words look. Many children stumble over words they know when those words have one or more affixes. An effective strategy for identifying long words with prefixes and suffixes is to show children how to peel affixes away from base words. The steps in the long word solving strategy consist of:

unbreakable

Step 1   Find the prefix and remove it.
            unbreakable – *un* = breakable
Step 2   Find the suffix and remove it.
            breakable – *able* = break
Step 3   Identify the syllables, and pronounce the base word.
            break
Step 4   Put the whole word back together. Pronounce it.
            un + *break* + *able* = unbreakable

Model this strategy and write the steps on a chart. Give children practice using this strategy to identify long words in the books they are reading in your classroom. Whenever children are stumped by familiar base words with prefixes and suffixes, refer to the chart and show children how to systematically peel off prefixes and suffixes.

For additional practice, ask children to work individually or with a partner to complete a long word solving guide (Figure 5–1). The words in the guide in Figure 5–1 are from F*rindle* (Clements, 1996). This chapter book tells the story of how a new word, frindle, enters an imaginary dictionary, thanks to a clever and inventive fifth grader. Fourth and fifth graders read books peppered with long, affixed words. Therefore, you will easily find words in other books to make long word solving guides tailored to the books children are reading in your classroom.

Once the children complete the practice guide, ask them to look up at least two of the words, using the page numbers written below the long words on the guide. Once children find sentences with the long words, children write the words at the top of a sticky note and stick the sticky note to the top of the pages on which the words are found. Call on individuals (or groups) to read the sentences they find, to write the target words on the board, and to underline the prefixes and suffixes. Look in the Reproducible Pattern Appendix (A–15) for a guide to duplicate for your own classroom.

■■■■■ ■ ■ ■ ■ SYLLABLES AND ACCENT

Syllables

The syllable is the basic unit of pronunciation in English words. Each and every English syllable has one and only one vowel sound. Syllables may have more than one vowel letter, but only one vowel sound. For instance, *street* and *set* are both one-

Long Word Solving

FIGURE 5–1 Long Word Solving

Step 1. Find the prefix and remove it.
Step 2. Find the suffix and remove it.
Step 3. Identify the syllables, and pronounce the base word.
Step 4. Put the whole word back together. Pronounce it.

Directions:
Read each word in the first column. Find the prefix, the suffix, and the familiar base word. If a word does not have a prefix or a suffix, leave the box blank. The first two words are done for you.

Long Word	Prefix Find the prefix. Remove it.	Suffix Find the suffix. Remove it.	Base Word Pronounce the base word.
1. unbreakable page 34	un	able	break
2. thoughtfully page 53		ful ly	thought
3. unstoppable page 32	un	able	stop
4. forbidden page 85		en	forbid
5. useless page 61		less	use
6. advertisements page 57		ment, s	advertise
7. complications page 78		tion, s	complicate
8. emphasized page 40		ed	emphasize
9. fascinating page 28		ing	fascinate
10. uneasily page 80	un	ly	easy
11. closer page 37		er	close
12. apologized page 4		ed	apologize
13. forgotten page 90		en	forgot

Words from: Clements, A. (1996). *Frindle*. New York: Simon and Schuster Books for Young Readers.

syllable words. *Set* has one vowel letter and one vowel sound, the short /e/, while *street* has two vowel letters and one vowel sound, the long /e/. In other words, every vowel sound equals one syllable. This is true for short and long words. Try saying *replacement*. Count the vowel sounds you hear. Re / place / ment has three vowel sounds and three syllables. Even vowel-like sounds represent syllables. To illustrate this, pronounce *rattle* (rat / tle). The vowel in the last syllable, *tle*, is not a distinct vowel but rather the vowel-like sound "*tul.*" Therefore, when we listen for the syllables in words, we listen for vowels and vowel-like sounds. Every vowel or vowel-like sound in a word equals one syllable.

Children who know and understand letter patterns determine the number of syllables in a long, unfamiliar word by counting the distinct vowel patterns. Each vowel letter pattern represents one vowel sound and hence the number of vowel patterns equals the number of syllables. For instance, *thirteen* has two vowel patterns: the

Vr pattern *ir* and the VV pattern *ee*. These two vowel patterns represent one vowel sound each and, therefore, *thirteen* is a two-syllable word. The vowels in *thirteen* are pronounced just as we would expect from the Vr and VV letter patterns.

Nine Ways to Recognize Syllables

In order to pronounce long and unfamiliar words, children must recognize which letters form syllables and which do not. There are nine useful guidelines for dividing long words into syllables. Teach children to look for the following:

1. *Closed Syllable*   A closed syllable ends in a consonant sound and the vowel is usually short. The VC short vowel pattern is a closed syllable, as in *pan*, *chick*, and *strap*. Knowing that the closed syllable ends with a consonant helps children decide where to break long words into pronounceable syllables. When two consonant letters separate two vowels, as in *napkin*, the syllable usually divides between the two consonants. Following this guideline, we would divide *napkin* into *nap / kin*, *lantern* into *lan / tern*, and *canyon* into *can / yon*. When words have double consonants, as in *nugget*, the syllable divides between the two like consonants, *nug / get*. Two adjacent consonants are a cue to the closed syllable, short vowel pattern. In pronouncing a closed syllable, suggest that children first try the short vowel sound. Then, if the short vowel sound does not form a word that makes sense in the sentence, advise children to try the long sound.

2. *Open Syllable*   An open syllable ends in a vowel sound. The vowel in an open syllable often represents a long vowel sound. The CV pattern (*me*, *she*, *be*) is an open syllable. Many two-syllable words have one open syllable. When the first vowel in a two-syllable word is followed by a single consonant (*silent*, *fever*, *bacon*), the syllable division is often right after the long vowel (*si / lent*, *fe / ver*, *ba / con*). Suggest that children first try a long vowel sound for an open syllable (*si / lent*, *fe / ver*, *ba / con*) and, if that does not result in a word that fits the context, try the short vowel sound.

3. *le Syllable*   When a word ends in a consonant plus *le*, the consonant and the *le* usually form the last syllable. The consonant preceding the *le* typically begins the syllable, and the vowel is pronounced as a schwa, an /uh/. Hence, the *dle* in *candle* is pronounced as "*dul*," the *fle* in *waffle* as "*ful*," and the *ble* in *stumble* as "*bul*." *le* syllables are easy to spot because the telltale *le* is the last letter group in words (with the exception of words that have suffixes, of course). Examples of the *consonant + le* syllable include the *ble* in *bubble*, *cle* in *cycle*, *dle* in *candle*, *fle* in *rifle*, *gle* in *giggle*, *kle* in *twinkle*, *ple* in *people*, *sle* in *hassle*, and *zle* in *drizzle*.

4. *Vowel-vowel Syllable*   Adjacent vowel letters usually belong in the same syllable. Vowel pairs may represent a long sound (*train*), a short sound (*head*), or a diphthong (*oil*, *owl*), as well as other sounds such as those in *hook*, *food*, *awful*, *caught*, and *blew*. When a long word has two vowels side-by-side, children should first try pronouncing the vowels as though they belong in the same letter pattern (*stew / ard*, *cau / tion*, *chow / der*).

5. *Silent e Syllable*   The silent *e* syllable is the VCe long vowel pattern. In stressed syllables the first vowel usually represents the long sound (*ad / miré*), with a few notable exceptions. Suggest that children try the long vowel first, just as they normally would when encountering the VCe pattern. If the long sound does not make a real word that fits the reading context, then the silent *e* pattern is probably in an unaccented syllable (*cap´ / tive*). Unaccented syllables do not receive much stress in pronunciation. The vowel in an unaccented syllable may represent a schwa or short *i* (*cap´ sule*, *cab´ bage*).

6. *r-controlled Syllable*   The r-controlled syllable contains a Vr pattern in which the vowel is neither long nor short (*mar / ble*). The Vr syllable is relatively easy to identify, as it contains a vowel pattern that occurs frequently in English words.

7. *Prefix and Suffix Syllables*   Prefixes and suffixes usually represent separate syllables, with the exception of *-s/es*, and *-ed* when the *-ed* is pronounced /t/, as in the word *packed* (/pakt/). This simplifies identifying the syllables in long words. When children see an affix (with the two exceptions we just mentioned), the children automatically know the prefix and suffix: (1) represent separate syllables and (2) affect word meaning.

8. *Compound Word Syllables*   Divide compounds between the two words (*rail / road; flash / light*). Words glued together have the same syllable count as when they are pronounced separately. Therefore, *snowman* has two syllables, one for *snow* and one for *man*. *Motorcycle* consists of *motor / cycle*. Each individual word consists of two syllables (*mo / tor* and *cy / cle*). Hence, motorcycle is a four-syllable word. Knowing that there is an automatic syllable break between the two words in a compound helps children separate long words into smaller, pronounceable segments.

9. *Syllables with Consonant Clusters and Digraphs*   If three consecutive consonants include a consonant cluster or digraph, divide the syllables either before or after them (*ex / tra*) or digraph (*dol / phin*).

Accent

The syllables in long words are pronounced with different amounts of stress or emphasis. The syllable that gets the most voice emphasis is called a *stressed syllable*. The vowels in stressed syllables tend to be pronounced as we would expect from the letter patterns in which they occur. Vowels in syllables that do not receive the main stress are often pronounced with a soft, or short, sound, usually the sound of "uh" as in the *en* in *chicken* or a short /i/ as in *planet*. *Chicken* consists of two syllables, *chick´/en*. The vowel sound in the stressed syllable (*chick*) is consistent with the VC short vowel pattern. However, the letter *e* in the last syllable (*en*) does not sound like the short *e* in *set*. Instead, the *e* represents a schwa, a soft "uh" sound. When we shift the accent, we also change the pronunciation. For example, when we put the stress in the first syllable in *con´ tent*, we refer to the substance, gist, or meaning of something. By simply shifting the accent to the last syllable, *con tent´*, we refer to a sense of satisfaction. In one instance the word is a noun, *con´ tent*; in the other the word is an adjective, *con tent´*. Use the clues to the placement of accent in Table 5–5 to help children determine which syllable receives the primary accent in long words.

1. *One-syllable Words*	All one-syllable words are accented.	**TABLE 5–5** Clues to the Placement of Accent
2. *Compound Words*	The primary accent usually falls on the first word in a compound (*snow´ / man, life´ / boat*).	
3. *Prefixes and Suffixes*	We do not usually accent prefixes and suffixes.	
4. *Two-syllable Words*	The primary accent often falls on the first syllable in a two-syllable word (*ta´ / ble, or´ / bit*).	
5. *Double Consonants*	In words that have double consonants, the primary accent usually falls on the syllable that closes with the first consonant (*din´ / ner, yel´ / low*).	
6. *Words Ending in -tion*	The primary accent usually falls on the syllable preceding the *-tion* (*na´ / tion, pre / dic´ / tion*).	
7. *Words Ending in -le*	Generally speaking, *le* syllables are not accented (*bram´ ble*).	
8. *Syllables Ending in -ck*	Syllables that end in *ck* are often accented (*crick´ et*).	
9. *Two-syllable Words with No Clear Indication as to the Accented syllable*	If there is no clue as to accent in a two-syllable word, try accenting the first syllable (*fin´ ish*).	

LEARNING ABOUT WORD STRUCTURE IN THE ALPHABETIC AND CONSOLIDATED WORD FLUENCY STAGES

Stage 3. Alphabetic Word Fluency Stage: First and Second Grade

Annalyse (Figure 5–2) is just beginning the second half of first grade. Consequently, she is learning about word families, letter patterns, and high utility suffixes. She adds suffixes when writing (*annamols*) and recognizes words with common suffixes when reading. Table 5–6 shows the weekly teaching guide for children in the second half of first grade. While the major focus of word study in the second half of first grade is on letter patterns, her teacher devotes some time to teaching contractions, frequently used compound words, and high utility suffixes (Table 5–6). First graders like Annalyse benefit from learning about *-s/es*, *-ed*, *-ing*, and compound words because they encounter these structures when reading and wish to spell words with these structures when writing.

Table 5–7 shows the teaching guide for the second grade. By second grade, children have a large and growing fluent reading vocabulary. Second graders become proficient at reading and spelling comparative suffixes (the *-er* in *bigger* and the *-est* in *biggest*) and high frequency prefixes, such as the *un-* in *unhappy* and *re-* in *redo*. By the end of second grade, children have a good working knowledge of high utility suffixes, a handful of prefixes, and know often-used contractions, and compound words. Children recognize these structural units by sight (spelling), sound, and meaning.

Stage 4. Consolidated Word Fluency: Third, Fourth, and Fifth Grade

While the main focus in the first and second grade is on teaching word families, letter patterns, and frequently used affixes and contractions, the third, fourth, and fifth

FIGURE 5–2 Alphabetic Writing Sample (Animals)

Annamols.
Annamols can be nacher and annamols can be trand you can bye them from the pet store and hope ther not a pain. Some annamols have spots and some annamols dont some annamols have strips and some dont. Annamols look difrint like me and you annamols dont look like enyyone not evan pooh.

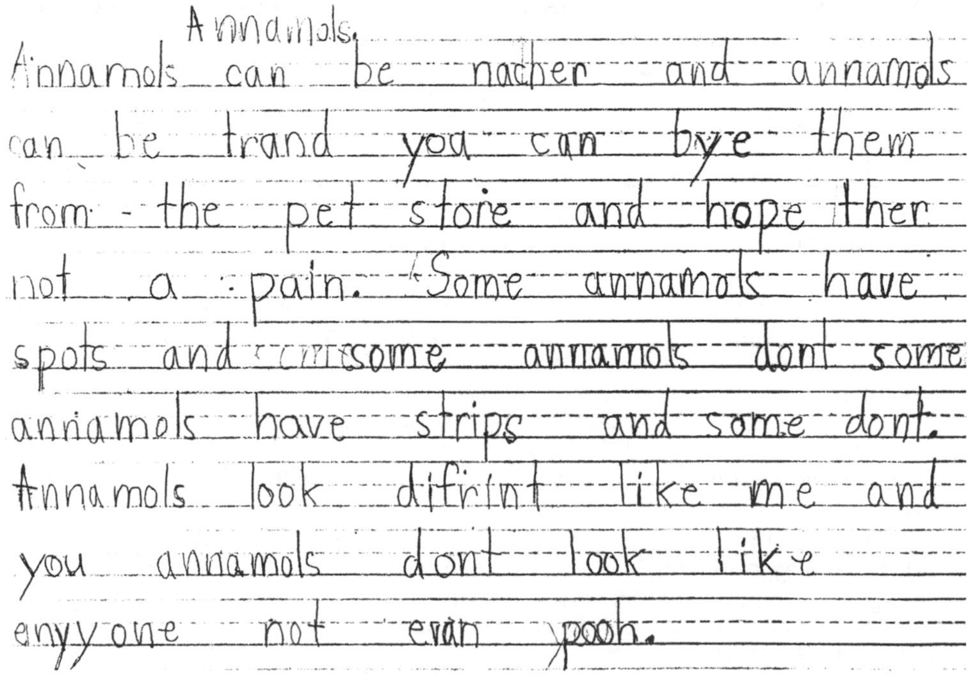

FIGURE 5–2   Continued.

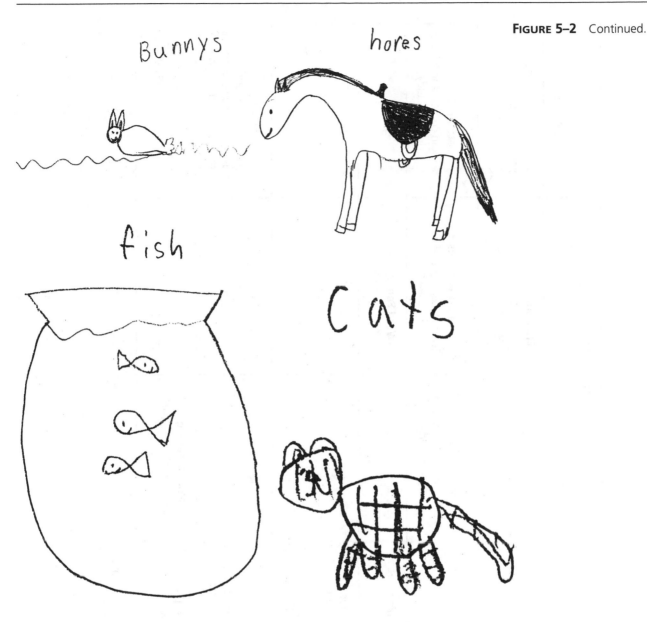

grades concentrate solely on teaching structural analysis. Tamika (Figure 5–3) is a third grader in the consolidated word fluency stage. Joshua (Figure 5–4) is a fifth grader in the same word fluency stage. Both children read long words, and recognize compound words, contractions, prefixes, and suffixes. The difference between the two children is that Tamika knows less about the structural elements in words than does Joshua.

Table 5–8 (page 158) shows the weekly teaching guide for third grade, which is a transition year. Children are leaving the early grades behind and are moving into the higher grades where content area study dominates the curriculum. Before children go to the fourth grade, they must be proficient at recognizing and using letter patterns, high utility compound words, prefixes, suffixes, and contractions. Consequently, the third grade weekly guide shows two optional days to review letter patterns, preferably with spelling. The two optional days are beneficial only for children who are not yet proficient at using letter patterns to read, spell, and learn new words.

TABLE 5–6 First Grade Weekly Teaching Guide: Second Half of the Year for Children in the Alphabetic Word Fluency Stage*

MONDAY	TUESDAY	WEDNESDAY	THURSDAY	FRIDAY
			Phonemic Awareness Beginning, middle, and ending sounds, and blending ⟺	**Phonemic Awareness** Beginning, middle, and ending sounds, and blending (as needed) ⟺
		Letter Patterns Teach in context and with focused study	**Letter Patterns** Teach in context and with focused study	**Letter Patterns** Teach in context and with focused study
Word Family Words (as needed)	**Word Family Words** (as needed)		**Word Family Words** (as needed)	
Structural Analysis High utility prefixes, suffixes, and compound words Teach in context and with focused study	**Structural Analysis** High utility prefixes, suffixes, and compound words Teach in context and with focused study			
	Fluency Letter patterns, word family words, rapid word recognition, or oral reading fluency			**Fluency** Letter patterns, word family words, rapid word recognition, or oral reading fluency
Word Meaning Teach in context and with focused study	**Word Meaning** Teach in context and with focused study	**Word Meaning** Teach in context and with focused study		

Teach phonemic awareness along with phonics, when appropriate.
* For children who do not have developmental or learning disabilities.

TABLE 5–7 Second Grade Weekly Teaching Guide for Children in the Alphabetic Word Fluency Stage*

MONDAY	TUESDAY	WEDNESDAY	THURSDAY	FRIDAY
		Phonemic Awareness (optional) ⟷		
		Letter Patterns Teach in context and with focused study	**Letter Patterns** Teach in context and with focused study	**Letter Patterns** Teach in context and with focused study
Structural Analysis High utility prefixes, suffixes, compound words, and contractions Teach in context and with focused study	**Fluency** Letter patterns (if needed), word structure, rapid word recognition, oral and silent reading fluency	**Structural Analysis** High utility prefixes, suffixes, compound words, and contractions Teach in context and with focused study		**Fluency** Letter patterns (if needed), word structure, rapid word recognition, oral and silent reading fluency
Word Meaning Teach in context and with focused study	**Word Meaning** Teach in context and with focused study			**Word Meaning** Teach in context and with focused study

Teach phonemic awareness along with phonics, when appropriate.
* For children who do not have developmental or learning disabilities.
** For children who cannot consciously manipulate the sounds in words.

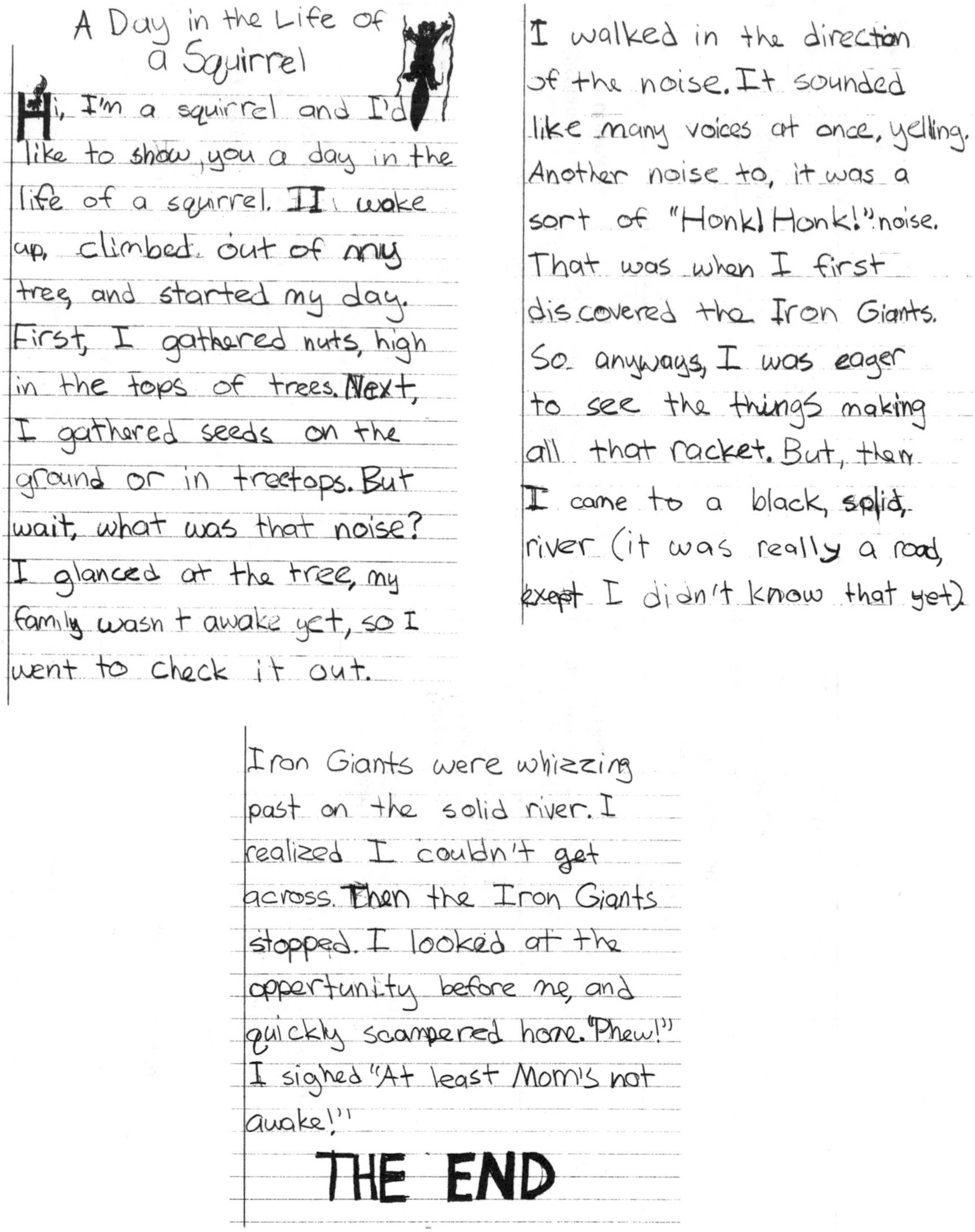

> ### A Day in the Life of a Squirrel
>
> Hi, I'm a squirrel and I'd like to show you a day in the life of a squirrel. I woke up, climbed out of my tree, and started my day. First, I gathered nuts, high in the tops of trees. Next, I gathered seeds on the ground or in treetops. But wait, what was that noise? I glanced at the tree, my family wasn't awake yet, so I went to check it out.
>
> I walked in the direction of the noise. It sounded like many voices at once, yelling. Another noise to, it was a sort of "Honk! Honk!" noise. That was when I first discovered the Iron Giants. So anyways, I was eager to see the things making all that racket. But, then I came to a black, solid, river (it was really a road, exept I didn't know that yet)
>
> Iron Giants were whizzing past on the solid river. I realized I couldn't get across. Then the Iron Giants stopped. I looked at the oppertunity before me, and quickly scampered home. "Phew!" I sighed "At least Mom's not awake!"
>
> ## THE END

FIGURE 5–3 Consolidated Writing Sample (A Day in the Life of a Squirrel)

As children's attention begins to shift toward large multi-letter groups in words, structural analysis becomes prominent in the third-grade language arts program. Fluency in recognizing letter patterns in words is fully developed in some children. For children who are not fluent in letter patterns, spend teaching time to bring these patterns to fluency. For children who fluently recognize patterns, spend instructional time on bringing to fluency contractions, prefixes, suffixes, whole word recognition (Chapter 6), oral reading, and silent reading (Chapter 7). Teaching word

Title: The Cobras Have Come.

> My mom, and my grandma were pushing my sister Sammy and I on the swings in our back yard, talking with eachother when they were enterupted by a hissing noise. I asked my mother, "What was that?" she answered, "Oh nothing." But then we all saw what the noise had been, we stared in awe as thousands of poisonous cobras emerged from the trees. The deadly snakes were all completely black except for the dark green around their eyes.
>
> The huge snakes came slithering madly at us! with their fangs showing!!! My mom, my sister, my grandma and I all ran into the house slamming the door behind us to protect us from the hissing snakes. The snakes imdiately stoped hissing. We sat on the floor listening to the snakes rustling around in the leaves. Then one cobra hissed and stuck, its head under the door!! We all yet out a yell of horror as more cobras began promptly

> sticking their head under the door and hissing. A few minutes later one of the largest cobras had wriggled under the door and was approaching me. I crawled backwards swiftly until I reached the wall, then I had nowhere to go. Before I knew it the cobra was about to bite me when I awoke with sweat trickling down my face. I peered down at my leg expecting to see the cobra but only saw a blanket tightly wrapped around my leg. I pulled off the blanket got out of bed. as I plodded downstairs I thought to myself, "It was only a nightmare, a very scary nightmare.

FIGURE 5–4 Consolidated Writing Sample (The Cobras Have Come)

meaning is increasingly important for supporting word learning and reading comprehension. Previous to the third grade, almost all of the words children met in text were words in their speaking vocabularies. The major challenge for first and second graders is to associate sounds with letters so as to recognize words in speech. In the third grade children encounter more and more words that they either: (1) do not know in speech or (2) have heard in speech but are not entirely sure of the meaning. Now children are challenged to learn new words in text that they cannot automatically recognize in speech. Therefore, it is important to teach vocabulary in context whenever possible. You may want to teach the meaning of especially nettlesome words in focused study and then give children opportunities to apply their knowledge of word meaning when reading and writing.

Table 5–9 shows the weekly teaching guide for the fourth and fifth grade. This guide is markedly different from the third-grade guide, and a world away from the guides for first and second graders. Fourth and fifth graders are increasingly tuned into large structural elements and use this knowledge when reading and spelling. Joshua reads and writes many multi-syllable words, and he is developing a good working knowledge of less-common prefixes and suffixes. Joshua reads fifth-grade content area books and chapter books that are chock full of long, multi-syllable words. Therefore, it is beneficial to teach Joshua about the syllables in words, and to help him develop fluency in splitting long words into pronounceable syllables.

Some of the long words that Joshua meets in text consist of roots borrowed from Latin and Greek. In the fifth grade we want to spend some time introducing children to the more frequently occurring root words, as shown in Appendix III. There are more root words in Appendix III than you will want to teach in the fourth and fifth grade. Select the root words that appear most frequently in the books children read and in the words children wish to spell. By the fourth and fifth grade, children like Joshua are fully independent readers whose attention is almost solely on comprehension. Therefore, the amount of time spent teaching about word structure is far less than the portion of the school day that is devoted to word families and letter patterns in the first and second grades.

TABLE 5–8 Third Grade Weekly Teaching Guide for Children in the Latter Portion of the Alphabetic Word Fluency Stage or Children in the Consolidated Word Fluency Stage*

MONDAY	TUESDAY	WEDNESDAY	THURSDAY	FRIDAY
Review Letter Patterns with spelling (as needed)				**Review Letter Patterns** with spelling (as needed)
	Structural Analysis Prefixes, suffixes, compound words, base words, and syllables Teach in context and with focused study		**Structural Analysis** Prefixes, suffixes, compound words, base words, and syllables Teach in context and with focused study	
Fluency Letter patterns (if needed), word structure, rapid word recognition, oral and silent reading fluency		**Fluency** Letter patterns (if needed), word structure, rapid word recognition, oral and silent reading fluency		**Fluency** Letter patterns (if needed), word structure, rapid word recognition, oral and silent reading fluency
	Word Meaning Teach in context and with focused study	**Word Meaning** Teach in context and with focused study	**Word Meaning** Teach in context and with focused study	

* For children who do not have developmental or learning disabilities.

TABLE 5–9 Fourth and Fifth Grade Weekly Teaching Guide for Children in the Consolidated Word Fluency Stage*

MONDAY	TUESDAY	WEDNESDAY	THURSDAY	FRIDAY
Structural Analysis Prefixes, suffixes, base words, root words, and syllables Teach in context and with focused study		**Structural Analysis** Prefixes, suffixes, base words, root words, and syllables Teach in context and with focused study		
	Fluency Word structure, rapid word recognition, oral and silent reading fluency		**Fluency** Word structure, rapid word recognition, oral and silent reading fluency	
	Word Meaning Teach in context and with focused study	**Word Meaning** Teach in context and with focused study		**Word Meaning** Teach in context and with focused study

*For children who do not have developmental or learning disabilities.

Many of the words Joshua meets in content area textbooks are not in Joshua's speaking vocabulary. What's more, the authors of novels for fifth graders may use words that Joshua has never heard (spoken language) or seen (reading and spelling). The goal in the fourth and fifth grades is to develop the vocabulary children need to be successful readers and writers in middle school. To this end, fourth- and fifth-grade teachers combine the teaching of word meaning and word structure. Knowing about word structure supports adding long, and often exotic, words to children's fluent reading vocabulary. The more children know about word structure and word meaning, the more likely they are to effortlessly read long, complex words. Of course, adding words to children's fluent reading vocabulary supports the comprehension of challenging content subject textbooks.

■ ■ ■ ■ HANDS-ON ACTIVITIES FOR TEACHING STRUCTURAL ANALYSIS

English is the product of centuries of borrowing words, speech changes that were never incorporated into spelling, and a plethora of foreign language influences. The strength of structural analysis is that it directs children's attention to the large, multi-letter groups in words. On the one hand, if children know a word in spoken language but do not recognize it in print, syntactic and semantic context cues strengthen the structural analysis by helping children select pronunciation that fits the context. On the other hand, if children do not know a new word in speech or in print, structural cues give children a much-needed insight into word meaning.

Knowledge of word structure affects fluency through its contribution to vocabulary learning. In teaching word structure, you help children develop the tools they need to identify and learn complex words. When children analyze words in large multi-letter structures, they have fewer units to blend than when analyzing words into letter patterns, and hence word identification is faster. When the structures themselves give children insight into word meaning, adding new words to children's reading vocabularies becomes much more efficient. The more words children automatically recognize, the better positioned they are to become accomplished fluent readers.

Activities for Recognizing Prefixes and Suffixes in Long Words

▷ LARGE GROUP
SMALL GROUP
PREFIXES AND
SUFFIXES

STICKY-NOTE PREFIX AND SUFFIX BOOKS

Children write words with suffixes on sticky notes and then put the sticky notes together to create sticky-note suffix books. Use this activity to give children practice with base words which change spelling when suffixes are added, such as *happily;* to practice adding -*s* (*plays*) and -*es* (*benches*); and to explore the prefixes added to the beginning of words.

MATERIALS: Sticky notes; pencils; staplers; chart paper; marker; construction paper.

DIRECTIONS: Discuss selected prefixes and/or suffixes. Talk about how the affixes affect word meaning and, when appropriate, word usage. Also talk about instances in which the base word spelling changes when certain suffixes are added. Write base words on the board, and have children add the designated affixes. Make a chart of words with prefixes or suffixes. Then, when children are familiar with the affixes, ask them to work with a partner to make sticky-note prefix or suffix books.

Ask each child to write one affix on a sticky note, then have children write one base word + affix on other sticky notes. Challenge children to write as many different words as they can. When finished, children put all the sticky notes together and staple them at the top (Figure 5–5). The advantage of writing suffixed words on sticky notes is that any word with a suffix can be written on the sticky notes, regardless of changes in base word spelling, such as changing the

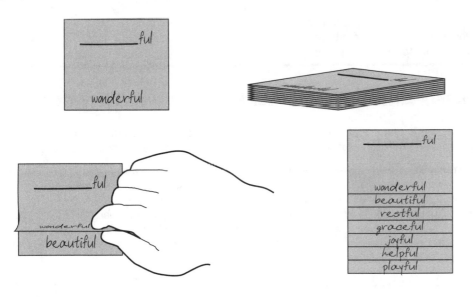

FIGURE 5–5 Sticky-note Suffix Book

final *y* to *i* before adding a suffix. Invite partners to flip through their sticky-note books, reading words as they flip pages. Use thumbtacks to put the sticky-note books on a bulletin board.

You may also want to make an extra large sticky notebook as a large or small group activity. Instead of sticky notes, cut 8 1/2 × 11 construction paper in half or in fourths. Write the affix on one page, and then write the base word + affixes on other individual sheets. Ask the group to suggest words with the affix, and have children tell you (or whomever is doing the writing) how to spell the words. Add a few blank pages to the back of the book, and staple the whole thing together. Leaf through the book as children read the different words. Display the book; leave a marker handy so children can add more words with the affix.

SPINNING PREFIXES AND SUFFIXES

> **SMALL GROUP PREFIXES AND SUFFIXES**

Children turn a spinner that stops randomly on an affix. Children then decide if the affix can be added to words on cards that they hold. If so, children write words with prefixes or suffixes on a small white board.

MATERIALS: One large circle of heavy tagboard; a copper-colored brad; tagboard arrow; marker; at least five word cards for each child; white board, dry erase markers. To make a spinner, divide a tagboard circle into pie-shaped wedges equaling the number of prefixes and suffixes you wish to give children to practice. Write one prefix or suffix in each wedge (Figure 5–6). Laminate the tagboard circle. Use a brad to fasten an arrow to the center of a tagboard circle, thus completing the spinner.

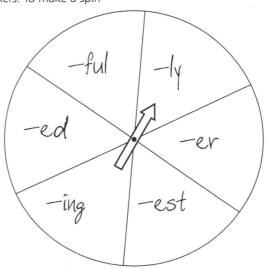

DIRECTIONS: Ask a small group to join you at a table. Place the spinner in the center and distribute from five to eight word cards to each child. Children take turns spinning the spinner. When the arrow stops on a prefix or suffix, children look at their word cards to see if they can add the prefix or suffix to any of the words they are holding. If so, children write the base word + affix on a white board. For example, suppose the spinner stops on *-ly*. A child holding a card with *happy* would write *happily*, while a child holding a card with *bad* would write *badly*. Children then show everyone in the small group the words they wrote and read the words to the group. Reading and writing words brings together the spoken and written language forms of affixed words. Using the spinner to select affixes and then looking through word cards for an appropriate match adds an extra challenge, as well as a bit of excitement, to this activity. You may want to turn this into a game by awarding one point for

FIGURE 5–6 Spinning Prefixes and Suffixes

every time a child spins and successfully adds an affix to a word he or she is holding. Children must say and write a word to earn a point. Table 5–4 lists frequently occurring affixes, which are appropriate for this activity.

SMALL GROUP
PREFIXES OR
SUFFIXES

PREFIX AND SUFFIX TRANSPARENCY CONCENTRATION

This game is played just like a regular concentration game, with one important exception: Words with prefixes or suffixes are written on an overhead instead of on cards.

MATERIALS: Overhead transparencies containing rows of words with prefixes or suffixes children are learning; small sticky notes to cover the words; scissors; permanent marker; as many colors of non-permanent markers as there are children in a small group. Write two of the same words with a prefix or suffix randomly on a transparency. Write a numeral over each column and a capital letter beside each row. Cut small sticky notes in half or in thirds. Trim the bottom and sides of the sticky notes so that they just cover the words on the overhead transparency. Cover the words with the sticky notes (Figure 5–7).

	1	2	3	4
A	Contentment	lively	happiness	joyous
B	Contentment	hoping	boastful	hopped
C	lively	happiness	joyous	boastful
D	resourceful	hoping	hopped	resourceful

	1	2	3	4
A				joyous
B		hoping		
C			joyous	
D		hoping		

FIGURE 5–7 Prefix and Suffix Transparency Concentration

DIRECTIONS: Write each child's name on the board and put a color word beside the name. The color identifies the children who make matches during the game. Explain that children are going to play concentration by remembering where two words with the same prefix (or suffix) are written on an overhead transparency. Children look at the overhead, and tell you the word number (designated by the column number) and the row (designated by an uppercase letter). For example, a child might ask you to uncover the second word in row A and the fifth word in row C. If the two words match and the child reads both words, use the designated colored marker to draw an X through both words. The child with the most Xs (matched words) wins. At the end of the game, review the word matches, and have children identify the prefixes or suffixes in each pair of words.

SMALL GROUP
PREFIXES AND
SUFFIXES

PREFIX AND SUFFIX CHAINED WORDS

Children build words by adding prefixes or suffixes to base words, and then chain the words to show the common structural unit. Put the chains on a bulletin board so that children can add words to them. Also write the words on charts to provide ready references for spelling affixed words.

MATERIALS: A selection of base word cards; a selection of suffixes on 3 × 5 cards; a chained word guide for each small group (see Appendix A–16 for a Reproducible Master); colored markers; large tagboard circles; dictionaries; overhead projector (optional). Figure 5–8 shows a chained word guide for suffixes. Adapt this handout by substituting prefix for suffix on the guide.

DIRECTIONS: Review the prefixes or suffixes that you have previously taught. Ask children to put their dictionaries on their desks and to work with a buddy. Give each set of buddies a selection of base word cards, one card with a prefix or suffix, and one chained word guide. This activity is most effective when different sets of partners work with different affixes. For instance, one set of partners might be working with *-ful,* while other sets of partners might be working on making words with *-ness, -able,* or *-less.* Have partners write one affixed word in each link on the chained word guide. Advise partners to check their dictionaries if they are not sure if an affix +

Date: _____

Members in your group: _____

_____

_____

FIGURE 5–8   Prefix or Suffix
Chained Words

Word Chain

Suffix ___-ness_____

Directions

Match word cards with suffix cards to build new words. Check new words in the dictionary.
Write one new word in each circle to make a chain.

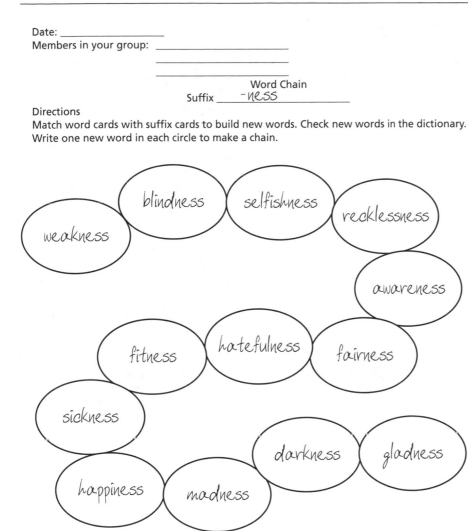

base word combination makes a real word. When finished, each set of partners shares their words and the whole group cross-checks to make sure that every word is, indeed, a real word.

INTERACTIVE BULLETIN BOARD   Pass out tagboard circles and colored markers. Have the children write words with affixes in the circles. Ask children to use the same color marker for words with the same affix. For example, all base word + -*est* combinations might be in red, base word + -*ful* combinations might be in green, and base word + -*ly* combinations might be in blue. Create an interactive bulletin board by having the partners recreate the chained words by writing each word in color on a large circle and, with your help, fastening the circles to the bulletin board. Leave a few blank circles and colored markers near the bulletin board. Challenge children to add words to the chains so as to make the chains as long as possible. When the chains become too long for the bulletin board, use masking tape loops to chain the words around the room. Children are amazed at how many words they make by adding prefixes or suffixes to known base words.

CATERPILLARS   You may want to turn the large chains into a caterpillar. Make caterpillar heads from large circles, adding colorful eyes, noses, and mouths. Write a prefix or suffix on each head. Invite children to add sections to the caterpillar by writing words that contain the prefix or suffix on the blank circles. Leave blank circles, markers, and masking tape in a learning center or in a convenient place so that children can add affixed words to the caterpillars.

▷ LARGE GROUP
SMALL GROUP
SUFFIXES

SUFFIX FLIP BOOKS

These flip books, constructed from sentence strips, have different base words on small pages and a suffix on a large page. When the small pages are flipped, different base word-suffix combinations are created. Use this activity with base word-suffix combinations in which the base word spellings do not change when a particular suffix is added.

MATERIALS: Sentence strips cut into 2-inch sections and 4-inch strips; markers or pencils; stapler. Cut as many 4-inch strips as there are children in a group. Make a lot of 2-inch strips. In selecting base word-suffix combinations, use base words in which the spelling does not change with the addition of a certain suffix. For example, *fool* and *harm* are good base words (*fooled, harmed*), whereas *cap* and *bag* are not (*capped, bagged*). If using -*ed*, -*est*, -*er*, -*s/es*, or -*ing*, select words that do not end in a VC syllable or a final *y*.

DIRECTIONS: Discuss the suffixes children are learning or need to practice. Make charts showing the suffixes added to familiar base words, then pass out one 4-inch strip to each child. Have children write a suffix on the far right half of the strip. Each child may write a different suffix or all the children may write the same suffix. Distribute the 2-inch strips. Children find words on classroom charts, on the word wall, and in books, newspapers, and magazines. Children then write the base words on the 2-inch strips, with one word per strip. Staple all the tagboard strips together to create individual suffix flip books (Figure 5–9).

FIGURE 5–9 Suffix Flip Book

▷ LARGE GROUP
SMALL GROUP
PREFIXES AND
SUFFIXES

SUFFIX T-CHARTS

T-charts are a paper-and-pencil way to sort words into groups with different affixes. Children may sort: (1) base words that do and do not change spelling when a suffix is added, (2) by different suffixes, or (3) by different prefixes.

MATERIALS: T-chart guides (look at Appendix A–17 for a Reproducible Pattern); base word cards or lists of base words.

DIRECTIONS: Discuss base words and prefixes or suffixes. Distribute the base word cards (or base word lists) and T-chart guides. Have children work individually or with a partner to read the base words and complete the T-chart. Write a prefix or a suffix (or any combination of affixes you choose) on the board. Explain that children are to decide if the affix you wrote on the board can be added to the base words. If so, children write the base word + affix in a designated column on the T-chart. There are many ways to use a T-chart to write and sort words with prefixes or suffixes. For example, you might ask children to:

1. Add suffixes to words and to write all words that do not change spelling on one side (*hoped*) and words that do change spelling on the other side (*hopped*).
2. Separate words into groups depending on the suffixes that are added to them.
3. Separate words into groups by different prefixes.
4. Divide words into groups depending on meaning, such as *pre-*, meaning before, and *re-*, meaning over again; or -*ed*, meaning past action, and -*s/es*, meaning current action.

Figure 5–10 shows a T-chart for sorting base words to which the suffix -*est* is added.

▷ SMALL GROUP
PREFIXES AND
SUFFIXES

LONG WORD SEARCH

Children look on specified pages of content area textbooks to find words with certain prefixes or suffixes. This activity simulates a game in that partners earn points for the words that they find.

Suffix T Chart

FIGURE 5–10 Suffix T-chart

Name: _Darla_

Directions:
Add _-est_ to the base words: tall, happy, pretty, big, fat, ugly, short, fair, mean, loud, fast, green, round, hungry, weird, near, sweet, flat.

Write words with -*est* in Column A if the base word spelling <u>does not</u> change.
Write words with -*est* in Column B if the base word spelling <u>does</u> change.
The first one is already done.

Column A	Column B
Base word + *est*	Base word + *est*
Base word spelling <u>does not</u> change.	Base word spelling <u>does</u> change.
tallest	happiest
shortest	prettiest
fairest	biggest
meanest	fattest
loudest	ugliest
fastest	hungriest
greenest	
roundest	
weirdest	
nearest	
sweetest	

MATERIALS: Copies of content area textbooks; a long word search game for each set of partners. Figure 5–11 shows an activity guide which corresponds to pages D14 through D23 in "Learn About Space Exploration" in *Harcourt Science* for fifth graders (Frank et al., 2000). Appendix A–18 has a blank game board to duplicate and tailor to the specific needs of the children whom you teach.

DIRECTIONS: Discuss the structure of the long words in children's content textbooks. Ask children to point out commonly used prefixes and suffixes, then have children work with a partner to complete the long word search game. We will use a science book to illustrate long word searching. In this example, you would ask children to get out a copy of their science books (or another content area book). Pass out the long word search to partners and explain that children are to look on the designated pages of their content area textbook to find words with specific prefixes and suffixes. Children then write the word they find on the line in each box. Do the first box as a whole group, so that children develop a clear idea of what they are to do. Words from the science book in this example are: (1) exploration, observations; (2) telescope; (3) scientific; (4) environment; (5) removal; (6) electricity; (7) international, station, exploration; (8) moons; (9) invention, station or stations, rotation; (10) permanent; (11) redesigned; (12) powerful; (13) technology; (14) supersonic; (15) British; (16) finally; (17) geologist, scientist; (18) safety; and (19) visualize. Check the finished guides together in a large group. Ask volunteers to write the words on the board and to underline the designated prefix or suffix. You might also want to divide the words into syllables to illustrate syllable-by-syllable decoding.

FIGURE 5–11 Long Word Search

Names of Partners: _____   _____

Directions: The page number, a hint for finding the word, and the points for each word are in each box. Search for the words, and write them on the line in each box.
Total Points: _____

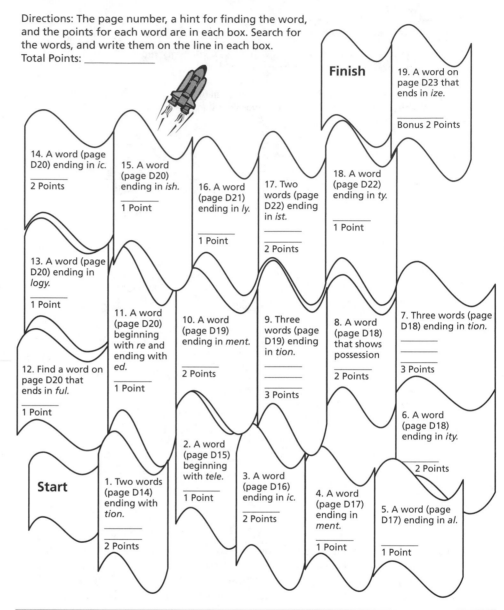

19. A word on page D23 that ends in *ize.*
_____
Bonus 2 Points

Finish

14. A word (page D20) ending in *ic.*
_____
2 Points

15. A word (page D20) ending in *ish.*
_____
1 Point

16. A word (page D21) ending in *ly.*
_____
1 Point

17. Two words (page D22) ending in *ist.*
_____
2 Points

18. A word (page D22) ending in *ty.*
_____
1 Point

13. A word (page D20) ending in *logy.*
_____
1 Point

11. A word (page D20) beginning with *re* and ending with *ed.*
_____
1 Point

10. A word (page D19) ending in *ment.*
_____
2 Points

9. Three words (page D19) ending in *tion.*
_____
3 Points

8. A word (page D18) that shows possession
_____
2 Points

7. Three words (page D18) ending in *tion.*
_____
3 Points

12. Find a word on page D20 that ends in *ful.*
_____
1 Point

6. A word (page D18) ending in *ity.*
_____
2 Points

Start

1. Two words (page D14) ending with *tion.*
_____
2 Points

2. A word (page D15) beginning with *tele.*
_____
1 Point

3. A word (page D16) ending in *ic.*
_____
2 Points

4. A word (page D17) ending in *ment.*
_____
1 Point

5. A word (page D17) ending in *al.*
_____
1 Point

▷ SMALL GROUP
PREFIXES AND
SUFFIXES

AFFIX WEBS

Children analyze the semantic connections among words with the same affixes and create webs to illustrate these connections.

MATERIALS: Dictionaries; paper and pencil; large chart paper; marker; yarn (optional); tagboard spider (optional); tagboard spiders with words or word cards (optional).

DIRECTIONS: Discuss the meaning of the affixes. Have children point out words with the affixes. Explore variations in word meaning or grammatical class that are produced when adding affixes to base words. Ask small groups to focus on different affixes. Children make a list of words with the affix they are working on. When children have a list of words with the affix, ask children to write the affix in the center of a piece of paper. Have groups arrange the affixed words into a web showing meaningful connections. Children connect the words in the web by drawing lines among the words. Groups complete webs by defining, at the bottom of the page, the meaning of the affix. Groups share the finished webs with their classmates. Display webs on the board. Make two or three large webs. Put them on pieces of chart paper (as shown in Figure 5–12). Put the webs on the bulletin board and challenge children to add words with the same affixes to the webs.

BULLETIN BOARD   Make a spider web affix bulletin board. String yarn so as to simulate a spider web. Put a tagboard spider with an affix on it in the middle of the web. Have children find words to which the affix might be attached. Children write words with the affix on tagboard bugs or spiders, or on small word cards. Arrange the affixed words on the web to show the meaningful relationships among words.

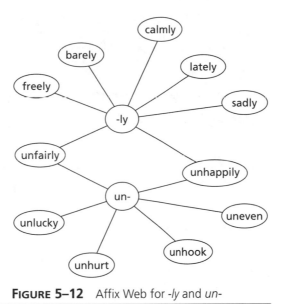

FIGURE 5–12   Affix Web for *-ly* and *un-*

PREFIX AND SUFFIX CROSSWORD PUZZLES

▷ SMALL GROUP
INDIVIDUAL
PREFIXES AND
SUFFIXES

Children solve these crossword puzzles by identifying the prefixes or suffixes in words and writing the prefixes or suffixes in the correct blanks.

MATERIALS: Crossword puzzles (Figure 5–13); words with prefixes or suffixes the children are learning to read and write.

FIGURE 5–13   Suffix Crossword Puzzle

Across	Down
1. sheepish	1. active
2. brightest	3. longer
5. stronger	4. calmly

DIRECTIONS: Show children the crossword puzzle. Explain that children are to read the words under the columns *Across* and *Down,* identify the prefixes or suffixes in the words, and write *only* the prefixes or suffixes in the correct blanks. Figure 5–13 shows a suffix crossword puzzle.

Recognizing and Understanding Common Clipped Words
CLIPPED WORD FOLD-OVERS

▷ LARGE GROUP
SMALL GROUP
CLIPPED WORDS

Clipped words are shortened forms of long words, such as *vet* for *veterinarian.* Fold-overs, made out of manila folders cut into strips, show the clipped words on the outside and, when the folder strip is open, reveal the long word and an illustration of the word's meaning.

MATERIALS: Manila folders cut into strips about two to three inches wide; markers.

DIRECTIONS: Discuss clipped words, such as *ad* for *advertisement.* Write a few long words on the board; underline the clipped words inside the long words (*ad*vertisement). Help children understand that, while most clipped words are shortened spellings of their long word counterparts, there are some exceptions, as in *fax* for *facsimile, bike* for *bicycle,* and *pix* for *picture.* Table 5–2 lists different clipped words.

Demonstrate how to make a clipped word fold-over. Write a clipped word on the front of the manila folder strip. Write the long word on the right side of the open strip and draw an illustration of word meaning on the left side. Have children make their own individual clipped fold-overs. When all the clipped word fold-overs are finished, it is time to share. Individual children first show the clipped word to the group. Then the group says (or guesses) the long word. Figure 5–14 is an example of a completed fold-over. You may also want to have children make clipped word fold-overs as a learning center activity.

FIGURE 5–14 Clipped Word Fold-overs

Recognizing and Understanding Compound Words
COMPOUND WORD BUILDING

▷ SMALL GROUP
COMPOUND WORDS

Small groups build as many compound words as possible from a set of base words.

MATERIALS: Compound word building guides (Appendix A–19).

DIRECTIONS: Ask children to work with a partner. Distribute a compound word building guide to each set of partners. Instruct the partners to use the base words to build different compounds and to write the compounds in the squares on the guide. Have partners check their dictionaries if they are not sure whether two base words make a real compound (Figure 5–15). Use the compound words in Appendix II to select base words.

Date: _____

FIGURE 5–15 Compound Word Building Guide

Partners: _____   _____

Directions:

Combine the base words to make compound words. You may use the base words more than once.

Base Words

fire	shoe	play	light	snow	foot	over	sun	boat
room	horse	man	house	mail	ball	rain	coat	sail

How may compounds can you make from the base words?

1. firehouse
2. snowman
3. fireman
4. snowball
5. mailman
6. ballroom
7. lighthouse
8. sunlight
9. sunroom
10. horseman
11. firelight
12. raincoat
13. snowshoe
14. playhouse
15. sailboat
16. overcoat
17. football
18. playroom
19. horseshoe
20. houseboat

COMPOUND SEARCH AND SORT

▷ LARGE GROUP
SMALL GROUP
COMPOUND WORDS

Children analyze compound words according to whether the compound meaning is nearly the same or quite different from the base word meaning. In so doing, children develop a better understanding of the meaning of the compound words they read in text.

MATERIALS: A variety of books children are currently reading; 3 × 5 or 5 × 8 index cards; a compound sorting guide (Appendix A–20); markers; masking tape.

DIRECTIONS: Introduce this activity by writing a familiar compound word, such as *toothbrush*, and asking children to define the compound and the base words. Then write another compound word that has a meaning which is rather far afield from the meaning of its individual base words, such as *butterfly* or *doughnut*. Discuss the meaning of the compound and the individual base words, pointing out that sometimes the meaning of compound words has little relationship to the meaning of individual base words. Pass out blank note cards and ask the children to look for compound words in the books they are reading, in magazines, on classroom displays, and in announcements posted in the hallways of the school. Children write the compound words on the cards. Locating compounds is surprisingly easy. For example, children found 122 different compounds in *Lizard Music* (Pinkwater, 1976) alone.

Shuffle and pass out the word cards. Ask children to sort compound words into two groups and to write them on the compound sorting guide. Group 1 consists of compounds with meaning that is anticipated from combining the two base words (*tooth* + *brush* = *toothbrush*). Group 2 consists of compounds with meaning that is very different from the meaning of individual base words (*butter* + *fly* = *butterfly*). When children are finished, discuss compound words and help children become aware of compound words whose meaning cannot be inferred from gluing together the meanings of the individual base words.

FIGURE 5–16 Compound
Word Sorting Guide

Date: _____

Names of Children in Your Group: _____
_____
_____

Directions: Sort the compound words into two groups.
Group 1   You can figure out the meaning of the compound by putting the meaning of the two base words together. Example: <u>toothbrush</u>.
Group 2   You cannot figure out the meaning of the compound by putting the meaning of the two base words together. Example: <u>butterfly</u>.

Group 1   **Group 2**

Base Word + Base Word =   Base Word + Base Word ≠
Compound Meaning   Compound Meaning

Group 1	Group 2
toothbrush	butterfly
lifeguard	bulldog
houseplant	eggplant
snowshoe	seesaw
sunlight	doughnut
firelight	turtleneck
playroom	dragonfly
foghorn	greenhorn
fishpond	honeymoon
earthworm	roughneck

INTERACTIVE BULLETIN BOARD   Another way to highlight compounds with meaning that can and cannot be discovered from the base words is to make a bulletin board. Put two headings on a bulletin board: *Base Word + Base Word = Compound Meaning* and *Base Word + Base Word ≠ Compound Meaning,* in which the ≠ represents *does not equal.* Pass out compound word cards. Ask children to put compound word cards on the bulletin board under the appropriate headings. Invite children to add their own compound words to the lists on the bulletin board. Figure 5–16 is an example of a completed sorting guide.

▷ **LARGE GROUP**
SMALL GROUP
COMPOUND WORDS

ILLUSTRATED COMPOUNDS

Children explore compound words by illustrating the two individual words and then writing an equation that combines the words into a single compound.

MATERIALS: List of compounds (Appendix II); paper; pencils, crayons, or colored markers.

DIRECTIONS: Explore compound words. Talk about compounds in which the meaning of the compounds is close to the meaning of the two words individually. Talk, too, about compounds in which the meaning of the compounds is far afield from the two individual words. Ask children to select two or more compound words. Have children write one compound at the top of their papers, then have children write the two words individually and illustrate each word. Ask

Figure 5–17
Illustrated Compound Words

children to write a "+" between the words, and place the combined compound after an "=" (*bull + frog = bullfrog*), as shown in Figure 5–17. Once the compounds are illustrated, put the papers on the bulletin board. You might then ask children to sort compounds into a group in which the compound meaning can be inferred from the individual words (*snowman*) and into a group in which the compound meaning has little or no relation to the meaning of the combined words (*cliffhanger*).

CREATE YOUR OWN COMPOUND

▷ **Large Group**
Small Group
Compound Words

Children create their own compound words by gluing together two words and defining their creative compounds.

Materials: Paper, pencils, crayons.

Directions: Once children are familiar with the concept of compound words, invite them to glue together two words to make a new compound. Have children illustrate their new compound word and write a complete definition, as shown in Figure 5–18.

Figure 5–18   Create Your Own Compounds

Recognizing Syllables on Long Words

SYLLABLE-BY-SYLLABLE DECODING

Children find syllables in long words written on sentence strips and then use the syllables to pronounce the long words.

MATERIALS: Sentence strips; black markers; long words from content area, guided reading, or leisure reading books; dictionaries; multiple copies of content area, guided reading, or leisure reading books.

DIRECTIONS: Write a long word on a sentence strip, such as *explosion*. Take the end of the strip and gently fold it over so that only the first syllable, *ex,* shows. Explain that there is a long word on the sentence strip, but that only the first syllable is showing. Ask children to read the first syllable, *ex.* Reveal the second syllable, *plo,* and ask children to read it. Then ask the children to read the two syllables together, *explo.* Reveal the last syllable, *sion.* Have children read the whole word, *explosion.* Use several other words to model syllable-by-syllable word identification, such as *enormous* (*e-; enor-; enormous*), *forgotten* (*for-; forgot-; forgotten*), and *tolerate* (*tol-; toler-; tolerate*).

You may also use this activity to demonstrate the effect of accent on vowel pronunciation. Compare and contrast words from current texts in which the vowel sound is influenced by the accent given to the syllable, such as *engage* (*en gage'*), which has a long *a* in the accented syllable; and *manage* (*man'age*), which has a short *i* in the unaccented syllable.

Contextualize syllable-by-syllable decoding by writing cloze sentences using sentences from the books children are reading. Select several sentences, write each on the board, and leave one multi-syllable word out of each sentence, replacing it with a blank. For instance, if children are reading *Stuart Little* (White, 1973), you might replace *extremely* with a blank in the sentence: "During his illness, the other members of the family were _____ kind to Stuart (p. 49)." You could also replace *penetrate* with a blank in the sentence: "But his voice was not strong enough to _____ the thick wall (p. 48)." Write each missing word on a sentence strip.

Read the first sentence. Show children the first syllable in *extremely (ex).* Ask them to use the semantic cues, syntactic cues, and the first syllable to predict the missing word. Next add the second syllable (*extreme*). The children now need only to use semantic and syntactic cues to determine the suffix (*extremely*). With *penetrate,* begin by revealing the first syllable (*pen*). Ask children to use context cues plus the first syllable to predict the word, then add the second syllable (*pene*), again asking children to predict the word's identity. Finally, reveal the third syllable (*penetrate*). Model how you figure out word identity with semantic cues, syntactic cues, and syllable cues. Give children practice predicting long words in other cloze sentences.

SYLLABLE BOXES

Children count the syllables in long words, and then separate words into syllables by writing individual syllables in joined boxes.

MATERIALS: Long words; as many joined boxes as there are syllables in long words (Figure 5–19).

DIRECTIONS: Ask children to count the syllables in long words by tapping their pencils for each syllable they hear. Remind children that each syllable has one and only one vowel sound. Then write a few long words on the board. Ask the children to count the number of syllables in each word. For example, *rabbit* has two syllables, *traveling* has three syllables, and *entertaining* has four syllables. Draw a box for each syllable, and join the boxes together. Have the children spell each syllable, and write the letters in each box. Next, pronounce the sounds of each syllable and blend the syllables into a word. Use the syllable boxes (Figure 5–19) to give children extra practice identifying the syllables in long words.

Directions:
Read the words. Write the syllables in the boxes below the words.

FIGURE 5–19   Syllable
Boxes

rabbit

traveling

entertaining

(Answers)

rab	bit

tra	vel	ing

en	ter	tain	ing

planet

sandwich

third

(Answers)

plan	et

sand	wich

third

HAIKU POETRY

Children explore syllables and meaning as they write Haiku, a form of Japanese poetry, which consists of words of no more than seventeen syllables that are arranged in only three lines.

MATERIALS: Books about famous Japanese writers of Haiku; Haiku collections; several pieces of large chart paper; markers; index cards; masking tape; Haiku rules chart; colored construction paper; colored chalk or crayons.

DIRECTIONS: Haiku written in English has three lines of seventeen syllables arranged in a five-seven-five syllable pattern. Write a Haiku poem on the chalk board, read it aloud, and explain that for over 300 years Japanese poets have been writing Haiku about the beauty of nature, the seasons, plants, and animals. Share books about famous Japanese writers of Haiku, such as *Cool Melons—Turn to Frogs! The Life and Poems of Issa* (Gollub & Stone, 1998) and *Grass Sandals: The Travels of Basho* (Spivak, 1997). Write *Seeing, Hearing, Touching,* and *Smelling* on separate pieces of chart paper. Talk about these four senses, then take children outside. Have the children sit on the ground and concentrate on one special thing, such as a cloud, the wind, a tree, or a small pebble. Ask the children to think of words that describe the thing they are paying attention to. Back inside the classroom, distribute index cards and ask children to write two or three words that describe something they remember from the outdoors. Make class lists of describing words by fastening masking tape loops to the describing word cards and taping them to the chart paper.

Post the rules of writing Haiku, as shown below:

Writing a Haiku Poem
Write only three lines.
Line one has five syllables.
Line two has seven syllables.
Line three has five syllables.
Haiku does not rhyme.
Do not use the words *like* or *as.*
Describe nature.

Select a theme, and write a whole group Haiku poem using some of the describing words from the charts. Count the syllables to make sure that the Haiku follows the five-seven-five-syllable formula. A group of third graders wrote "After the Rain" (Figure 5–20) after a spring shower.

When the children are comfortable with Haiku, ask them to write their own Haiku poems. Guide children as they write their first Haiku by suggesting that children write the subject of their poem on the first line, where the subject is found on the second line, and what the subject does on the third line. Set aside the draft

▷ LARGE GROUP
SMALL GROUP
IDENTIFYING
SYLLABLES IN WORDS

After the Rain

Mushy, soggy mud
Blue jays chirping cheerfully
Cool, refreshing breeze

FIGURE 5–20   Haiku

poems for editing later. A day or two later, ask children to work with a partner to edit the first drafts of their Haiku poems.

Examples of Literature Connections

Gollub, M., & Stone, K. (1998). *Cool melons—Turn to frogs! The life and poems of Issa.* New York: Lee & Low Books.

> This book explores the life of Issa, an 18th-century Haiku poet, and includes a selection of poems translated into English.

Hearn, L. (1998). *The boy who drew cats and other Japanese fairy tales.* Mineola, New York: Dover Publications.

> Here is a short (sixty-four page) collection of traditional Japanese tales fourth and fifth graders enjoy.

Hooks, W. H. (1992). *Peach Boy.* New York: Bantam Books.

> Here is another version of this Peach Boy Japanese legend, available in the Bank Street Ready to Read series, Level 3.

Kimmel, E. (2000). *Sword of the Samurai: Adventure stories from Japan.* New York: HarperCollins Juvenile Books.

> This book is a collection of action-packed adventure tales, each with a brief introduction to put the short story in a cultural context.

McAlpine, H. (1989). *Japanese tales and legends.* New York: Oxford University Press.

> This is a collection of retellings of traditional Japanese legends and tales.

Osborne, M. P. (1995). *Night of the ninjas.* New York: Scholastic.

> This book is the fifth chapter book in the Magic Tree House series.

Sakuari, G. (1994). *Peach boy: A Japanese legend.* Mahwah, NJ: Troll Communications.

> This is an easy-to-read (only thirty-two pages) translation of a Japanese fairy tale that the struggling readers in your classroom enjoy.

Spivak, D. (1997). *Grass sandals: The travels of Basho.* New York: Atheneum Books for Young Readers.

> This book describes the life of the famous Japanese poet, Basho, and includes many of his poems.

▷ LARGE GROUP
SMALL GROUP
IDENTIFYING
SYLLABLES IN WORDS

ACROSTIC POEMS

In acrostic poems, a word is read vertically, and the lines of the poem are read horizontally. Because each letter of the word begins a line of the poem, it is similar to a word puzzle and a good medium for describing concepts and individuals, as well as for exploring long, multi-syllable words.

MATERIALS: Words from mathematics, science, social studies, or guided-reading books; thesauruses; crayons, chalk, or colored markers (optional); construction paper (optional).

DIRECTIONS: Explain how to write an acrostic poem. Show children how to: (1) Select a special word and write it, letter-by-letter, down the left side of the page. (2) Think of describing words. Write the words. (3) Begin each line with a word that starts with the letter on that line. (4) Count the number of syllables in each line, and write the syllable count at the end of each line. (5) Edit. Have fourth and fifth graders use the thesaurus to find long words to replace overused words. Ask children to exchange short, one-syllable words for long multi-syllable words. Talk about using inventive words. Look for words that paint images in readers' minds. (6) Write the final draft. (7) Illustrate with a poster or drawing. If children have not written acrostics before, write a whole-class acrostic about a content area or curriculum theme before asking children to write their own poems.

Acrostic poems are a good way to conclude a curriculum unit. When children write an acrostic poem for a key word related to the curriculum unit,

I magination can make magic in your mind.
M any people use thier imagination every day.
A ny time you can use your imagination,
G ood people use their imagination.
I n your imagination anything can appear
N othing works better than your imagination
A uthors use their imagination to write
T he imagination mind is very wild.
I like to use my imagination to do art
O ur imagination helps us learn
N othing can stop your Imagination.

FIGURE 5–21   Acrostic Poem: Imagination

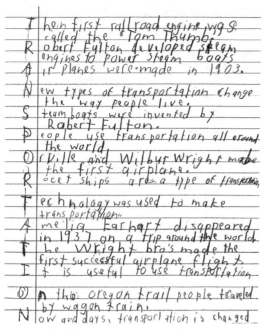

FIGURE 5–22   Acrostic Poem: Transportation

they review in their own minds the important points they have learned. Because the acrostic poems are unfettered by conventions of rhyme and meter, students bring their full imagination to bear as they write. For example, a teacher whose class was finishing a unit of study on imagination asked her students, as part of the culminating experience, to write an acrostic for the word *imagination* (Figure 5–21). The acrostic poem in Figure 5–22 was written for the word *transportation,* which is a social studies unit of study.

BUILDING TWO-SYLLABLE WORDS

▷ LARGE GROUP
SMALL GROUP
BUILDING WORDS
WITH SYLLABLES

Two-syllable word building helps children identify the syllables in two-syllable words. When children build content area words syllable-by-syllable, they are encouraged to identify new content area words syllable-by-syllable rather than letter pattern-by-letter pattern.

MATERIALS: A selection of two-syllable words from social studies, science, health, or guided-reading books; 5 × 8 cards with syllables. Divide words into syllables. Write the syllables on 5 × 8 cards. Write the first syllables, in random order, in one column and the second syllables in another column, as shown in Figure 5–23.

DIRECTIONS: Begin by modeling syllable-by-syllable word building. Let us, for the sake of illustration, assume that children are reading about countries and cultures in their social studies book. Write the syllables *try, ture, coun,* and *cul* on the board. Explain that these four syllables, when combined, make two social studies words. Show children how to combine the syllables into words: *coun + try = country* and *cul + ture = culture.*

Pass out 5 × 8 syllable cards to cooperative groups. Ask children to build social studies words (or words from other content areas) by combining the syllables in the first column with the syllables in the second column. Should children have questions about the two-syllable words they are building, tell them to look in a specific chapter in the textbook or in the glossary to find words that begin with the syllables in the first column. You may also want to ask the children to find the definition for each word in their textbook. If the children have personal word banks, have them write some of the words on cards, along with definitions, and put the words in the word banks. These words are then at the children's fingertips when needed. Figure 5–23 shows

FIGURE 5–23 Building
Two-syllable Words

Examples of Syllable Cards to Build Social Studies Words

Syllable Card		Words
is	ban	island
rur	urb	rural
cul	land	culture
ur	ture	urban
sub	al	suburb

Syllable Card		Words
de	yon	Kiva
cac	sert	canyon
mis	va	cactus
can	sion	mesa
me	tus	mission
Ki	sa	desert

Syllable Card		Words
com	lect	index
in	coln	contrast
may	or	elect
con	trast	compare
Lin	gress	mayor
con	dex	Lincoln
e	pare	congress

Syllable Card		Words
ex	el	channel
chan	gine	steamboat
po	port	express
trans	ny	transport
Eng	ton	engine
Ful	boat	Fulton
en	land	pony
fu	press	fuel
steam	nel	England

Syllable Card		Words
pro	port	process
har	source	harvest
farm	cess	farming
re	lic	resource
ro	vate	robot
pri	bot	private
ex	ing	export
im	vest	import
pub	port	public

Syllable Card		Words
lo	thor	local
fic	ty	fiction
au	tion	author
re	ing	research
ci	cil	city
meet	cal	meeting
coun	search	council

examples of six syllable cards for syllable-by-syllable word building that a third-grade teacher used with her class.

LARGE GROUP
SMALL GROUP
IDENTIFYING
SYLLABLES IN LONG
WORDS

LONG WORD SPLITTING

Children identify syllables in long words and gain insight into the principle that one vowel sound equals one syllable, irrespective of the number of vowel letters.

MATERIALS: Words from content area books, reading books, or spelling lists; a long word splitting guide (Appendix A–21).

DIRECTIONS: Review the syllables in spoken words by reminding children about how to tap a pencil for each syllable. For example, children might join you in tapping once for the /a/ in *afraid* and once again for /fraid/. Write on the board the headings: *Word, Number of Vowel Sounds (Pencil Taps), Number of Vowel Letters,* and *Number of Syllables (Pencil Taps)*. Model how to count syllables in spoken and written words. Use a common two-syllable word, like *market,* as an example. Ask children to tap out the syllables, count out the vowels, and figure out the number of syllables. Do this with several words.

Long Word Splitting

FIGURE 5–24 Long Word Splitting

Date: _____

Name: _____

Directions: Read each word. Use your pencil to tap the number of syllables. Write the number of pencil taps in Box 1. Count the vowel letters. Write the number of vowel letters in Box 2. Write the number of syllables in the word in Box 3. Which two boxes have the same number? Why? The first word is done for you.

Line 15 does not have a word. Look in a book you are reading. Find a word that is at least two syllables long. Write the word on line 15, and fill-in the boxes. Write the title of the book at the very bottom of the page.

Hint—Each syllable has only one vowel sound.

Word	Box 1 Number of Vowel Sounds (Pencil Taps) Tap It Out	Box 2 Number of Vowel Letters Count It Out	Box 3 Number of Syllables (Pencil Taps) Figure It Out
1. reason	2	3	2
2. basketball	3	3	3
3. satisfy	3	3	3
4. football	2	3	2
5. snowy	2	2	2
6. selection	3	4	3
7. tolerate	3	1	3
8. wonderful	3	3	3
9. butterfly	3	3	3
10. rewrite	2	3	2
11. delightful	3	3	3
12. whispered	2	3	2
13. preview	2	3	2
14. vanish	2	2	2
15. headquarters Stuart Little by E. B. White	3	4	3

Word	Number of Vowel Sounds (Pencil Taps) Tap It Out	Number of Vowel Letters Count It Out	Number of Syllables (Pencil Taps) Figure It Out
market	2	2	2
leapfrog	2	3	2
decorate	3	4	3

Distribute the long word splitting guide. Ask children to work with a partner to figure out the number of syllables in each word. The last line is blank. Have partners write a long word of their own choosing in the blank or ask children to select a long word from the words they are learning to spell (Figure 5–24). When the partners are finished working, draw children's attention to the headings on the board. Ask volunteers to share the words they found and split on their own. Discuss the principle that the number of syllables equals the number of vowel sounds we hear in a word, not the actual number of vowel letters.

DOUBLE CONSONANT SYLLABLE SNIP AND BUILD

Children work in small groups to cut words with two adjacent consonants (*rabbit* or *window*) into syllables. Children then trade syllables with other groups and then build as many words as possible from the individual syllables. Groups compare and contrast the original words with the words built from separate syllables.

MATERIALS: Plastic sealable bags; *permanent* markers; scissors; double consonant sort and build guide (Appendix A–22); multiple copies of 3 × 5 cards with two-syllable words on them. All the two-syllable words should either have two adjacent identical consonants (*rabbit*) or two adjacent unlike consonants (*window*). You will find a reproducible pattern for double consonant syllable snip and build in Appendix A–21.

DIRECTIONS: Review the principle that long words are generally divided between two adjacent consonants, if the consonants do not form a cluster or digraph. Ask children to work in an equal number of small groups. Have children get out paper and pencils, and pass out to each group one plastic bag, one permanent marker, a double consonant sort and build guide (Appendix A–21), and one set of word cards (either double like consonants or double unlike consonants). Review the steps on the double consonant sort and build guide. Discuss words with double consonants that are just alike (*rabbit*) and words with double consonants that are different letters (*window*). Explain that each set of partners is to write the words on their resealable bags, and to cut words into syllables (Steps 1 and 2). Then have the group exchange syllables with another group (Step 3). Caution each set of partners to keep the words on their own bags a secret from their partner group for the time being. Challenge each partner group to use the syllables to build as many words as they can. Have each group write the words they build (Step 4). Finally, have the partner groups get together and compare the words built with the whole words on the sealable bags (Step 5). Ask the groups to discuss the words and to cross-check any questionable words in the dictionary. Before turning to another lesson or activity, ask each group to put the syllable cards into the plastic bag with the whole words written on it. Save these bags to use in centers or as extra practice for individual children.

TEN-MINUTE FLUENCY ACTIVITIES FOR STRUCTURAL ANALYSIS

Like all fluency activities in this book, the following activities are for children who already know prefixes, suffixes, compounds, and syllables, but who are inaccurate or slow using this information. The goal of fluency activities is to bring information to a level where children use it accurately, rapidly, and effortlessly. The fluency activities are timed and take only ten minutes of class time.

SPEEDY WORDS

In this beat-the-clock fluency activity, children add suffixes to as many words as they can within a teacher-designated time.

MATERIALS: One speedy word fluency guide for each child (Appendix A–23); a timer. Table 5–10 has twelve sets of base word and suffix combinations for speedy words.

DIRECTIONS: Select base words that are already in children's fluent reading vocabulary. Likewise, the suffixes should have been previously taught, either by you (this year), or by the children's former teacher (last year). If some of the children in your classroom are not fluent at reading and writing words with the suffixes taught in previous grades, then bring those suffixes to fluency first. Make this fluency activity more challenging by adding more base words and suffixes, or easier by reducing the number of base words and suffixes.

Before distributing the speedy words fluency guide, explain that each child is going to write as many base words with suffixes as possible. Explain further that there are lines under the car, and each line has a base word and suffixes. Children read the base words, decide which suf-

Name: _____

Date: _____

FIGURE 5–25 Speedy Words

Speedy Word Score ___*19*___

Speedy Words with Suffixes

Directions: Combine the base words and the suffixes to write new words. Write as many words as you can before the timer goes off. Every word counts for one lap on the Speedy Word Race Track.

Base Word	+	Suffix =	Speedy Words
cheer		-less, -ful, -ing	cheerful cheerless cheering
power		-less, -ful, -ing	powerless powerful
neglect		-less, -ful, -ing	neglecting
law		-less, -ful, -ing	lawless lawful
resent		-less, -ful, -ing	resentful
mercy		-less, -ful, -ing	merciless merciful
doubt		-less, -ful, -ing	doubtful doubting doubtless
care		-less, -ful, -ing	careless caring
wonder		-less, -ful, -ing	wonderful
thank		-less, -ful, -ing	thankless thankful

fixes can be added to the base word, and then write the words with suffixes on the line. Stress that words must be real, not make believe. Remind children to cross-check, asking themselves if they know the word, have heard it before, or have seen it before. Figure 5–25 has ten examples of base word and suffix combinations for speedy words.

Place a speedy words guide face-down on the desks. Tell children how much time they have to write the speedy words; ask them to hold their pencils in the air, and begin the countdown; "Five, four, three, two, one—Go!" Writing stops when the timer goes off or when individual children cannot think of any more words to write (Figure 5–25). Count the number of correctly spelled words, and write that number in the space provided at the top of the paper. Give the children two, three, or more chances, on different days, to write words from the same set of base words and suffixes. Giving children repeated opportunities to create words from the same set of base words and suffixes promotes fluency in recognizing and manipulating the structural elements. When the number of words is recorded in the corner of each child's paper, individuals are motivated to beat their own previous high score. Stress that each child is competing against himself or herself, not against others in the class.

TABLE 5–10 Twelve Sets of Base Word and Suffix Combinations for Speedy Words

Set 1

Base Word +	Suffix =	Speedy Words
short	-er, -est	shorter, shortest
tall	-er, -est	taller, tallest
big	-er, -est	bigger, biggest
wide	-er, -est	wider, widest
great	-er, -est	greater, greatest
kind	-er, -est	kinder, kindest
nice	-er, -est	nicer, nicest
long	-er, -est	longer, longest
fast	-er, -est	faster, fastest
dark	-er, -est	darker, darkest

Set 2

Base Word +	Suffix =	Speedy Words
clean	-ly, -ing, and -er	cleanly, cleaning, cleaner
quick	-ly, -ing, and -er	quickly, quicker
warm	-ly, -ing, and -er	warmly, warming, warmer
neat	-ly, -ing, and -er	neatly, neater
dry	-ly, -ing, and -er	dryly, drying, dryer
open	-ly, -ing, and -er	openly, opening, opener
play	-ly, -ing, and -er	playing, player
joke	-ly, -ing, and -er	joking, joker
name	-ly, -ing, and -er	namely, naming
time	-ly, -ing, and -er	timely, timing, timer

Set 3

Base Word +	Suffix =	Speedy Words
trace	-s, -es, -ed, -ing	traces, traced, tracing
jump	-s, -es, -ed, -ing	jumps, jumped, jumping
ride	-s, -es, -ed, -ing	rides, riding
throw	-s, -es, -ed, -ing	throws, throwing
touch	-s, -es, -ed, -ing	touches, touched, touching
reach	-s, -es, -ed, -ing	reaches, reached, reaching
hunt	-s, -es, -ed, -ing	hunts, hunted, hunting
paint	-s, -es, -ed, -ing	paints, painted, painting
paste	-s, -es, -ed, -ing	pastes, pasted, pasting
color	-s, -es, -ed, -ing	colors, colored, coloring

Set 4

Base Word +	Suffix =	Speedy Words
bold	-ly, -ness, -er	boldly, boldness, bolder
eager	-ly, -ness, -er	eagerly, eagerness
fair	-ly, -ness, -er	fairly, fairness, fairer
fierce	-ly, -ness, -er	fiercely, fierceness, fiercer
great	-ly, -ness, -er	greatly, greatness, greater
hopeful	-ly, -ness, -er	hopefully
kind	-ly, -ness, -er	kindly, kindness, kinder
polite	-ly, -ness, -er	politely, politeness
playful	-ly, -ness, -er	playfully, playfulness
prompt	-ly, -ness, -er	promptly, promptness, prompter

TABLE 5–10 Continued.

Set 5

Base Word +	Suffix =	Speedy Words
cheer	-less, -ful, -ing	cheerless, cheerful, cheering
power	-less, -ful, -ing	powerless, powerful, powering
neglect	-less, -ful, -ing	neglectful, neglecting
law	-less, -ful, -ing	lawless, lawful
resent	-less, -ful, -ing	resentful, resenting
mercy	-less, -ful, -ing	merciless, merciful
doubt	-less, -ful, -ing	doubtless, doubtful, doubting
care	-less, -ful, -ing	careless, careful, caring
wonder	-less, -ful, -ing	wonderful, wondering
thank	-less, -ful, -ing	thankless, thankful, thanking

Set 6

Base Word +	Suffix =	Speedy Words
dark	-ish, -ly, -er	darkish, darkly, darker
baby	-ish, -ly, -er	babyish
noise	-ish, -ly, -er	noisily, noisier
red	-ish, -ly, -er	reddish, redder
warm	-ish, -ly, -er	warmish, warmly, warmer
small	-ish, -ly, -er	smallish, smaller
sick	-ish, -ly, -er	sickish, sickly, sicker
sweet	-ish, -ly, -er	sweetish, sweetly, sweeter
plain	-ish, -ly, -er	plainly, plainer
late	-ish, -ly, -er	latish, lately, later

Set 7

Base Word +	Suffix =	Speedy Words
merry	-ly, -er, -est	merrily, merrier, merriest
probable	-ly, -er, -est	probably
keen	-ly, -er, -est	keenly, keener, keenest
harsh	-ly, -er, -est	harshly, harsher, harshest
humble	-ly, -er, -est	humbly, humbler, humblest
superb	-ly, -er, -est	superbly
improper	-ly, -er, -est	improperly
grave	-ly, -er, -est	gravely, graver, gravest
scare	-ly, -er, -est	scarier, scariest
young	-ly, -er, -est	younger, youngest

Set 8

Base Word +	Suffix =	Speedy Words
fear	-less, -ing, -ed	fearless, fearing, feared
purpose	-less, -ing, -ed	purposeless
flavor	-less, -ing, -ed	flavorless, flavoring, flavored
weight	-less, -ing, -ed	weightless, weighing, weighed
fault	-less, -ing, -ed	faultless, faulting, faulted
flaw	-less, -ing, -ed	flawless, flawed
harm	-less, -ing, -ed	harmless, harming, harmed
limit	-less, -ing, -ed	limitless, limiting, limited
penny	-less, -ing, -ed	penniless
wire	-less, -ing, -ed	wireless, wiring, wired

TABLE 5–10 Continued.

Set 9

Base Word +	Suffix =	Speedy Words
correct	-(t)ion, -able, -ing	correction, correctable, correcting
prevent	-(t)ion, -able, -ing	prevention, preventable, preventing
infect	-(t)ion, -able, -ing	infection, infecting
describe	-(t)ion, -able, -ing	description, describable, describing
object	-(t)ion, -able, -ing	objection, objecting
produce	-(t)ion, -able, -ing	production, producing
predict	-(t)ion, -able, -ing	prediction, predictable, predicting
recognize	-(t)ion, -able, -ing	recognition, recognizable, recognizing
comfort	-(t)ion, -able, -ing	comfortable, comforting
collect	-(t)ion, -able, -ing	collection, collectable, collecting

Set 10

Base Word +	Suffix =	Speedy Words
mystery	-ous, -ed, -ing	mysterious
poison	-ous, -ed, -ing	poisonous, poisoned, poisoning
vary	-ous, -ed, -ing	various, varied, varying
wonder	-ous, -ed, -ing	wondrous, wondered, wondering
advantage	-ous, -ed, -ing	advantageous, advantaged
humor	-ous, -ed, -ing	humorous, humored, humoring
luxury	-ous, -ed, -ing	luxurious
marvel	-ous, -ed, -ing	marvelous, marveled, marveling
danger	-ous, -ed, -ing	dangerous
rebel	-ous, -ed, -ing	rebellious, rebelled, rebelling

Set 11

Base Word +	Suffix =	Speedy Words
govern	-ment, -ing, -able	government, governing, governable
believe	-ment, -ing, -able	believing, believable
achieve	-ment, -ing, -able	achievement, achieving, achievable
employ	-ment, -ing, -able	employment, employing, employable
punish	-ment, -ing, -able	punishment, punishing, punishable
pay	-ment, -ing, -able	payment, paying, payable
recognize	-ment, -ing, -able	recognizing, recognizable
excite	-ment, -ing, -able	excitement, exciting, excitable
breath	-ment, -ing, -able	breathing, breathable
move	-ment, -ing, -able	movement, moving, movable

Set 12

Base Word +	Suffix =	Speedy Words
correct	-able, -ing, -(t)ion	correctable, correcting, correction
invent	-able, -ing, -(t)ion	inventing, invention
collect	-able, -ing, -(t)ion	collectable, collecting, collection
protect	-able, -ing, -(t)ion	protecting, protection
determine	-able, -ing, -(t)ion	determining, determination
detect	-able, -ing, -(t)ion	detectable, detecting, detection
discuss	-able, -ing, -(t)ion	discussing, discussion
imagine	-able, -ing, -(t)ion	imaginable, imagining, imagination
prevent	-able, -ing, -(t)ion	preventable, preventing, prevention
celebrate	-able, -ing, -(t)ion	celebrating, celebration

RAPID LONG WORDS

LARGE GROUP
SMALL GROUP
FLUENCY WRITING
WORDS WITH
PREFIXES AND
SUFFIXES

Children write as many multi-syllable words with prefixes and suffixes as possible within five minutes. This fluency activity is more challenging when you designate the exact prefixes and/or suffixes children are to use, and easier when children are free to write words with any prefixes or suffixes of their choosing.

MATERIALS: Timer; paper; pencils.

DIRECTIONS: Explain that children are to write as many words with prefixes or suffixes as they can within five minutes. Look around the classroom for words with affixes; write a few examples on the board to get children started thinking about words they might write. Remind children that spelling counts. Have children put their pencils in the air to signal they are ready to begin. When everyone is poised to write, say, "Ready. Set. Go!" Set the timer for five minutes (or more, depending on the needs and ability of the children whom you teach). Writing stops when the timer goes off. Count the number of words with affixes; have children underline each prefix or suffix, and write the number at the top of the paper. Encourage each child to write more words on successive trials. You may also want to put some words "off limits" if you find that children routinely inflate their scores by adding simple suffixes like -ed or -s (-es) to words.

RAPID PREFIX/SUFFIX SEARCH

SMALL GROUP
FLUENCY READING
WORDS WITH
PREFIXES AND
SUFFIXES

Children quickly scour newspapers, magazines, or cereal boxes for words that begin with prefixes or end with suffixes. Children use a highlighter to identify the found words, all within a time limit that you specify.

MATERIALS: Newspapers, magazines, or cereal boxes; as many highlighters as there are children in a group.

DIRECTIONS: Explain that the children are going to search for words with prefixes and suffixes in a newspaper or magazine, or on a cereal box, and highlight the words they find. Explain further that children have only four minutes (more or less time, depending on the ability of the group and the amount of text children will be searching) to find and highlight as many words as they can. Have children put their highlighters in the air to indicate they are ready to search. Set the timer. After the timer goes off, have the children trade papers with a neighbor. Count the number of highlighted words. Make sure each highlighted word has a prefix or suffix. Write the number in the top corner and return the papers to their owners.

SYLLABLE PATTERN SORT

SMALL GROUP
FLUENCY IDENTIFYING
SYLLABLE PATTERNS
IN WORDS

Children sort words into groups based on the pattern of the last syllable. Words may be one or two syllables long. Children sort according to two or three ending syllable patterns, such as le (tumble), r-controlled (paper), open (be), closed (back), and VCe (same).

MATERIALS: Cards with words that have the designated syllable patterns.

DIRECTIONS: Children sort words according to two or three syllable patterns. Direct children to think about the pattern in one-syllable words or the last syllable in two-syllable words. Alternatively, children who have learned about the effects of accent on vowel pronunciations might also sort according to whether the vowel in the last syllable does or does not represent the expected sound; in other words, whether the last syllable is or is not stressed. Set the timer for up to five minutes. When sorting is complete, check the sort as a whole-group activity; write words on the board according to the category into which they were sorted. Repeated opportunities to sort by syllable patterns are one means of developing fluency identifying common syllable patterns. These patterns, in turn, assist children as they figure out the pronunciation of new words.

▷ LARGE GROUP
SMALL GROUP
FLUENCY READING
LONG WORDS
FLUENCY READING
WORDS WITH
PREFIXES AND
SUFFIXES

FAST PITCH BASEBALL

Fast pitch baseball is a game in which opposing teams move around the bases on a chalk board by quickly and accurately reading: (1) phrases or short sentences with multi-syllable words or (2) words that have prefixes and suffixes the children need to be brought to fluency.

MATERIALS: Cards with words in short phrases or sentences that include multi-syllable words and/or words with prefixes and suffixes that the children need to fluently recognize; chalk board or white board; colored chalk or dry erase markers.

DIRECTIONS: Draw a baseball diamond and a scoreboard on the chalk board. Divide the children into two teams; write a logo for each team on the scoreboard. Draw a batter's box on the floor. There are no home runs in this game, only base hits. In order to keep the game moving quickly from team to team, two players, one from each team, can be on a base at the same time. Players from opposing teams alternate being at bat. Fast pitch baseball rules are as follows:

1. The teams line up facing the chalk board. A batter from Team A steps into the batter's box. The teacher or assistant shows the batter a card with a short phrase or sentence with multi-syllable words and/or words with prefixes and suffixes. If the batter reads the phrase or sentence within three seconds, the team logo is written near first base, and the batter goes to the end of the line.
2. The player from Team B goes to the batter's box and takes a turn at bat. If that player reads the phrase or sentence within three seconds, and all the multi-syllable and/or affixed words are read correctly, the team's logo is also written next to first base. A member from each team is now on first base.
3. The next-in-line player from Team A goes to bat. If that player reads the phrase or sentence within three seconds, the Team A logo moves to second base. Each time a team member correctly reads a phrase or sentence, that team's logo progresses around the bases.
4. An out is earned if a batter takes more than three seconds, misreads a word, or gets help from teammates. When one team gets three outs, the game is over. The team with the most runs wins.

▷ SMALL GROUP
INDIVIDUAL FLUENCY
FLUENCY READING
LONG WORDS
FLUENCY READING
WORDS WITH
PREFIXES AND
SUFFIXES

BULL'S EYE RAPID REPEATED WORDS, PHRASES, AND SENTENCES

This word fluency activity challenges children to read, within a specified amount of time, words, phrases, or sentences that include multi-syllable long words and/or words with prefixes and suffixes the children need to bring to fluency. Children who reach the word, phrase, or sentence reading goal score a bull's eye, and their names are written in the center of an archery-type target. This activity is quick, highly motivating, and easily adapted for readers of every ability level.

MATERIALS: A stopwatch or watch that shows seconds; cards with words, phrases, or sentences that include multi-syllable long words and/or words with prefixes and suffixes the children need to bring to fluency; construction paper arrows with children's names on them; a timer; a bull's eye target.

The bull's eye target consists of an inner circle and three outer rings. Add more rings or subtract one, depending on what is most suitable for your classroom teaching situation. Cut four circles: a red circle, a slightly larger yellow circle, an even larger blue circle, and a somewhat bigger green circle. Fasten the largest circle (green) to the center of a bulletin board. Put the next biggest circle, the blue one, over the green circle so that several inches of the green circle are visible. Then put the yellow circle on top of the blue circle and fasten the red circle in the center, thus creating a bull's eye target.

DIRECTIONS: Explain that each child in a small group is to read a stack of word, phrase, or sentence cards within a certain amount of time, such as two minutes. If a child correctly reads all the cards within two minutes, the child fastens the arrow with his or her name in the center of the bull's eye. Children who take longer than the designated time fasten their arrows to one of the three outer circles, depending on how much extra time is taken to read the words, phrases, or sentences. You specify the range, in seconds or minutes, that each outer ring of the bull's eye represents.

Let's assume, for the purpose of illustration, that we decide each circle beyond the red bull's eye represents an additional thirty seconds. Let us also assume that we set two minutes as the target time. Two minutes and thirty seconds places the arrow on the yellow circle, three minutes on the blue circle, and three minutes and thirty seconds falls on the green circle (Figure 5–26). Any time over three minutes and thirty seconds puts the arrow outside the parameter of the green circle. Stress that children are striving for speed while maintaining accuracy. If a child miscues, the miscue must be corrected and the time required for self-correcting figures into the total reading time. Have the children read the same word, phrase, or sentence cards until the children are proficient; that is, until the children hit the bull's eye.

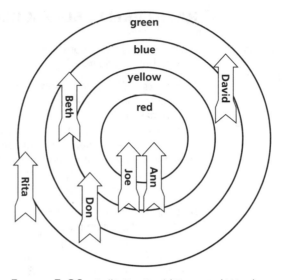

FIGURE 5–26 Bull's Eye Rapid Repeated Words, Phrases, and Sentences

WORD AND PHRASE WHACK

In this team game, the teacher pronounces either: (1) a multi-syllable word, (2) a phrase with a multi-syllable word, (3) a word with a prefix, or (4) a word with a suffix. One player from each of two teams races to be the first to whack the word or phrase on the chalk board with a fly swatter. This activity moves quickly, requires no prior preparation, and encourages children to increase their word recognition speed while maintaining accuracy.

▷ LARGE GROUP
SMALL GROUP
FLUENCY READING
LONG WORDS
FLUENCY READING
WORDS WITH
PREFIXES OR
SUFFIXES

MATERIALS: Chalk board or white board; chalk or dry erase marker; two fly swatters; single words or phrases that consist of: (1) multi-syllable words or (2) words with prefixes and suffixes the children need to bring to fluency.

DIRECTIONS: Draw a line down the center of the chalk board. On each side of the dividing line, write individual words or short phrases that consist of multi-syllable words or words with prefixes and suffixes the children need to bring to fluency. Randomly write the words and phrases on each side of the board so that words and phrases are in different places on either side. Divide the children into two teams of equal word recognition ability. Line up the teams facing the chalk board. Play the phrase whack according to the following rules:

1. The whacker is the team member at the head of the line. A whacker from each team stands in front of the chalk board, holding a fly swatter.
2. The teacher or assistant pronounces a word or phrase consisting of at least one multi-syllable word or at least one word with a prefix or a suffix.
3. The whacker for each team finds the word or phrase and whacks it with the fly swatter as fast as possible.
4. The whacker who whacks the word or phrase first earns one point for the team.
5. The whacker gives the fly swatter to the next player and goes to the back of the line.
6. In case of a tie, both teams earn one point.

Once words or phrases are whacked, you can: (1) leave the phrases on the board to give other players practice recognizing them, or (2) erase the words or phrases, which makes the game easier for team members at the back of the line because there are fewer phrases from which to choose.

One of the potential drawbacks to using fly swatters is that some children may become a bit overzealous whacking the board. If this should happen, give children a small rag and ask them to race to be the first person who completely erases the designated word or phrase. Caution children that if they mistakenly erase a portion of a nearby word or phrase, the team forfeits the point and that point then goes to the opposing team. This cautionary word helps children remember to take a certain amount of care when erasing targeted words and phrases.

▷ LARGE GROUP
SMALL GROUP
FLUENCY READING
WORDS WITH
PREFIXES AND
SUFFIXES

RAPID PREFIX/SUFFIX BINGO

Children quickly find words on bingo cards that consist of prefixes and/or suffixes the children need to bring to fluency.

MATERIALS: Bingo cards (Appendix A–24); lists of words with prefixes or suffixes children need to bring to fluency; tokens to cover bingo spaces; watch with a second hand.

To make bingo cards, pass out blank bingo sheets (Appendix A–24 is a reproducible bingo pattern). Read or write on the board about fifty words with prefixes and suffixes. Have children write on the cards twenty-four of the words. Children may choose any words they like and should write the words randomly on the cards. You may want to have each child make two different cards, thus creating a stockpile of assorted bingo cards. Stress that children are to use their best handwriting; laminate the cards.

DIRECTIONS: Explain that children are going to play bingo, but this version is somewhat different in that children have only five seconds to find the word on their bingo card. If children have the word on their bingo card, they cover it with a token, as usual. However, in this version of speedy bingo, children have only five seconds to look for the word on their cards. Draw words at random, and read each one. Repeat the words twice and, after five seconds, set the word aside and go on to the next word. Children enjoy the challenge of rapid bingo and, coincidentally, sharpen their listening skills, especially when there is a special reward for getting a bingo, such as a homework pass or an extra ten minutes of free time on Friday.

■■■■■ ■ ■ ■ ■ **REFERENCES**

Carlisle, J. F. (2000). Awareness of the structure and meaning of morphologically complex words: Impact on reading. *Reading and Writing: An Interdisciplinary Journal, 12,* 169–190.

Clements, A. (1996). *Frindle.* New York: Simon and Schuster Books for Young Readers.

Combs, M. (2002). *Readers and writers in primary grades: A balanced and integrated approach,* 2nd edition. Upper Saddle River, NJ: Prentice Hall.

Frank, M. S., Jones, R. M., Krockover, G. H., Lang, M. P., Leod, J. C., Valenta, C. J., & Deman, B. A. (2000). Changes to Earth's surface. In *Harcourt science* (pp C6–C11; D14–D23). Orlando, FL: Harcourt School Publishers.

Gollub, M., & Stone, K. (1998). *Cool melons-turn to frogs! The life and poems of Issa.* New York: Lee & Low Books.

Hearn, L. (1998). *The boy who drew cats and other Japanese fairy tales.* Mineola, New York: Dover Publications.

Hooks, W. H. (1992). *Peach Boy.* New York: Bantam Books.

Kimmel, E. (2000). *Sword of the Samurai: Adventure stories from Japan.* New York: HarperCollins Juvenile Books.

Leong, C. K. (2000). Rapid processing of base and derived forms of words and grades 4, 5 and 6 children's spelling. *Reading and Writing: An Interdisciplinary Journal, 12,* 277–302.

McAlpine, H. (1989). *Japanese tales and legends.* New York: Oxford University Press.

Nagy, W. E., Diakidoy, I. A. N., & Anderson, R. C. (1993). The acquisition of morphology: Learning the contribution of suffixes to the meanings of derivatives. *Journal of Reading Behavior, 25,* 155–170.

Osborne, M. P. (1995). *Night of the ninjas.* New York: Scholastic.

Pinkwater, D. M. (1976), *Lizard music.* New York: Bantam Doubleday Dell Books for Young Readers.

Sakuari, G. (1994). *Peach Boy: A Japanese legend.* Mahwah, NJ: Troll Communications.

Singson, M., Mahony, D., & Mann, V. (2000). The relation between reading ability and morphological skills: Evidence from derivational suffixes. *Reading and Writing: An Interdisciplinary Journal, 12,* 219–252.

Spivak, D. (1997). *Grass sandals: The travels of Basho.* New York: Antheneum Books for Young Readers.

White, E. B. (1973). *Stuart Little*. New York: Harper and Row.

White, T. G., Power, M. A., & White, S. (1989). Morphological analysis: Implications for teaching and understanding vocabulary growth. *Reading Research Quarterly, 24,* 283–304.

White, T. G., Sowell, J., & Yanagihara, A. (1989). Teaching elementary students to use word-part clues. *The Reading Teacher, 42,* 302–308.

Use these word structure activities with first through fifth grades in:

▶ **The Alphabetic Word Fluency Stage**

▶ **The Consolidated Word Fluency Stage**

6 DEVELOPING FLUENCY WITH ACTIVITIES FOR WORD MEANING AND RAPID RECOGNITION

Imagine that you are waiting in a long, slow line at the checkout counter of your neighborhood grocery story. Nestled among assorted types of candy are various magazines and weekly publications. All of a sudden, you start reading the captions and headlines on the magazines even though you had no intention of doing so. The publishers of those startling headlines and evocative article titles count on your inclination to instantly recognize and understand messages in your environment. Fluent readers have at their beck and call the spelling, letter patterns, pronunciation, and meaning of the words they instantly recognize (Ehri & Wilce, 1985).

Sarah (Figure 6–1) quickly recognizes many words at any time and any place. She knows them whether they are in context or in isolation, in books or on bulletin boards, or printed in color or in black and white. The words that Sarah rapidly recognizes are in her fluent reading vocabulary. As a matter of fact, rapid word recognition *is* fluent word recognition. Fluent word recognition is the immediate, accurate, and effortless ability to read and understand words. Rapid, fluent word recognition is the dominant word recognition strategy of children like Sarah who are in the consolidated stage of word fluency (Aaron et al., 1999).

The ability to recognize a large number of words rapidly, accurately, and effortlessly is crucial for both comprehension and fluency (Hasbrouck, Ihnot, & Rogers, 1999). It's no wonder, then, that fluent readers recognize 99 percent of the words they encounter (Vacca, Vacca, & Gove, 2000). By the time children are in the third grade, good readers are markedly faster at word recognition than poor readers (Aaron et al., 1999). Rapid word recognition is so important that even minor word identification difficulties have a major effect on comprehension (Foorman, Francis, Shaywitz, Shaywitz, & Fletcher, 1997). Of course, fluent readers occasionally change a word or two in text during the natural course of oral reading. However, children who primarily pay attention to ideas and understandings typically ignore these minor miscues when they do not affect text meaning. If, however,

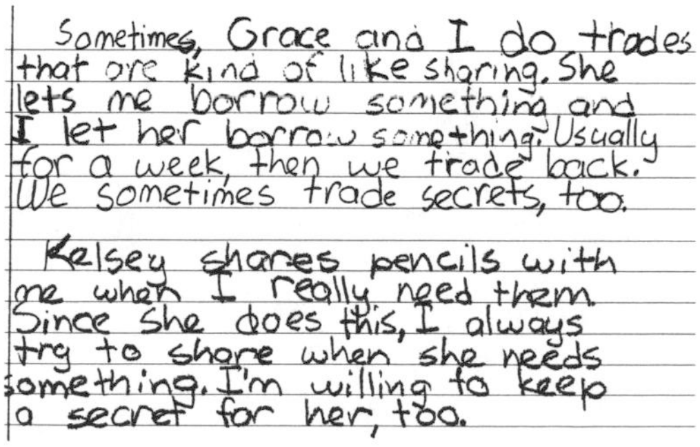

> Sometimes, Grace and I do trades that are kind of like sharing. She lets me borrow something and I let her borrow something. Usually for a week, then we trade back. We sometimes trade secrets, too.
>
> Kelsey shares pencils with me when I really need them. Since she does this, I always try to share when she needs something. I'm willing to keep a secret for her, too.

FIGURE 6–1 Sharing Reaction

children do not self-correct miscues that affect meaning, then their teachers must step in to help children correct the mispronunciations (Barksdale-Ladd & King, 2000). High-fluency readers monitor their own understanding of text and correct miscues that interfere with their ongoing comprehension (NCES, 1995).

So long as word recognition is fast, accurate, and effortless, children pay attention to understanding the text. However, when children do not understand word meaning or when word recognition is slow and inaccurate, children are torn between paying attention to comprehension and paying attention to the words. Under this circumstance, readers shift their attention back and forth between comprehension and word recognition. Attention switching drains some of the vital attention that should be going into comprehension, and hence comprehension suffers.

Readers may use six strategies to compensate, at least somewhat, for poor word recognition (Walczyk, 2000). Readers may:

1. slow their reading rate so as to have more time to recognize words.
2. look back in text to verify information.
3. mumble or say words to themselves in order to hear the words read aloud.
4. pause briefly at phrase and sentence boundaries to give themselves time to better understand the grammatical structure of the text.
5. shift their attention back and forth between comprehension and word recognition.
6. reread text one or more times.

While the first four strategies result in poor reading efficiency, none are as disruptive as shifting attention and rereading (Walczyk, 2000). Sarah has a large vocabulary of words that she recognizes rapidly. Therefore, she seldom uses these six strategies. Because Sarah rapidly recognizes almost all the words in text, she is able to pay full attention to comprehension. Consequently, she reads faster and her understanding is far better than that of her classmates who recognize fewer words fluently, and who take more time to read.

USING CONTEXT CUES TO RECOGNIZE WORDS ■ ■ ■ ■ ■ ▬▬

The reading context helps readers narrow down which words might logically and meaningfully fit into a sentence. There are three cues to word identification and word recognition: syntactic cues, semantic cues, and graphophonic cues. *Syntactic cues* consist of the grammatical relationships among words in sentences. *Semantic cues* consist of the meaningful connections among words in phrases, sentences, and passages. *Graphophonic cues* consist of the letters and letter groups in words, punctuation, and any other print-related cues on the page. In using context cues, children combine what they know about:(1) the words in spoken language; (2) the words in written language; (3) the real world; (4) the meaningful connections among words in sentences, paragraphs, and passages; (5) the grammatical relationships among words in sentences; and (6) knowledge of the letter and sound structure of English words.

Syntactic Cues

English grammar prescribes particular word sequences in sentences. Because only certain types of words are permissible in certain language structures, children limit their word choices to just those words that fit a particular grammatical structure. For purposes of illustration, let us consider the following sentence:

The farmer planted six one-acre fields of c_____n.

In using syntactic cues, children ask themselves, "Does this seem like language?" Because children speak English everyday, they are already familiar with English syntax. Therefore, children intuitively know that the missing word is a name of something (a noun), not a verb, adjective, adverb, or preposition. Children expect written language to make sense and expect words to be arranged in conventional grammatical structures.

Semantic Cues

Semantic cues are meaning clues. When children use semantic cues to help them solve the identity of an unfamiliar word, they ask themselves, "Does this make sense?" Semantic cues help children narrow down their choices to those words that make sense. The engaged reader brings background knowledge to bear on word recognition. The reader knows that farmers grow crops for a living and so the missing word must be a cash crop. The engaged reader also infers from the sentence meaning that the missing word is a particular cash crop that is grown in fields rather than orchards. The question is, which crop did the farmer plant?

Combining Semantic Cues, Syntactic Cues, and Graphophonic Cues

We have now reduced thousands of possible nouns down to just a few. If the text is lavishly illustrated with pictures that explain or expand meaning, we might combine semantic and syntactic cues with picture cues to guess the correct word. If, however, the text is not lavishly illustrated, then we might rely on a three-way combination of semantic cues, syntactic cues and *graphophonic cues*. Graphophonic cues are clues to word recognition, plus punctuation. Word recognition clues include single letter-sounds, letter patterns, prefixes, suffixes, compound words, base words, root words, contractions, and syllables. In this example, we can predict that *corn* or *cotton* is the missing word. C*orn* and *cotton* "make sense" and "look like language."

Good readers do not guess without considering graphophonic cues. Therefore, we want to look for familiar letters and letter patterns. Since we have already considered the beginning and ending letter-sound cues, we will now look inside the word for letter patterns and for structural elements. Let us assume that the unidentified word, which we already know begins with a *c* and ends with an *n*, is very short and has an *or* in the middle. This automatically suggests to us that *corn* is the missing word. Corn "makes sense," "looks like language," and "sounds right." We are now satisfied that *corn* is, indeed, the missing word.

The process we just used to verify that *corn* fits the context is called *cross-checking*. Cross-checking is the process in word identification in which the reader verifies that a word makes sense, conforms to English grammar patterns, and looks and sounds right. Readers use syntactic cues, semantic cues, and graphophonic cues in cross-checking. When word recognition is rapid, children concentrate on passage meaning; however, when words are not rapidly recognized, children shift their attention away from comprehension to word identification. Graphophonic cues help children figure out pronunciation. Syntactic and semantic cues help children in cross-checking for meaning and grammar. As children read and write, they meet the same words over and over again. Practice eventually results in adding more and more words to the fluent reading vocabulary. A large fluent reading vocabulary, in turn, frees children to concentrate on passage meaning rather than on the individual words in sentences.

WHICH WORDS TO TEACH AND WHY ■ ■ ■ ■ ▬▬▬

All words are not created equal. Some words are relatively easy to learn, while others take more reading and writing experience. There are several factors that affect how easy or how hard it might be for the children in your class to learn a particular word. Some of the factors are related to the children's abilities and preferences; other factors are related to the words themselves. *Hippopotamus*, for example, may be recalled after only one reading, while *was*, an often-confused word, may bedevil readers for a year or more. *Hippopotamus*, with its great length, unusual appearance, and meaningful association with an exotic animal, has many distinctive features in its favor. *Was*, however, looks a lot like *saw* (with which it is frequently confused) and does not conjure up an image of a physical object or action.

In addition to visual distinctiveness (*hippopotamus* versus *was*), there are four other word-level factors to consider when teaching vocabulary: (1) words authors use frequently; (2) words that sound alike but do not look alike; (3) words that look alike but do not sound alike; and (4) special words that children are interested in learning. Of course, you will want to help children learn words that are part of the overall language arts curriculum, used in storybooks and context area texts, and generally expected to be learned by good readers and writers in the grade you teach.

High-frequency Words

Children need wide reading experiences to develop a large fluent reading vocabulary, but they also need direct instruction, especially when it comes to high-frequency words, hard words, or content area-specific words (Johnson, 2001; Nagy, Anderson, & Herman, 1987; Snow, Burns, & Griffin, 1998). High-frequency words occur often in text. Out of the 1,000 most frequently used words, a mere 300 account for a whopping 65 percent of the words in written text. These common words are the basic grist for writers and readers (Fry, 1994), and children absolutely have to learn to read and spell them fluently. The *Merriam-Webster's Elementary Dictionary* (2000) boasts that it has the meanings and uses of over 32,000 words and phrases. The words in this dictionary roughly fall into two categories: content words and function words.

Content words carry meaning. Most of the words we teach and most of the words children encounter in reading are content words. Examples of content words include nouns (*boy, car*), verbs (*jump, hop*), adverbs (*fast, plodding*), and adjectives (*beautiful, flimsy*).

Function words hold sentences together by connecting and relating meaning-carrying words. Function words include prepositions (*in, for*), articles (*the, an, a*), conjunctions (*and, but*), pronouns (*she, we*), and helping verbs (*could, was*).

Function words are not associated with sensory images and, hence, we cannot picture them in our minds; in other words, whereas we can create a mental image for *boy* and *jump*, no particular image comes to mind for *but* and *was*. Because function words do not have meaning in and of themselves, children are often tempted to neglect them. Children may skip function words entirely or substitute visually similar words, such as reading *"where"* for *"when."* Some function words cannot be decoded with phonics (*were, they*); others are not easily recognized because they have so many letters in common with other function or content words (*when – where; her–here; then – them*). These difficult-to-recognize factors are somewhat counterbalanced by the fact that function words tend to be relatively easy to predict in phrases and sentences. Readers may instinctively know the function words in sentences because syntactic and semantic cues suggest word identity, as in the examples below:

- Tommy ate _____ biggest cookie. (*the*, an article)

- Use a knife to spread the peanut butter _____ the bread. (*on*, preposition)

- Farmer Smith _____ going to milk his favorite cow. (*was*, helping verb)

- The mother rabbit fed _____ babies. (*her*, pronoun)

These sentences illustrate two key points for successfully teaching children to quickly, accurately, and effortlessly recognize function words:

1. Teach function words in phrase and sentence contexts.
2. Teach function words early and teach them well.

It is necessary to teach function words early because these words are in all the books that beginning readers read. If you teach in the upper grades and are working with children who struggle with grade-level material, be sure to spend time teaching function words. You can expect children to be better readers and, not coincidentally, better writers when they have many function words in their fluent reading and writing vocabularies. Since function words are used frequently, you can expect word fluency to increase when children rapidly, accurately, and effortlessly recognize function words.

Table 6–1 is a list of high-frequency function words taken from Fry's 1,000 high-utility words (1994) and a list of 500 words children most often use in writing (Gentry & Gillet, 1993). The most frequently occurring pronouns in Table 6–1 are: I, *you*, *he*, *she*, *it*, *we*, and *they*. Common helping verbs are: *shall*, *will*, *could*, *would*, *should*, *may*,

TABLE 6–1 High-frequency Function Words*				
a	but	is	so	whether
about	by	it	some	which
above	can	its	someone	while
across	could	itself	something	who
after	did	like	than	whose
against	do	many	that	will
all	down	me	the	with
along	during	mine	their	within
although	each	most	them	without
am	either	much	themselves	would
among	everybody	must	then	yet
and	everyone	my	there	you
another	everything	myself	these	your
any	except	near	they	yourself
anything	few	nor	this	
are	for	nothing	those	
around	from	of	though	**Contractions**
as	had	off	to	can't
at	has	on	toward	didn't
away	have	one	through	doesn't
back	he	or	under	don't
be	her	other	until	I'd
been	him	our	up	I'll
because	himself	over	upon	I'm
before	his	past	us	isn't
behind	how	round	was	it's
below	I	several	were	that's
beside	if	she	what	we'll
between	in	should	when	you're
both	into	since	where	

*Some words on this list may function as different parts of speech, depending on the sentence: The kitten is hiding in the back of the television. His back is badly sunburned.

must, can, have, had, has, do, did, and forms of the verb *be: is, are, was, were, am,* and *been.* The most commonly used prepositions consist of: *of, at, by, for, in, on, to,* and *with.* Let us use an easy book, called *And I Mean It, Stanley* (Bonsall, 1974), to illustrate the importance of teaching high-frequency words. This book for beginning first graders has only fifty-seven words. Twenty-eight, or 49 percent, are on the high-frequency function word list in Table 6–1. When we consider high-frequency content words, we find that twenty-four words are on Fry's (1994) list. Taken together, 89 percent of the fifty-seven words in *And I Mean It, Stanley* (Bonsall, 1974) are among the most frequently used words in written language.

Children need lots of reading and writing experiences to develop fluency recognizing high-frequency content and function words. Give the children in your classroom ample opportunities to read and reread the same text. For children who need extra practice, look in familiar books for phrases and sentences that include function and content words, and write the phrases and sentences on cards. Put the cards in children's word banks and use the cards in games and for direct practice, if necessary (Tan & Nicholson, 1997; van den Bosch, van Bon, & Schreuder, 1995). Word banks are small boxes in which children store high-frequency words, words they want to learn, words they need to know in order to read grade-level text, and content area words. Children naturally use function words in writing, so you will have many opportunities to teach these low-meaning words when children revise and edit.

Homonyms: Sound-alike Words

Hom (or *homo*) comes from the Greek language, and means "the same." Homonyms (also called *homophones*) sound alike, but differ in spelling and meaning (*son – sun*). Children are far more likely to misspell homonyms than they are to mispronounce them. First-, second-, and third-grade teachers introduce and teach the simpler homonyms, such as *sail–sale; by–buy; deer–dear; break–brake; flour–flower;* and *hear–here.* Third-, fourth-, and fifth-grade teachers single out for special attention the homonyms that children routinely mix up in writing, such as *its–it's; there–their–they're; your–you're; threw–through; to–too–two;* and *whose–who's.* Fourth- and fifth-grade teachers also introduce and teach homonyms with more challenging distinctions, as in *peace–piece; rain–reign; principal–principle; compliment–complement;* and *patience–patients.*

Table 6–2 is a list of homonyms children may encounter in reading or may wish to spell. Use modified cloze sentences to give children practice with homonyms in context. *Cloze sentences* have one or more words removed and replaced by a blank. One way to modify a cloze sentence is to write two homonyms under a blank. In filling in the blank, children choose which of the two sound-alike words fit the sentence context. Write two cloze sentences, one for each homonym in a pair. This helps children learn to use syntactic and semantic cues to identify homonyms that fit the sentence context, as we see in the examples below:

1. Both Juan and June brought _____ lunch to school.
   there, their

2. Put your book over _____.
   there, their

1. _____ going on the field trip?
   Who's, Whose

2. _____ jacket has red buttons?
   Who's, Whose

Homonyms present an opportunity to increase children's speaking and reading vocabularies, as well as a good belly laugh at the humorous aspects of our

FIGURE 6–2   Homonym
Riddles

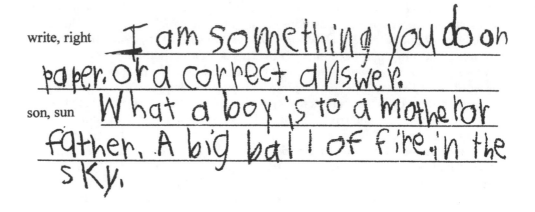

write, right   I am something you do on paper. Or a correct answer.

son, sun   What a boy is to a mother or father. A big ball of fire in the sky.

language. Children's literature for teaching homonyms include mind tickling homonym riddles, such as those found in *Eight Ate a Feast of Homonym Riddles* (Terban, 1982), and the homonym adventures of Peggy Parish's Amelia Bedelia in books like *Amelia Bedelia Helps Out* (1979), as well as humorous books like *A Little Pidgeon Toad* (Gwynne, 1990), *The King Who Rained* (Gwynne, 1988b), and *A Chocolate Moose for Dinner* (Gwynne, 1988a). Third, fourth, and fifth graders especially like to make their own homonym riddles. First read and share some of Terban's (1982) riddles, and then ask children to follow Terban's model in writing their own riddles. Mark (Figure 6–2) wrote homonym riddles for *write/right* and *son/sun*. Have children select which homonym pairs they would like to write riddles for and then, when the riddles are finished, have children present their riddles to the class. Your class might also enjoy making its own homonym riddle book.

Read and share books about homonyms, have children hunt for homonyms, put homonyms on a wall chart, and make up silly poems with them. Fourth and fifth graders enjoy writing their own humorous homonym stories. Once the stories are edited, have the groups read their stories aloud to their classmates. The listeners then decide which homonyms are in the story and how they are spelled. This is great fun and quite a mind-engaging challenge for the readers, writers, and listeners.

Homographs: Look-alike Words

Words that look alike but do not sound alike are called *homographs*. Homographs differ in pronunciation, meaning, and word origin. When children encounter a homograph, they might assume that they know the homograph because it looks like a familiar word. Should this happen, children may not appreciate the need to expand their reading and speaking vocabularies. For instance, children may recognize and understand *min´–ute* in the sentence, *Wait a minute*, but may not realize that the same letters represent *mi–nute´* in the sentence, *The difference between the twins is minute* (*mi–nute´*). We cannot assume that children who know the meaning of *min´–ute* also know the meaning and pronunciation of the homograph *mi–nute´*.

Visually there is no difference between *dove* (the bird) and *dove* (past tense of dive). Because homographs look alike, the key to pronunciation and meaning is in the sentence structure. This makes homographs a good tool for helping children concentrate on the meaningful connections among words in sentences, and focus on using semantic and syntactic cues. Homograph riddles make children aware of homographs, are fun to solve, are mentally challenging, and call attention to meaning cues. You will find a good selection of riddles in *The Dove Dove: Funny Homograph Riddles* (Terban, 1988) and *Eight Ate a Feast of Homonym Riddles* (Terban, 1982). You might, for example, use these books to introduce children to homographs and to

add	ad	compliment	complement	in	inn
aid	aide	coral	choral	insight	incite
air	heir, err	cord	chord	its	it's
aisle	isle, I'll	core	corps	kernel	colonel
allowed	aloud	council	counsel	knew	new, gnu
alter	altar	course	coarse	lair	layer
an	Ann	creek	creak	leak	leek
ant	aunt	cruel	crewel	lean	lien
ark	arc	cue	queue	least	leased
ate	eight	current	currant	led	lead
ax	acts	days	daze	lesson	lessen
bail	bale	dear	deer	lie	lye
ball	bawl	die	dye	links	lynx
band	banned	do	dew, due	loan	lone
baron	barren	doe	dough	loot	lute
base	bass	duel	dual	made	maid
based	baste	earn	urn	mail	male
basis	bases	ewe	yew	mall	maul
bazaar	bizarre	facts	fax	main	mane
be	bee	faint	feint	manner	manor
beach	beech	fair	fare	marry	merry, Mary
bear	bare	fairy	ferry	maze	maize
beat	beet	feet	feat	meet	meat, mete
bell	belle	foul	fowl	metal	mettle, medal
birth	berth	flare	flair	might	mite
bite	byte	flea	flee	miner	minor
blue	blew	flew	flue	moat	mote
board	bored	flower	flour	moose	mousse
bore	boar	four	for, fore	more	moor
boulder	bolder	fourth	forth	morn	mourn
bow	beau	freeze	frieze	morning	mourning
bow	bough	fur	fir	muscle	mussel
bowl	boll	gate	gait	naval	navel
brake	break	grease	Greece	need	kneed
bread	bred	great	grate	new	knew
bridle	bridal	grown	groan	night	knight
broach	brooch	guilt	gilt	no	know
brows	browse	gym	Jim	none	nun
build	billed	hail	hale	nose	knows
burro	burrow	hair	hare	not	knot
bury	berry	hall	haul	oh	owe
by	bye, buy	have	halve	one	won
caller	collar	hay	hey	or	oar, ore
capital	capitol	heard	herd	our	hour
carrot	carat	heel	heal	ours	hours
cart	carte	he'll	heel	overdo	overdue
cash	cache	here	hear	owe	oh
cast	caste	hi	high	pail	pale
cause	caws	him	hymn	pain	pane
cereal	serial	hoard	horde	pair	pear, pare
cheap	cheep	hole	whole	past	passed
chili	chilly	horse	hoarse	patience	patients
choose	chews	hue	hew	pause	paws
claws	clause	I	eye	pedal	peddle, petal
close	clothes	idle	idol	peek	peak, pique

TABLE 6–2 Continued.

piece	peace	seize	seas, sees	thrown	throne
pier	peer	sell	cell	tide	tied
plane	plain	seller	cellar	tighten	titan
pole	poll	sense	cents	time	thyme
poor	pour, pore	senses	census	toad	towed
presence	presents	sent	cent, scent	toe	tow
prey	pray	shear	sheer	tray	trey
pride	pried	shoe	shoo	two	to, too
prince	prints	shoot	chute	vale	veil
principal	principle	shown	shone	vein	vane, vain
profit	prophet	side	sighed	vial	vile
purr	per	sight	site, cite	wade	weighed
quarts	quartz	sleigh	slay	wait	weight
rack	wrack	so	sew, sow	warn	worn
rain	reign, rein	sole	soul	waste	waist
raise	rays, raze	some	sum	way	weigh
read	reed	sore	soar	we	wee
red	read	stair	stare	we'd	weed
real	reel	stationary	stationery	week	weak
right	write, rite	steak	stake	we've	weave
ring	wring	steal	steel	whale	wail
road	rode	straight	strait	which	witch
roll	role	sun	son	whine	wine
rose	rows	surf	serf	who's	whose
rough	ruff	sweet	suite	wore	war
rung	wrung	sword	soared	would	wood
sacks	sax	tail	tale	wrap	rap
sail	sale	tea	tee	wrote	rote
sealing	ceiling	team	teem	wry	rye
see	sea	tear	tier	yolk	yoke
seed	cede	tense	tents	you	ewe
seem	seam	there	their, they're	you'll	yule
seen	scene	threw	through	you're	your

sensitize them to differences in sound and meaning. Once children are sensitive to homographs, have them work in small groups, individually, or with the whole class to make up their own homograph riddles, using Terban's books as an inspiration.

Special Words Children Want to Learn

Every child, whatever the age or grade, wants to learn a few special words. Find out the words children want to learn, put these words in word banks, add them to your weekly spelling list (if you use such a list), and put them on the word wall. Children's personal names and the names of their parents or caregivers, brothers, sisters, cousins, friends, and teachers hold a special fascination for beginning readers. The ever-popular word, *dinosaur* (as well as the names of particular dinosaurs), and the names of other animals are center stage for some of our young readers. Holiday words, favorite foods, and the names of toys and television characters also figure prominently in children's preferences in the early grades. As children begin reading chapter books, they may be intrigued by words for special characters and events. Strange words fascinate third through fifth graders. Children are interested in the longest words in English; words with odd letter combinations; palindromes (words which are spelled the same forwards and backwards, such as *peep* and *pop*); tongue tickling words like those found in rhyming poetry and jingles; and onomatopoeic words (words that resemble the sounds around us, such as "meow" for a cat's call, and "tick tock" to approximate the sound of a clock ticking).

Onomatopoeic Words: Special Sounding Words

Children are fascinated by onomatopoeic words because of the unique sounds these words represent. These words create images in our minds of the sounds we associate with actions and objects, such as *baa* for a sheep and *cock-a-doodle doo* for a rooster, as shown by the onomatopoeic words in Table 6–3. Many books, including books by Dr. Seuss, are filled with wonderful onomatopoeic words. For example, *Dig Wait Listen: A Desert Toad's Tale* (Sayre, 2001) is an expository book that uses many onomatopoeic words to describe the life of a desert toad. Words like *plop* and *thunk* describe the sound of rain, *thump thump* tells about the sound the toads make, and *tsk tsk tsk* imitates the hissing of the snake. Use books like this to start a class collection of onomatopoeic words. Invite children to select their favorite onomatopoeic words and add them to their word banks. Encourage children to sprinkle their stories and poems with onomatopoeic words to spice up their writing with special sounds.

Palindromes: Words Spelled Forwards and Backwards

Palindromes are words that are spelled the same backwards and forwards, such as *pop, level, mom,* and *peep*. It is thought that palindromes were first used by a Greek in 276 BC who wrote a palindrome lampooning a sour-faced ruler. Palindromes have been popular ever since. They make for great word fun in the third, fourth, and fifth grades. Children are fascinated with the way that the letters spell the same words,

TABLE 6–3
Onomatopoeia: Words that Spell the Sounds We Hear Around Us

				Animal Sounds
babble	drip	psst	tick tock	baa (sheep)
bang	eek	rattle	tinkle	bow wow (dog)
bell	fizz	rip	twang	buzz (bee)
boing	giggle	rumble	ugh	cheep (bird)
bonk	goo goo gaa gaa	sizzle	vroom	chirp (bird)
boom	grrr	slop	whack	cluck (chicken)
brrr	gurgle	slurp	wheeze	cock-a-doodle doo (rooster)
burp	ha-ha	snap	whir	hee-haw (donkey)
clack	he-he	sniff	whoosh	hiss (snake)
clang	hiccup	sniffle	yahoo	honk (goose)
clank	hiss	splash	yak	meow (cat)
clatter	honk	splish	yuck	moo (cow)
click	murmur	splish splash	zap	neigh (horse)
clip-clop	ooze	splush	zip	oink (pig)
coo	ow	squeak	zonk	peep (chick)
crackle	phew	squish	zoom	quack (duck)
cuckoo	ping	swish		ribbit (frog)
ding	plop	thud		squeak (mouse)
ding-dong	pow	thump		tsk tsk (snake)
				tweet (bird)
				woof (dog)

no matter whether the word is read from right-to-left or left-to-right. The keen interest in palindromes is part and parcel of upper-grade children's overall fascination with the strange and unusual aspects of English words. Challenge children to see how many palindromes they can find, use the words in silly sentences, create poetry that includes palindromes, and make a palindrome dictionary. For books that feature words and phrases that can be read forwards and backwards, look for *Go Hang a Salami! I'm a Lasagna Hog! and Other Palindromes* (Agee, 1999a), *Sit on a Potato Pan, Otis!: More Palindromes* (Agee, 1999b), and *So Many Dynamos!: and Other Palindromes* (Agee, 1997). *Too Hot to Hoot: Funny Palindrome Riddles* (Terban, 1985) has many riddles, all of them in palindromes.

Words in Poetry

Poetry is a wonderful way to explore words and to heighten children's interest in word learning. Rhyming poetry encourages children to think about word meaning, word sound, and creative expression all at once. Many professional books have a good stock of ideas for teaching rhyming poetry, such as the ideas in *Write Me a Poem: Reading, Writing and Performing Poetry* (Wilson, 1994). Poetry that does not rhyme, such as Haiku and free verse, focus children's attention on word meaning and on using words to express our emotions, observations, and reactions to our environment. As children consider the words they wish to use in poetry writing, they develop a better understanding of how the words in our language express meaning, emotions, and ideas. As children read poetry, they develop deeper understandings of word meaning and written expression.

Explore special words, play games with words, and write riddles and poems. The more opportunities children have to read, write, talk about, play with, and enjoy the words in our language, the more likely it is that children will expand their rapid reading vocabularies. Additionally, you can combine ongoing classroom language exploration with some of the activities in this chapter to develop rapid word recognition.

GUIDELINES FOR USING HANDS-ON WORD RECOGNITION ACTIVITIES

The twenty-six hands-on activities in this chapter develop and reinforce one of the four key components for developing a fluent reading vocabulary. The first five activities develop word meaning. There are five alternatives for using cloze sentences and two masking techniques for enhancing children's ability to use the context cues. The next six activities develop word recognition accuracy, and the last eight activities develop rapid recognition, or fluency. When you use the twenty-six activities in your classroom, follow the two key guidelines for success:

1. *Use Word Recognition Activities to Supplement Ongoing Reading, Writing, and Language Arts Activities.*   The word recognition activities in this chapter are supplementary. The activities should augment, not supplant, the ongoing word study and language arts learning in your classroom. The activities should in no way replace book reading. Wide reading in and of itself helps increase the size of children's reading vocabulary (Fielding, Wilson, & Anderson, 1986). Ensure that children have plenty of time to read in school and at home, and that they have many books from which to choose.

2. *Give Children Repeated Exposure to the Same Words.*   Be sure that children read and write the same words over and over again, in different contexts, and for different purposes. Children need to see, hear, write, and say words many times (Logan, 1997). We do not know how many times a particular child needs to read and write a

word before that word is always recognized and written quickly, accurately, and ef-fortlessly. The individual differences among children may affect how easy or hard a particular word or set of words is for children to learn. For example, children may differ in their personal interest in a particular word, in their ability to use English, in their cultural and home backgrounds, or in the availability of print at home, just to mention a few. And, of course, the words themselves differ. Differences that affect how easy or difficult a word is to learn include the word's visual characteristics, the frequency with which the word appears in text, whether the word is decodable, and the meaningfulness of a given word (*the* versus *cat*). By giving children many oppor-tunities to read and write the same words, you assure that children have the liter-acy experiences they need to develop large fluency reading vocabularies.

LEARNING ABOUT WORD MEANING AND DEVELOPING RAPID WORD RECOGNITION IN THE ALPHABETIC AND CONSOLIDATED WORD FLUENCY STAGES

The alphabetic stage begins, for most children, in late kindergarten or early first grade and lasts to the middle or end of the second grade (Ehri, 1997; Ehri, 1998; Ehri & McCormick, 1998; Gaskins, Ehri, Cress, O'Hara, & Donnelly, 1997). The consoli-dated stage may begin in the late second grade or early third grade, and lasts through the fifth grade. To benefit from the word-level activities in this chapter, children must have phonemic awareness and letter pattern knowledge in order for these word recognition activities to be effective (Aaron et al., 1999; Stuart, Master-son, & Dixon, 2000).

Children in the alphabetic and consolidated stages learn words through the use of many different strategies, especially through wide and extensive reading. Children must understand the meaning of the words they meet in books, and chil-dren absolutely must be able to recognize those words quickly, accurately, and ef-fortlessly. The number and difficulty of words children learn depends on the chil-dren's word fluency stage and on children's opportunities to engage in wide reading and extensive writing. Our goal is to get children into books and to get them to meaningfully use words by reading and writing every day. As we do this, we want to assure that children understand word meaning and effortlessly recognize the words they encounter in text.

HANDS-ON ACTIVITIES FOR TEACHING WORD MEANING

Children develop a fluent reading vocabulary through practice in reading and writ-ing the same words over and over again for different purposes in a variety of learn-ing contexts. Children also develop a large fluent reading vocabulary when their teachers use direct instruction that actively involves children in their own learning (Searfoss, Readence, & Mallette, 2001; Stuart, Masterson, & Dixon, 2000; Tan & Nicholson, 1997; van den Bosch, van Bon, & Schreuder, 1995). Use the meaning-focused activities to enlarge and expand children's understanding of, and appreci-ation for, the words in our language.

WORD ASSOCIATION LOOPS

▷ LARGE GROUP
SMALL GROUP
WORD MEANING

Children select words from a familiar book and then create a word loop in which each word is connected to the previous word and to the following word through its use in the story or in the content subject textbook. In creating loops, children find, read, and write words; think about meaning; and relate meaning to story events or the information in content textbooks.

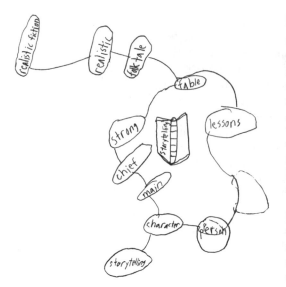

FIGURE 6–3 Word Association Loop

MATERIALS: Paper and pencils.

DIRECTIONS: Demonstrate how to create a word association loop by writing on the board: (1) a pivotal word from a book children have read, (2) a concept word from a content area textbook, or (3) a key word from a current curriculum theme. Discuss word meaning in relation to the story, information in the content textbook, or the curriculum theme. Ask children to think of a word that is associated with the target word, then use the second word to trigger a third word, and so on. Connect words one-by-one, with each word having a meaningful association or relationship with its immediate predecessor. In adding words to the loop, children explore word meaning and the meaningful relationships among words.

Once children are familiar with how to make a word association loop, ask them to work with a small group or individually to create loops which show their own understandings and perceptions of the relationships among words and ideas or the information in text. The word association ring in Figure 6–3 expresses connections made among words, events, and ideas in a story about a legend.

▷ LARGE GROUP
SMALL GROUP
WORD MEANING
FOLLOWING
DIRECTIONS
UNDERSTANDING
FUNCTION WORDS

DIRECTIONS FOR DRAWING

Children read and follow directions to draw pictures and patterns in specific locations on their papers. The directions include many function words, which gives children practice reading function words in contexts where accurate recognition is critical for drawing the correct pictures in the right places on papers.

MATERIALS: Paper; simple directions; crayons or markers. Sets of directions for drawing various pictures on paper, as shown in Figure 6–4.

FIGURE 6–4 Directions for Drawing

Set 1
1. Draw a yellow ball.
2. Draw a green ball beside it.
3. Make a sad face under the yellow ball.
4. Draw a house with two windows beside the balls.
5. Draw a boy or girl under the balls.
6. Write a silly sentence under the picture.

Set 2
1. Draw a yellow balloon on your paper.
2. Draw a blue balloon beside the yellow one.
3. Draw a purple balloon under the yellow balloon.
4. Draw a red ballon near the purple balloon.
5. Draw a green balloon below the red one.
6. Make a long red tail on any balloon.
7. How many balloons did you draw?
8. Write the number of balloons in the corner of this paper.

Set 3
1. Draw a house on your paper.
2. Draw a swing beside the house.
3. Draw a ball near the swing.
4. Draw a tree on the other side of the house.
5. Draw a kite over the tree.
6. Put a long tail on the kite. Make it dangle below the kite.
7. Draw a sun over the house.
8. Write something about the family who lives in the house.
9. Write the sentence under the picture.

Set 4
1. Draw a snowman on your paper.
2. Draw two black circles for his eyes.
3. Draw a mouth under his eyes.
4. Draw a purple carrot in his mouth.
5. Draw a blue scarf around his neck.
6. Put a yellow sun over his head.
7. Draw two balls beside him.
8. Make one ball green.
9. Make the other ball pink.
10. Draw a yellow sun above the snowman.
11. Draw two other things. You may draw anything you wish. Use only two colors when you draw.
12. Turn the paper over. Write your name on the back.

FIGURE 6–5 Directions for Drawing

DIRECTIONS: Prepare a set of directions, as shown in Figure 6–4. Ask children to get out their crayons or markers, and then give each child a blank piece of paper and a set of directions for drawing. Children read and follow the directions to draw pictures on the blank paper. When the drawings are complete, ask the children to compare their papers. Read the directions with the group; share pictures and papers; and talk about the function words children need to bring to fluency.

Set 1 is the easiest of the four examples; set 4 is the hardest. Function words in Set 1 are: *a, beside, it, under, the, with, or,* and *all.* Function words in Set 2 are: *on, your, a, beside, the, one, near, below, any, under, many, did, you, of,* and *in.* Function words in Set 3 consist of: *a, on, your, beside, the, near, other, side, of, over, it, below, something, about, who,* and *under.* Function words in Set 4 consist of: *on, your, for, his, a, under, in, around, over, beside, him, one, the, other, above, other, may, anything, back,* and *when.* Directions are easy to write. Use the high-frequency function words in Table 6–1, as well as any other function or content words the children need to recognize, read, and understand. Figure 6–5 shows a set of completed directions for the drawings in Set 1.

SEMANTIC FEATURE ANALYSIS

▷ **LARGE GROUP**
SMALL GROUP
WORD MEANING

Semantic feature analysis helps children learn word meanings, compare and contrast words, and apply prior knowledge when learning new words.

MATERIALS: A grid showing words and attributes, characteristics, or features of words as shown in Figure 6–6. To make grids, decide on the words and features. Write the features across the top of the grid, and the words on the left-hand side.

DIRECTIONS: Have children work individually or with a buddy to decide which attributes or characteristics are attributable to important words from the books children are reading in your class. Discuss the words and features before children complete the grid. When children finish the semantic feature analysis grid, review and discuss the attributes of words. Talk about instances when children differ in their views or opinions.

FIGURE 6–6 Semantic Feature Analysis

	Living	Fur	Pet	Four-Footed	Large
cat	+	+	+	+	0
cow	+	+	–	+	+
dinosaur	–	–	–	0	0
spider	+	–	–	–	–
hamster	+	+	+	+	–
fish	+	–	+	–	0

0 = Sometimes
+ = Yes
– = No

▷ LARGE GROUP
SMALL GROUP
WORD MEANING

WORD WEBS

Word webs show how the meanings of new words are connected to the meaning of known words and concepts. Word webs are useful for: (1) exploring words that have multiple meanings, (2) developing alternatives to overused words in writing, such as *said* and *go* (Lafromboise, 2000), or (3) developing content area vocabulary concepts.

MATERIALS: Large pieces of paper; markers or pencils.

DIRECTIONS: Make several word webs as a whole group activity before having children make webs in small groups. The general procedure is to discuss a special word from a chapter book children are reading in your classroom or from a content area textbook. Write the word in the center of a large piece of paper or the board. Write important meanings and characteristics connected to the side of the center word. Include words that are related to the center word through sharing similar meanings, characteristics, or attributes. Draw lines between the center word and related words, thus creating a web-like structure. Some webs have all the words in circles, while others just have words connected with lines (sometimes called strands) to the center word. Figure 6–7 shows a word web for *water,* created after children had studied the salt and fresh water ecosystems.

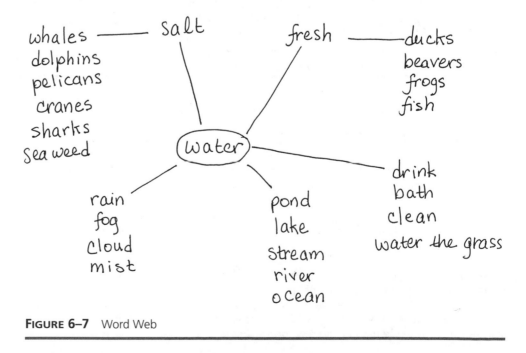

FIGURE 6–7   Word Web

ADD-ON SENTENCES

Add-on sentences develop an understanding of nouns, verbs, adjectives, and adverbs in sentence contexts.

MATERIALS: Word cards; masking tape loops to stick the cards on the board.

DIRECTIONS: Write a sentence on the board and replace a noun, verb, adjective, or adverb with a line. Stick the word cards randomly on the board. Read the sentence. Discuss the type of word (noun, verb, adjective, or adverb) that makes sense in the blank. Ask children to take turns selecting a card, reading the word on the card, and deciding whether the word fits the context. If it does, the word is added to the sentence by sticking the card under the blank. If not, the card is set aside. Each time a word is added to the sentence, have the group read the new, longer sentence in chorus. Examples of finished sentences are shown below.

Adding-on Different Adjectives

Robin ate a _____ sandwich.

delicious	*Words set aside:*
large	hopping
scrumptious	hungry
fattening	swishing
jumbo	satisfied
gooey	falling
tasty	
and	
yummy	

Adding-on Synonyms for the word Large

The house is _____.

enormous	*Words set aside:*
gigantic	intelligent
spacious	speedy
huge	tasty
roomy	chipper
colossal	clumsy
immense	
and	
massive	

In addition to using add-on sentences to identify and use parts of speech, use add-on sentences to explore synonyms for overused words. Repeatedly reading these sentences helps build fluency, which is another benefit of this add-on sentence activity.

HANDS-ON ACTIVITIES FOR USING CONTEXT CUES ■ ■ ■ ■ ■ ▬▬▬

Context cues include the semantic, syntactic, and graphophonic cues. Not all cues are equally helpful in each reading situation. In one setting, semantic cues may be extremely helpful and, hence, children may pay more attention to meaning clues than to syntactic and graphophonic cues. In other situations, syntactic or graphophonic cues may be a better source of information. Beyond wide reading and writing, perhaps the best way to give children structured practice using context cues is to create cloze sentences.

The cloze procedure is an informal assessment technique used: (1) to find out if reading material is too difficult, just right, or too easy for children; and (2) to find out how well children are able to read certain passages. To use the cloze procedure to assess reading, find a 250- to 300-word passage that is typical of the type of books children are reading in class. Leave the first and last sentence intact and delete every fifth word from the remaining sentences. Replace the deleted words with blanks.

Another way to use the cloze procedure is to construct cloze sentences that give children practice using context cues to identify the missing words. We will use several versions of the cloze procedure to give children practice identifying words in context. You may wish to use cloze sentences that are available commercially or you may wish to construct your own cloze sentences. Regardless of the source of the cloze sentences, you will want to match the specific type of cloze sentence with the needs of the children in your classroom. The descriptions of the various options help you match the type of cloze sentence to the abilities children need to develop further.

▷ LARGE GROUP
   SMALL GROUP
   CONTEXT CUES

CLOZE SENTENCES

Cloze sentences are a useful tool to give children practice using semantic, syntactic, and graphophonic cues. The cloze sentences themselves vary depending on the type of cue you wish to emphasize.

1. High-Meaning Word Deletion

MATERIALS: Sentences from classroom reading material.

DIRECTIONS: Delete one high-meaning word from a sentence. Replace that word with a blank. Make all blanks the same length so children do not have a clue as to word length. The following sentences are from *Sarah, Plain and Tall* (MacLachlan, 1985):

"A bonnet!" he cried. "I see a yellow _____!" (p. 18)	(bonnet)
The hail crunched and melted _____ our feet. (p. 50)	(beneath)
Papa took the reins and Sarah climbed down from the _____. (p. 56)	(wagon)

Cues used: Semantic cues, syntactic cues, and punctuation cues.

In each of these cloze sentences, children must use semantic cues and syntactic cues to fill in the blanks. Since there are not letters to suggest possible words, children do not draw on how a word is spelled, its letter patterns, its affixes, or its syllables. The missing word in each cloze blank can be deduced from the sentence context by thinking about meaning and syntax alone.

2. Partial Word Deletion: Pronounceable Letter Patterns

MATERIALS: Sentences from classroom reading material.

DIRECTIONS: Decide on a letter pattern cue you would like children to use, and then selectively delete all portions of words except that pattern. There are two options for deleting letters in words:

1. You may focus children's attention on beginning letters, ending letters, or vowel patterns by deleting all parts of the words *except* the beginning letters (tr_____), all parts of the words *except* the ending letters (_____nt), or all parts of the words *except* the vowel pattern (_____oi_____). In this option, children use their knowledge of beginning letters, ending letters, or vowel patterns to figure out the identity of the missing word.
2. You might delete just the beginning letters (_____ead), just the ending letters (poi_____), or just the vowel pattern (p_____nt). In this option, children consider all the letters surrounding the deleted letter pattern and then use semantic and syntactic cues to infer the identity of the missing word.

USING BEGINNING LETTER CUES   One way to help children use beginning letters in combination with semantic and syntactic cues is to write the beginning letter in the blank, as shown by the examples of sentences from *Fantastic Mr. Fox* (Dahl, 1970):

• In the woods there was a huge tr_____. (p. 15).	(tree)
• For a long t_____ they kept on digging. (p. 52)	(time)
• Peering through the jars, th_____ saw a huge woman coming down the cellar. (p. 78)	(they)

Cues used: Semantic cues, syntactic cues, and beginning letter cues.

In these sentences, children simultaneously consider meaning cues, grammatical cues, and the beginning letter and sound cues in order to fill in the blanks. In these examples, children are asked to use their knowledge of: (1) a beginning consonant cluster (the *tr* in *tree*), (2) a single beginning consonant (the *t* in *time*), and (3) a consonant digraph (the *th* in *they*). Children focus specifically on the beginning graphophonic cues provided and use these cues to help them identify a word that makes sense in the sentence context.

Using Vowel Pattern Cues   You can construct cloze sentences to help children get practice using specific vowel letter patterns, as in the following examples from *Revolutionary War on Wednesday* (Osborne, 2000):

- All they had to do was p_____nt to a picture and wish to   (point)
  go there. (p. 1)
- Jack pulled his sc_____f tighter. (p. 11)   (scarf)
- He found a picture of the b_____ts on the riverbank. (p. 32)   (boats)

Cues used: Semantic cues, syntactic cues, vowel pattern cues.

Each of the selective deletions in these sentences requires children to focus on a particular vowel pattern. In the first sentence children focus on the *oi* diphthong pattern, in the second on the r-controlled (*ar*) pattern, and in the last sentence on the V V long vowel pattern (*oa*). You may delete any type of vowel letter pattern that children are learning in your classroom. In so doing, children get practice using their knowledge of the vowel letter patterns in the context of meaningful sentences.

3. Partial Word Deletion: Structural Analysis

Materials: Sentences from classroom reading material.

Directions: Decide on the structural units (affixes, contractions, compound words, syllables) you want children to practice using in context, and then delete all portions of the words except that pattern. You might delete only prefixes (_____play), suffixes (play_____), letters deleted from contractions (did_'_, didn'_, did_'t), or syllables (_____dle). You might also delete only a portion of a compound word.

Using Cues to Prefixes and/or Suffixes   Deleting just a prefix or a suffix helps children think about the contextually appropriate affixes that are attached to words, as in these examples from *The Lizard and the Sun; la Lagartija y el Sol* (Ada, 1999):

- But the sun did not come out, and everything remained
  in dark_____. (p. 4, unnumbered)   (darkness)
- It shone so bright_____ that it seem_____ to glow.   (brightly, seemed)
  (p. 9, unnumbered)
- She _____turn_____ to where the rock lay and tried   (returned)
  to move it. (p. 17)

Cues used: Semantic cues, syntactic cues, prefix and/or suffix structural cues.

In these examples children fill in the missing prefix or suffix to spell a word that fits the grammatical structure of the sentence. Children must not only be familiar with the affixes, but must also be sensitive to English syntax. Before asking children who speak languages other than English at home to complete this type of cloze, make sure that the children are aware of, and able to use, the syntactic patterns in which the affixed words appear.

Using Cues to Contractions   Give children practice identifying contractions in context by deleting just a portion of the contraction from words in sentences contained in familiar books, such as *The Tower of the Elf King* (Abbott, 2000):

- Eric remembered the last time he'_____ seen the wicked   (he'd)
  sorcerer. (p. 15)
- "It feels like we'_____ moving," said Julie. (p. 25)   (we're)
- "Now let'_____ get the thieves, too!" Khan said. (p. 49)   (let's)

Cues used: Semantic cues, syntactic cues, and contraction cues.

In addition to having children fill in the appropriate letters in each contraction, you might use the high-meaning word deletion option. Here you would write both words under the line and have children write the contraction on the line, as follows:

- Eric remembered the last time _____ seen the wicked   (he'd)
  sorcerer. (p. 15)   *he had*

- "It feels like _____ moving," said Julie. (p. 25)   (we're)
      we are
- "Now _____ get the thieves, too!" Khan said. (p. 49)   (let's)
      let us

Filling in the missing letters in contractions or writing contractions from two clue words helps children think about the two words that make up the contractions and, additionally, assures that children fully understand the contractions they read and write.

USING SYLLABLE CUES   Words in familiar text are written, but only the first syllable in a two-syllable word is provided as a cue. This is a particularly good strategy to help children identify key words in chapter books and content area books. For three-syllable or longer words, delete only one syllable, as in *gi_____tic* or *gigan_____* for *gigantic* and *en_____gy* or *ener_____* for *energy.* The sentences below are from *The Giant Germ* (Capeci, 2000), the sixth book in the Magic School Bus chapter book series:

- I saw my sandwich on the ground next to the
    pic_____ table. (pp. 12–13)   (picnic)
- After we landed, Mrs. Frizzle handed out rub_____ boots   (rubber)
    and a safety helmet. (p. 13)
- Yeast cells form buds that devel_____ into new yeast   (develop)
    cells. (p. 18)

Cues used: Semantic cues, syntactic cues, and syllable cues.

Rather than selecting single sentences from familiar text, you might wish to write a whole paragraph, deleting one syllable from key multi-syllable words. An entire paragraph gives children stronger context cues and, additionally, allows children to practice using their syllable knowledge while reading connected text.

USING COMPOUND WORD CUES   English is peppered with compound words. Compound words are generously used by authors of children's books, as illustrated by the sentences from *The Cabin Faced West* (Fritz, 1958):

- It was the only place the day_____ had a chance to   (daylight)
    come in. (p. 9)
- In desperation, she blew into the fire_____, hoping to   (fireplace)
    revive a hidden spark. (p. 40)
- Little spots of sun_____ trickled through the trees and
    grape_____, and lay flickering on the road. (p. 43)   (sunshine, grapevines)

Cues used: Semantic cues, syntactic cues, and compound word cues.

Generally speaking, children will not have much, if any, difficulty recognizing the individual words in compounds. The challenge, then, is for children to realize that some of the long words in text are compound words, and that in pronouncing both words together children can say the compound words aloud.

4. Partial Word Deletion with Clues to Word Length

This form of cloze differs from those previously mentioned in that you write one line for each deleted *letter.* One line for each missing letter gives children word length information that contributes to using graphophonic cues. For example, in deleting portions of the word *thorn,* you might write th _ _ _. The three blanks indicate just how long the word is and this, in turn, helps children narrow down their choices, as in *The th _ _ _ pricked her finger.*

5. Word Choice Clues

A fifth version is to write two or three words below the blank. The words from which children choose may offer them choices that differ in meaning, grammatical class, or graphophonic cues. Children may choose from among two or three words.

USING SEMANTIC CUES   To focus children's attention on meaning clues, give children choices between two words that differ in meaning but belong to the same grammatical class. An example of a cloze sentence that focuses on semantic cues is:

- Mrs. Black baked _____ for the party.
        (***cookies, sandwiches***)

USING SYNTACTIC CUES   Children think about both syntax and meaning clues when the words represent different grammatical classes, as in:

- Mrs. Black baked cookies for the _____.
        (***push, good, party***)

USING GRAPHOPHONIC CUES   Print cues become especially important when words look a lot alike, as we see in:

Mrs. Black baked cookies for the _____.   Mrs. Black _____ cookies for the party.
        (***pretty, party***)   (***backed, baked***)

USING HOMONYM CUES   Cloze sentences with homonyms for choices are particularly challenging and, coincidentally, an effective way to give children practice thinking about homonym word meaning:

- John ate a bowl of _____ for lunch.
        (***chili, chilly***)
- John _____ a bowl of _____ for lunch.
    (***eight, ate***)   (***chili, chilly***)

Though homonyms sound alike, the differences in spelling have a profound effect on meaning. The cloze procedure with synonyms combines all types of cues and, additionally, helps sensitize children to the presence of synonyms in our language and helps children focus on meaning when identifying words.

MASKING

▷ LARGE GROUP
SMALL GROUP
CONTEXT CUES

Masking is a technique in which you temporarily cover up all or a portion of a word in a sentence, poem, or connected familiar text.

1. Sticky Note Masks

MATERIALS: Sticky notes; familiar text on charts, or on overhead transparencies.

DIRECTIONS: Sticky notes may be placed over an entire word or may be used to cover up only certain portions of a word.

2. Index Card Masks

MATERIALS: Index cards; pocket chart; wide sentence strips with sentences written on them.

DIRECTIONS: Write a sentence from a familiar book on a sentence strip and place the strip in the pocket chart. Before asking children to gather around the pocket chart, place an index card over words you wish to mask. Have children then read the sentence either individually or aloud in chorus. Call attention to the masked words. Ask children to predict the hidden words, using meaning and sentence structure cues. You may also use the index card to cover up all but the beginning letter-sound in words, thereby focusing children's attention on semantic cues, syntactic cues, and beginning letter cues.

HANDS-ON ACTIVITIES FOR WORD RECOGNITION ACCURACY ■ ■ ■ ■ ▬▬

Remembering the unique letter sequence of each word is an essential part of fast, accurate, and effortless word recognition. This is particularly true for short words that do not have many of the distinctive features (*was*) that longer words provide (*hippopotamus*). Many high-frequency words are short words: Only 31 percent of the first 300 words in Fry's list have more than one syllable; only 18 percent have more than five letters; and two-thirds are four letters or less. Some of the accuracy activities help children pay attention to the distinct letter sequence in words, while other activities give children practice reading or writing words while developing the children's understanding of word meaning.

▷ LARGE GROUP
SMALL GROUP
ACCURATE WORD
RECOGNITION
WORD MEANING
IN CONTEXT

PERSONAL WORD BANKS

Personal word banks are small boxes in which children store high-frequency words, words they want to learn, and words they need to know in order to read grade-level text and content area words. Word cards are filed alphabetically, which reinforces the children's memory of alphabetical order. Personal word banks are also ready resources for the words children wish to spell when writing. You may also use the word cards in personal word banks to informally assess children's ability to fluently recognize words and to understand word meaning.

MATERIALS: A small box (a small recipe box is just the right size) for each child; note cards that fit inside the box; tabs; pencils.

DIRECTIONS: Put tabs on twenty-six cards; write one letter of the alphabet on each tab. Use the tabbed cards to file word cards alphabetically. Fill the boxes with word cards. Write one word on the front of each card; write a phrase or sentence with the word on the back.

Generally speaking, the meaning of pronouns (*her* ice cream cone) and articles (*the* car) is clear in short phrases. Some prepositions and some conjunctions should be in complete sentences (He went *aboard* the ship. Jim stayed home *because* he was sick.). Select familiar sentences or phrases from books children are reading, or ask children to make up their own sentences to write on the cards. For example, phrases and sentences from *Owl at Home* (Lobel, 1975) include: *Winter ran around the room* (p. 11); *Owl was at home* (p. 5); and *Owl opened the door* (p. 6). Sentences like these contextualize words, yet are short enough for young readers to feel comfortable reading them. Older readers might want to copy sentences from books they are reading or from content area texts. The following phrases and sentences come from *Owl at Home* (Lobel, 1975):

Side One	Side Two
Winter ran <u>around</u> the room.	around
Owl was at <u>home</u>.	home
covered with <u>snow</u>	snow
Owl opened the <u>door</u>.	door

- Have children file the word cards in alphabetical order and use the cards in games or for direct practice, if necessary (Tan & Nicholson, 1997; van den Bosch, van Bon, & Schreuder, 1995).

- Ask children to review their words with a partner. Children remove all or part of the word cards from their personal banks, trade stacks with a partner, and then take turns showing each other the word cards.
- Have a good reader, or an assistant, an older student, or a parent help struggling readers review their word cards.
- You may occasionally want to use the personal word bank cards as an informal check of children's rapid recognition vocabulary. Use the cards as flash cards by showing children cards as rapidly as possible. Words recognized without hesitation are fluent words; those which require self-correction, are misread, or cause hesitations are not in children's rapid recognition vocabulary. Charting progress by the number of words that children add to their fluent reading vocabularies is a useful way to document progress. Knowing which words children are able to recognize rapidly and which words cause problems help you decide on words to emphasize in practice activities, word play, and word games.

HIDE-AND-THINK WORDS

▷ **Large Group**
Small Group
Accurate Word
Recognition

Use this easy activity to develop children's memory for words, particularly the letter sequence in similarly spelled words. Hide-and-think words fit nicely into even the smallest amount of time, and are therefore especially good for transition times.

Materials: Cards with visually confusing words.

Directions: Follow these seven simple steps:
1. Show children a word card and ask them to read the word aloud in chorus.
2. Children spell the word in chorus.
3. Hide the word behind your back. Tell the children to close their eyes and to "see" the word in their minds.
4. Children should spell the word in chorus with their eyes closed.
5. While children's eyes are closed, turn around so that your back is to the children. Pick up a second word card.
6. Ask the children to open their eyes. Show the children both words.
7. Have children indicate which word they read before.

Other options include: showing children one word to "see" (*there*) in their minds and then giving them a choice among three words (*there, their, where*). Or asking children to "see" two words (*there, where*) in their minds and then showing them three word cards (*there, their, where*).

In using Hide-and-think Words, we find that it is better to start with words that are dissimilar in spelling (*come–go*) and then to gradually use words that are visually similar (*where–there*).

WORD HUNTS

▷ **Large Group**
Small Group
Accurate Word
Recognition

Word hunts sensitize children to the presence of the same words in a variety of materials and contexts.

Materials: Old magazines, newspaper articles, and books; pencils, pens, crayons, or highlighters.

Directions: Ask children to look in newspaper and magazine articles, in books, and in your classroom for particular words. Parts of speech, such as nouns, verbs, adverbs, or adjectives, are good words for older children to find. Younger children might hunt for words that describe things we see, smell, touch, or taste. Another alternative is to invite fourth and fifth graders to scour books and the environment for words that are especially intriguing. Children might look for short words, long words, funny-sounding words, and unusual words. Bring in some of your favorite and unusual words, too. Put the words on a large bulletin board or make charts listing the words children find. In a very short time your classroom will be awash with strange and fun words. Encourage the children to use these words in writing poetry and stories.

▷ LARGE GROUP
SMALL GROUP
ACCURATE WORD
RECOGNITION
CONVENTIONAL
SPELLING

COUNT AND SPELL

In this activity, children are asked to remember the number of letters in a word, represent the number with squares, and then spell the word from memory.

MATERIALS: Large index cards on which you have written hard-to-remember or difficult-to-spell words; several paper squares for each child in the group; a blank piece of paper and a pencil for spelling words.

DIRECTIONS: Pass out paper squares to each child in a small group, then follow these ten steps:
1. Show children an easily confused word, such as *where*.
2. Children read the word in chorus.
3. Ask children to say the word again, and to count the letters as they point to each one.
4. Children line up as many paper squares as there are letters in the word. In the example of *where*, children line up five paper squares.
5. Children point to each paper square and say the letter name that the square represents. In this example, children point to the first square and say "*w*," to the second while saying "*h*," to the third while saying "*e*," to the fourth while saying "*r*," and to the fifth while saying "*e*."
6. Remove the word card. Ask children to spell the word from memory. Children may look at the five squares on their tables to help them remember the letters in the word.
7. Once the children finish spelling, show them the card for *where* again. Read *where* in chorus and spell *where* in chorus.
8. Have children spell *where* by writing one letter on each square.
9. Scramble the squares.
10. Ask children to line up the squares to spell *where*.

Follow this procedure with three or four more words. Say, for example, you use this activity to reinforce their memory and spelling of *where, here, there,* and *they* on one day. On another day you might use the activity with the same words, add a new word, *then,* or delete a word children know and replace it with another hard-to-remember word.

▷ SMALL GROUP
ACCURATE WORD
RECOGNITION

FOUR CARD DRAW

This card game gives children experience reading and rereading function words in short phrases.

MATERIALS: Stickers with four copies of the same picture; fifty-two 3 × 5 index cards.
To make books of four cards each, put one of four look-alike stickers on each of four cards. Make thirteen books of four cards for a fifty-two-card deck. Write a short phrase or sentence with one function word on each card. Four cards should have the same function word, but in different sentences. For example, four cards with a yellow flower sticker may have: *Where* are you going? She forgot *where* she put her pencil. Do you know *where* my book is? *Where* is the blue crayon? Four cards with a bird sticker might have: *Which* car is the fastest? She didn't know *which* book to choose. *Which* crayon should I use? *Which* way did he go? Laminate the cards. If you decide to make more than one deck, use index cards in different colors so as to differentiate the decks.

DIRECTIONS: From two to four children play this game. The rules are as follows:
1. The dealer gives each player six cards. The remaining cards are placed face-down.
2. Players take turns asking for cards with a certain sticker. For example, a player might say, "I would like a card with a yellow flower."
3. If another player has a yellow flower sticker, that player lays the card, sentence up, on the table. The player who requested the card then reads the face-up sentence. If the player correctly reads the sentence, the player keeps the card. If the player does not correctly read the entire sentence, the card is returned to its original owner.
4. Players ask only for a card with a sticker that matches a card in the player's hand.
5. Every player takes one card from the face-down pile after asking for a card, whether the player kept a card or returned it to the original owner.
6. When a player has four cards with the same sticker picture, the player puts all the cards on the table and reads the sentences.
7. The winner is the first player to go out; that is, to have no cards left to play.

WIPE-AWAY WORDS

LARGE GROUP
SMALL GROUP
ACCURATE WORD
RECOGNITION

This is a good activity for those few spare minutes during transition times throughout the day. Using wipe-away words is an effective and highly motivational activity that reinforces children's visual memory for the unique letter sequence of easily confused words.

MATERIALS: No special materials are necessary.

DIRECTIONS: Write one easily confused word on the chalk board. Leave it on the board for two seconds (longer for younger children or less-able readers). Erase the word. Ask the children to tell you the word, then have children spell the word while you write it on the board again.

To use this activity while getting children ready to leave for lunch or at the end of the day, have each child whisper the word in your ear as he or she lines up to leave the room. You may also ask children to write the word on a scrap of paper, to put their name on the paper, and to drop it in a special box. In this option, all correct words earn children one point. The children with the most points, or who reach a certain number of points, might get a special treat on Friday, such as an extra fifteen minutes to pursue a personal interest or a homework pass.

TEN-MINUTE FLUENCY ACTIVITIES FOR RAPID WORD RECOGNITION

Use these hands-on activities with children who recognize words accurately but slowly and who, therefore, need just a little more practice in order to add words to their fluent reading vocabularies. Set a limit on the time to complete the activities. Setting time limits increases speed without decreasing accuracy (van den Bosch, van Bon, & Schreuder, 1995). Some of these activities present words in isolation, while others present words in context. Recognizing words quickly and accurately is effective whether words are practiced in isolation, or in phrase or sentence contexts. This kind of practice is effective for average and struggling readers (Tan & Nicholson, 1997).

RED LIGHT RAPID WORDS AND PHRASES

SMALL GROUP
WORD RECOGNITION
FLUENCY

Children take turns reading words or phrases on cards as fast as possible before a Red Light card turns up. When a Red Light card appears, the next child in the small group begins reading.

MATERIALS: Sets of cards on which you have written single words or short phrases that contain words children need to recognize faster. Make ten cards that have a red stop light on them. Shuffle the cards to intermix the word/phrase cards with the Red Light cards.

DIRECTIONS: Ask a small group to join you at a quiet table. Explain that you will show the cards one at a time to one child. The child reads the words (or phrases) as fast as possible. When a Red Light card turns up, the next child gets a turn. If a child misreads a word, the misreading acts just like a Red Light and the turn is also passed to the next player. Make sure that children read and reread the words and phrases at least three times in one sitting, as repetition builds speed and self-confidence. Add extra motivation by giving each child one point for every card read. The child with the most points wins. You may also want to lend the cards to children so that they may practice before the next Red Light rapid words or phrases reading game.

SPINNING WORDS

SMALL GROUP
INDIVIDUAL
WORD RECOGNITION
FLUENCY

Children sit in a circle and the teacher spins a disk while children take turns showing each other word cards. A designated child reads the word and catches the spinning disk before it falls over.

MATERIALS: One large lid that has absolutely flat sides, with no grooves whatsoever (flat-sided lids spin well; lids with grooves on the sides do not). In lieu of a flat-sided lid, use any circle-shaped disc that is large enough for children to grab as it spins. You also need cards with words children need to bring to fluency.

DIRECTIONS: Gather a small group around a large table or ask children to sit in a small circle on the floor. Place a stack of word cards face-down. Pass the stack to the child on your right. The child with the cards is called the "Card Holder." The teacher or the Card Holder chooses someone in the group to be the reader. The teacher says "Go!" and starts the disc spinning. At the word "Go!" the Card Holder shows the reader the first card in the stack. The reader must read the word correctly and grab the spinning lid before it falls over. The reader, if successful, becomes the Card Holder and designates another child to be the reader. A lid spins for only a few seconds, so the time limit for word recognition is quite short. This is a highly motivational activity which challenges children to increase their recognition speed and to maintain accuracy, and takes only a small amount of time.

▷ SMALL GROUP
INDIVIDUAL
WORD RECOGNITION
FLUENCY

TIMED RAPID WRITING

Children write as many words as they can think of in a teacher-specified time. On repeated rapid writing trials individuals try to beat their own score by writing more and more words in the same amount of time.

MATERIALS: Timer or a watch with a second hand; paper; pencils.

DIRECTIONS: Pass out paper and explain that you will set the timer for four minutes. Remind the children that spelling counts! Have the children put their pencil tips in the air. When the children are poised with their pencils in the air, set the timer and begin the countdown: "Ready. Set. Go!" Writing stops when the timer goes off. Count the number of words and write that number in the corner. Save the paper. Challenge individuals to write more words the next time the class does timed rapid writing. Ask children to use their mathematics skills to graph their own progress.

Rapid writing is easier when children write any words they can think of, and harder when the children write words that meet specific criteria, such as four or five letters long or more than one syllable. If you teach third, fourth, or fifth grade, set word length guidelines. Without word length guidelines, some children may choose to write only number words or short word family words (*at, cat, fat*), even though the children are fully capable of writing long and diverse words. General guidelines for word length are as follows: First and second graders may write any words they can think of, although you may want to encourage some children to write longer and longer words as their reading ability increases. Third graders should write words with at least six letters. Some high-frequency words like *school* may be declared "off limits" so as to encourage children to take risks writing more challenging words. Ask fourth and fifth graders to write words which are at least two syllables long; fifth graders may enjoy writing only special words, such as words with prefixes, or only words with suffixes.

▷ SMALL GROUP
INDIVIDUAL
WORD RECOGNITION
FLUENCY

TIMED REPEATED SPEED SORTS

Children recognize and categorize words under timed conditions, which helps children develop the ability to recognize words rapidly, accurately, and effortlessly (Bear, Invernizzi, Templeton, & Johnston, 2000).

MATERIALS: Word cards; timer or a stopwatch. Select words that under normal conditions children sort slowly and, therefore, need practice to sort with both speed and accuracy. Avoid words children do not have experience sorting.

DIRECTIONS: Give children from fifteen to twenty cards to sort. Explain that the timer is set for a certain amount of time, say four minutes, and that children should sort as fast as they can before the timer goes off. Have children sort the same set until sorting is fast and accurate. Timed, repeated speed sorts are closed; that is, you specify the sorting categories. First and second graders might sort words into naming words (nouns) and doing words (verbs), or into such categories as foods, toys, or animals. Third through fifth graders might sort words by nouns, verbs, adjectives, adverbs, or into categories of plants, animals, and minerals. Repeated speed sorting is also an excellent fluency activity for the words in children's content area textbooks.

RAPID SEQUENCE CARDS

▷ SMALL GROUP
INDIVIDUAL
WORD RECOGNITION
FLUENCY

This timed fluency activity challenges children to arrange flash cards into meaningful sentences within a teacher-specified time.

MATERIALS: Cards with words the children need to bring to fluency; cards with punctuation marks; a timer; envelopes to hold the cards. Select sentences from familiar books; make cards for the words; put words in envelopes; write the sentences on the outside of the envelopes.

DIRECTIONS: Ask a small group to join you at a table. Divide children into pairs. Give each pair a group of word cards. Explain that the children have a specified amount of time to arrange the words into a sentence. Each team that makes a sentence before the timer goes off earns one point. Use and reuse the same words in different combinations so as to give children practice making different sentences with some overlapping words.

SPEEDY CLOZE WORDS

▷ LARGE GROUP
SMALL GROUP
WORD RECOGNITION
FLUENCY

In this activity, children read a sentence with one missing word. The teacher shows children two words for a brief time, removes the words, and children write the word that fits the sentence context.

MATERIALS: Cards for words children need to bring to fluency; masking tape loops taped to the backs of word cards; sentences using the words; a stopwatch or watch with a second hand. This activity is especially good for bringing to fluency sound-alike words (homonyms).

DIRECTIONS: Pass out one sheet of paper to each child. You may write a cloze sentence on the board or you may read a sentence aloud. If you write a sentence, explain that children have exactly five seconds (shorter or longer, depending on the children whom you teach) to read the sentence to themselves. If you are going to read the sentence aloud, explain that you will read a sentence with a missing word. As soon as the sentence is read (either by the children or by you), tape two word cards to the board. The children have exactly five seconds (longer for younger or struggling readers) to study the words. After five seconds, take the words away. When you say, "Go!" the children write the word that makes sense in the sentence. Examples include:

Cards briefly on the chalk board:	Cloze sentences:
there their	Read-aloud sentence:
	The children ate _____ lunch.
Cards briefly on the chalk board:	Read-aloud sentence:
was saw	The rabbit _____ eating carrots.
Cards briefly on the chalk board:	Read-aloud sentence:
when where	Mario laughed _____ he saw the clown.

Have the children write the word at the top of their paper and hold up the paper when they are finished writing. On subsequent rounds, children fold their papers over so that only one word shows. You may want to give children one point for each conventionally spelled, correct word. Children who accrue a certain number of points earn something special, like a homework pass, or extra free time on Friday afternoon.

TIMED TOSS AND TAKE-AWAY WORDS

▷ SMALL GROUP
WORD RECOGNITION
FLUENCY

First through second graders gently toss a small, soft ball onto a chair that has a word card on it, rapidly read the word, and then pass the ball on to another child, all within a specified amount of time. Children keep the words they correctly read.

MATERIALS: A chair for each child; 5 × 8 cards with words the children need to bring to fluency; masking tape loops; a soft, small ball; a timer or a watch with a second hand.

DIRECTIONS: Place the chairs in a *small* circle, with the seats facing inward. Have the children stand behind one chair each. Tape (or place) one word card on each chair. Explain that children have five minutes to gently toss a ball onto chairs with words, and to read the words on the chairs. Children begin to toss and read when you set the timer and say, "Ready. Set. Go!" Challenge the small group to see how many words they can read in five minutes. To give children repeated practice reading the same words, leave the words in place until the timer buzzes. To give children practice reading a variety of words, replace each correctly read word with a new word.

▷ **LARGE GROUP**
SMALL GROUP
WORD RECOGNITION
FLUENCY

HASTY WORDO

Wordo is played just like bingo, except there is no free space and the number of squares may range from sixteen to twenty-eight. The game may be used with any words children need to bring to fluency.

MATERIALS: As many Wordo cards as there are players; tokens to cover Wordo squares; sentences with words. Appendix A-25 is a reproducible blank Wordo card with twenty-four squares. Hasty Wordo is appropriate for all kinds of words. For purposes of illustration, we will use sound-alike words (homonyms), as shown in Figure 6–8. Select sound-alike words children routinely confuse (Table 6–2).

Get the children involved in making Wordo cards and sentences. Write a list of words on the board (more words than there are squares on the Wordo cards) and ask children to randomly write one word in each Wordo square. Have children write sentences on slips of paper and put them in a box. Before playing Hasty Wordo, read through the clue sentences. Select the best ones, and read them when playing Hasty Wordo.

FIGURE 6–8 Hasty Wordo (Homonyms)

WORDO!

their	blew	too	due
hear	high	new	who's
meet	there	do	knew
whose	weigh	they're	way
here	meat	blue	to

Two sets of clue sentences:

<u>Their</u> house is red.
She <u>blew</u> out the candle.
Homework is <u>due</u> tomorrow.
Did you <u>hear</u> the news?
The bike is brand <u>new</u>.
<u>Who's</u> going on the trip?
Let's <u>meet</u> after lunch.
<u>Do</u> you have a pencil?
John <u>knew</u> the song.
How much does your dog <u>weigh</u>?
<u>They're</u> going to the movie.
Our dog likes to eat <u>meat</u>.
Tim has a <u>blue</u> balloon.

<u>Their</u> dog is barking.
The hat is <u>too</u> big.
The report is <u>due</u> today.
The kite is <u>high</u> in the sky.
Mary has a <u>new</u> car.
<u>They're</u> having a party
Put the box down <u>there</u>.
<u>Do</u> you want to go?
<u>Whose</u> socks are these?
Elephants <u>weigh</u> a lot.
Do you know the <u>way</u> home?
<u>Here</u> is the book you wanted.
I like hamburger <u>meat</u>.
Go <u>to</u> the store.

The wind <u>blew</u>.
Jack wants to go, <u>too</u>.
I <u>hear</u> the bell.
How <u>high</u> can you jump?
<u>Who's</u> finished eating lunch?
<u>Meet</u> me before school.
<u>There</u> is no place to sit.
Gabriel <u>knew</u> the answer.
<u>Whose</u> jacket is on the floor?
<u>They're</u> eating lunch.
Which <u>way</u> is the lake?
Put the pencil <u>here</u>.
Maria has a <u>blue</u> jacket.
Let's go <u>to</u> the movie.

DIRECTIONS: Give each child a Wordo card and tokens. Explain that you are going to: (1) pronounce a word (in our example a sound-alike homonym), (2) use the word in a clue sentence, and (3) pronounce the word a second time. Explain further that when children hear the word the second time, they have exactly five seconds to find the word on their Wordo cards. To win, children cover vertical, horizontal, and diagonal lines. The winner spells each word to verify that the proper squares are covered.

In addition to these word meaning, accuracy, and fluency activities, model your own fascination with words by sharing words that are special to you. You might, for example, select a few high-imagery words from favorite poems, say the words, and ask children to paint a picture of the words in their minds. Ask children what they imagine when they paint word pictures in their minds. Share your own mental images. Have children draw pictures of what they imagine about word meaning. As you share your interest in words, build into your classroom language arts curriculum time for specific, direct instruction in vocabulary, as well as ample time for reading and writing. A large and ever-expanding cache of words that are recognized rapidly, accurately, and automatically is one of the bases for text-level fluency.

REFERENCES ■ ■ ■ ■ ▬▬▬

Aaron, P. G., Joshi, R. M., Ayotollah, M., Ellsberry, A., Henderson, J., & Lindsey, K. (1999). Decoding and sight-word naming: Are they independent components of word recognition skill? *Reading and Writing: An Interdisciplinary Journal*, 11, 89–127.

Abbott, T. (2000). *The tower of the elf king*. New York: Scholastic.

Ada, A. F. (1999). *The lizard and the sun: la lagartija y el sol*. New York: Bantam Doubleday Dell Books for Young Readers.

Agee, J. (1997). *So many dynamos!: and other palindromes*. New York: Farrar Straus & Giroux.

Agee, J. (1999a). *Go hang a salami! I'm a lasagna hog! and other palindromes*. New York: Econo-Clad Books.

Agee, J. (1999b). *Sit on a potato pan, otis!: More palindromes*. New York: Farrar Straus & Giroux.

Barksdale-Ladd, M. A., & King, J. R. (2000). The dilemma of error and accuracy: An exploration. *Reading Psychology*, 21, 353–372.

Bear, D. R., Invernizzi, M., Templeton, S., & Johnston, F. (2000). *Words their way: Word study for phonics, vocabulary, and spelling instruction*. Columbus, OH: Merrill.

Bonsall, C. (1974), *And I mean it, Stanley*, New York: Harper & Row.

Capeci, A. (2000). *The giant germ*. New York: Scholastic.

Dahl, R. (1970). *Fantastic Mr. Fox*. New York: Puffin Books.

Ehri, L. C. (1997). Sight word learning in normal readers and dyslexics. In B. Blackman (Ed.), *Foundations of reading acquisition and dyslexia: Implications for early intervention* (pp. 163–189). Mahwah, NJ: Lawrence Erlbaum Associates.

Ehri, L. C. (1998). Grapheme-phoneme knowledge is essential for learning to read words in English. In J. L. Metsala & L. C. Ehri (Eds.), *Word recognition in beginning literacy* (pp. 3–40). Mahwah, NJ: Lawrence Erlbaum Associates.

Ehri, L. C., & McCormick, S. (1998). Phases of word learning: Implications for instruction with delayed and disabled readers. *Reading & Writing Quarterly: Overcoming Learning Difficulties*, 14, 135–163.

Ehri, L. C., & Wilce, L. (1985). Movement into reading: Is the first stage of printed word learning visual or phonetic? *Reading Research Quarterly*, 20, 163–179.

Fielding, L., Wilson, P., & Anderson, R. (1986). A new focus on free reading: The role of trade books in reading. In T. E. Ralhpel and R. Reynolds (Eds.), *Contexts of literacy-based school learning* (pp. 146–160). New York: Random House.

Foorman, B., Francis, D., Shaywitz, S., Shaywitz, B., & Fletcher, J. (1997). The case for early reading intervention. In B. Blachman (Ed.), *Foundations of reading acquisition and dyslexia* (pp. 243–264). Mahwah, NJ: Lawrence Erlbaum Associates.

Fritz, J. (1958). *The cabin faced west*. New York: Puffin Books.

Fry, E. (1994). *1,000 instant words: The most common words for teaching reading, writing, and spelling*. Laguna Beach, CA: Laguna Beach Educational Books.

Gaskins, I. W., Ehri, L. C., Cress, C., O'Hara, C., & Donnelly, K. (1997). Procedures for word learning: Making discoveries about words. *The Reading Teacher*, 50, 312–327.

Gentry, J. R., & Gillet, J. W. (1993). *Teaching kids to spell*. Portsmouth, NH: Heinemann.

Gwynne, F. (1988a). *A chocolate moose for dinner*. New York: Aladdin Books.

Gwynne, F. (1988b). *The king who rained*. New York: Aladdin Books.

Gwynne, F. (1990). *A little pidgeon toad*. New York: Aladdin Books.

Hasbrouck, J. E., Ihnot, C., & Rogers, G. H. (1999). Read naturally: A strategy to increase oral reading fluency. *Reading Research and Instruction*, 39, 27–38.

Johnson, D. D. (2001). *Vocabulary in the elementary and middle school*. Boston, MA: Allyn and Bacon.

La Fromboise, K. L. (2000). Saidwebs: Remedy for tired words, *The Reading Teacher*, 53, 540–546.

Lobel, A. (1975). *Owl at home*. New York: Harper Collins.

Logan, G. D. (1997). Automaticity and reading: Perspectives from the instance theory of automatization. *Reading and Writing Quarterly: Overcoming Learning Difficulties*, 13, 123–146.

MacLachlan, P. (1985). *Sarah, plain and tall*. New York: Harper and Row, Publishers.

Merriam-Webster's elementary dictionary: The student's source for discovering language (2000). Springfield, MA: Merriam-Webster.

Nagy, W. E., Anderson, R. C., & Herman, P. A. (1987). Learning word meanings. From context during normal reading. *American Educational Research Journal*, 24, 237–270.

National Center for Education Statistics. (1995). *Listening to children read aloud: Oral fluency*. [Online] 1 (1). Available FTP: National Center for Education Statistics: nces.ed.gov Directory: pubs/95762.html.

Parrish, P. (1979). *Amelia Bedelia helps out*. New York: William Morrow & Company.

Osborne, M. P. (2000). *Revolutionary war on Wednesday*. New York: Random House.

Sayre, A. P. (2001). *Dig wait listen: A desert toad's tale*. New York: Green Willow Books.

Searfoss, L. W., Readence, J. E., & Mallette, M. H. (2001). *Helping children learn to read: Creating a classroom literacy environment, 4th edition*. Needham Heights, MA: Allyn and Bacon.

Snow, C. E., Burns, M. S., & Griffin, P. (Eds) (1998). *Preventing reading difficulties in young children*. Washington, D.C.: National Academy Press.

Stuart, M., Masterson, J., & Dixon, M. (2000). Spongelike acquisition of sight vocabulary in beginning readers. *Journal of Research in Reading*, 23, 12–27.

Tan, A., & Nicholson, T. (1997). Flashcards revisited: Training poor readers to read words faster improves their comprehension of text. *Journal of Educational Psychology*, 89, 276–288.

Terban, M. (1982). *Eight ate a feast of homonym riddles*. New York: Houghton Mifflin.

Terban, M. (1985). *Too hot to hoot: Funny palindrome riddles*. New York: Houghton Mifflin.

Terban, M. (1988). *The dove dove: Funny homograph riddles*. New York: Clarion Books.

Vacca, J. A. L., Vacca, R. T., & Gove, M. K. (2000). *Reading and learning to read, 4th edition*. New York: Longman Publishing Group.

van den Bosch, K., van Bon, W. J. J., & Schreuder, R. (1995). Poor readers' decoding skills: Effects of training with limited exposure duration. *Reading Research Quarterly*, 30, 110–125.

Walczyk, J. J. (2000). The interplay between automatic and control processes in reading. *Reading Research Quarterly*, 35, 554–566.

Wilson, L. (1994). *Write me a poem, reading, writing, and performing poetry*, Portsmouth, NH: Heinemann.

DEVELOPING READING FLUENCY

Use these fluency activities with first through fifth graders in:

▶ **The Alphabetic Word Fluency Stage**

▶ **The Consolidated Word Fluency Stage**

When fifth grader Jamie curls up on her bed with a library book and begins reading to her younger sister, she could read by pausing between short phrases: "Once upon / a time / there was / a chihuahua / named Rita, / and she / had / a friend / named Rosie." She could also pause at every word: "Once / upon / a / time / there / was / a / chihuahua / named / Rita, /and / she / had / a / friend / named / Rosie." Likewise, she might read: "Once upon a time / there was a chihuahua named Rita, / and she had a friend named Rosie." Stopping abruptly between short oral phrases or pausing between words disrupts the natural flow of language, hinders comprehension, and interferes with enjoyment. The last option, smooth oral reading, is the kind of fluent reading we expect from a fifth grader. The best way to develop reading fluency is to have children read in your classroom everyday, read at home for pleasure, read widely, and read often. In addition to wide and frequent reading, there are specific oral and silent reading activities that you may use to help children improve their fluency.

WHAT IS READING FLUENCY? ■ ■ ■ ■ ▬▬

Fluent reading is smooth and expressive, sounds like talk, approaches the speed of normal conversation, and preserves the author's syntax. Fluent readers pay attention to punctuation and think about meaning, as meaning is foremost in their minds. Consequently, fluent readers decide where to pause and where to place emphasis so as to make meaning clear (National Institute of Child Health and Human Development, 2000). High-fluency readers comprehend better, read faster, and are more accurate than low-fluency readers (National Center for Education Statistics, 1995). High-fluency readers differ markedly from their low-fluency classmates, and these differences are readily noticeable by the fourth grade. In a nationwide study of reading fluency, the National Center for Education Statistics (NCES) found that high-fluency fourth graders read with expression and group words into meaningful phrases, whereas low-fluency fourth graders ignore sentence structure and read in one- or two-word phrases (1995). Fluent readers concentrate on understanding what they are reading and on reading smoothly and expressively.

Fluent readers are automatic at decoding (Samuels & Flor, 1997). In fact, fluent, expressive oral reading is a good indication of decoding fluency in children. You can assume that if children read a text at a certain level, say fifth grade, with good expression and accuracy, in a normal speaking voice, and with good comprehension, then children are fluent, or automatic, decoders of text written at a fifth-grade level. Likewise, because fluent readers recognize words accurately, rapidly, and automatically, they put their energy into understanding and learning from text, not into word recognition. You can also assume that if children are fluently reading fifth-grade text they have also reached word fluency at a fifth-grade level. Oral reading fluency is an audience-oriented ability; that is, oral readers read to communicate with a listening audience. However, we should not forget or lose sight of the overarching goal of fluency, which is to open up a world of ideas, self-growth, curiosity, new knowledge, and uncharted horizons.

Four Levels of Reading Fluency

Through most of the last century, fluency was more or less ignored (Allington, 1983). Fluency came into the spotlight in the mid-1990s, probably because fluency was then acknowledged to be a fundamental part of good reading (National Institute of Child Health and Human Development, 2000). Thanks to the National Assessment of Education Progress (NAEP), we now have a way to judge oral reading fluency. The NAEP uses a four-level scale to rate fluency (NCES, 1995).

1. *Level 1*   At the poorest level, Level 1, reading is primarily word-by-word.
2. *Level 2*   At the second level, children primarily read in two-word phrases, along with some three- and four-word phrases. Phrasing is awkward and unrelated to text meaning.
3. *Level 3*   At Level 3, children use three- and four-word phrases, along with a few smaller word groupings. While Level 3 phrasing is generally appropriate and preserves text meaning, readers read with little or no expression.
4. *Level 4*   Level 4, fluent reading, consists of smooth and expressive reading using large, meaningful phrases. When Level 4 readers miscue, their misreadings do not affect text meaning and do not detract from the overall story structure. Nationally, 13 percent of fourth graders read at Level 4, 42 percent read at both Level 2 and 3, and 7 percent read at Level 1.

■■■■■ ■ ■ ■ ■ **GUIDELINES FOR DEVELOPING READING FLUENCY**

Reading fluency develops gradually and incrementally in the presence of a working knowledge of letter names, letter-sounds, letter patterns, meaningful multi-letter word structures, and when classroom instruction includes developing a meaning-based fluent reading vocabulary and practice in reading a variety of texts for a variety of purposes. Follow these seven fluency-teaching guidelines when developing oral reading fluency:

1. *Have Children Read Silently Before Reading Aloud*   Children should always read passages silently, at least once, before they read passages aloud. The only time we ask children to read passages aloud without first reading them silently is when we wish to assess children's oral reading.
2. *Model Fluent Reading for Children*   Model and demonstrate fluent reading (Richards, 2000). In modeling and demonstrating fluency, teachers give children opportunities to follow along with a fluent reader while imitating the intonation, expression, and flow of fluent reading.

3. *Give Feedback and Guidance*   Giving children feedback and guidance on their oral reading improves the effectiveness of fluency lessons when children reread familiar text (National Institute of Child Health and Human Development, 2000).

4. *Help Children Read in Phrases*   Ensure that children are sensitive to phrases and know how to read in meaningful phrase groups (Rasinski & Padak, 2001). Show children how to group words into phrases, demonstrate good phrasing, give children opportunities to imitate the phrasing of fluent reading, provide children with hands-on opportunities to identify meaningful phrases, and to read in meaningful word groups.

5. *Use Text Just Below Instructional Level*   The text for developing oral reading fluency should be just below the children's instructional level. The goal is to find passages in which children recognize nearly all the words and, hence, concentrate on reading smoothly and expressively in phrases that preserve the author's syntax and meaning. Decoding, while a fine goal, does not have a role in oral reading fluency lessons.

6. *Keep Passages Relatively Short*   Passages for developing oral reading fluency should be short, ranging from fifty to several hundred words, depending on the reading ability of the children.

7. *Have Children Reread Text*   Opportunities to read and reread the same text over and over again are essential and effective for developing fluency (National Institute of Child Health and Human Development, 2000).

Providing practice in reading aloud with expression is essential for building oral reading fluency. This raises the question of what type of text, when used for real reading practice, is the most likely to pay off in marked improvement in oral reading fluency.

WHAT TO LOOK FOR IN READING MATERIAL

Although some texts foster fluency development in children, other texts do not, and some may even interfere with fluency. Selecting just the right text is the first step in developing oral reading fluency. Look for these six types of text when selecting material for developing oral reading fluency:

1. *Text Written Just Below Instructional Level*   Choose books that are just below children's instructional level. Look for text that has words children already know and sentences that are relatively easy for the children to understand. Avoid text in which children are likely to get bogged down in identifying unfamiliar words or sorting out confusing sentences. In reading books with known words and familiar sentence patterns, children are free to concentrate on reading in meaningful phrases and with good expression. Reading books that are too hard results in frustration, poor phrasing, misunderstandings, and low confidence. If you use text on children's instructional level, supply ample support before, during, and after reading (Rasinski & Padak, 2001).

2. *Text with Natural Language Patterns*   Select text that uses language patterns; in other words, texts that, when read aloud, sound like real language rather than book language (Richards, 2000). The ideal material for developing oral reading fluency flows in a natural language cadence when read aloud. The familiar, natural language structures are easily read aloud and, therefore, encourage children to pay attention to meaningful phrases and to read with expression. The type of text you choose, its length, and the use of words, phrases, and sentences depends on the age, grade, and oral reading fluency of the children in your classroom.

3. *Predictable Text: Patterned Books*   Predictable books, such as I *Went Walking* (Williams, 1992), use the same language pattern over and over again. This type of text is especially beneficial for developing fluency in beginning readers who do not yet have an extensive fluent recognition vocabulary. The first page in I *Went Walking* shows a child walking, and the second page poses the question "What did you see?" and gives a picture hint as to the answer to the question. Text on the third page answers the question, "I saw a brown horse looking at me," and the fourth page has a picture of the horse. Children quickly pick up the predictable pattern, and this, in turn, supports fluent reading. Have the children read and reread the same predictable books over and over again.

While beginning readers read predictable books with greater fluency than non-predictable text, fluency improves only after readers figure out and remember the predictable patterns. Furthermore, predictable text may well encourage overdependence on the pattern (Hiebert & Martin, 2001). When this happens, children "read" the books by turning the pages, cueing in on the illustrations, and reciting the text from memory. The advantage of predictable books, however, is that they are well suited for developing fluent oral reading in emergent readers. To sidestep the problem of children simply memorizing the patterned text, have children read the text without the pictures. You may cover up the pictures or rewrite portions of the text on a large chart. Ask a small group to read in chorus, and then ask individuals to read designated sentences. To find out which words in a predictable book the children have learned to recognize, write the words on plain 3 × 5 cards and ask the children to read them (Richek, Caldwell, Jennings, & Lerner, 2002). Children read fluent words quickly and accurately.

4. *Predictable Text: Rhyming Poetry, Limericks, and Rhyming Stories*   Rhyming poetry, limericks, and rhyming stories have a natural cadence that invites readers to group words into phrases. In reading rhyming poetry, children may use the predictable rhyme patterns to help them get a sense of when it is appropriate to pause between phrases. Rhyming poetry appeals to children of all ages, and is therefore a good choice for developing fluency from kindergarten through fifth grade. Model fluent reading, have the group read aloud in chorus, and then invite individuals to take turns reading different lines. Limericks are a special kind of rhyming poetry that tell a story in only five lines. Limericks tantalize the reading appetite of older students, perhaps because the rhythm and rhyme scheme almost always makes limericks sound comical when they are read aloud. The same rhythm and rhyme scheme that makes limericks seem funny also encourages smooth, expressive oral reading. In choosing books written in rhyming verse, be sure to look for good rhyming stories. These stories are much more prevalent in books for children ages four through eight than for older children. Rhyming stories tend to be relatively short, and encourage the use of good phrasing and expression.

5. *Lyrics to Popular Songs and Favorite Tunes*   Songs do not have to be sung in order for the lyrics to capture rhythmic, and often rhyming, language. Upper elementary children especially enjoy reading the lyrics of popular songs. Choose songs with natural language patterns and write them on charts. Read the lyrics in chorus, and talk about their meaning. Model fluent oral reading, and show children how to use good phrasing and expression to help convey meaning. In teaching young children, write the lyrics to old favorites, such as *The Wheels on the Bus*, and then read and reread the lyrics in chorus. The rhythm of predictable language, rhyming verse, and natural language act as a bridge to oral reading fluency. Coincidentally, the lyrics to popular songs capture children's interest and motivate them to read fluently as well.

6. *Plays Written Just Below Instructional Level*   When using plays to increase oral reading fluency, children read lines during performances rather than reciting lines from memory. Plays have all the ingredients for fostering oral reading fluency. The lines of individual characters are usually short, which gives oral readers bite-size bits

of text to practice for fluency. The text itself is written in natural language. Since the goal is a performance in front of an audience, the children who read their parts are encouraged to read with feeling. Plays have distinct characters with personalities that invite oral interpretation, which encourages reading with expression. Plays also have a clear-cut plot line that tells a story and, therefore, the lines spoken by each character are of paramount importance to the overall meaning of the play. Another benefit is that plays are rehearsed, which calls for reading the same text over and over again. Rereading plays is purposeful; children practice their lines so as to perfect their performance. Rereading is a powerful tool for improving reading fluency. The performance is the highpoint. Performances consist of reading scripts with feeling to classmates or to a neighboring class. Toss in a few props, like hats, brooms, and pails, and you have a bonafide performance that improves reading fluency, develops self assurance, and gives children a way to share their literacy with others.

DEVELOPING READING FLUENCY IN THE ALPHABETIC AND ■ ■ ■ ■ ▬▬▬ CONSOLIDATED WORD FLUENCY STAGES

As children first enter into the alphabetic stage, they can only read orally (Ehri, 1997; Ehri, 1998; Ehri & McCormick, 1998; Gaskins, Ehri, Cress, O'Hara, & Donnelly, 1997). They seem to need to hear themselves say the words before they understand word meaning. Children do not always read "out loud," however. Children may mumble under their breath or quietly move their lips without uttering a single sound. As children move into the alphabetic stage, they begin to amass words in their fluent reading vocabularies. By mid-first grade, the fluent reading vocabulary is large enough to support some preliminary instruction in oral reading fluency. Second graders have enough words in their fluent reading vocabularies to benefit from participating in the oral and silent reading activities. All the fluency activities are appropriate for third through fifth graders who are in the consolidated word fluency stage. Fluency activities help these children to understand and respond to text quickly and effortlessly. As children improve their ability to quickly understand and respond to text, they become better able to read increasingly more difficult text.

HANDS-ON ACTIVITIES FOR INCREASING ■ ■ ■ ■ ▬▬▬ ORAL READING FLUENCY

Most strategies for developing oral reading fluency involve reading and rereading the same text over and over again, the teacher modeling fluent reading, or a combination of both repeated reading and teacher modeling. Table 7–1 lists teaching strategies and gives a brief description of each one.

REPEATED READING

Repeated reading is simply reading and rereading the same text several times. After an extensive review of the research on fluency, the National Reading Panel concluded that repeated reading with teacher guidance and feedback is an effective way to improve fluency up through the fifth grade (National Institute of Child Health and Human Development, 2000). Repeatedly reading familiar text improves children's ability to read smoothly with expression, and also improves self-monitoring, self-correcting, error detection, and problem-solving strategies (Askew, 1993). Repeated reading is easy to use, does not take a large slice of the school day, and children do not get bored rereading the same familiar passages. There are two major ways to implement repeated reading in your classroom: taped repeated reading and paired repeated reading.

▷ SMALL GROUP
INDIVIDUAL
ORAL READING
FLUENCY

TABLE 7–1 Strategies for Developing Oral Reading Fluency

Strategy	Grouping for Instruction	Description
Taped Repeated Reading	Individual	A child rereads the same text over and over again into a tape recorder until the text is read fluently.
Paired Repeated Reading	Small Group	Pairs of children take turns reading the same text three times and asking questions about the text.
Choral Reading	Large Group, Small Group	Children read familiar text aloud together.
Shared Reading	Large Group, Small Group	Teachers read big books with emergent readers, and on repeated readings children join in to read repetitive sentences, predictable language, or special phrases.
Guided Reading	Large Group, Small Group	Includes prereading to activate prior knowledge and set purposes, reading text individually, and post reading, which may involve rereading portions of the text, which helps develop fluency.
Fluency Development Lesson	Large Group, Small Group	A multi-phase lesson combining teacher modeling, repeated reading, paired repeated reading, performance, and vocabulary study.
Echo Reading	Small Group, Individual	The teacher reads a short section of text and children imitate the teacher's fluent reading.
Neurological Impress Method (NIM)	Individual	The teacher and child read text together, with the teacher modeling fluency.
Marking Phrases	Individual	The teacher and child use colored markers to designate phrases in text, and then take turns reading in meaningful word groupings.
Readers' Theater	Large Group, Small Group	Children read plays, using their voices to supply the dramatic interpretation.
Read-arounds	Small Group	Children read their favorite portions of a familiar text.
Taped-assisted reading	Individual	Children listen to a tape recording of a story or short selection, and follow along with the text.
Language Experience Approach	Individual, Small Group, Large Group	Children dictate stories to their teacher. The stories are reread by the group.
Radio Reading	Large Group, Small Group	A classroom approximation of a radio broadcast in which children communicate with any audience through oral reading.

Taped Repeated Reading   We have successfully used this one-on-one teaching strategy with children of all ages and reading abilities.

MATERIALS: Tape recorder; short selections just below the child's instructional level; a pencil; homemade rating scale. Passages of fifty words or less work best. We use an informal scale, shown in Figure 7–1, consisting of five faces: one smiley face with the word "Superb"; one with a slight smile that says "Outstanding"; one with a straight-mouth face saying "Okay"; one with a slightly turned-down mouth that says "Not too bad"; and one with a mouth turned-down a little more that says "Not so great." The child is responsible for judging his or her own reading.

DIRECTIONS: The steps of taped repeated reading are:

1. *Introducing the Text*   Explain that the child is to silently read a short passage, followed by reading the passage aloud into the tape recorder. Discuss the importance of reading in phrases and with expression.
2. *Taping Reading*   The child reads the entire passage aloud.
3. *Listening to Taped Reading*   Rewind the tape and play back the oral reading. Have the child follow along in the text as the child listens to the taped reading. Listening to the taped reading gives you an opportunity to give feedback on the oral reading, offer tips, and guide the child in understanding what types of behaviors need improving.
4. *Evaluating the Taped Reading*   Hand the rating scale to the child and ask, "How would you rate your own reading?" Talk about the child's self-evaluation. Repeat steps 2, 3, and 4 until the child reads fluently and the self-evaluation reflects a Superb! oral reading.
5. *Graphing Progress*   Make a simple graph, as shown. Each time you use taped repeated reading, graph how many repetitions it takes to reach fluency on each passage. Over time, children decrease the number of repetitions needed for fluency and markedly improve their overall reading fluency.
6. *Sending Text Home*   Send the text home with the child to share with family and friends. Since the child has practiced reading the text fluently, reading at home puts the child in the most favorable light, which builds self-confidence.

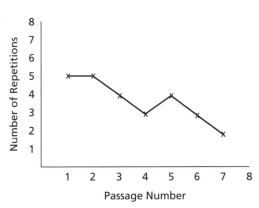

Another variation of repeated reading does not use a tape recorder, but instead relies on the teacher to record the miscues and reading rate for each repetition. Here the teacher sets a goal expressed in speed, accuracy, or both speed and accuracy. The teacher discusses miscues and phrasing with the child after each reading. The child rereads a single selection until the goal is reached. Results are graphed to show progress.

| Superb! | Outstanding | Okay | Not too Bad | Not so Great |

Figure 7–1   Taped Repeated Reading Self-Evaluation

Paired Repeated Reading   Paired repeated reading involves two children taking turns reading aloud to one another (Koskinen & Blum, 1986). As described by Koskinen and Blum, children of different reading abilities are teamed for paired reading, such as placing first grader with a low-achieving fifth grader.

Materials: Passages of about fifty words, written just below instructional level.

Directions: To use paired repeated reading, follow these steps:

1. *Creating Pairs*   Select children to work together as partners. You may select an older child to work with a younger child, a better reader to work with a weaker reader, or pair children based on shared interests, such as shared sports activities or shared after-school activities.
2. *Selecting Reading Material*   The children in each pair select material to read or the teacher supplies the reading materials.
3. *Practicing Reading with a Partner*   One child reads the passage three times aloud, while the other partner listens carefully. After the second and third readings, the listening partner asks the reader several questions. The partners switch roles after the third reading.

We have used this strategy effectively with children up through the sixth grade, and we have formed partners within the same classrooms, rather than across grades (Fox & Wright, 1997).

CHORAL READING

Reading in chorus is quite similar to singing in chorus; everyone joins together in a performance that blends many voices into one voice. The teacher models fluent reading, then the children practice, in chorus, reading the text. Both teacher modeling and repeated reading are essential parts of the choral reading teaching strategy.

MATERIALS: Short passages or poems that lend themselves to expressive reading.

DIRECTIONS: The steps involved in choral reading are:

1. *Selecting Choral Reading Materials*   Select material that is written in natural language patterns and that can be easily divided into bite-size parts. Rhyming poetry is well suited for choral reading because the selections are relatively short and the rhyming language lends itself to expressing the natural rhythm of language. Narrative passages that have lots of dialogue or that lend themselves to emotive reading are also very good for choral reading. We also enjoy reading in chorus books written in verse.
2. *Modeling Fluent Reading*   Read the selection aloud to model fluent reading. Discuss oral interpretation and reading in meaningful word groups.
3. *Dividing the Selection into Sections*   Skip this step if everyone is going to read the entire selection in chorus. Some selections lend themselves to division. Song lyrics and poems with a refrain, or chorus, are especially good for easing children into choral reading. Familiarize children with choral reading by having children read just the refrain in chorus (Tierney & Readence, 2000).
4. *Reading in Chorus*   Read the selection in chorus. Reread the selection several times until the choral reading is smooth and expressive. Tape record the reading and play it for children so that they hear themselves reading in chorus. Have children present their choral reading performance to their classmates or to other children in the same grade.

We have found choral reading to be especially beneficial for less-fluent readers when we specifically encourage these children to join in the chorus. Sometimes enunciation is problematic in large groups. Less-fluent readers may mumble or may read just a little behind the group in an effort to copy more-fluent readers. Solve these problems by repeatedly reading the text until all children enunciate clearly and read in unison. Avoid passages that are so short that the children memorize them, and be sure to use a generous dose of teacher modeling. It is especially important for you to show children how to group words into phrases and how to read with expression.

SHARED READING

This early literacy teaching strategy sets the stage for life-long reading fluency. It includes teacher modeling, repeated reading, and opportunities for even the youngest readers to successfully imitate fluency.

MATERIALS: Big books with evocative pictures and text that reflect natural language patterns.

DIRECTIONS: Follow these steps when using shared reading to develop reading fluency:

1. *Introducing the Big Book*   Introduce the big book by reading the title, discussing illustrations, and encouraging children to relate their background experiences to the pictures and to make predictions about the story content.
2. *Reading the Big Book*   Read the story aloud, pointing to the text as it is read. During reading, track words by pointing to each word as it is read. Tracking not only illustrates voice-print match (one spoken word matches one written word), but also demonstrates left-to-right directionality. Talk about the illustrations, the author, and the story content.
3. *Rereading with Child Participation*   Reread the book once or twice. Sometimes teachers reread the same big book on the next day. On repeated readings, ask the children to join in reading the whole text, repetitive text, predictable text, or special phrases. As children

read in chorus, they imitate their teacher's fluent reading, and in so doing begin to read smoothly with expression right from the start.

4. *Reading Little Books*   Give children their own little copies of the big book, and have children read independently or with a buddy. This gives children an opportunity to imitate the flow of natural language that they heard when you read aloud and when the group read portions of the big book in chorus. Even when children simply read from memory, rather than focusing on words, the act of imitating fluent reading establishes a valuable benchmark for what oral reading ought to sound like.

5. *Exploring Story Language*   Find an interesting word in the big book. Talk about the word, discuss word meaning, and add it to the word wall. Sometimes teachers focus on the beginning letter-sound in the word and engage the children in finding other words in the big book and on the word wall that begin with the letter-sound. Teachers may also highlight rhyming words by helping children listen for rhyme in poetry, playing games with rhyming words, and, perhaps, calling attention to the rime in rhyming words. While studying a special word does not directly teach reading fluency, word study does help children develop a reading vocabulary that supports fluent reading.

6. *Applying Language*   Ask children to retell the story in their own words or to write a group story that uses the same formula as the big book. Send the stories home with children to share with their families.

While shared reading has many advantages, the particular benefit for fluency development is that children's first oral reading experiences are modeled on the fluent reading of their teachers and, therefore, reflect the habits and behaviors of fluent readers.

GUIDED READING

▷ **LARGE GROUP**
SMALL GROUP
ORAL READING
FLUENCY

Guided reading develops strategies in the context of reading carefully selected literature and is typically used in the elementary grades.

MATERIALS: A copy of a book for everyone in the guided reading group.

DIRECTIONS: The steps in guided reading include:

1. *Selecting Literature*   Carefully select age-appropriate literature that is written on an instructional reading level.
2. *Introducing the Selection*   Introduce the text to build enthusiasm for reading and to familiarize children with concepts, vocabulary, and language patterns that might impair comprehension and reading pleasure.
3. *Reading*   Children read the text individually, in small groups, or with partners.
4. *Postreading*   Discuss with children the literature selection, reread and revisit text, and extend learning. Children may, for example, reread for certain information, discuss important ideas, discuss predictions, and explore vocabulary.
5. *Follow-up*   Assess, informally and observationally, children's reading progress with an eye toward documenting the children's ability to read increasingly more difficult and challenging text.

Rereading text, especially in the context of developing strategies and concepts, gives children opportunities to read portions of the same text more than once, which, in turn, helps build oral reading fluency.

FLUENCY DEVELOPMENT LESSON

▷ **SMALL GROUP**
ORAL READING
FLUENCY

Fluency development lessons combine several elements of good fluency instruction (Rasinski & Padak, 2001). As described by Rasinski and Padak, these lessons are estimated to last between ten and fifteen minutes.

MATERIALS: Text that is from 50 to 150 words.

DIRECTIONS: Follow these five steps:

1. *Modeling Fluency*   Each child has a copy of the text. As the children follow along, you read and reread the text to model fluent reading.
2. *Talking about Fluent Reading*   Discuss with children the text and the way that you read the text with expression and good phrasing.
3. *Choral Reading*   The group reads and rereads the text in chorus.
4. *Rereading with a Partner*   Children reread the text with a partner, using the paired repeated reading procedure.
5. *Performing the Text*   Groups of two to four students perform the text for school personnel and children in other classes. Special words are selected for closer study and for inclusion in children's personal word banks. Finally, the children take copies of the text home to share with their families.

▷ SMALL GROUP
INDIVIDUAL
ORAL READING
FLUENCY

ECHO READING

Echo reading is a small-group teaching strategy, although it can be used with individual children.

MATERIALS: One copy of text for every child.

DIRECTIONS: There are few steps in this easy procedure:

1. *Teacher Modeling*   Read a sentence or a few lines aloud while a small group listens.
2. *Imitating*   The children read the same sentence or a few lines by echoing your fluent reading.

Echo reading, when used in this manner, gives children a model of fluent reading to imitate and an opportunity to immediately reproduce that model. Short selections that allow the teacher to demonstrate, and the children to echo expressive reading work best. Excerpts from narrative text, especially narrative text with exciting dialogue, offer many opportunities for teachers to demonstrate, and for children to practice, expressive reading.

▷ INDIVIDUAL
ORAL READING
FLUENCY

NEUROLOGICAL IMPRESS

Neurological impress (Heckelman, 1969) is a one-on-one teaching strategy in which the teacher models fluent reading and the child echoes or imitates the model. The assumption is that the child develops fluency by listening to and imitating fluent reading. When first using the Neurological impress method, the reading materials should be on the child's easy reading level. Later, as the child develops fluency, reading materials may be moved up to the child's instructional level.

MATERIALS: Text on the child's easy reading level or instructional level, depending on the child's fluency.

DIRECTIONS: The four steps in the neurological impress method are:

1. *Sitting Side-by-side*   The child sits just a little in front of you. You sit to the side of the child so that your mouth is close to the child's ear. You and the child hold the book together.
2. *Reading in Unison with the Teacher's Voice Leading the Child's Voice*   Read the text in unison. When reading aloud, you should read in a slightly louder voice and slightly ahead of the child, thereby providing a clear model for the child to follow. Track the text by moving your finger under each word as it is pronounced. Maintain a comfortable pace even when the child slows down or encounters difficulty. Do not stop when the child stumbles on a word. No sounding-out is permitted.
3. *Child Tracking Text*   As the child becomes more fluent, the child tracks the text. If the child loses his or her place, you gently show the child where to track, and may even hold the child's finger while the child is tracking the words.
4. *Unison Reading with the Child's Voice Leading the Teacher's Voice*   With further increases in the child's fluency, your voice becomes softer, thereby reducing the modeling effect. Eventually the child's voice leads your voice in fluent reading.

Generally speaking, this teaching strategy is recommended for low-progress readers (Richek, Caldwell, Jennings, & Lerner, 2002).

PHRASE MARKING

▷ INDIVIDUAL
ORAL READING
FLUENCY

Phrase marking helps children in reading meaningful word groups by physically marking the phrases in text. Phrases may be shown with slashes or colored highlighters. We use colored highlighters to indicate phrases; we model how to find meaningful word groups in text, and ask the child to also mark phrases. The child then uses the marks on the page to read in meaningful word groups.

MATERIALS: Two copies of text, written just below instructional level; two different color highlighters, or colored pens.

DIRECTIONS: Follow these steps in using colored highlighters to mark phrase boundaries:

1. *Previewing Text*   Preview the reading material, discuss the title, relate background information, and predict the text content.
2. *Teacher Modeling How to Find Phrases and Reading in Phrases*   Hand a highlighter or a colored pen to the child; pick up another highlighter or pen in a different color for your own use. Read the first sentence to the child. Draw a line under the phrases with a highlighter or pen and read the sentence again to demonstrate good phrasing. Discuss how to use punctuation and syntax as guides for grouping words into meaningful phrases. Demonstrate how to group a second sentence into meaningful phrase units and demonstrate good phrasing by reading this sentence aloud.
3. *Child Marking Phrases and Reading in Phrases*   The child reads the next sentence silently, and then uses a different colored highlighter or pen to underline phrases. The child then reads the sentence aloud, according to the marked phrases. Discuss with the child the phrases, how to read in phrase units, and how to group words into meaningful units.
4. *Taking Turns Marking Phrases*   Take turns identifying phrases, marking phrases in color, and reading the text in meaningful word groups. Portions of the text may be read and reread several times to practice good phrasing.

   Another option is to write sentences on chart paper or sentence strips and to indicate phrases with slash marks (Brozo, Schmelzer, & Spires, 1983). At first children read the phrases in the order in which they appear in text; later the phrase strips are cut apart, rearranged, and flashed randomly. Keep reading selections short and slightly below instructional level when first marking phrases (Rasinski & Padak, 2001). After children have successfully read the text with the phrases marked in color or by slashes, have them read and reread the unmarked text.

READERS' THEATER

▷ LARGE GROUP
SMALL GROUP
ORAL READING
FLUENCY

Readers' theater is a vocal dramatization of a well-rehearsed script. In readers' theater, children and their teacher rewrite familiar literature so as to create scripts and then the children dramatically read the scripts. Little or no action accompanies the script reading; instead, the children's reading voices supply the dramatic interpretation. Sometimes minor props are used to add a little spice to the vocal dramatizations. This teaching strategy includes the teacher modeling fluency, repeated reading, an emphasis on communicating through emotive reading, and performing for an audience. Readers' theater improves the fluency of average (Martinez, Roser, & Strecker, 1999) and low-progress readers (Millin & Rinehart, 1999; Rinehart, 1999). It calls for children to work cooperatively with their classmates, and rereading occurs naturally as children prepare to perform the script for an audience.

MATERIALS: Literature with a strong plot line, which the teacher and child rewrite to create readers' theater scripts. Alternatively, intact plays written just below instructional level may be used. As many scripts as there are children in the group are needed.

DIRECTIONS: Readers' theater includes the following six steps:

1. *Selecting Text and Developing a Script*   Select a text that lends itself to rewriting in a script format. Fairy tales are excellent sources for readers' theater scripts, as are stories from guided reading lessons. An alternative to rewriting literature is to use an intact play, of which there are many available. Look for something that is just below children's instructional level and focuses on a theme that is of interest to the group.
2. *Silent Reading with a Buddy*   Children read the text silently with a buddy. Alternatively, the teacher may read the text aloud while the children follow along.
3. *Trying on Roles*   The children reread the play in a group, exchanging parts so as to get a feel for the roles in which children feel the most comfortable and to get a sense of the characters' emotions and personalities.
4. *Assigning Roles*   Decide which children will read specific roles, based on the children's preference from previous reading experiences and your understanding of the needs of the readers themselves.
5. *Practicing and Rehearsing*   Read and reread the parts, emphasizing expressive and emotive reading. Assist children with phrasing, intonation, and vocal expression.
6. *Performing*   When children are fully prepared to give a dramatic reading of the script, they present the play for their classmates or children in neighboring classrooms. Readers may sit, stand, or change positions while delivering the script. Props are minimal, though we have found that a few assorted props lend interest and an air of the professional theater to our productions.

We frequently forego rewriting text and use instead intact plays written just below the children's instructional level. Happily, there are many plays from which to choose. The following plays are examples of reproducible scripts: *25 Just-right Plays for Emergent Readers* (Pugliano-Martin, 1998) includes simple plays for beginning readers; *25 Emergent Reader Plays Around the Year* (Pugliano-Martin, 1999) is a collection of plays with seasonal and holiday themes; *Easy-to-Read Folk and Fairy Tale Plays* (Pugliano, 1997) offers a selection of seven plays for first- and second-grade readers; *Tall Tales Read-aloud Plays* (Pugliano-Martin, 2000) is a collection of eight adaptations of traditional stories that may be integrated with social studies, math, language arts, and art in the third through the fifth grades; *Revolutionary War Read-aloud Plays* (Murphy, 2000) is a collection of five plays set during the American Revolution and appropriate for children in the fourth through eighth grades; and *5 Easy-to-Read Plays Based on Classic Stories* (Scholastic, 1999) includes adaptations of the classics appropriate for fifth-grade readers. With the combination of teacher modeling, repeated reading, an emphasis on expressive reading, and the excitement of a real performance, readers' theater offers teachers a pedagogically sound strategy for developing fluency and offers children an opportunity to show off their expressive fluent reading (Tyler & Chard, 2000).

▷ LARGE GROUP
SMALL GROUP
ORAL READING
FLUENCY

READ-AROUNDS

Read-arounds is an activity in which children share their favorite portions of a familiar selection (Tompkins, 2001). This is a wrap-up activity that focuses on the positive, enjoyable passages in text and that celebrates literacy through sharing and honoring children's choices and preferences.

MATERIALS: One copy of a familiar literature selection for each child in a small group.

DIRECTIONS: The steps are as follows:

1. *Reading and Exploring Text*   Read and explore text with children, following the lesson sequence that you typically use with literature. This might include guided reading, basal book reading, or other teaching procedures.
2. *Children Selecting their Favorite Short Passages*   The children select their favorite passages. Passages may be as short as a sentence or as long as a paragraph (Tompkins, 2001).
3. *Practicing Reading*   Once favorite passages are selected, the children practice or rehearse reading their favorites. Children may rehearse individually or with a buddy.
4. *Reading Favorite Short Passages*   The children share their favorite portions with their classmates by reading the portions aloud. Children take turns reading, with reading mov-

ing from one child to another around the group, hence the name *read-arounds*. The teacher does not ask questions or interrupt the read-around. Several children may read the same passage. Favorite passages may be read in any order, with the children jumping in on their own. The teacher does not call on individuals, and children are not required to read aloud if they do not wish to do so. Teachers read their favorite passage aloud, too. The read-around ends when all the children who want to share their favorite passages have read aloud to the group.

TAPED-ASSISTED READING

▷ INDIVIDUAL
ORAL READING
FLUENCY

In taped-assisted reading, children listen to a tape recording of a story or short selection, and follow along in the text.

MATERIALS: Tape recorder; tape of a story; a print copy of the taped story; headphones.

DIRECTIONS: The steps for taped-assisted reading are as follows:

1. *Selecting a Tape*   Select a tape that is age-appropriate for the listener.
2. *Listening and Following Along*   The child listens to the tape and follows along in the text, imitating the intonation, expression, and phrasing of the fluent reading.

In using taped-assisted reading, take steps to assure that the listener actually attends to the text as it is being read. If the child is not actively following along with the reading, then taped-assisted reading becomes a listening activity, rather than a listening *and reading* activity.

LANGUAGE EXPERIENCE

▷ LARGE GROUP
SMALL GROUP
INDIVIDUAL
ORAL READING
FLUENCY

In this approach, children dictate stories and then read their dictated stories. Sometimes teachers and children edit stories, while at other times first-draft stories are read and enjoyed. The assumption is that children are motivated to read stories that reflect their own experiences. As part of the language experience approach, the children and their teacher reread portions of the text together, and the children read and reread all, or part, of the text individually.

MATERIALS: Chart paper; markers; common experiences to write about.

DIRECTIONS: The steps in language experience are:

1. *Developing a Shared Experience*   This crucial step creates a common experience that forms the basis for the language experience story. A shared experience may be as simple as a walk around the school grounds, a visit to the library, or making and blowing soap bubbles.
2. *Discussing the Experience*   Talk with children about their experience. Discuss what the children did, what they saw, what they touched, and what they felt. Use many different words and take this opportunity to introduce some new spoken words. In addition to developing language, you want to help children elaborate on their thinking so that the dictated story describes the complete shared experience.
3. *Writing the Story*   Begin by asking children something like, "What are we going to write about our walk in the playground?" Write the story on chart paper, saying each word as you write it. Write just the way the children dictate their story, using the children's own vocabulary and language patterns. Reread each sentence after it is written, tracking the words as they are read. Invite children to take turns dictating sentences.
4. *Reading and Rereading the Story*   Read the story aloud to children, so as to model smooth, expressive reading. Have the children read the story in chorus several times. You might ask individuals to come up to the chart to point out and read words, phrases, or sentences. Leave the story on display. Make copies for individual children.
5. *Elaborating*   Many different activities may be used for elaboration, among them: (1) writing sentences on sentence strips and having the children match the sentence

strips to the sentences in the story; (2) writing the words in a sentence on cards and asking the children to arrange the words into the familiar sentence; (3) having individual children illustrate their copies of the story; and (4) asking the children to select words in the story that they would like to learn to read and write. Eventually the stories are sent home for children to share with their families.

The repeated reading of familiar text written in the children's own language about the children's own experiences is expected to help children develop greater fluency. This teaching strategy is most appropriate for early emergent readers.

▷ LARGE GROUP
SMALL GROUP
ORAL READING
FLUENCY

RADIO READING

As the name implies, radio reading is a classroom approximation of a radio broadcast in which the reader is responsible for communicating, through oral reading, with a listening audience (Searfoss, Readence, & Mallette, 2001). The focus is on communication rather than on accuracy.

MATERIALS: Materials from literature or content textbooks.

DIRECTIONS: The steps in radio reading are as follows:

1. *Reading Aloud*   Each child reads a paragraph or two from a story or content area textbook, while the rest of the group listens. The goal is for the reader to communicate a message to the listeners, just as a radio announcer communicates with radio listeners. The reader may ask for help with word recognition. Unfamiliar words are immediately given to the reader; there is no sounding-out because this would potentially interfere with transmitting a meaningful message.
2. *Listening*   The audience listens to the reader, concentrating on understanding the message. The audience does not have a copy of the text.
3. *Talking About Meaning*   After reading aloud, children engage in a brief discussion to check for meaning. Select listeners to briefly rephrase the message.
4. *Clarifying Misunderstandings*   Should listeners misunderstand the message, then confusing portions of the text are reread.

Radio reading does not require silent reading before oral reading; does not offer children opportunities to reread, except when listeners are confused; and does not offer teachers opportunities to give children feedback and guidance. This activity would be strengthened by having children read passages silently before reading them orally and by providing some means of rehearsing (rereading) with teacher feedback before actually reading to a listening audience. After rehearsal, children then put on a radio show in which the goal is to communicate familiar text to a listening audience.

■■■■■ HANDS-ON ACTIVITIES FOR INCREASING SILENT READING FLUENCY

Fluency develops when classroom instruction includes practice in reading a variety of texts for a variety of purposes; activities that develop strategies for monitoring comprehension and correcting misunderstandings; reading and writing experiences to develop a large rapid recognition vocabulary; enough phonics and word structure instruction to develop a working knowledge of how written language represents speech; and sufficient attention to letter-level instruction so that readers quickly and accurately identify letters by name and by sound (Snow, Burns, & Griffin, 1998). Reading a variety of texts for a variety of purposes is essential. This means that teachers must carve time out of the school day for children to actually read text for children's own purposes and for children's own pleasure. Sustained Silent Reading (SSR) and Drop Everything and Read (DEAR) are the names of such classroom initiatives.

SSR AND DEAR

LARGE GROUP
SMALL GROUP
INDIVIDUAL
SILENT READING
FLUENCY

In SSR and DEAR, the teacher sets aside time during the day for children to read, uninterrupted by class changes, questions, or participation in group activities. SSR and DEAR aim to provide children with real, bonafide reading time, and in so doing to develop fluency and a love of reading.

MATERIALS: A variety of text written on a variety of levels.

DIRECTIONS: The steps in SSR and DEAR activities include:

1. *Setting Guidelines* Before children engage in SSR or DEAR, you will need to set silent reading guidelines, including the following: everyone reads; no one interrupts for any reason; no talking to your neighbors; children read anything they wish; and no one writes a book report or does any other school-related assignments in connection with reading.
2. *Reading Silently* Set a time for reading. Times may differ, depending on children's reading ability and the daily schedule. Children should have enough time, however, to become engaged in what they are reading. Everyone reads during the set-aside time, including the teacher.
3. *Sharing* Children may wish to talk about books they are reading or encourage their friends to read the same texts.

Results of research on SSR and DEAR reveal a mixed picture. The National Reading Panel concluded that, while it is not proven that techniques like SSR result in actual achievement gains, the concept of having children read more has merit (National Institute of Child Health and Human Development, 2000). Certainly increased interest in reading is beneficial for children who become engaged in reading as a consequence of classroom reading experiences, and demonstrating that reading is important and fun is laudable. The caution is to not use SSR or DEAR as the only approach to improving comprehension and reading achievement (National Institute of Child Health and Human Development, 2000). The wise teacher also bends the "free choice" rule just a bit when the teacher observes children reading, or attempting to read, material that is far above the children's instructional level. In this case, teachers may gently guide children toward text that is just below instructional level, rather than allowing children to struggle with text that is far too difficult. Ideally, children select and read literature written just below instructional level. It is also critical to have ample reading materials available so that, if children do not bring literature from home, they can find something of interest to read at school.

TIMED READING

LARGE GROUP
SMALL GROUP
INDIVIDUAL
SILENT READING
FLUENCY

Timed readings differ from SSR and DEAR in that in timed reading you select the passages, and children read for a specified time, followed by answering comprehension questions. The purpose of timed reading is to increase the reading rate without sacrificing comprehension.

MATERIALS: Text just below instructional level, one copy for each child.

DIRECTIONS: The steps are as follows:

1. *Selecting Passages* Select passages ranging from 100 to 300 words long. If the passages already have comprehension questions associated with them, use those questions. If not, devise up to ten questions per passage.
2. *Reading Silently* Children read passages silently. You write the minutes on a chalk board as the children read. As children finish silent reading, they raise their hands to signal that they have finished. Children then write the minutes shown on the chalk board at the top of their papers.

3. *Answering Comprehension Questions* After having read the selection silently and recording the time, children answer the comprehension questions.
4. *Determining Rate* Use the following formula to figure out reading rate:

$$\text{number of words} \times 60 \div \text{number of seconds} = \text{words per minute}$$

For example, if Marcia read a 250-word passage in two minutes, we would calculate $250 \times 60 = 15{,}000$. Then we divide 15,000 by 120 (two minutes) to get a rate of 125 words per minute (wpm). Silent reading rates steadily increase as children move through the upper grades and through high school. Leslie and Caldwell (2001) suggest general guidelines for silent reading at various grades. According to their calculations, the upper levels of reading rates, rounded to the nearest whole number, are as follows: second grade, 120 wpm; third grade, 170 wpm; fourth and fifth grades, 170–180 wpm; middle school, 230 wpm; and high school, 330 wpm.

5. *Calculating Comprehension* Correct the comprehension questions, writing the number correct at the top of the page.
6. *Graphing Results* Make a graph showing the rate and the number of correct answers to the comprehension questions. The idea is to increase the rate while maintaining high comprehension.
7. *Practicing* Practice timed reading once or twice a week.

When timing reading, never ask children to "read as fast as you can" without also emphasizing comprehension. Ignoring comprehension can have disastrous consequences. Use timed reading to improve the rate only when comprehension is emphasized, assessed, and maintained. The McCall-Crabbs Standard Test Lessons (1995) is a published set of small, graded booklets of short passages, with comprehension questions, that make it easy to calculate rate and comprehension.

High-fluency readers are efficient, confident, and relaxed readers who have the mental resources to focus on understanding and for whom the actual act of reading is so effortless that the whole process is a source of new information, successful learning, pleasure, and relaxation. High-fluency readers have the strategies they need to use reading as a learning tool for a lifetime, to excel in high school, and to graduate from college. In addition, high-fluency readers find reading so effortless and so natural that they give themselves over to the joy of reading, to the pleasure of a good story, to the excitement of a well-written mystery, to the imagery of fantasy, and to the mind-engaging issues of contemporary and traditional classics.

REFERENCES

Allington, R. (1983). Fluency: The neglected reading goal in reading instruction. *The Reading Teacher*, 36, 556–561.

Askew, B. J. (1993). The effect of multiple readings on the behaviors of children and teachers in an early intervention program. *Reading & Writing Quarterly: Overcoming Learning Difficulties*, 9, 307–315.

Brozo, W., Schmelzer, R., & Spires, H. (1983). The beneficial effect of chunking on good readers' comprehension of expository prose. *Journal of Reading*, 26, 442–445.

Ehri, L. C. (1997). Sight word learning in normal readers and dyslexics. In B. Blackman (Ed.), *Foundations of reading acquisition and dyslexia: Implications for early intervention* (pp. 163–189). Mahwah, NJ: Lawrence Erlbaum Associates.

Ehri, L. C. (1998). Grapheme-phoneme knowledge is essential for learning to read words in English. In J. L. Metsala & L. C. Ehri (Eds.), *Word recognition in beginning literacy* (pp. 3–40). Mahwah, NJ: Lawrence Erlbaum Associates.

Ehri, L. C., & McCormick, S. (1998). Phases of word learning: Implications for instruction with delayed and disabled readers. *Reading & Writing Quarterly: Overcoming Learning Difficulties*, 14, 135–163.

5 easy-to-read plays based on classic stories. (1999) New York: Scholastic.

Fox, B. J., & Wright, M. P. (1997). Connecting school and home literacy experiences through cross-age reading. *The Reading Teacher*, 50, 382–403.

Gaskins, I. W., Ehri, L. C., Cress, C., O'Hara, C., & Donnelly, K. (1997). Procedures for word learning: Making discoveries about words. *The Reading Teacher, 50*, 312–327.

Heckelman, R. G. (1969). Using the neurological-impress reading technique. *Academic Therapy Quarterly, 4*, 277–282.

Hiebert, E. H., & Martin, L. A. (2001). The texts of beginning reading instruction. In S. B. Neuman & D. K. Dickinson (Eds.), *Handbook of early literacy research* (pp. 361–376). New York: Guilford Press.

Koskinen, P., & Blum, I. (1986). Paired repeated reading: A classroom strategy for developing fluent reading. *The Reading Teacher, 40*, 70–75.

Leslie, L., & Caldwell, J. (2001). *The qualitative reading inventory III*. New York: Longman Publishing Group.

Martinez, M., Roser, N. L., & Strecker, S. (1999). "I never thought I could be a star": A readers' theatre ticket to fluency. *The Reading Teacher, 52*, 326–334.

McCall, W. A., & Crabbs, L. M. (1995). *McCall-Crabbs Standard Test Lessons*. New York: Teachers College Press.

Millin, S., & Rinehart, S. D. (1999). Some of the benefits of readers theater participation for second-grade title I students. *Reading Research and Instruction, 39*, 71–88.

Murphy, D. (2000). *Revolutionary war read-aloud plays*. New York: Scholastic.

National Center for Education Statistics (NCES). (1995). *Listening to children read aloud: Oral fluency*. [Online] 1 (1). Available FTP: National Center for Education Statistics: nces.ed.gov. Directory: pubs/95762.html.

National Institute of Child Health and Human Development. (2000). *Report of the National Reading Panel. Teaching children to read: An evidence-based assessment of the scientific research literature on reading and its implications for reading instruction: Reports of the subgroups* (NIH Publication No. 00-4754). Washington, D.C.: U.S. Government Printing Office.

Pugliano, C. (1997). *Easy-to-read folk and fairy tale plays*. New York: Scholastic.

Pugliano-Martin, C. (1998). *25 just-right plays for emergent readers*. New York: Scholastic.

Pugliano-Martin, C. (1999). *25 emergent reader plays around the year*. New York: Scholastic.

Pugliano-Martin, C. (2000). *Tall tales read-aloud plays*. New York: Scholastic.

Rasinski, T. V., & Padak, N. D. (2001). *From phonics to fluency: Effective teaching of decoding and reading fluency in the elementary school*. New York: Longman Publishing Group.

Richards, M. (2000). Be a good detective: Solve the case of oral reading fluency. *The Reading Teacher, 53*, 534–539.

Richek, M. A., Caldwell, J. S., Jennings, J. H., & Lerner, J. W. (2002). *Reading problems: Assessment and teaching strategies, 4th edition*. Boston: Allyn and Bacon.

Rinehart, S. D. (1999). "Don't think for a minute that I'm getting up there": Opportunities for readers' theater in a tutorial for children with reading problems. *Journal of Reading Psychology, 20*, 71–89.

Samuels, S. J., & Flor, R. F. (1997). The importance of automaticity for developing expertise in reading. *Reading & Writing Quarterly: Overcoming Learning Difficulties, 13*, 107–121.

Searfoss, L. W., Readence, J. E., & Mallette, M. H. (2001). *Helping children learn to read: Creating a classroom literacy environment*. Boston: Allyn and Bacon.

Snow, C. E., Burns, M. S., & Griffin, P. (Eds.). (1998). *Preventing reading difficulties in young children*. Washington, D.C.: National Academy Press.

Tierney, R. J., & Readence, J. E. (2000). *Reading strategies and practices: A compendium, 5th edition*. Boston, MA: Allyn and Bacon.

Tompkins, G. E. (2001). *Literacy for the 21st century: A balanced approach, 2nd edition*. Columbus, OH: Merrill.

Tyler, B. J., & Chard, D. J. (2000). Using readers' theater to foster fluency in struggling readers: A twist on the repeated reading strategy. *Reading & Writing Quarterly, 16*, 163–168.

Williams, S. (1992). *I went walking*. New York: Harcourt, Brace.

8 DEVELOPING WORD RECOGNITION AND FLUENCY IN CHILDREN WHO SPEAK A LANGUAGE OTHER THAN ENGLISH AT HOME

Suppose you have enrolled in a college course or in-service offering and, on attending the first session, realize that the teacher speaks a language you do not understand. Your home language is not useful in this class. Though the teacher and your new classmates talk to you, you are not able to understand what they are saying. The sounds are strange, the messages are meaningless, and you cannot make out the words. You cannot read the writing in the textbook, either. Some of the pictures show familiar objects and activities, but others do not.

Children who do not speak English and who attend schools where instruction is only in English find themselves in a similar situation. These children are plunged into a language culture, a school culture, and a social culture that is unfamiliar and often confusing. The language that serves children so well at home is not the same language that is spoken at school. The sounds of the school language are strange, words are unrecognizable, and meaning is elusive. Ideally, we would develop children's native language and literacy before teaching them to speak and read a second language. In the natural order of things, speech develops before reading. Since children already have competence speaking in their home language, learning to read that language is then based on a strong foundation in speech.

Classroom situations, school district resources, the number of different languages spoken in a single school, the philosophy of policymakers and parents, and access to teaching materials are but a few factors that determine whether children first learn to read in their home language or are taught to read English. When we turn to teaching children to read English, we must begin with speech. Reading instruction builds on children's ability to speak English. Neither you nor I would consider learning to read a second language, say Italian, without any knowledge whatsoever of spoken Italian. We would first learn something about the words, sounds, and structure of the Italian language. Then we would begin to learn to read Italian. Likewise, children who do not speak English as their first language need to know something about English words, sounds, and structure before we teach them to read English. The speaking-before-reading sequence is especially critical for languages like English, which is written in an alphabet.

Written language began about 20,000 years ago as a series of pictures that represented events. About 3500 BC, people living in present day Iraq developed symbols to represent words and syllables. Alphabetic writing, the last great innovation, emerged some 2,000 years later. In order to read picture writing a person only needs to interpret drawings of familiar objects. To read symbols that represent words, a person needs to memorize the symbol–meaning connections. However, to read an alphabet a person must know something about the sounds and the words of the language. Readers must memorize the specific letters that represent the specific sounds in the words of a particular language.

For example, in Spanish *ñ* represents the sound in *señor* (ny), which we hear in ca*ny*on. The vowels, *a, e, i, o,* and *u,* represent the sounds *ah, eh, ee* (long e), *oh* (long o), and *oo* (as in spoon). An *rr* represents an /r/ that is rolled two or three times, whereas the single *r* represent an /r/ that is rolled only slightly. The Spanish *j* stands for the English /h/, as in *Julio,* and the Spanish *h* is silent, as in *hablar* (to speak), pronounced *ah-blahr.* The Spanish *v* represents a soft English /b/. Of the fourteen Spanish vowel diphthongs, only one is a match for English (the *oi,* pronounced /oy/ as in the English *oil*). We cannot read Spanish without first identifying Spanish sounds, knowing the letters that represent the sounds, and understanding Spanish words. Likewise, children who speak Spanish must recognize English sounds, words, and structure before they are able to read English text.

LEVELS OF EMERGING BILINGUALISM IN YOUR CLASSROOM

Children who speak languages other than English at home bring a wide range of language and literacy competencies to school. Some are learning English for the first time, while others are proficient English speakers. We use the term *English as a second language,* or ESL, to describe children who speak a non-English language at home and who are learning to speak English in school. *Bilingual* describes children and adults who speak two languages with some proficiency. The closer the home language is to English in its sounds, words, and structure, the greater the overlap between the two languages. When overlap is high, children bring more knowledge from their first language (L1) to learning English (L2). However, when overlap is low, children have less information to bring from their home language in speaking and reading English.

There are four possible combinations of language and literacy that children might bring to your classroom. Children might be able to: (1) speak and read their home language and English; (2) speak and read their home language, and speak English well enough to quickly learn to read English; (3) speak and read their home language, and speak English, but without enough competence to quickly learn to read English, and (4) speak their home language only. We will now consider each of these broad categories in light of what they mean for teaching reading.

Proficiency in Speaking and Reading the Home Language and English

Children might be proficient in speaking and reading both their home language (L1) and the English language (L2). These children are already literate in two languages. They are able to read content area textbooks, enjoy literature, and write in both their home language and English. These children, and all children who speak English as a second language, live in one culture at home and another culture at school. While these cultures are more alike than different, the values and social interactions in children's home cultures are not a perfect match with the school culture.

For example, Navajo children grow up in a non-competitive culture (Smith, 1992). Activities that stress "being first," such as competitive games and spelling bees, run counter to the Navajo culture of cooperation and group cohesion. Navajo children respond best when they are part of a group or compete against themselves (Smith, 1992). Literacy activities that stress group work and reaching personal goals are most successful because these activities are compatible with the cultural values Navajo children bring to school.

Proficiency in Speaking and Reading the Home Language, and Proficiency in Speaking English

Children might be proficient in speaking and reading their home language (L1) and might also be proficient in speaking English (L2). These children have already developed the knowledge and abilities that are common to the reading process in any language. They understand what reading is and what it means to be literate. Children who read an alphabetic language transfer their understanding of the alphabetic principle when they learn to read English (Meyers, 1993). These children already view text from left-to-right and from top-to-bottom. In addition, if the children's home language uses the Roman alphabet, these children may already be familiar with most of the letters in our English alphabet.

Children who read an alphabetic language know how the alphabetic principle works and how to learn to read in a language in which the symbols (letters) systematically represent the sounds (phonemes). When the sounds in children's first language overlap with English sounds, we see a positive transfer from the children's home language to English (Wade-Woolley & Geva, 2000). It is relatively easy for literate children to generalize and transfer phoneme identification from one language to another. In other words, when children develop the conceptual understanding that words are constructed of individual phonemes, they are able to apply this concept to the sounds in a second language. For example, the child who reads French as a first language already knows that words consist of sounds and that letters represent the sounds in French words. This same child, in learning to read English, applies this conceptual framework to learning to read English. The literate French child listens for, manipulates, and associates English sounds with letters. This child already knows how to go about learning to read an alphabet, including the need to segment and blend the sounds in words.

Conversely, children who read a language like Chinese, which does not use an alphabet, do not have experience decoding and learning an alphabet. Though these children may take somewhat longer to learn to read English, they still read for meaning, apply comprehension strategies, self-monitor, and cross-check. Since children are fully competent English speakers, learning to read English is supported by their understanding of the words, sounds, and structure of the English language. These children learn to read and write English with focused instruction, as well as many and varied opportunities to use language, share literature, and read and write everyday.

Proficiency in Speaking and Reading the Home Language and Some Ability to Speak English

Children might be able to speak and read in their home language (L1) and speak English (L2), but without enough competence to support independent learning in English-only classrooms. LEP, or *limited English proficient*, is a term sometimes used to describe these children, who speak well enough to have English-only friends, participate in classroom activities, fit into the school routine, and interact socially. Generally speaking, it requires about two years for children to gain this level of proficiency in speaking the English language (Meyers, 1993).

At first blush, using English in social settings should be enough to support literacy, yet these children often struggle with reading and writing English. The structure of book language seems to be a problem for limited English proficient children. These children do not yet have enough English language fluency to read and understand the formal language in many textbooks (Williams, 2001). The language in content subject textbooks tends to be complex, peppered with technical terms, and rather abstract. Even storybooks and easy chapter books use language that is more formal than the dynamic give-and-take of everyday speech. It may take children from five to nine years to develop the kind of English language fluency that supports reading abstract, formal text (Meyers, 1993).

Limited English proficient children need to develop the same language competence that any child needs to learn to read English. Children learn English words through classroom discussions, wide reading, word study, and listening to their teachers read aloud. Children develop English language proficiency when they write letters to pen pals, keep journals, write short stories and poems, and work with groups to write brief reports on content area topics. Further support for literacy comes by preteaching difficult English vocabulary, using graphic organizers to show children how information is structured, selecting books that are relevant to the children's home culture, and pairing children with English-proficient learning partners.

Proficiency in Speaking the Home Language

A fourth possibility is that children are proficient in speaking, but not reading, their home language (L1) and are unable to speak or read English (L2). These children understand and use their home language everyday to interact socially and to learn. They do not understand English, nor do they necessarily understand why people read, where to find print on a page, how to hold books, and what it means to be literate. These children pass through all of the phases of second language learning.

DEVELOPING PHONEMIC AWARENESS ■ ■ ■ ■ ▬▬▬

Children may come to your classroom with different levels of phonemic awareness. Children who read a home language that is written in an alphabet can identify and blend sounds in their native language. Consequently, phonemic awareness in the children's home language may transfer to a second language (Denton, Hasbrouck, Weaver, & Riccio, 2000), provided that children are aware of and discriminate the sounds in the new language they are learning. Identifying and separating sounds is relatively easy when the sounds occur in the same positions in words in both the first and second language, such as at the beginning of words but not at the end of words. However, children may have difficulty identifying and manipulating the sounds if the same sounds occur in different positions in the words of different languages, such as at the end of words in the first language, but never at the end of words in the second language (Wade-Woolley & Geva, 2000).

Difficulty in learning to read is strongly linked to phonemic awareness whether children are native English speakers or are learning English as a second language (Chiappe & Siegel, 1999). Children who are not literate in their home languages or who read a native language that is not written in an alphabet benefit from learning to separate and blend the sounds in English words. Because different languages use different sounds, all second language learners must learn to identify and blend English sounds. Children need to identify and blend the English phonemes that overlap with their first language, as well as the English phonemes that are not part of their native language. In teaching phonemic awareness, therefore, it is important to highlight English phonemes, which, in turn, may help second language learners identify English sounds that are not in their home languages. Combine activities to develop sounds awareness, as explained in Chapter 2, with language development, reading, and writing instruction.

■■■■■■ TEACHING CHILDREN WHO ARE NOT YET ENTIRELY FLUENT IN ENGLISH

Languages worldwide consist of three common features: syntax (word order), vocabulary (the words), and phonemes (sounds). The language a child speaks at home has a predetermined word order, particular words, and specific sounds, albeit not necessarily the same grammar, words, and sounds as in English. Consequently, when children begin to learn the English language, they know that word order is important. They understand that language consists of words and, therefore, listen for English words in the conversations they hear in school. As children listen for words, they pay attention to English sounds.

Four Stages of Second Language Learning

Second language learning follows a predictable pattern that begins with listening comprehension and ends with fluency. Children pass through four stages before they reach full fluency in a language, as shown in Table 8–1 (Díaz-Rico & Weed, 2002; Richard-Amato, 1996). While the stages of second language learning are identifiable, children move through the stages at different rates. The time needed to move through the second language learning stages depends on the level of support for English language learning at school and at home, plus many other individual, cultural, and classroom variables. We support literacy by matching the content and strategies of reading instruction to the stages of second language learning.

The Preproduction Stage   Preproduction is called the silent period. Children speak little or no English and communicate mainly through gestures, facial expressions, objects, and pictures. They hold back from conversation, unsure of how to interact and uncertain of how to use the new language they are learning. In the preproduction stage, children develop listening comprehension and begin to learn English words. They ask yes/no questions, understand key English words, and may also use a few English words or phrases for special purposes.

When you talk with children, speak clearly and avoid idioms. Speak a little slower than usual and use normal intonation, except when pronouncing a few key words. Draw attention to key words by pronouncing them with a little more emphasis. For instance, you might say "book" with a little more emphasis when you say, "Show me the *book*," or "Give Amanda the *book*," or "This is a *book*." Support language development with questions that ask children to: "Find the _____." "Point to _____." "Is this a _____?" "Put the _____ on/under/over/beside the _____." "Which picture/object is the _____?" Develop children's listening comprehension through reading aloud, simple questions, facial expressions, easy-to-recognize pictures, objects, and demonstrations.

Strategies for Teaching Children in the Preproduction Stage   The classroom literacy program begins with spoken language and proceeds to written language. That is, children first recognize and understand spoken words and then learn to read written words. We begin, therefore, by developing listening comprehension and a listening vocabulary. Teachers use gestures, physical demonstrations, pictures, and objects to communicate and build language meaning, as described in four teaching strategies on the next page.

Preproduction: The Silent Period

TABLE 8–1 Stages of Second Language Learning

Children in the preproduction stage:

- Are developing listening comprehension.
- Communicate through gestures, facial expressions, objects, and pictures.
- Ask yes/no questions.
- Understand key English words.
- May memorize and use specific English words or phrases for specific purposes.

Early Production

Children in the early production stage:

- Are beginning to understand English.
- Use their home language most of the time.
- Use single English words or two-word phrases.
- Are learning more about English words, sounds, and structure.
- Repeat words the teachers model.
- May memorize and use key English words and phrases for specific purposes.
- Are learning to understand and use English in social settings.

Speech Emergence

Children in the speech emergence stage:

- Feel more comfortable and confident using English.
- Have a limited English speaking vocabulary.
- Have a good understanding of spoken English.
- Have a larger listening vocabulary than speaking vocabulary.
- Use simple sentences.
- Uses phrases, words, and simple sentences to answer questions.
- Can discuss concrete ideas.
- Speak more often, take more chances using English, and volunteer information.
- Make word order errors.
- Speak in complete sentences.

Intermediate Fluency

Children in the intermediate fluency stage:

- Initiate and sustain long conversations.
- Have good comprehension.
- Use more complex sentences.
- Make word order errors that reflect a more complex understanding of English.
- Interact socially with their classmates.
- Participate spontaneously in classroom activities.
- Sometimes recognize and correct their own word order errors.
- Use English to learn new information.
- Discuss and explain more abstract ideas.
- Use English to express and develop higher-order thinking skills.

　1. *Demonstrate, Through Physical Actions, the Words and Meaning of English Words, Phrases, and Sentences*　Use physical movement and actions to help children learn the English words that name familiar concepts. For instance, you might pantomime words like *eating* and *sleeping*, and demonstrate words like *jumping, reading, writing,* and *coloring.* Children naturally use gestures and demonstrations to communicate, so it is beneficial to give them opportunities to use pantomime to demonstrate concepts and words.

　2. *Use Pictures and Real Objects to Clarify Meaning and to Teach English Words*　Display real objects, miniature objects, and pictures. Point to objects, name objects,

and have children find objects by name. As children begin to understand English words, ask them to find objects, pick up objects, or point to objects. Get children to touch and manipulate objects by having them hand you objects by name, sort objects by their function, or line up objects according to the words you name. Show children pencils, crayons, papers, desks, doors, windows, and books as you say the English words. Ask children to manipulate and name the miniature farm and zoo animals in children's play sets, and the plastic food and dinner settings in house-keeping toy sets. Show children an assortment of doll furniture, and ask children to use English words to name the everyday household items.

3. *Read Aloud at Least Once a Day, or More if Your Classroom Schedule Permits*   Explain pictures, name objects in pictures, and use facial expressions to enhance meaning. Children may not automatically understand the meaning of all the words in the storybooks we read aloud; therefore, we want to amplify meaning by pronouncing words clearly, explaining pictures, and using facial expressions to show the characters' feelings and reactions.

4. *Read Predictable Storybooks, and Read Poems and Sing Songs that Repeat the Same Lines Over and Over Again*   Recurrent words, phrases, and sentences give children repeated exposure to the same English sentence structures. In hearing phrases or sentences repeated often, children have more opportunities to absorb and internalize the sounds, words, and structure of English. Songs in which lines are repeated include *Wheels on the Bus*, *If You're Happy and You Know It*, *Old MacDonald*, *The Bear Went Over the Mountain*, *Frog Went A-Courtin'*, and *Mary Had a Little Lamb*. The National Environmental Health Sciences website offers a wide selection of children's songs, patriotic songs, and long-time favorite tunes, along with lyrics and musical accompaniments (http://www.niehs.nih.gov/kids/musicchild.htm).

The Early Production Stage   Children enter the early production stage when they begin to feel more comfortable and confident with English. Comprehension is still limited, and children still use their home language most of the time. However, children are now beginning to understand more English and to use English in social settings. They repeat words the teacher models, may repeat simple poems from memory, and may be able to join their classmates in singing often-repeated songs. Children try out their developing language competence with single words or two-word phrases. They might respond with "yes" to the question, "Do you see the dog in the picture?" Children also might ask you to pay attention to their work by saying something like "look" or "see." Children may ask you to join them with a single word, "come," or may use short phrases, such as "Teacher come" or "Look this."

Ask children to answer either/or questions and prompt them to respond in two- or three-word phrases (Díaz-Rico and Weed, 2002), but do not force children to speak. Use the pictures in familiar storybooks to engage children in conversations. For example, after reading *The Practically Perfect Pajamas* (Brooks, 1972) you might point to a picture of Percy the polar bear asleep in his bright red pajamas and ask, "What is Percy doing?" (sleeping) "Yes, Percy is sleeping in his bed." "What is Percy wearing?" (red pajamas) Turning to a picture of several bears, you might ask, "How many bears are wearing pajamas?" (four) "Yes, four bears are wearing pajamas. Let's count the bears." (one, two, three, four) "Is this bear a girl or a boy?" (girl) "What is on the girl's pajamas?" (yellow flower) "Yes, this bear is wearing pajamas with a yellow flower. She is happy to be wearing pajamas with a pretty yellow flower." Encourage children to listen for meaning, to participate, and to use the language that they already understand. Give children positive feedback on their use of language, link language to meaningful stories and illustrations, and demonstrate language use by elaborating on shared ideas, observations, and feelings.

Strategies for Teaching Children in the Early Production Stage   Reading teaching strategies are much like the strategies we use to teach native English speaking children to read. The main difference is that teaching strategies put a greater emphasis on learning English words, listening for English sounds, and understanding the meaning and structure of spoken and written English.

Teaching strategies motivate children to use the English words and structures that they already know. Strategies also help children associate whole spoken words with whole written words (Chapter 6), identify English sounds (Chapter 2), and learn letter names and letter-sounds (Chapter 3). Additionally, it is important to continue to develop children's oral language with teaching strategies like those recommended for children in the preproduction stage.

1. *Label the Objects in Your Room and Refer to Them When Pronouncing English Words* (*Richard-Amato*, 1996)   Write words on cards and tape the cards to the objects they name. Ask designated children to find a familiar object and to bring you the word card for that object. For instance, you might ask a child to bring you the word "door." The child then goes to the door, takes the word card from the door, and brings it to you. Give the same word card to a different child and have that child put the word card back on the classroom door.

2. *Read Alphabet Books*   Use alphabet books to teach letter names, to develop an understanding of English words, and to introduce children to the sounds of individual letters (Chapter 3). Look for books with easy-to-recognize pictures, ball-and-stick letters, and letters in upper- and lowercase. Use the pictures in alphabet books to develop children's speaking vocabulary and the letters in alphabet books to help children learn beginning letter-sounds.

3. *Use Key Words and Pictures as Mnemonics for the Single Letter-Sounds in English Words*   If you have an alphabet strip in your classroom, you may wish to use the key words and pictures on the strip to help children recall and use letter-sound associations (Chapter 3).

4. *Chant Letter and Sound Associations*   Simple chants help children recall key words, letters, and letter-sounds, as well as increase awareness of the rhythm and structure of spoken English. For example, children might chant, "B (letter name) /b/ /b/ /b/ boat." "S (letter name) /s/ /s/ /s/ sun." "A (letter name) /a/ /a/ /a/ apple" (Chapter 2).

5. *Write Language Experience Stories*   After sharing an experience and reviewing the sequence of events, children dictate a story or explanation of events while you write down what the children say. The children then read and reread their story, find words in the story, and sequence word cards to recreate sentences in the story.

6. *Make a Picture Dictionary for Each Child*   A picture dictionary consists of pages that feature a picture and a word for that picture. Begin by having children find pictures in magazines and glue them onto unlined paper, or by asking children to draw their own original art to illustrate words. Write the English word under each picture. Some words might be written in both English and the children's native language. Invite a parent or community volunteer who speaks the home language to write words in the native language. Ask volunteers to help children connect the native language spoken words they know with the English words they are learning.

7. *Make Simple Picture-word Puzzles*   Make puzzles that feature a picture of a familiar object on one side and the English word on the other (Richard-Amato, 1996), as shown in Figure 8–1. You might also place two, three, or four objects (or pictures) on a table and ask children to match the words with the objects, as shown in Figure 8–2.

8. *Have Children Sort Objects or Pictures According to Beginning Sounds or Beginning Letters*   To sort words by beginning sounds, tape one picture to several different tubs (or small buckets). Place in each tub several objects or pictures that begin with the same sound as the word in the picture. Dump the objects and pictures from two tubs on the floor or table, and ask children to sort the objects and pictures by putting them into the tub with the picture that begins with the same sound. To sort words by beginning letter-sounds, write a letter on each tub and have children sort

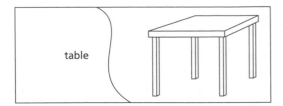

FIGURE 8–1   Picture-word Puzzle

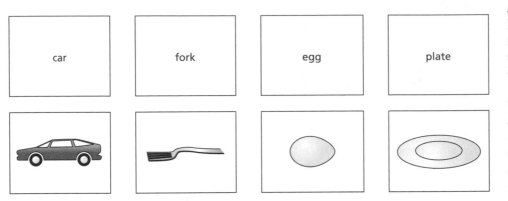

FIGURE 8–2   Matching Objects with Words

them according to the beginning sounds in the object or picture name that matches the letter written on each tub. For example, if one tub has a Bb and another has an Ss, children would put a small *ball* into the Bb tub and a picture of a *sun* into the Ss tub (Chapter 3).

9. *Ask Children to "Read Around the Room"*   Give children a special hat or pair of decorative glasses and something to use to point to words and logos. Wearing the special hat or glasses, children read all the labels, signs, and logos in your classroom.

The Speech Emergence Stage   Children are more relaxed and comfortable using English in the speech emergence stage. Children understand more words than they use in conversation. Though their English vocabulary is still limited, children construct simple sentences, talk about concrete topics, and use language in social situations. Children speak more often, take more chances using language, and are quicker to answer questions and volunteer information in and out of class.

Children draw on their first language (L1) to speak English (L2). Consequently, English language mistakes often reflect the sounds, words, and structure of the children's home languages. Children might, for example, say, "Why you go?" or "Who go here?" or "You like book?" Mistakes may make conversation with the children difficult to understand. Children in the speech emergence stage may rephrase statements in order to make their messages clearer.

Strategies for Teaching Children in the Speech Emergence Stage   Children in the speech emergence stage know enough about English to support learning to read known English words (Chapter 6), identify English sounds (Chapter 2), learn letter patterns that represent English sounds (Chapter 4), and identify common prefixes and suffixes (Chapter 5).

1. *Use Charts and Displays to Illustrate and Demonstrate the Letter Patterns in Written Words*   For example, you might write *bl* at the top of a chart and then write words that are spelled with this cluster. Ask children to find words with *bl* on the word wall, on bulletin boards, and in their dictionaries or word banks. Should children offer words in their home language that begin with the letter pattern, write down these words, too. Display the charts in your classroom, and refer to them when children encounter the patterns in new words or wish to write words with sounds that the patterns represent.

2. *Make Large Word Murals*   Divide a long piece of butcher paper into columns. Write a letter pattern at the top of each column and put words in the columns that are spelled with the patterns. Large murals, because they include several different patterns, offer opportunities to compare and contrast letter patterns and the sounds they represent in English words. Leave a marker nearby so that children can add words that are spelled with the different patterns on the mural.

3. *Solve by Rhyming, Play Rhyming Games with Puppets, Share Rhyming Poetry, and Read Rhyming Stories*   The goal is to help children develop sensitivity to rhyming words by exploring rhyme in all sorts of language contexts. Use chants, poems, and

songs with rhyming words that are spelled alike (*pail – snail*, but not *pale – snail*). You might, for instance, pose a riddle like: "I am a pet. My name rhymes with hat. I am a _____" or "I shine in the sky. I rhyme with run. I am the _____." Play rhyming games with a puppet. For instance, the puppet might ask children to identify rhyming words, saying, "Which words belong together: can, man, or cat?" Or the puppet could ask children to identify the non-rhyming words, asking, "Which word does not belong: big, hat, or pig?" Have children join you in chants with rhyming words (Chapter 2), singing songs with rhyming words, and reading books written in rhyme. Share rhyming poetry. Once children are familiar with a poem, mask the rhyming words and ask children to supply the missing rhymes.

4. *Play Bingo with High-Frequency Words and Words Spelled with Letter Patterns Children Are Learning in Your Classroom* Use the bingo template in Appendix I. Write in the bingo squares high-frequency words or words with letter patterns the children are learning. Connect bingo games with children's home language by writing a special word from the children's native language on the bingo cards. Select a word that you have pretaught or that you are sure children already know how to read.

5. *Use Stories on Tapes and CD-ROMs to Encourage and Support Language and Literacy Development* In listening to tapes and in viewing CD-ROMs, children have opportunities to see written words as they hear the words pronounced.

6. *Read in Chorus* Have children read familiar poems and short passages aloud and with appropriate voice intonation. Ask the group to read and reread the same poem or passage. Make sure that everyone participates, and tape the final reading. Play the tape and share it with others in your school or family at home.

7. *Sort Words According to Shared Letter Patterns* Glue one picture of a word that includes the sound of a target letter pattern to each of several sacks. For example, if children are to sort words by the beginning consonant digraphs *sh*, *ch*, and *th*, you might glue pictures of a *shark*, a *chicken*, and a *thumb* to each of three sacks. Write words that begin with *sh*, *ch*, or *th*. Have children read the words and put them into the sack with the picture that represents the beginning sound (Chapters 3 and 4).

8. *Play Games with Words that Are Spelled with the Letter Patterns or Affixes Children Are Learning in Your Classroom* Write words with letter patterns or affixes on index cards and use the cards in games in which children identify target letter patterns and read English words (Chapters 4 and 5). Children might, for example, play a card game where they collect books of four cards with words that have the same letter pattern or affix. Children might play concentration by matching words with the same letter patterns or affixes. Team games are also useful for reinforcing knowledge and, additionally, are highly motivational. Melting snowman, letter pattern checkers, and 100 yard dash in Chapter 4, and fast pitch baseball and bull's eye in Chapter 5 are examples of games that may be played in small groups.

9. *Use the Cloze Procedure* The cloze procedure gives children practice using letter patterns, meaning, and structure cues to identify or write words that fit sentence meaning. There are several useful variations of cloze; look in Chapter 6 for ways to modify the cloze to meet the needs of the children whom you teach.

The Intermediate Fluency Stage As children move into the intermediate fluency stage, they begin to initiate and sustain long conversations. Children interact and participate spontaneously in classroom activities, and use language to learn new information. Language comprehension is good, and children generally understand classroom explanations. However, some of the subtle nuances of language may be misunderstood or unrecognized. Visual cues and graphic aids are still important for helping children comprehend classroom instruction and directions. While children discuss more abstract ideas, they lack specific vocabulary in content area subjects.

Children at this stage use more complex sentences, and their syntax errors reflect a more complex understanding of English. These children make mistakes using

English vocabulary and grammar. However, they may recognize their own word order errors and may even correct their own English usage. Children talk with their classmates about all sorts of topics and function well socially. In classroom discussions and social interactions, children may have difficulty following the conversations if the topics shift quickly or unpredictably. Therefore, it is important to guide discussions so as to clearly indicate topic shifts and to use visual aides to help children interpret meaning.

Strategies for Teaching Children in the Intermediate Fluency Stage   Children in the intermediate fluency stage bring a sufficiently developed understanding of how to read and write English for all sorts of purposes. These children understand and read long words. They benefit from exploring word structure (Chapter 5), from expanding their rapid reading vocabulary (Chapter 6), and from increasing reading fluency (Chapter 7).

1. *Encourage Children to Correspond with an English-speaking Pen Pal in Your School or in Another School*   Children can correspond with youngsters in the same grade in other schools, cities, or countries. Good books about letter writing include *Messages in the Mailbox: How to Write a Letter* (Leedy, 1991), which explains how to write all sorts of letters and notes; *The Long, Long Letter* (Spurr, 1997), a humorous story about an extraordinarily long letter; and *Pen Pals* (Holub, 1997), which has a humorous twist children will enjoy. You may want to use the Internet for correspondence, if you have Internet access in your classroom. Free e-mail is available on certain websites, such as Hot Mail at www.hotmail.com. Children can also use America Online's Instant Messenger to converse real-time with their peers in other schools, cities, or countries.

2. *Use Cartoons to Help Children Learn to Read and Write English Words*   There are two ways to use cartoons to support literacy: (1) Find cartoons with two to four frames, cut them into individual frames, and laminate the frames. Scramble the frames, and then ask children to read each frame and put the frames in sequential order. (2) You might cut cartoons into frames, erase the words in the dialogue balloons, and then make individual copies for children. Have children write their own English dialogue in the balloons (Richard-Amato, 1996).

3. *Ask Children to Work with Partners to Write Stories and Short Reports*   Have children work with a partner to write stories about familiar events, to retell familiar stories in their own words, or write brief reports about content area topics. Children work together to revise and edit their work. Publish children's writing. Make the writing available in your classroom and encourage children to read each other's published books, poems, and reports.

4. *Use Readers' Theater to Develop Oral Reading Fluency*   Select plays that relate to the content subjects children are studying in your classroom. Plays are available commercially (look in Chapter 7 for suggestions). Many plays are linked to social studies, holidays, and seasons, or they may explore the lives of famous people. Find plays written on many different levels of reading difficulty and for children in different grades.

5. *Make Definition Webs*   Definition webs are useful for developing English vocabulary and clarifying word meaning. The advantage of definition webs is that children are called on to think of examples or characteristics of English words, which, in turn, helps children develop a more in-depth understanding of word meaning. Making definition webs is a good group or partner activity (Figure 8–3).

6. *Explore Greek and Latin Roots that Appear Frequently in English Words*   Make word webs (Chapter 6) to illustrate the meaningful connections among English words that share the same Greek or Latin roots (Figure 8–4). Select words in content area books which include Greek or Latin

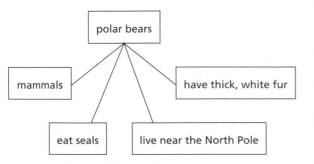

FIGURE 8–3 Definition Web

roots, and then use webs to expand children's understanding of the content words and other English words that have the same root.

7. *Predict Story Endings*   Ask children to read part of a short story and then have them work with a partner to predict the ending. Ask the children to write (or orally tell) their ending. Share the story endings with the group, and then read the whole story. Talk about how children's endings are alike or different from the author's ending.

8. *Count and Identify the Syllables in Long Words*   Ask children to count the syllables they hear in long words. Use activities like syllable-by-syllable decoding and syllable boxes (Chapter 5) to help children identify the letters in the syllables in long words.

9. *Show Children How to Peel Off Prefixes and Suffixes to Identify Long English Words*   Demonstrate how to identify words with prefixes and suffixes. Use the long word solving activity in Chapter 5 to show children how to identify words with prefixes and suffixes. Give children opportunities to find words with prefixes and suffixes in newspapers, magazines, on the word wall, and in textbooks. Make lists of words with the same prefixes and suffixes, and talk about how the prefixes and suffixes affect word meaning.

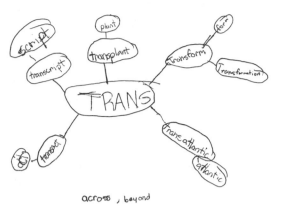

FIGURE 8–4   Word Web for Trans–

ELEVEN WAYS TO CREATE A SUPPORTIVE CLASSROOM LEARNING ENVIRONMENT ■ ■ ■ ■ ▬▬

Children bring to our classrooms a rich language heritage grounded in their home cultures and learned naturally through family life and early interactions with members of their cultural and language community. The amount of overlap between the school culture and children's home cultures affects English language learning in your classroom (Díaz-Rico & Weed, 2002). Classroom activities that reflect common values, behavior patterns, and social interactions naturally make sense to children, while other activities that do not correspond to children's cultural background may be confusing or misunderstood. Supportive classrooms acknowledge children's countries of origin and honor children's home cultures in many different ways.

Talk About Countries of Origin

Talking about countries of origin helps children feel more comfortable and accepted in your classroom. Display maps showing children's countries of origin and discuss where these countries are in relation to your own school. Talk about the geographical location, the weather, the climate, prominent geographical features (rivers and mountains, for example), customs, clothing, and food. Make posters that feature countries of origin, read books about countries, and invite parents or community members to share their experiences of living in their countries of origin.

Honor Familiar Customs and Celebrations

Make children feel at home in your classroom by recognizing those customs and holidays that are important in their home cultures. Honoring familiar customs and celebrations of home cultures lets children know that these cultures are valued and have a high status in your classroom. When children share and celebrate their common ideas and shared values, the classroom learning environment not only supports second language learners, but also creates a harmonious, accepting classroom atmosphere in which all children feel comfortable and welcome.

Read Books that Honor Children's Cultural Heritage

Many books have themes, setting, and characters that connect directly to children's home cultures and countries. For example, *The Gullywasher* (Rossi, 1995), *This House Is Made of Mud* (Buchanan, 1991), and *Blanca's Feather* (Madrigal, 2000) are engaging read-aloud stories that are set in Mexico. *Daughter of the Mountains* (Rankin,1993) is an exciting adventure of an Indian girl that can be read aloud or read independently by accomplished fifth graders. *The Golden Mare, the Firebird, and the Magic Ring* (Sanderson, 2001) is a beautifully illustrated Russian folk tale that children enjoy as a read-aloud book or that fifth graders may enjoy reading on their own. Examples of books about China include *Beautiful Warrior: The Legend of the Nun's Kung Fu* (McCully, 1998), which is a picture book about young women warriors, or *A Ticket to China* (Riehecky, 1999), which describes intriguing sights and places in China.

Share Books that Use Words from Children's Home Languages

Depending on the language spoken at home, you may find books that either present text in two languages, the home language (L1) and the second language (L2), or books which use L1 words in English text. For example, *The Unbreakable Code* (Hunter, 2000) tells the story of the Navajo code talkers of the Second World War, and includes the original code with Navajo pronunciations and their links to English letters and words. *A is for Asia* (Chin-Lee, 1999) presents the English alphabet with examples of words from the Indonesian, Arabic, Chinese, Hindi, Vietnamese, Korean, Burmese, Urdu, Japanese, Russian (the Cyrillic alphabet), Turkish, Korean, Tagalog (Philippines), and Mongolian languages. *Carlos and the Cornfield—Carols y la milpa de maiz* (Stevens, 1995) is written in both English and Spanish, and uses a few key Spanish words to flavor the English text.

Use Some Words from Children's Home Languages in Your Classroom

Introduce a few key words from children's home languages into your classroom discussions. Use common nouns or verbs, write the words on charts, and encourage children who only speak English to learn the words. Invite parents or community members who speak the children's native language to visit your classroom and to share words from their native language. There are two immediate advantages for introducing words from children's home languages in your classroom: (1) children who speak languages other than English have a vocabulary with which to communicate with their peers, and (2) you introduce English-only language speakers to a tapestry of words that enrich their learning.

Develop Concepts Before Teaching English Words

English language learners bring different prior experiences, native language vocabulary, and concepts to our classrooms. We cannot assume that all children already have the concepts to connect with English words. Make sure that children have the concepts they need to learn English words. There are two possible connections among spoken meaning, concepts, and written word meaning.

1. Children may have the concepts and the words for these concepts in their home languages, but may not know the English labels for the familiar concepts. For example, children may know the word *dog* in their home language. Children recognize dogs when they see them, and can explain what dogs look like, what dogs eat, and how dogs sound when they bark. These children need to learn the English word (*dog*) for a familiar concept and native language word they already know. Once children recognize the English word "dog," they are then ready to learn the written word for dog.

2. Children may have a concept but have not learned the native language word for that concept. Should an English word represent a concept that children do not understand, we must help children develop the concept as well as the English word for that concept. For example, children may not understand the concept of *erosion*. These children need to develop both the concept and the English word for that concept. Simply teaching the English word is not helpful because children do not understand the meaning of the English word they are learning.

Make sure that children understand the concepts that English words label. If children have not had the opportunity to develop concepts, create learning opportunities through films and CD-ROM, by taking field trips, by discussing pictures that represent concepts, and by reading text that explains them.

Teach Cognates to Children Who Are Literate in Their Home Languages

Cognates are words that have a common origin across two different languages. Cognates look alike and may also sound somewhat similar. It follows, then, that children who recognize a cognate in their home language have some insight into the meaning of that same word in English. Because cognates look quite similar, children who are literate in their native language are likely to recognize cognates when these words are written in English. Cognates are a window to teaching Spanish-speaking children how to read English (Rodríguez, 2001; Williams, 2001), as well as windows for teaching English to children who speak other native languages.

The more overlap that exists between English and children's home languages, the greater the possibility that there are many cognates for developing English vocabulary. Cognates may be identically spelled, spelled almost the same, or sound similar but look dissimilar. Table 8–2 shows examples of cognates in Spanish, French, and German. In teaching cognates, check to be sure that words that appear to be cognates are, indeed, really cognates. Sometimes words that appear to be cognates do not mean the same thing in two languages. These words are called *false friends* or *false cognates*. False friends are confusing and, if inappropriately used, can cause considerable misunderstanding and confusion. For example, the French word *brave* means *nice*, not *courageous*; *embarazada* in Spanish means *pregnant*, not *embarrassed*; the word *delito* in Spanish means *crime*, not *delight*. You might start a classroom list of cognates, make a cognate dictionary, or create a bulletin board that shows the many cognates that link one language to another. Invite children to participate in making lists, cognate dictionaries, and bulletin boards (Williams, 2001).

Use Pictures, Objects, Demonstrations, and Displays to Contextualize Learning

Pictures, objects, demonstrations, and displays ground English words in meaningful contexts. The display in Figure 8–5 is an example of how you might combine pictures and words to represent the sound associated with the letter Bb. Figure 8–5 includes both English and Spanish words that begin with the letter Bb and the sound

TABLE 8–2 Examples of Spanish, French, and German Cognates

English	Spanish	English	French	English	German
alphabet	alfabeto	artist	l'artiste	arm	arm
calendar	calendario	bicycle	bicyclette	banana	banane
carpenter	carpintero	biology	biologie	cola	cola
delicious	delicioso	blue	bleu	computer	computer
direction	dirección	construction	construction	feather	feder
elephant	elefante	danger	danger	finger	finger
exit	éxito	dictionary	dictionnaire	fish	fisch
general	general	edition	edition	hamburger	hamburger
journal	jornal	finish	finir	hand	hand
letter	letra	hazard	hasard	hair	haar
mathematics	matemáticas	institution	l'institution	hound	hund
music	música	mountain	montagne	house	haus
notice	noticia	November	novembre	milk	milch
number	número	radio	radio	mother	mutter
pharmacy	farmacia	rapid	rapide	mouse	maus
radio	radio	sincerely	sincerement	olive	olive
sandal	sandalia	soup	soupe	tea	tee
special	especial	table	table	telephone	telefon
television	televisión	theory	théorie	toast	toast
visit	visita	train	train	tofu	tofu

of /b/. The second language learners in your classroom bring to school concepts, ideas, and knowledge, albeit expressed in their home languages. By including words from the children's home language in displays, such as the one shown in Figure 8–5, you create an opportunity for children to connect familiar first language words with the English words and English letter-sounds.

The use of familiar first language words creates a scaffold upon which spoken and written English might be learned, especially when children are already literate in their native language. Additionally, the children's home language is honored, and the English-only speakers in your classroom have real-life opportunities to learn a little about other languages. It is not always possible to connect the words, letters, and sounds in children's home language with English. English phonemes may not be a part of children's native language, or the same letters may represent different sounds in the two languages. However, when there are clear-cut connections between English and the children's home language, using words in the children's first language brings this first language into your classroom in a meaningful way.

Pair Second Language Learners with Children Who Speak English as a First Language

When a new child who speaks English as a second language enters your class, ask a congenial English-speaking child to be the special partner for the new child. Support the relationship by seating the children near each other, by having them visit the same centers, and by ensuring that they are partners whenever possible. Pairing children gives the English language learner an opportunity to communicate with, and learn from, a child who already speaks English and, additionally, benefits the English-only speaking child by giving that child closer contact with another language.

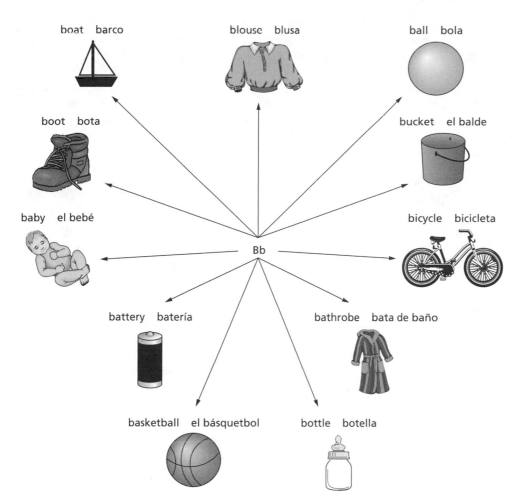

FIGURE 8–5   Picture Display of Words that Begin with the Letter Bb in English and in Spanish

Ask More-proficient Second Language Learners to Translate Key Messages for Less-proficient English Language Learners

Children who are more proficient in English have a definite role to play in supporting the communication of their less-English-proficient classmates. Sometimes children who are just beginning to learn English need extra help communicating their ideas to their teachers. Likewise, teachers sometimes have special messages they need to communicate with second language learners. In these situations, asking one child to help translate for another child serves the purposes of: (1) increasing the accurate exchange of ideas and (2) letting less-proficient children know that they are welcome in your classroom and that their ideas and input are valued.

Welcome Parents and Native Language Speaking Community Members into Your School and Classroom

Open your classroom to parents. Welcome them into the classroom as volunteers, translators, visitors, and helpers. Make friends with the children's parents. If you cannot speak the home language, look for someone in your school who is proficient in that language. Organize small clubs or groups of parents who speak the same language. Help parents contact one another by finding a meeting space at school. Encourage parents to form friendly relations with other teachers and staff, and be available to support parents whenever you can. In return, parents will feel honored and welcome in your school and classrooms, home languages and cultures will be validated, and children will have a caring and nurturing place to learn.

Cultures are continually changing; they often overlap, and there is variation within the same culture. Language, like cultures, share the common features in that all languages have syntax, words, and sounds. However, languages differ in word order, in vocabulary, and in the sounds that make up words. Learning to read English requires that children understand English word order and English words. Because English is written in an alphabet, children must also be aware of English sounds, connect those sounds to letters, and use this knowledge to identify and learn English words. Base your classroom literacy program on developing competence in spoken English, make it consistent with the children's stage of English language learning, and honor the children's home language and culture. In so doing, the second language learners in your classroom become fully bilingual, and the English-only speaking children whom you teach learn about and come to value other languages and cultures.

REFERENCES

Brooks, E. (1972). *The practically perfect pajamas*. Delray Beach, FL: Winslow Press.

Buchanan, K. (1991). *This house is made of mud*. Flagstaff, AZ: Rising Moon Books.

Chiappe, P., & Siegel, L. S. (1999). Phonological awareness and reading acquisition in English- and Punjabi-speaking Canadian children. *Journal of Educational Psychology, 91*, 20–28.

Chin-Lee, C. (1999). *A is for Asia*. New York: Orchard Books.

Denton, C. A., Hasbrouck, J. E., Weaver, L. R., & Riccio, C. A. (2000). What do we know about phonological awareness in Spanish? *Reading Psychology, 21*, 335–352.

Díaz-Rico, L. T., & Weed, K. T. (2002). *The crosscultural, language, and academic development handbook: A complete K-12 reference guide, 2nd edition*. Boston, MA: Allyn and Bacon.

Holub, J. (1997). *Pen pals*. New York: Grosset and Dunlap.

Hunter, S. H. (2000). *The unbreakable code*. Flagstaff, AZ: Rising Moon Books.

Leedy, L. (1991). *Messages in the mailbox: How to write a letter*. New York: Holiday House.

Madrigal, A. H. (2000). *Blanca's feather*. Flagstaff, AZ: Rising Moon Books.

McCully, E. A. (1998). *Beautiful warrior: The legend of the nun's kung fu*. New York: Arthur A. Levine Books.

Meyers, M. (1993). *Teaching to diversity: Teaching and learning in the multi-ethnic classroom*. Toronto, Canada: Irwin Publishing.

Rankin, L. (1993). *Daughter of the mountains*. New York: Puffin Newbery Library.

Richard-Amato, P. A. (1996). *Making it happen: Interaction in the second language classroom, from theory to practice, 2nd edition*. White Plains, New York: Addison-Wesley Publishing Group.

Riehecky, J. (1999). *A ticket to China*. Minneapolis, MN: Carolrhoda Books, Inc.

Rodríguez, T. A. (2001). From the known to the unknown: Using cognates to teach English to Spanish-speaking literates. *The Reading Teacher, 54*, 744–746.

Rossi, J. (1995). *The gullywasher*. Flagstaff, AZ: Rising Moon Books.

Sanderson, R. (2001). *The golden mare, the firebird, and the magic ring*. New York: Little Brown.

Smith, K. J. (1992). Using multimedia with Navajo children: An effort to alleviate problems of cultural learning style, background of experience, and motivation. *Reading & Writing Quarterly: Overcoming Learning Difficulties, 8*, 287–294.

Spurr, E. (1997). *The long, long letter*. New York: Hyperion Paperbacks for Children.

Stevens, J. R. (1995). *Carlos and the cornfield – Carlos y la milpa de maiz*. Flagstaff, AZ: Rising Moon Books.

Wade-Woolley, L., & Geva, E. (2000). Processing novel phonemic contrasts in the acquisition of L2 word reading. *Scientific Studies in Reading, 4*, 261–266.

Williams, J. A. (2001). Classroom conversations: Opportunities to learn for ESL students in mainstream classrooms. *The Reading Teacher, 54*, 750–757.

REPRODUCIBLE PATTERNS

FIGURE A–1
Sound Pulling

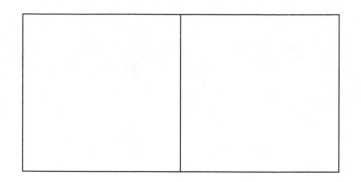

FIGURE A–4 Clothes for
the Alliteration Clothesline

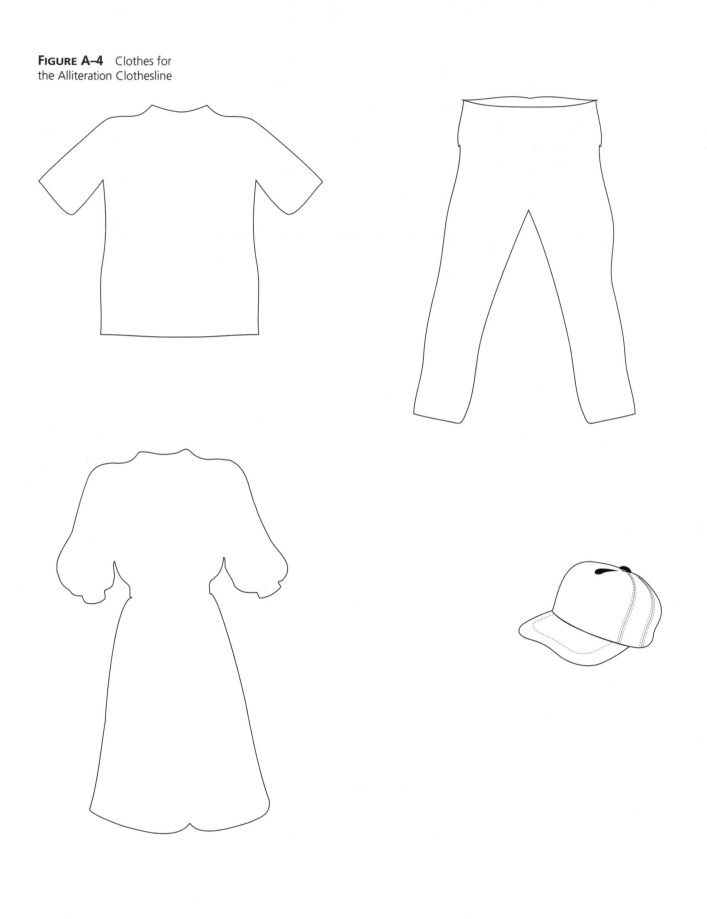

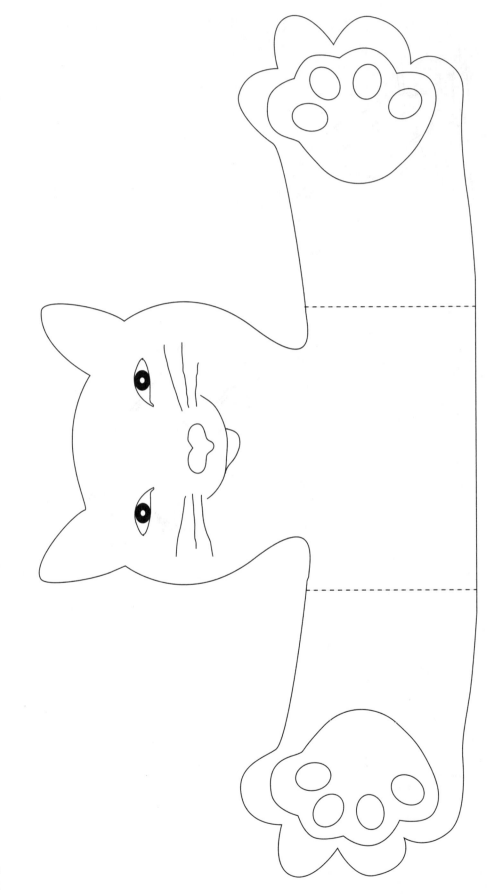

Cat Fold Pattern

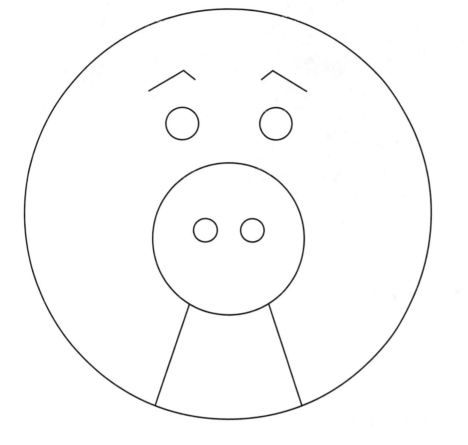

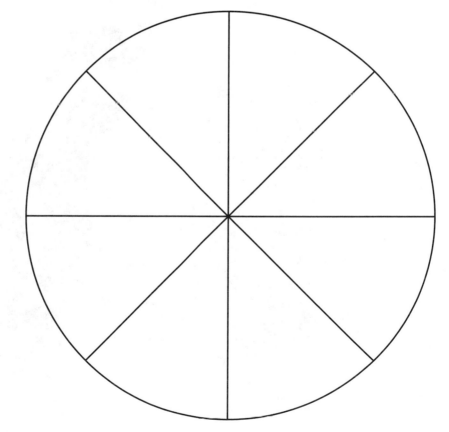

FIGURE A–9 Duck Word
Building Guide Pattern

Date: _____

Name: _____

Use the letters to build as many words as you can.
Vowel Letters   a   i   o
Consonant Letters   n   t   b   g   d   s

Draw a picture of a duck above each line:

_____ _____ _____   _____ _____ _____

Draw a picture of a duck above each line:

_____ _____ _____   _____ _____ _____

Draw a picture of a duck above each line:

_____ _____ _____   _____ _____ _____

Super Duck

(Draw a picture of a duck looking quite brave and fine in a gladiator outfit or some other super looking costume.)

_____

_____

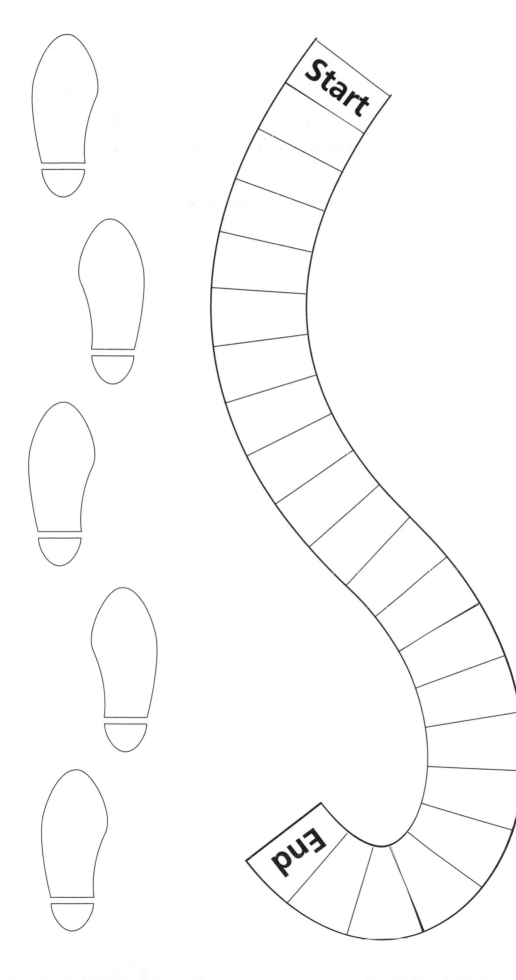

Figure A–11 100 Yard Dash Game Pattern

Start

End

FIGURE A–12 Rapid Balloons for Word Family Words

Name: ______________________

Date: ______________________

Look at the balloons below. Use the letters to make **real** words. Write your words on the lines below!

Beginning Sounds Ending Sounds

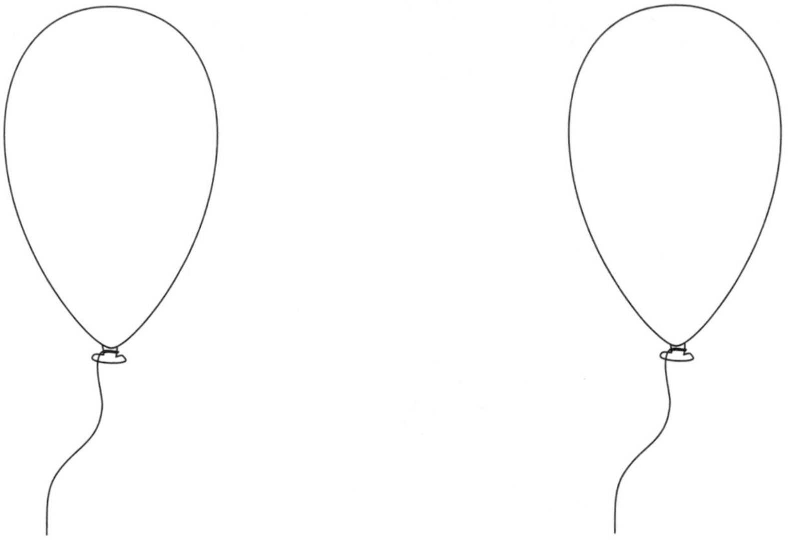

FIGURE A–13
Rapid Balloons for Pronounceable Letter Patterns

Name: ______________________
Date: ______________________

Look at the balloons below. Use the letters to make **real** words. Write your words on the lines below!

Beginning Middle End

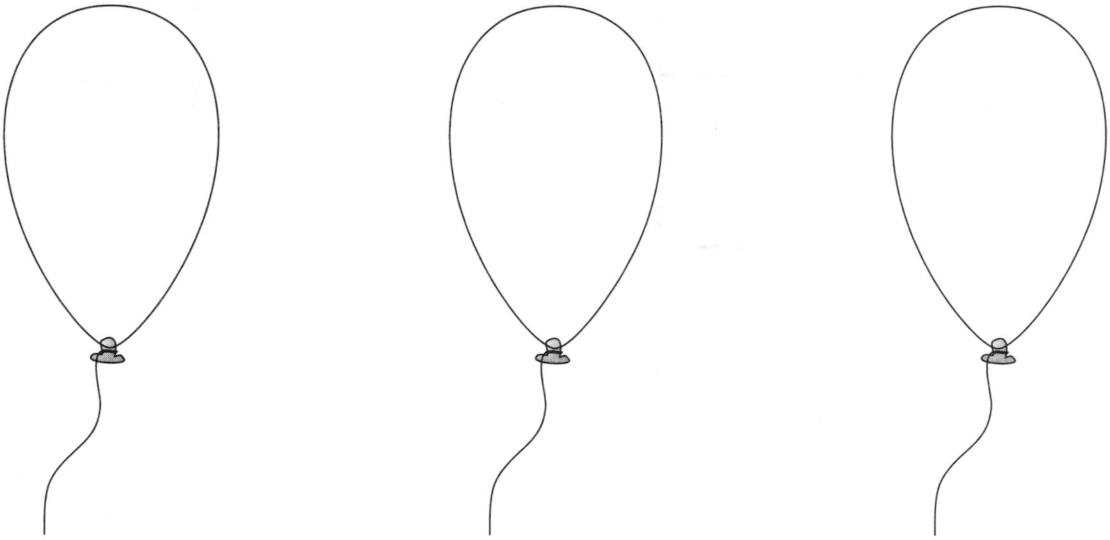

Write the words you make on the lines below.

FIGURE A–14 Word Race Pattern

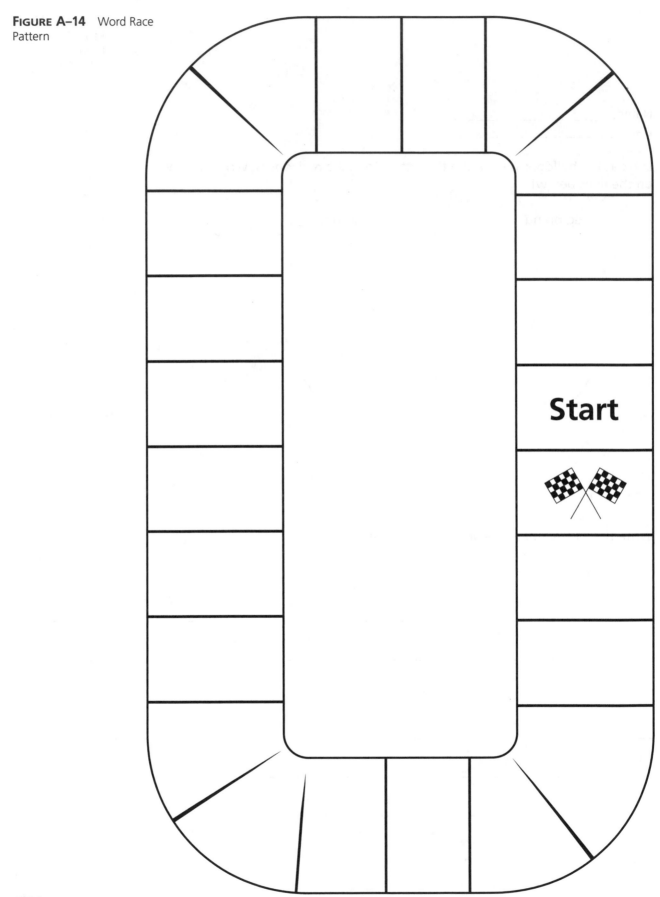

Start

Long Word Solving Steps

Step 1. Find the prefix and remove it.
Step 2. Find the suffix and remove it.
Step 3. Identify the syllables, and pronounce the base word.
Step 4. Put the whole word back together again. Pronounce it.

Directions:

Read each word in the first column. Write the prefix in the Prefix Box. Write the suffix in the Suffix Box. Write the base word in the Base Word Box. If a word does not have a prefix or a suffix, leave that box blank. The first word is done for you.

When you finish, pick two words. Look them up in the book. Find the sentences with the words. Write each word on a sticky note. Put each sticky note on the page where you find the word in a sentence.

Long Word	Prefix Box Find the prefix. Remove it.	Suffix Box Find the suffix. Remove it.	Base Word Box Pronounce the base word.
1. unbreakable	un	able	break
2.			
3.			
4.			
5.			
6.			
7.			
8.			
9.			
10.			
11.			
12.			
13.			

Name: _____

Date: _____

Members in Your Group: _____
_____
_____

Word Chain

Suffix _____

Directions:

Match word cards with suffix cards to build new words. Check new words in the dictionary. Write one new word in each circle to make a chain.

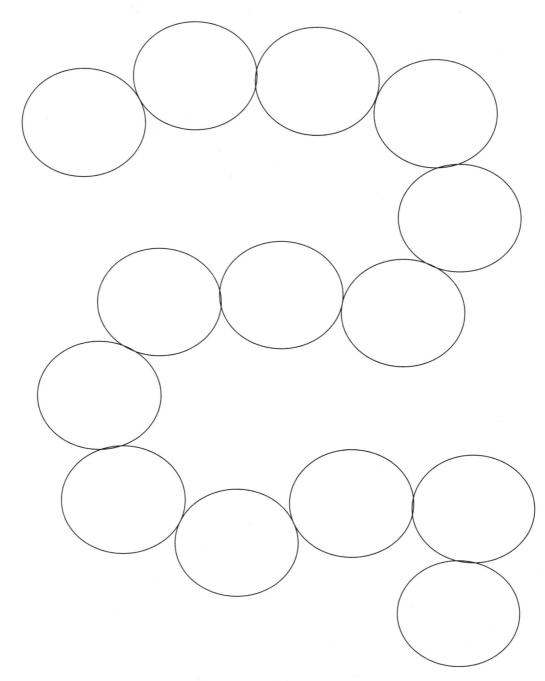

FIGURE A–17 Prefix and Suffix T-chart

Name: ______________________________

Directions:

Add to the base words ________________________________.

Write words on the right that ____________________________.

Write words on the left that _____________________________.

Base word +	Base word +

Names of Partners: _____   _____

Directions: The page number where you can find each word
and the points for each word are in each box. Search for
the words, and write them on the line in each box.
Total Points: _____

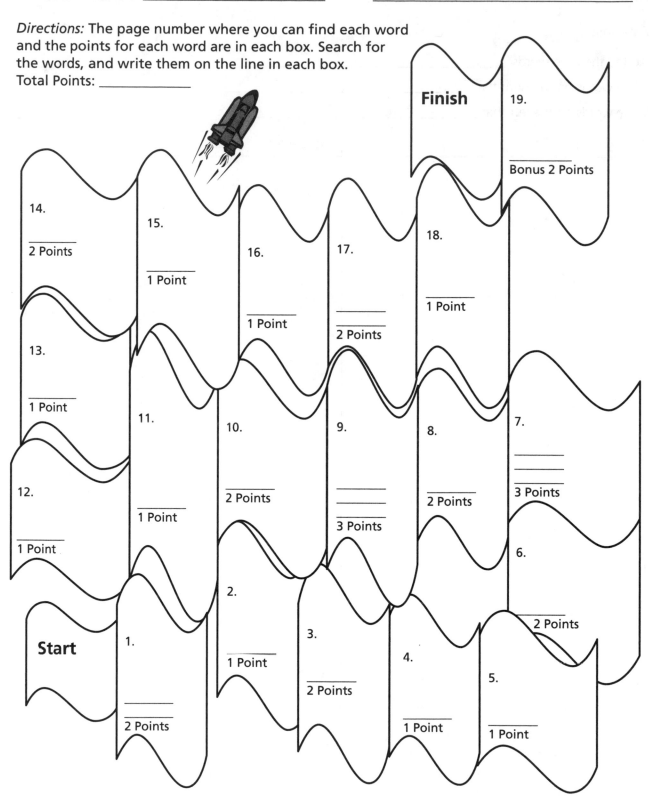

Finish

19.
_____
Bonus 2 Points

14.
_____
2 Points

15.
_____
1 Point

16.
_____
1 Point

17.
_____
2 Points

18.
_____
1 Point

13.
_____
1 Point

11.
_____
1 Point

10.
_____
2 Points

9.
_____
3 Points

8.
_____
2 Points

7.
_____
_____
3 Points

12.
_____
1 Point

6.
_____
2 Points

Start

1.
_____
2 Points

2.
_____
1 Point

3.
_____
2 Points

4.
_____
1 Point

5.
_____
1 Point

FIGURE A–19
Compound Word Building Guide

Date: ____________________

Partners: __________________   ____________________

Directions:

Combine the base words to make compound words. You may use the base words more than once.

Base Words

How many compounds can you make from the base words?

1. ____________________	11. ____________________
2. ____________________	12. ____________________
3. ____________________	13. ____________________
4. ____________________	14. ____________________
5. ____________________	15. ____________________
6. ____________________	16. ____________________
7. ____________________	17. ____________________
8. ____________________	18. ____________________
9. ____________________	19. ____________________
10. ____________________	20. ____________________

FIGURE A–20
Compound Word Sorting
Guide

Date: _____

Names of Children in Your Group   _____
                                  _____
                                  _____

Directions: Sort the compound words into two groups.

Group 1   You can figure out the meaning of the compound by putting the meaning of the two base words together. Example: <u>toothbrush</u>.
Group 2   You cannot figure out the meaning of the compound by putting the meaning of the two base words together. Example: <u>butterfly</u>.

Group 1	**Group 2**
Base Word + Base Word = Compound Meaning	Base Word + Base Word Ø Compound Meaning
toothbrush	butterfly

270

Long Word Splitting

Date: _____

Names: _____   _____

Directions: Read each word. Use your pencil to tap the number of syllables. Write the number of pencil taps in Box 1. Count the vowel letters. Write the number of vowel letters in Box 2. Write the number of syllables in the word in Box 3. Which two boxes have the same number? Why? The first word is done for you.

Line 15 does not have a word. Look in a book you are reading. Find a word that is at least two syllables long. Write the word on line 15, and fill-in the boxes. Write the title of the book at the very bottom of the page.

Hint - Each syllable has only one vowel sound.

Word	**Box 1** Number of Vowel Sounds (Pencil Taps) Tap It Out	**Box 2** Number of Vowel Letters Count It Out	**Box 3** Number of Syllables (Pencil Taps) Figure It Out
1. reason	2	3	2
2.			
3.			
4.			
5.			
6.			
7.			
8.			
9.			
10.			
11.			
12.			
13.			
14.			
15.			

Workers in Your Group

_____   _____

_____   _____

Workers in Your Partner Group

_____   _____

_____   _____

Directions: Put a check beside each step as it is completed. Turn in the bags, syllable cards, and word lists after you complete Step 5.

Step 1   Write all the words on a sealable bag.
Complete ___

Step 2   Cut the words into syllables. Put the syllables in a stack.
            Save the bag with the words on it.
Complete ___

Step 3   Trade the syllable cards with your partner group.
Complete ___

Step 4   Use the syllable cards from your partner group to build as many words as you can.
            Write the words you build on a piece of paper.
Complete ___

Step 5   Work together with your partner group.
            Compare the words that each group built with the whole words on the bags.
            Check any different words in the dictionary to make sure they are real words.
Complete ___

Name: _____

Date: _____

Speedy Word Score _____

Speedy Words with Suffixes

Directions: Combine the base words and the suffixes to write new words. Write as many words as you can before the timer goes off. Every word counts for one lap on the Speedy Word Race Track.

Base Word   +   Suffix   =   Speedy Words

_____

_____

_____

_____

_____

_____

_____

_____

_____

B	I	N	G	O
		FREE		

WORDO!

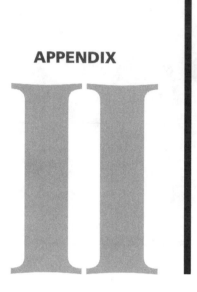

COMPOUND WORDS

In two-syllable compound words, the break comes between the words (e.g., *after / noon*; *back / door*; *camp / fire*). Three-or-more-syllable compound words are divided between the words, and are additionally divided within long words (e.g., *pil / low / case*; *cot / ton / tail*; *bus / y / bod / y*).

Aa afterdeck, aftermath, afternoon, aftershock, airbrush, aircraft, airdrop, airfield, airflow, airline, airmail, airplane, airport, airsick, anchorwoman, anyone, anything, anyway, anywhere, applejack, applesauce, armband, armchair, armpit, arrowhead, awestruck

Bb backache, backboard, backbone, backdoor, backfield, backfire, background, backhand, backlog, backpack, backrest, backside, backstage, backstroke, backtrack, backyard, badmouth, bagpipe, ballpoint, ballroom, bandbox, banknote, barbell, bareback, barefoot, barnyard, baseball, basketball, bathhouse, bathrobe, bathroom, bathtub, battlefield, battleship, beachhead, bedrock, bedroom, bedside, bedspread, bedtime, beefsteak, beehive, beeswax, beforehand, bellybutton, bighorn, billboard, billfold, birdbath, birdbrain, birdcage, birdhouse, birthday, birthmark, birthplace, birthright, blackberry, blackbird, blackboard, blackhead, blackjack, blacklist, blackmail, blackout, blacksmith, blacktop, blastoff, blindfold, blockhead, blockhouse, bloodhound, bloodshot, bloodstream, bloodthirsty, blowhard, blowhole, blowout, blowpipe, blowtorch, blowup, bluebell, blueberry, bluebird, bluebook, bluefish, bluegrass, bluenose, blueprint, boathouse, bodyguard, bombshell, bonehead, bookcase, bookend, bookkeeper, bookmobile, bookmark, bookshelf, bookstore, bootlick, bottleneck, bowlegged, boxcar, boyfriend, brainchild, brainstorm, brainwash, breakdown, breakfast, breakneck, breastbone, bridegroom, bridgehead, broadcast, broomstick, brownout, brushwork, buckskin, bucktooth, buckwheat, bulkhead, bulldog, bulldozer, bullfight, bullfrog, bullhead, bumblebee, bunkhouse, bushwhack, businessman, businesswoman, busybody, buttercup, butterfat, butterfly, buttermilk, butternut, butterscotch, buttonhole, buyback, bystander

Cc callbox, campfire, campground, candlestick, candlewick, canvasback, cardboard, carefree, caretaker, carfare, carsick, cartwheel, cashbox, catbird, catfish, cattail, cattleman, chairman, chairperson, chairwoman, chalkboard, checkbook,

checkerboard, checklist, checkmate, checkout, checkroom, checkup, cheekbone,
cheerleader, cheeseburger, chessman, chestnut, chickpea, childbirth, chipboard,
choirboy, chopsticks, clambake, clamshell, classmate, classroom, clergyman,
cliffhanger, clockwise, clodhopper, clothesline, clothespin, cloudburst, clubhouse,
coastline, cobblestone, cobweb, cockroach, codfish, collarbone, comeback,
congressman, congresswoman, cookbook, cookout, copperhead, corkscrew,
corncob, cornmeal, cornstalk, cottonmouth, cottontail, countdown,
counterclockwise, counterpart, countryman, countryside, countrywoman,
courthouse, courtyard, cowboy, cowgirl, cowhand, cowhide, cowlick, craftsman,
crisscross, crossbow, crosshatch, crossroad, crosswalk, crossword, crowbar,
cupboard, cupcake, cutback, cutout, crybaby

Dd daredevil, darkroom, database, daybreak, daydream, daylight, daytime,
deadbeat, deadhead, deadline, deadlock, deadpan, deathtrap, desktop, dipstick,
dishcloth, dishpan, dockhand, doghouse, dogwood, doorbell, doorknob,
doorman, doorstep, doorway, doughnut, downcast, downpour, downright,
downshift, downstairs, downstream, downtown, downward, downwind, draftsman,
dragonfly, drainpipe, drawback, drawbridge, drawstring, dreamland, dreamlike,
dressmaker, driftwood, driveway, dropout, drugstore, drumbeat, drumhead,
drumstick, dugout, dumbbell, dunderhead, drywall

Ee earache, eardrum, earmuffs, earphone, earring, earshot, earthquake,
earthworm, eavesdrop, eggplant, eggshell, elsewhere, Englishman,
Englishwoman, everglade, evergreen, everlasting, everybody, everyday,
everyone, everything, everywhere, expressway, extraordinary, extraterrestrial,
eyeball, eyebrow, eyedropper, eyeglasses, eyelash, eyelid, eyesight, eyeteeth,
eyetooth, eyewash, eyewink, eyewitness

Ff facecloth, faceplate, fairground, fairway, fairyland, fallback, fallout, faraway,
farewell, farmhand, farmland, farsighted, fastback, fathead, feedback, fiberglass,
fiddlestick, figurehead, fingernail, fingerprint, firearm, fireball, firebird, firebox,
firecracker, firefighter, firehouse, firelight, fireman, fireplace, fireproof, fireside,
firewater, firewood, fireworks, firsthand, fisherman, fishhook, fishpond, fishtail,
flagpole, flapjack, flashback, flashbulb, flashcube, flashlight, flatboat, flatcar,
flatfish, flatland, flintlock, floodlight, floorboard, floorwalker, flophouse, flowerpot,
flyby, flycatcher, flyspeck, flytrap, foghorn, folklore, football, footbridge, foothill,
footlights, footloose, footnote, footpath, footprint, footrest, footstep, footstool,
forever, forklift, formalwear, fortuneteller, fourposter, foxhole, foxhound,
framework, frankfurter, freehand, freelance, freeload, freestyle, freeway, freewheel,
freewill, Frenchman, Frenchwoman, freshman, freshwater, frogman, frostbite,
fruitcake, fruitwood, fullback, furthermore, fussbudget

Gg gangland, gangplank, gangway, gatepost, gateway, gearbox, gearshift,
gentleman, gentlewoman, gingerbread, gingersnap, girlfriend, goalkeeper,
godfather, godmother, godparent, goldbrick, goldenrod, goldfinch, goldfish,
goldsmith, goodhearted, gooseneck, grandchild, granddad, granddaughter,
grandfather, grandma, grandmother, grandpa, grandparent, grandson, grandstand,
grapefruit, grapevine, grasshopper, grassland, gravestone, graveyard, greasepaint,
greenback, greenbelt, greengrocer, greenhorn, greenhouse, Greenland,
greenroom, greyhound, gridiron, gridlock, grindstone, gristmill, groomsman,
groundhog, groundwater, groundwork, grubstake, gumdrop, gumshoe, gunlock,
gunpowder, gunsmith

Hh haircut, hairdo, halfback, halfhearted, halfway, hallway, hamburger,
hammerhead, handbag, handball, handbook, handcuff, handlebars, handmade,
handout, handrail, handshake, handsome, handspring, handwriting, hangnail,
hardware, hardwood, hatbox, hayloft, haystack, headache, headband, headboard,

headdress, headfirst, headgear, headland, headlight, headline, headlock, headlong, headman, headmen, headphone, headpiece, headquarters, headrest, headroom, headset, headstand, headstone, headstrong, headwater, headway, hearsay, heartbeat, heartbroken, heartsick, hedgehog, heirloom, henpeck, hereafter, herself, hideout, highland, highway, highwayman, hillside, hilltop, himself, hindmost, hitchhike, hogshead, hogwash, holdup, hollyhock, homeland, homemade, homeroom, homesick, homespun, homework, honeybee, honeycomb, honeydew, honeymoon, honeysuckle, hopscotch, horseback, horsefly, horseman, horseplay, horsepower, horseshoe, horsewoman, hotbox, hothouse, hotshot, hourglass, houseboat, housefly, household, housekeeper, houseplant, housewife, housework, however, huckleberry, hummingbird, humpback, hunchback

Ii icebound, icebox, icebreaker, icecap, icehouse, Iceland, icemaker, inchworm, inkwell, innkeeper, inside, ironclad, ironside, itself

Jj jackknife, jackpot, jackrabbit, jaywalk, jellyfish, jigsaw, joystick, junkyard

Kk kettledrum, keyboard, keyhole, keypunch, keystone, kickback, kickoff, kidnap, kingfisher, knapsack, kneecap, knickknack, knockdown

Ll lackluster, ladybug, lamppost, landlady, landlord, landmark, landscape, landslide, larkspur, lawsuit, leapfrog, leftover, letterhead, lifeboat, lifeguard, lifelike, lifelong, lifesaving, lifetime, lighthearted, lighthouse, lightwave, limelight, limestone, lipstick, livestock, loathsome, lockjaw, locksmith, lodestone, loganberry, loggerhead, lonesome, longhand, longhorn, lookout, loophole, lopsided, loudmouth, loudspeaker, lovesick, lowland, lumberjack, lunchroom, lunchtime, lunkhead

Mm mailbox, mailman, mainframe, mainland, mainstay, makeshift, makeup, manhandle, manhole, mankind, manslaughter, marketplace, marshland, masterpiece, masthead, matchbox, matchstick, maybe, meadowlark, meantime, meanwhile, meatball, merrymaking, milepost, milestone, milkmaid, milkman, milkshake, milkweed, millpond, mincemeat, minefield, minuteman, mockingbird, moneymaking, moonbeam, moonlight, moonshine, moonstruck, moreover, motorboat, motorcycle, mousetrap, mouthpiece, myself

Nn nailhead, nametag, nearsighted, necklace, necktie, needlework, network, nevertheless, newborn, newcomer, newfound, Newfoundland, newscast, newspaper, newsstand, nickname, nightfall, nightgown, nightmare, nightstick, nighttime, nobleman, noblewoman, noontime, northeast, northwest, nosebleed, notebook, nowadays, nowhere, numbskull, nursemaid, nutcracker, nuthatch, nutshell

Oo oaktag, oatmeal, oddball, offhand, offset, offshoot, offshore, offspring, oilcloth, oncoming, oneself, onset, onto, otherwise, ourselves, overcoat, oxcart

Pp padlock, paintbox, paintbrush, pancake, paperback, parkway, passageway, passport, password, patchwork, paycheck, payroll, peacock, peanut, peephole, penknife, penmanship, peppermint, pickax, picklock, pickpocket, pickup, piggyback, pigpen, pigsty, pigtail, pillbox, pillowcase, pincushion, pineapple, pineland, pinkeye, pinpoint, pinwheel, pipeline, pitchfork, platform, playback, playground, playhouse, playmate, playpen, playroom, plaything, playwright, pocketbook, pocketknife, polecat, policeman, policewoman, ponytail, popcorn, porthole, postbox, postcard, postman, postmark, postmaster, potluck, potshot, printout, proofread, pullback, purebred

Qq quakeproof, quarterback, quicksand

Rr racehorse, racetrack, racquetball, radioactive, ragweed, railhead, railroad, railway, rainbow, raincoat, raindrop, rainfall, rainproof, rainspouts, rainstorm, ramrod, ratfink, rattlesnake, rawhide, razorback, redcoat, redwood, restroom, ringworm, roadbed, roadblock, roadrunner, roadside, roadwork, rollaway, rollback, roommate, rosebud, roughneck, roundabout, roundhouse, roundup, rowboat, rubberneck, runaway, runway

Ss sackcloth, saddlebags, safeguard, sagebrush, sailboat, salesman, salesperson, saleswoman, saltbox, saltshaker, saltwater, sandbar, sandbox, sandman, sandpaper, sandpiper, sandstone, saucepan, sawbuck, sawdust, sawmill, scarecrow, schoolhouse, Scotland, scoutmaster, scrapbook, screwdriver, seaboard, seacoast, seafaring, seafood, seaplane, seaport, searchlight, seashell, seashore, seasick, seaweed, secondhand, seesaw, setback, shadowbox, shellfish, shipshape, shipwreck, shipyard, shoebox, shoelace, shoplift, shortcoming, shorthorn, shortsighted, shortstop, sidekick, sideline, sideshow, sidestep, sidetrack, sidewalk, sideways, sightseeing, signpost, silkworm, silversmith, silverware, skateboard, skinhead, skydiving, skylark, skylight, skyline, skyrocket, skyscraper, slaphappy, slapstick, sledgehammer, sleepwalk, sleepyhead, slingshot, smallpox, smashup, smokestack, snapdragon, snapshot, snowball, snowbird, snowdrift, snowflake, snowman, snowmobile, snowplow, snowshoe, snowstorm, soapbox, softball, software, somebody, someday, someone, something, sometime, somewhat, somewhere, songbird, sorehead, soundproof, southeast, southwest, spacecraft, spaceship, spacesuit, spacewalk, spearhead, spearmint, splashdown, sportsman, spotlight, springboard, springtime, spyglass, stagecoach, staircase, stairway, starboard, starfish, statesman, steadfast, steamboat, steamroller, steamship, stepfather, stepladder, stepmother, stickball, stingray, stockyard, stoplight, stopwatch, storehouse, storekeeper, stowaway, straightforward, strawberry, streamline, streetcar, streetlight, strongbox, stronghold, sugarcane, suitcase, summertime, sunbathe, sunbeam, sunburn, sunburst, sundown, sunfish, sunflower, sunglasses, sunlight, sunrise, sunset, sunshine, sunshade, superrich, surfboard, swampland, swayback, sweatshirt, sweetheart, swimsuit, switchboard, swordfish

Tt tablecloth, tablespoon, tadpole, tailwind, takeoff, teacup, teakettle, teammate, teaspoon, teenage, textbook, Thanksgiving, themselves, thereafter, thereby, therefore, threadbare, throughout, throughway, throwback, thumbtack, thundercloud, thunderstorm, tideland, tieback, tightrope, timberline, timetable, tinderbox, tinfoil, tinsmith, tiptoe, toadstool, today, toenail, tomboy, tombstone, tomcat, tonight, toolbox, toothache, toothbrush, toothpaste, toothpick, topmost, topsoil, touchback, touchdown, trademark, trapdoor, treadmill, tribesman, trustworthy, tryout, tugboat, tumbleweed, turnout, turnpike, turntable, turtleneck, typecast, typewriter

Uu understand, upheaval, upheld, uphold, upkeep, upland, uplink, uppermost, upright, upstairs, upstream

Vv videocassette, videotape, vineyard, volleyball

Ww walkout, walkover, walkway, wallpaper, wardrobe, warehouse, warfare, warlike, warpath, warship, washcloth, wastebasket, watchdog, watchman, watercolor, watercress, waterfall, waterfront, watermelon, waterproof, watershed, watertight, waterway, waterwheel, waterworks, waveband, weathercock, weatherman, weathervane, wedlock, weekday, weekend, wellhead, wetland, whatever, wheelbarrow, wheelchair, whenever, whereabouts, whereupon, whichever, whirlpool, whitehead, whitewash, whoever, wholesome, widespread, wildcat, wildflower, wildlife, windmill, windowpane, windpipe, windshield, windsock, wingspan, wintergreen, wintertime, wisecrack, wishbone, withdraw, withdrawn, withdrew, within, withstand, withstood, without, woodblock, woodchuck, woodcutter, woodland, woodpecker, woodsman, woodwind, woodwork, wordbook, wordplay, wordsmith, wordstock, workbench, workbook, workbox, workman, worksheet, workshop, worldwide, worthwhile, wristwatch

Yy yardstick, yearbook, yearend, yourself

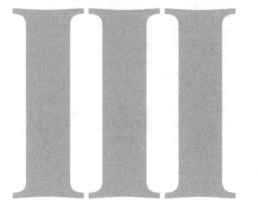

ROOT WORDS

Root Word	Examples
aqua (water)	aquarium, aquatic, aquanaut
art (skill)	artist, artisan
ast(er) (star)	asterisk, astronomy, astronaut
aut(o) (self)	automobile, automatic, autobiography
bi (two)	bicycle, bifocals, biped
bio (life)	biology, bionic, biotech
cap (head)	capitol, cap
ceive (take)	receive, conceive
chron (time)	chronicle, chronic
cycle (wheel)	bicycle, tricycle, unicycle
deci (ten)	decimal, decimeter
dem (people)	democracy, democratic
cycl (circle of wheel)	bicycle, motorcycle
fin (end)	final, finish, finite
firm (strong)	confirm, affirm
ge(o) (earth)	geography, geology
magn (great)	magnificent, magnitude
mal (poor)	malnutrition, maladjusted
man(u) (hand)	manual, manicure
mill (thousand)	millimeter, millipede
mit (sent)	transmit, mitigate
mob (move)	automobile, mobile
multi (many)	multiple, multiply
opt (see)	optical, optician, option
ped (foot)	pedal, pedestrian
phon (sound)	phonics, phonograph
phot (light)	photo, photocopy
poly (many)	polygon, poly
port (carry)	export, portable, transport
rupt (break)	interrupt, disrupt, erupt
sci (know)	science, conscience
scop (see)	telescope, microscope, stethoscope

Root Word	Examples
scribe (write)	inscribe, subscribe, scribe
tech (skill)	technician, technical
tele (distant)	telescope, television, telephone
therm (heat)	thermos, thermostat, thermometer
tri (three)	tricycle, triad, triple
un(i) (one)	uniform, unicorn, unicycle
vac (empty)	vacate, vacation
vid (see)	video, evident
voc (voice)	vocabulary, vocal

PREFIXES AND USEFUL EXAMPLES

Anti- (Against)	*Com-* (With, Together, or Jointly)
antiaircraft	commerce
antibiotic	commit
anticrime	common
antidemocratic	commune
antidumping	compact
antifraud	companion
antifreeze	compartment
antinoise	compatible
antirust	compete
antismoke	compile
antistick	compose
antistress	compost
antitheft	compound
antiviolence	comprehend
antiweed	compress
	compromise

Con- *(With, Together, or Jointly)	*De-* (Partly, From, Down, Away)
concern	debug
concert	decamp
concur	decertify
condominium	declassify
confer	decompose
congress	decompress
congruent	decontaminate
connect	defog
consequent	defrost
construct	depart
contact	deplane
contain	depress
contract	desalt
contribute	dethrone

Con- *(With, Together, or Jointly)

De- (Partly, From, Down, Away)

Con-	De-
convene	detour
convey	detrain

*In some instances, com- and con- are different spellings for the same prefix.

Dis- (Not, Apart From)

En-*, Em-* (In, On, Put Into, Cause)

Dis-	En-*	Em-*
disable	encircle	embalm
disadvantage	enclose	embank
disappear	endanger	embark
discomfort	enfold	embattle
disconnect	enforce	embed
discontent	enjoy	embitter
discontinue	enlarge	emblazon
disentangle	enliven	embody
dishonest	enrich	embolden
dishonor	enroll	embroil
disinterest	enshrine	empanel
dislodge	ensnare	empower
disloyal	entangle	
disorder	enthrone	
displace	entrap	
displease		

*In some instances, en- and em- are different spellings for the same prefix.

Fore- (Before, Former, In Front Of)

Il-, im-, in-, ir- (Not)

Fore-	Il-, im-, in-, ir-			
forearm	illegal	imbed	inaccurate	irrational
forecast	illegible	immature	inarticulate	irreclaimable
forefather	illegitimate	immeasurable	inaudible	irreconcilable
forefinger	illicit	immigrant	incapable	irrecoverable
forego	illiterate	immobile	incoherent	irredeemable
foregone	illogical	immoderate	incomparable	irreducible
foreground		immodest	incomplete	irrefutable
forehand		immoral	incorrect	irregular
foresee		immortal	indistinct	irrelevant
foreshadow		immovable	inept	irreparable
foresight		impassable	inexpensive	irrepressible
forestall		impatient	injustice	irreproachable
foretell		imperfect	insane	irreproducible
forethought		implausible	invalid	irresistible
foreworn		impractical	invisible	irresponsible

Mid- (Middle, Midst)

Mis- (Not, Bad, Wrong, Unfavorably)

Mid-	Mis-
midair	misaddress
midday	misadvise
midfield	misalign
midland	misapply
midline	misbehave
midnight	miscopy
midpoint	misdiagnose
midsection	misdial
midstream	misfile
midsummer	misgovern
midterm	misidentify
midtown	misinform

Mid- (Middle, Midst)	*Mis-* (Not, Bad, Wrong, Unfavorably)
midway	mismatch
midweek	misperceive
midwife	misprint
midyear	mistitle

Multi- (Many, More Than One)	*Non-* (Not)
multicolored	nonconformist
multicultural	noncredit
multidimensional	nondairy
multidisciplinary	nonessential
multiethnic	nonfat
multifaceted	nonfatal
multiform	nonfiction
multifunction	nonfunctional
multilingual	nonliving
multimedia	nonmember
multimillionaire	nonpoisonous
multinational	nonprofit
multipurpose	nonpublic
multiracial	nonsmoking
multistory	nontaxable
multiyear	nonstick

Out- (Surpassing)

outbid
outclass
outdistance
outdo
outgrow
outmaneuver
outnumber
outperform
outplay
outrun
outsell
outshine
outsmart
outtalk
outweigh

Over- (Too Much)	*Pre-* (Earlier, Preparatory, In Front)
overachieve	prearrange
overage	precook
overblown	predate
overbuild	predestine
overcharge	predetermine
overcrowd	preexist
overdress	preheat
overeat	prehistoric
overload	prejudge
overpay	premature
overpower	prepackage
overprice	prepay
overproduce	preset
oversleep	preshrunk
overstay	preview

Re- (Again, Anew, Backward)

readdress
readjust
reappear
rearrange
reawaken
reconnect
recopy
rediscover
redraw
reestablish
reheat
resell
restart
retie
rewash
rewire

Semi- (Half, Partly)

semiannual
semiautomatic
semicircle
semiconscious
semidarkness
semidetached
semidry
semifinal
semiformal
semiliterate
semimonthly
semiprivate
semiskilled
semisoft
semisweet
semitropical

Sub- (Under)

subcommittee
subcontract
subculture
subdivide
subfreezing
subgroup
subhuman
submarine
subnormal
subroutine
subset
subspecies
substructure
subsurface
subtitle
subway

Super- (Extra, Above, Greater)

supercharger
supercritical
superego
superfine
superhighway
superhero
superhuman
superimpose
superman
supermarket
supernatural
superpower
supersaturate
supersize
superstar
superstructure

Trans- (Across, Beyond, Through)

transact
transalpine
transatlantic
transfigure
transform
translucent
translunar
transmigrate
transmutation
transnational
transoceanic
tranship
transplant
transpolar
transport
transship

Un- (Not)

unbroken
unclear
uneven
unfair
unfinished
unfriendly
unhappy
unknown
unlucky
unnecessary
unpopular
unreal
unseen
unskilled
unspoiled
untrue

Under (Below, Under, Less)

underachieve
underage
undercharge
underdeveloped
underestimate
underfeed
underexpose
underground
underinsure
underpay
underplay
underrate
undershoot
undersized
undervalue
underweight

SUFFIXES AND EXAMPLES

-able (Capable of)

acceptable
changeable
employable
enjoyable
favorable
likable
lovable
noticeable
preferable
punishable
questionable
reachable
reliable
reusable
suitable
valuable

-al, -ial (Relating to)

arrival
burial
coastal
comical
denial
ethical
global
logical
magical
musical
removal
renewal
rental
tribal
tropical
tutorial

-ed (Past Tense)

asked
baked
called
copied
dropped
ended
farmed

-en (Relating to)

broken
chosen
darken
fallen
frozen
golden
hidden

-ed (Past Tense)

hoped
hugged
learned
mailed
needed
pretended
removed

-en (Relating to)

lessen
loosen
proven
sadden
shaken
soften
stolen

-ed (Past Tense)	*-en* (Relating to)
sailed	sunken
traveled	worsen

-er, -or (One Who)	*-er,* (More)
baker	bigger
banker	colder
camper	darker
farmer	fewer
jogger	fresher
miner	heavier
painter	louder
reader	muddier
robber	newer
singer	safer
skater	shorter
speaker	slower
swimmer	soapier
teacher	warmer
worker	wider
writer	winner

-est (Most)	*-ful* (Quality of)
brightest	beautiful
busiest	cheerful
darkest	colorful
fastest	delightful
freshest	faithful
happiest	graceful
heaviest	harmful
kindest	helpful
newest	meaningful
oldest	painful
prettiest	peaceful
scariest	playful
strongest	respectful
tiniest	skillful
warmest	successful
youngest	watchful

-ic (Like, Pertaining to)	*-ing* (Ongoing)
academic	baking
allergic	burning
angelic	carrying
aquatic	clapping
artistic	cutting
athletic	eating
barbaric	helping
genetic	hiding
historic	jumping
idiotic	looking
melodic	playing
nomadic	raining
numeric	riding
oceanic	singing
robotic	smiling
scenic	using

-ion, -tion, -ation, -ition
(Act, State of)

-ish (Like)

action	babyish
adaptation	childish
animation	clownish
alteration	elfish
collision	feverish
competition	fiendish
congratulation	foolish
decoration	selfish
education	sheepish
erosion	sluggish
graduation	snappish
hesitation	squeamish
introduction	stylish
invitation	ticklish
maturation	unselfish
rendition	youngish

-ity, -ty (State, Quality of)

-ive, -ative, -itive
(Tending to, Relating to)

chatty	active
crafty	cognitive
crusty	combative
drafty	decorative
faulty	elusive
frosty	erosive
fruity	evaluative
gravity	evasive

-ity, -ty (State, Quality of)

-ive, -ative, -itive
(Tending to, Relating to)

guilty	formative
knotty	intuitive
oddity	massive
purity	narrative
rarity	operative
safety	passive
sanity	repetitive
sporty	talkative

-less (Quality of)

-ly (Every, In the Manner of)

aimless	brightly
careless	calmly
cloudless	cleverly
endless	closely
flawless	evenly
friendless	exactly
harmless	faintly
helpless	greatly
homeless	happily
hopeless	lightly
pointless	neatly
powerless	neighborly
priceless	shyly
sleepless	truly
sugarless	weekly
useless	wisely

-*ment* (Result, State of)	-*ness* (Quality of)
agreement	boldness
ailment	calmness
confinement	coziness
development	dampness
employment	darkness
enjoyment	happiness
excitement	fairness
fulfillment	firmness
involvement	fondness
judgment	goodness
movement	haziness
placement	kindness
punishment	numbness
requirement	openness
settlement	uselessness
shipment	weariness

-*ous, -eous, -ious* (Full of, State of)	-*s, -es* (Plural)
advantageous	babies
courageous	dolls
dangerous	dresses
famous	elves
furious	families
glamorous	friends
glorious	games
humorous	horses
joyous	kings
marvelous	ladies
monstrous	monkeys
mountainous	nuts
murderous	pandas
mysterious	queens
poisonous	sandwiches
vigorous	wishes

-*ship* (State of, Quality of)	-*y* (Quality of, Full of)
apprenticeship	ability
assistantship	baggy
championship	beefy
citizenship	bossy
dealership	bumpy
directorship	chewy
friendship	curly
guardianship	dirty
hardship	dumpy
horsemanship	fishy
leadership	funny
membership	hairy
partnership	itchy
salesmanship	jumpy
sponsorship	leggy
township	lucky